America, Aristotle, and the Politics
of a Middle Class

America, Aristotle, and the Politics of a Middle Class

Leslie G. Rubin

BAYLOR UNIVERSITY PRESS

Cover design and custom illustration by *the*BookDesigners. Images © Shutterstock/blurAZ, MidoSemsem

An earlier version of chapter 1 appeared as "Aristotle's Politics on the Hoof: Sparta, Crete, and Carthage," in *Interpretation: A Journal of Political Philosophy* 39, no. 1 (2011): 3–36. It is republished here with permission.

Library of Congress Cataloging-in-Publication Data

Names: Rubin, Leslie G., 1954–2017 author.
Title: America, Aristotle, and the politics of a middle class / Leslie G. Rubin.
Description: Waco, Texas : Baylor University Press, [2018] | Includes bibliographical references and index.
Identifiers: LCCN 2017034039 (print) | LCCN 2017048668 (ebook) | ISBN 9781481308045 (web PDF) | ISBN 9781481308038 (ebook: Mobi/Kindle) | ISBN 9781481300568 (ePub) | ISBN 9781481300544 (cloth : alk. paper) | ISBN 9781481300551 (pbk. : alk. paper)
Subjects: LCSH: United States—Politics and government—Philosophy. | Aristotle. Politics. | Republics. | Middle class—Political activity.
Classification: LCC JK31 (ebook) | LCC JK31.R82 2017 (print) | DDC 320.01—dc23

Printed in the United States of America on acid-free paper with a minimum of 30 percent recycled content.

To Chas,

whose self-discipline has goaded me
and whose encouragement has never flagged
over thirty-six years.

CONTENTS

INTRODUCTION

POLITICS AND THE POLITICAL ANIMAL

Americans' attitudes toward politics resemble a dilemma as old as the first democracy. As in the story Socrates tells in Plato's *Republic* of Leontius' encountering the dead bodies of criminals, we are thoroughly disgusted by politics and yet we cannot look away.[1] American citizens who pay any attention to politics are wont to refer reflexively to their right to speak freely and to vote but also their dismay at the results of political debate and elections. Since the era of its founding, the American political system has depended upon both a certain amount of citizen support and a certain amount of citizen apathy. In addition to immeasurable blood, sweat, and tears spilled in making the United States independent, unprecedented numbers of citizens contributed opinions and arguments concerning the best institutions to govern them. The American founding did not merely set the stage for American politics; it was politics in action, according to Aristotle's definition: reasoned speech concerning the just and the unjust, the good and the bad among free and equal citizens.

AMERICAN FRAMERS' UNDERSTANDING OF "POLITICS"

The "improved" "science of politics" to which Publius (Alexander Hamilton and James Madison) appeals in Federalist Papers 9 and 47 reflects certain observations about human nature.[2] First, these Federalists argued that, because of insights recently derived from this science, the Constitution's representation system, established over an extended area, would help to "break and control" the tendency toward disruptive faction exhibited by all societies of free men.[3] Second, the modern science of politics teaches the necessity to separate the

1

three basic powers of government in order to avoid tyranny and so to distribute them as to create checks and balances among the various bodies exercising those powers.[4] These influential founders saw both that human beings were entitled to be treated as equals and as free men by their political system, and that their equality and liberty, combined with natural human self-interest and passions, posed serious potential dangers to political stability in the form of factions.

Interestingly, its resistance to factional conflict is one of the prominent factors supporting Aristotle's claim that the republic based upon the middling element is the best regime for most cities and men. In addition, Aristotle not only speaks of the same three basic powers exercised by all governments, but also suggests that a founder or reformer can influence the way the powers interact in order to discourage a regime's tendency toward tyranny. Though Aristotle does not declare so boldly that "ambition must be made to counteract ambition,"[5] his description of the virtue of ambition, a mean between excessive and inadequate desire for justifiable honor,[6] harmonizes well with the willingness of the middling republic's citizen to rule and to be ruled in turn. The insights of the science of politics are not as new as Publius might suggest. Behind them lie assumptions comparable to those of Aristotle: that political life properly so called occurs among free citizens who are equal in significant ways and, therefore, that the best regime for which human beings can reasonably hope is a certain kind of republic. Some very significant "modern" insights concerning the benefits and the limits of the political authority of the people, associated with John Locke, Thomas Hobbes, and James Madison, were anticipated by Aristotle but never put together into a working regime until the American experiment. The founders rediscovered some long-ignored truths about human nature, and they had the resources, the political will, and the political culture required to put them into effect, while Aristotle did not. Aristotle and the American founders debate the good and the bad, the just and the unjust aspects of the rule of the many for the sake of the common good, and the insights that fuel their discussions are mutually instructive.

ARISTOTLE'S UNDERSTANDING OF "POLITICS" AND
THE POLITICAL

Aristotle observes that people are hardwired for politics: "The human being is by nature a political animal."[7] To be human is to thrive in a *polis*, a political society, discussing the good and the bad, the just and the unjust. The *polis* is a Greek invention, and the best arrangement of life within it was a matter of heated debate and sometimes armed struggle among the Greeks.[8] In the *Politics,* Aristotle looks back on a few centuries of history and political rhetoric and tries to make sense of politics' manifold ends and means. Which ends are most appropriate to political life per se? Which belong only in non-political orders, such as tyranny or kingship? Which forms of politics achieve the appropriate goals of a political order? The *Politics* begins with Aristotle's definition of a *polis* (a city and its supporting countryside) as a political association. The rest of the *Politics* gives this circular definition content. That it is an association means that it is aimed at a good common to the members, but Aristotle is at pains to discern what makes the *polis* different from other human associations.

Other ancient writers see political rule as merely a subcategory of another form of governance—kingship, tyranny, mastery, household management[9]— but Aristotle rejects these arguments: "Everything is defined by its function and its capacity, and if it is no longer the same in these respects it should not be spoken of in the same way, but only as something similarly termed."[10] People spoke loosely about politics then, just as modern Americans speak of office politics and sexual politics and governmental politics as if they were all subcategories of an essentially similar assertion of power. Politics strictly speaking, however, is distinctive in its task and power, its purpose and ruling arrangements. Aristotle distinguishes "between a large household and a small city" and between the science of kingly rule and that of political rule.[11]

Aristotle observes that humans do not use their voices like other animals. The *political* animal uses *logos*, speech that implies reason, to "reveal the advantageous and the harmful, and hence also the just and the unjust and the other things of this sort; and community in these things is what makes a household and a city."[12] The political association is based on common moral perceptions— not on place, leadership, or ethnic bonds, but on a common understanding of the good and the just.[13] It is not enough for a political analyst to focus on the economic pressures or the social relationships that seem to move people to form groups. If the fundamental moral consensus does not hold, there is no political whole.

So, talk about just and unjust makes us essentially political. As long as political life goes on, the talk goes on. If consensus about the common good makes the city in the first place, Aristotle must explain what is left to talk about. The sometimes frustrating inexhaustibility of political argument is tied to another reason that human beings are "by nature" political animals: our individual incompleteness. Human beings live in cities because the city is the association aimed at and best equipped to support human sufficiency.[14] Aristotle's analogy, the hand:the body::each person or household:the *polis*,[15] suggests that one reason he applies the adjective "natural" to politics is to evoke an organic relationship, without which the individuals and groups would not survive or would be defective (like a "stone hand"). Humans need others to survive and to "live well." The historical progression from man and woman to household to village to political order responds to the primal human needs both to live and to live well. Each member of these groups contributes to the sufficiency of the whole and contributes differently according to different abilities. Though those contributions are all necessary, they are viewed by differing community members as incommensurable.[16] Every sort of citizen will have a different opinion about the common good, because each makes different contributions to that good and each draws from the common different benefits to fulfill individual needs. Consequently, each has a different view of what justice requires. Even the city as a whole is never fully sufficient—it "aims at" sufficiency, but must continuously strive for it. Thus, another reason for endless debate about the good and the bad is the ever-changing state of the inhabitants' needs, both material and moral, and the resources available to fill them.

A *polis* is natural to humans, because they are political animals and because the city resembles an organism. There is yet a third sense in which city life, therefore politics, is natural to humans. The nature of a being includes its perfection, Aristotle asserts. An acorn's nature is to become a healthy, productive oak tree; a human being's nature, though more complicated, is to perfect its humanity. Associations are more perfect in the more sufficient form, and cities are more sufficient than villages or households. In its best form, a city aims to provide the requisites not merely for the maintenance of life, but for the good life, that is, the practice of the excellence appropriate to being human.[17] From these observations, Aristotle concludes that one who survives without a city is either a beast, "incapable of sharing," or a god, "in need of nothing through being self-sufficient."[18] The *Politics* is a treatise exploring the political nature of mankind, rejecting the subhuman and rarely referring to the divine, but taking quite seriously not only the cultured life of a leisured aristocracy, but the life of the majority of people who, without a *polis'* support, would live like beasts or be constantly at war. Politics is the underpinning of humanity itself.

While his emphasis at the beginning of the description of the political order is on natural necessity in at least three senses, Aristotle is careful to state that the institution of a specific regime is not merely an impulse of nature, but rather an intentional act. Cities are natural to human beings, but human beings must choose to live in a particular city. One is born into a household, and households only survive over time by the instinctual merging with others. Households form into villages, clustering together to stave off the challenges of natural necessity. On the other hand, that Aristotle calls the first man to give laws establishing a city a great benefactor indicates that he could have acted otherwise or not at all.[19] The particular characteristics of a city are determined by human choices combined with chance. It is natural only that the inhabitants benefit from living in a city as opposed to living "separated from law and adjudication."[20] While Book I is so abstractly written as to be indifferent to the justice or injustice of a specific regime,[21] it clearly argues that the locus of justice is the political order and thus accords to politics a crucial human function.

In the brief remarks of his first two chapters, Aristotle establishes the basic premises of his observations and arguments concerning politics. The city is the political association. Life in a city is natural to the political animal. The best political association will, therefore, be the best city, providing the best support for the flourishing of the political animal. When Aristotle henceforth distinguishes "political" arrangements and activities in actual or theoretical cities from other sorts of arrangements and activities, he adds to our understanding of the uniqueness of politics and the standards its practice requires. Communities have existed in the world and in men's minds that do not fulfill the requirements of political life strictly speaking. Some acorns grow into imperfect oak trees; some rot on the ground or are eaten by animals. Though all cities by nature may aim at full sufficiency and a good life, the human element or the need to choose particular arrangements under particular circumstances can cause the enterprise to go astray. Aristotle's organic metaphor is not to be taken too literally—unlike most acorns, which, once they germinate, grow into functioning oak trees, most associations of human beings do not grow into good political orders. When they do, it is more by human effort than by unaided intrinsic development.

The remainder of Book I, a discourse primarily dealing with the activities and organization of the household, makes few mentions of regimes or of politics as ordinarily understood. The household is a necessary step toward the political order and, as Aristotle argues later,[22] a necessary component of a successful city, but it is a subordinate part of the city. In the context of the account of household rule, the discussion of the conditions under which slavery could be considered natural and just and the discussion of the types of rule that obtain within the family will, however, have particular import as essential points of contrast in Aristotle's later analyses of types of political rule.

The Master-Slave Relationship Is *Not* Politics

Aristotle's notorious attention to slavery is occasioned by his overall purpose, to distinguish politics from other types of rule. A slave is a human being who is possessed and used as a tool by another human being. Anyone who is by nature incapable of ruling himself, of bringing his body and appetites under control for rational purposes—to put it bluntly, anyone who does not know how to take care of himself—is by nature slavish. Since, says Aristotle, it is necessary and advantageous that there be relationships of ruling and ruled in all aspects of life, and since the better and more rational should rule the worse and less rational, it is clear that the slavish man needs to be ruled by a master who can tame his body, so to speak, and force it to serve rational aims.[23] These rational aims are the aims of the more rational man—thus, the slave comes to serve the advantage of the master, but the relationship redounds to his own benefit. Though Aristotle shows that such utterly incompetent, mentally deficient men are not as common or as distinguishable as the practice of slavery is widespread,[24] he does make an argument for the naturalness of enslaving them, and only them.

In a distinction that will become crucial later on, Aristotle here sets up both political rule and kingly rule in opposition to the mastery of slaves—the former are more dignified because their subjects are rational human beings, for "the rule is always better over ruled things that are better."[25] Kingly rule, political association, and mastery all involve a common work, a common end. The first two are higher common efforts because they are not merely matters of one man's reason ruling another man's body, but matters of one or several persons' intellects ruling appetites and passions in people who are capable of self-restraint, people whose souls already rule their bodies. Just enslavement, according to Aristotle, requires that some people be as different from others as the soul is from the body, while political and kingly relations depend on human beings who differ only in the particular virtues they possess and display, and in the extent to which they control their appetites for the sake of higher ends.

Aristotle concludes the slavery discussion not by focusing on the questions of its justice, but by returning to his primary concern: "It is evident from these things . . . that mastery and political rule are not the same thing and that all the sorts of rule are not the same. . . . For the one sort is over those free by nature, the other over slaves; and household management is monarchy . . . while political rule is over free and equal persons."[26] As his first chapter anticipates, Aristotle's account of these subordinate parts of the city aims at distinguishing political rule from other types of rule with which it is often confused. The "expertise" of the master is merely to know the things he commands the slave to perform—a rather undignified expertise best relinquished to an overseer. The implication Aristotle makes here is that no political leader should view himself as a master of slaves or his rulership as merely commanding actions he would not perform himself.

THE MARITAL RELATIONSHIP *Is* POLITICAL

In another notorious section of Book I, Aristotle treats the relations between a husband and wife, and sheds more light on the distinctiveness of politics.

He calls marital rule "political," suggesting that husband and wife are equal in some important respect, in addition to being free. There may be a problem with securing obedience from a wife who is free and one's equal:

> In most political offices, it is true, there is an alternation of ruler and ruled, since they tend by their nature to be on an equal footing and to differ in nothing; all the same, when one rules and the other is ruled, the ruler seeks to establish differences in external appearance, forms of address, and prerogatives, as in the story Amasis told about his footpan. The male always stands thus in relation to the female. (*Politics* I.12.1259b4–10)

The male appropriates to himself permanent kingship in the family just as Amasis, a peasant, seized the Egyptian throne in a coup—unjustly.[27] In political life, conventional distinctions mask the *natural* equality between ruler and ruled. Aristotle asserts first that, in the "politics" of a marriage, the male is by nature more expert in leading than the female, but he later states the criterion differently: the deliberative element in the female soul is "not authoritative," so the male assumes permanent rule in the household.[28] He does not, however, say that the female has no capacity for leadership or deliberation. Her subordinate position may depend on her inequality in the requisite virtue of rule. It may also be that a woman's deliberative capacity has less authority because her husband refuses to listen to it, as did Ajax.[29] In this context, Aristotle's reference to Amasis' footpan and his quotation of Sophocles' *Ajax*—"to a woman silence is an ornament"—strongly suggest that a husband's permanent rule of his wife is merely conventional and grounded in force, rather than natural and supported by mutual agreement, and that a woman's enforced silence is not always justified and is sometimes unwise. Using the term "political" to illuminate the marital relationship also illuminates the political relationship: political citizens must respect and obey those who (temporarily) hold office over them, but not worship their rulers as the Egyptians worshiped the statue of a god made from Amasis' gold chamber pot, nor should they remain silent when their rulers are behaving like madmen.

Aristotle goes on to argue that the ruler in the larger sphere who deserves his office differs from his subjects not only in the greatness of his virtue, but in the types of virtues he exercises. Because ruling and being ruled differ in kind, the virtues necessary to their performance must differ in kind. Master and slave, husband and wife all require some virtues, for ruling well or for being ruled—different, but still human, virtues for different characteristic functions. The ruler of a city must have "complete virtue of character," presumably because his rulership is exercised over the largest and most complete association, aiming at complete human sufficiency and the good life.[30] If, in the marital relationship, there is potential for conflict because the ruler and ruled differ only in the degree that deliberation rules the soul, in the political realm, where ruling offices rotate among roughly equally deliberative persons, there could be a much greater problem: the ruled must have both certain virtues to be able to obey properly and other virtues when it is their turn to rule.

ARISTOTLE'S POLITICAL REGIME

The explicit and implicit definitions presented throughout the treatise demonstrate that Aristotle sees politics as the activity of ruling and being ruled among free human beings who are treated as free and who are roughly equal. A political unit cannot treat its members as slaves or as children, but must treat them as free adults, capable of some deliberate thought and entitled to a say in their collective future. Thus politics, strictly speaking, requires a rotation of offices; less force and more persuasion in the enforcement of the laws; a tolerance of the diversity of employments, wealth, and interests of the citizens; a certain scope for the private attachments of the citizens; and an arena, however mundane, for the activities of public virtue.

The combination of a fundamentally political nature with unavoidable contrariness moves Aristotle to describe and defend in the *Politics* a regime sometimes translated "polity," a regime that is Aristotle's republic. The best polity is the republic based on the middle class. This middling republic reveres a cluster of citizen virtues, while it takes measures to prevent the least virtuous from holding sway. The middling republic favors neither the wealthy nor the poor, the highly educated nor the ignorant, but rather encourages a class that occupies a middling economic status and a middling social status, with an interest in balancing the other classes and a predisposition to do so. The middling republic divides the work of the regime among various officials, so that no one holds too much power and everyone who wishes to participate has a reasonable chance at an office, but it allows most citizens to spend most of their time in the private pursuit of self-reliance. The American republic as envisioned by its founders, thus, bears some striking resemblances to Aristotle's middling republic.

Aristotle's observations on the messiness of the activity that defines human beings can help one understand why modern citizens of democratic regimes might say that they "hate politics" but still insist that they govern themselves. It is puzzling that the being whose greatest potential for happiness lies within a political regime *says* that he or she hates politics. Aristotle and the American founders thought that a properly constituted republic could accommodate this paradox, even build upon it as a foundation.

The permanent rule of a virtuous aristocracy or outstanding family, however superior in orderliness and in the encouragement of certain virtues, is not politics rightly understood. It can only be a just arrangement of society when there exists a superior person or group to whose rule all non-slaves agree. Even then, if all surrender their liberty to him or them permanently, nothing distinguishes this arrangement from either parental rule or (however benevolent) despotism. The "best regime" discussed in the last books of the *Politics* attempts to avoid becoming tyrannical,[31] but this regime is not, in Aristotle's strict sense, political. This aristocracy takes a paternalistic attitude toward the inhabitants: the city is run like a large household intent above all on the education of the youth in the virtues of leisure and attending to the orderly and respectful carriage of the citizens at all times. Toward the noncitizens, its artisans and slaves, the regime is despotic—akin to the head of the household's rule over the servants—subjecting to rule human beings who would be capable of some self-mastery if they lived in a different regime.[32] According to Aristotle's arguments, politics is not merely household rule over a larger number: the city encompasses and attends to a variety of elements; it is much less homogeneous than a household. Where all are free and roughly equal "in their nature," it is said to be unjust that some always rule and others are always ruled. Rather, some citizens should rule and some be ruled, but they must take turns.

Politics, therefore, requires equality, in the sense that equality is the appropriate public relationship among human beings capable of the exercise of some freedom. Politics is superior to non-political arrangements, even among somewhat unequal men, when existing inequalities are not great enough or obvious enough to justify the paternalistic or despotic rule of the superior. Despotism is justified only in the case of natural slaves and natural masters (persons of vastly unequal and observable innate capacities) as long as the relationship is mutually beneficial, and kingship and aristocracy are good regimes only when the rulers are truly superior in political wisdom and virtue to their subjects, but none of these arrangements based on extreme inequality is shown unequivocally to be just or stable in the *Politics*. The republic based upon a large middle class is Aristotle's political regime par excellence.

A CLASSICAL GREEK ON AMERICAN POLITICS

On one subject the poles of contemporary American politics seem to agree: America is in trouble. Of course, there is a range of descriptions of its troubles— economic stagnation or income inequality, excessively loose immigration enforcement or excessive bigotry against immigrants, decay of the family and other social bonds or refusal to embrace unique individuals' lifestyles, inattention to racial disparities or excessive attention to racial differences, to name only a few—but the feeling of crisis seems pervasive.

Economists of all stripes attribute much of our social and political conflict to free market capitalism. Competition and individual advancement are baked into the system; therefore, we should not be surprised that the financial interests that competition spawns result in deeply felt political differences. Unfortunately for this position, there are economically successful as well as less successful practitioners of all sorts of livelihoods on all sides of the current debates. Though economic interests are extremely important, they cannot explain the current polarization any more than they explain periods of relatively greater consensus.

The international situation—long-term military involvement in foreign wars, stress in long-held alliances, bold assertions by powers with anti-American agendas, international economic instability—could explain some citizens' perceptions of crisis in America's public policies. The actions of other nations have, however, always been beyond America's control. Furthermore, periods of international tension have often resulted in national unification, rather than exacerbated division.

While "social conservatives" might attribute the current situation to rapid changes in the definition of family and in the social atmosphere surrounding moral education and citizenship expectations, "social progressives" might attribute it to the delays and obstacles placed in the way of full individual self-definition of social relationships or ethnic and "gender" identity. America has always defined itself in terms of individual rights as well as rights of association and free exercise of religion. What causes the nation to break into such deeply divided interpretations of these rights at this time?

Why do Americans differ so much even on what it means to abide by the Constitution or to embody in law the principles behind the Constitution? A full understanding of the way out of this clash of passions and interests requires a step away from the poles and a clear understanding of how the country reached this level of uncivil disagreement. One way to step away without crossing into uncharted terrain is to ask what in the essential makeup of the American way of life supports both ends of the polarity, what underlies the endless debate and might even foster irreconcilable tensions. Not only can one see better the relation of certain trees to the forest as a whole, but one might also understand the inner workings of each type of tree by looking at the reason it is in the forest in the first place. To risk a runaway metaphor, no successful forest is made up of a single species of tree, and no successful tree is cultivated in a hostile forest environment.

It is conventional wisdom today that the middle class in the American republic is threatened, certainly economically and, for some observers, morally. If true, Aristotle would lament the disappearance of the able seamen and the ballast in the ship of state—those who may not chart the course but without whom the ship might capsize from the dominance of dynastic oligarchy or populist demagogy. Despite much lip service bestowed upon the middle class by politicians and political commentators, Aristotle and the founding generation might doubt that these leaders understand their own rhetoric. If most citizens—wealthy, middling, and poor alike—are not raised to appreciate the middling virtues (including the political/moral/social value of the middle class itself), to take a turn in some office beneficial to the community, to cultivate friendly relations across the economic spectrum, and to aspire to personal and community-wide excellence, the republic will suffer a decline. Above all, the middle class needs to understand that the way it lives is the best way for a citizen to live—best for the individual and the family, and best for a free society—and even non-middle-class citizens must recognize the middling virtues as the standards to which they should strive.

Using his strict definition of politics, ruling and being ruled among equal and free persons for the sake of a common good, Aristotle critiques the practical failures of other regimes and then describes the political order most associated with mankind's political nature, the middle-class republic. Looking at the arguments concerning the middle class and the significance of its virtues made by America's founding generation, it is possible to see their concerns paralleling Aristotle's in significant ways. The science of politics of the eighteenth century revealed some of the same characteristics of human nature that Aristotle saw and attempted to build a structure of rule that would lessen their ill effects. That structure is a middle-class republic in Aristotelian terms. Did the Americans succeed in making it possible for the vast majority to occupy a middling status in wealth and in educational/moral virtue in a free and roughly equal society so that they rule and are ruled in turn?[33]

The expectations of the founding generation regarding the social and moral characteristics of future American citizens may have been thwarted; a decline in the dominance of the middling class seems to be the result. In the writings of various political thinkers at the time, there are arguments as well as casual remarks to the effect that the rich had proven incapable of governing a just republic and the very poor and uneducated were not self-sufficient enough to be trusted to hold predominant power, but citizens of middling wealth and modest education represented the best prospects for republican government, that is, self-government. It is time to reexamine Aristotle's insistence that a community and its citizenry continually strive not only to achieve material self-sufficiency, but also to share "in happiness or in living in accordance with intentional choice," giving "careful attention to political virtue and vice."[34] It is possible that the founding generation relied too heavily on the apparently natural concomitants of middle-class life and left too far to the side the attention to political virtue, or perhaps that, in the intervening decades, the American people have chosen a different path to public peace and prosperity without understanding what they have sacrificed.

Taking it as obvious that the various participants in and commentators on the founding had various backgrounds in political thinking and that no one took any previous thinker as a complete guide to the task, we can simply learn from both Aristotle and the Americans about the practical task of creating and "keeping" a republic. The ways Aristotle defends the crucial factors of success that are similar in the American outlook highlight reasons for maintaining the American framework, despite temptations to alter or remove its load-bearing walls. The ways Aristotle criticizes the aspects that are different can supply us with a thoughtful understanding of America's challenges not only in the founding era, but also today. This comparison aims to illuminate both the brilliance and the weaknesses of the Philosopher's and the founders' expectations.

Part I

ARISTOTLE'S REPUBLIC

1

A Practical Republic

ARISTOTLE'S REAL-WORLD POLITICS

Aristotle will recommend the polity or republic as the "best" regime for "most cities and most human beings," suggesting that it is a goal that can be appreciated rationally and a goal to which most political communities can reasonably aspire. He proffers no guarantees of its success. Some populations are not characterized by the equality that a republic requires; chance or the wrong choices made at crucial times could derail the most prudent plans. In his analysis of real political experience in Sparta, Crete, and Carthage, Aristotle presents a case against the best intentions in politics, a case that modest aspirations are more likely to combine with most people's modest virtues to produce livable cities, while high aspirations will very likely end in rule of the few that is indistinguishable from tyranny. Beginning, as Aristotle does, with the fundamental principle that a just political order must recognize the equality and liberty of its members, the American founders used the improved "science of politics" to negotiate a constitutional structure that held out modest, attainable aspirations for their republic as well.

Lest he appear a mere sophist playing with the notion of the best regime, Aristotle insists he must dispose of the regimes, both actual and speculative, called noble by others before he describes his own "best regime." Only if these other regimes are "in fact not in a fine condition" can his enterprise be genuine and not sophistical.[1] Aristotle's discussions of Sparta, Crete, and Carthage prepare the rationale for pursuing a middling regime, rather than the rule of the best. He demonstrates that the painstaking lawgivers of these admired communities could not engineer a situation in which the citizens would be virtuous and the city stable. On the other hand, when these regimes did achieve some good political effects in terms of stability, they were not those at which the lawgivers originally aimed. Aristotle thus suggests that, as important as the initial lawgiver is for establishing the way of life of a regime, he cannot take all contingencies into account, and he cannot rely on future statesmen to maintain a truly aristocratic way of life against all odds. If chance must complicate human affairs, then certain characteristics of a political order will render it more able to weather the storm. The examination of these regimes reveals characteristics that the citizens must embody and the regime entail to guard the basic arrangements against inevitable decay: the institutional arrangements of a republic, which mixes the influence of the rich and the poor to create a regime that is admittedly not an aristocracy, but aims at a certain virtue. The Spartan, Cretan, and Carthaginian regimes mixed some democratic elements with quite a few oligarchic elements yet still failed. More, and more explicit, efforts at balance might have been beneficial.

THE REPUBLIC EMERGES FROM THE DEFINITION OF POLITICS

Throughout the *Politics*, Aristotle examines the historically new phenomenon of politics, both defining it strictly and defending it as a human activity. Before the regime (*politeia*) called "republic" (*politeia*)? is defined in Book III of the *Politics* and examined in depth in Book IV, the republic as a standard for a good regime and "political" as a standard for rule are mentioned in a number of contexts, most extensively in the assessments of highly regarded regimes in Book II. Aristotle first makes use of the term *politeia* in reference to a particular regime, rather than to regimes in general, in II.6, when he examines Plato's *Laws* and then again in describing the regimes of Crete and Carthage. He criticizes these regimes, as well as that of the Lacedaemonians, with reference both to the standards of the simply best regime (described in Books VII and VIII) and those of the republic. They clearly fail in Aristotle's eyes to achieve the simply best, but aspects that resemble the republic receive his praise. In the descriptions and criticisms of these regimes, Aristotle gives some indications of what is good in and what is required by the *politically best*, as opposed to the *simply best*, regime.[3] The best political association provides the best support for the flourishing of the political animal. When Aristotle distinguishes "political" arrangements and activities from other sorts of arrangements and activities, he adds to our understanding of the uniqueness of politics and the standards its practice requires.

If politics and the city are natural to human beings, Aristotle has not yet explained why it is so hard to find a stable and self-sufficient city. Though all cities by nature may *aim* at full sufficiency and a good life, human fallibility and the need to choose particular arrangements under particular circumstances can cause the enterprise to go astray. The good news is that optimum politics requires what appear to be suboptimal conditions—for example, that there be no clearly superior human being to rule justly and beneficially. Insofar as political rule is natural, the hierarchy of ruler and ruled should have its roots in the soul. Because the city is, by definition, an organization of free and equal citizens, however, much controversy surrounds the problem of distinguishing the best souls for ruling and satisfying the ruled that they should obey others who are, in some sense, their equals. The inequalities of offices, even when they are temporary, cause resentment, potentially instability. Again, this controversy flourishes on the level of selfish motives, but it represents a serious question. It is difficult to delineate the standards according to which a city should choose the best rulers among the souls of equals.[4] If political rule is among equals and stability rests on the satisfaction of all parts of the regime, the best *political* regime does not require the simply best people to rule, but only those the city can be persuaded are the best in the circumstances.

In Book II, as Aristotle criticizes the "city in speech" Socrates builds in Plato's *Republic*, he elaborates this issue. A city is not a household. First, truly political rule is not permanent but rotated; those who are ruled also know how to rule. Second, it is necessary for the sufficiency of the political association that the citizens be many and differ greatly.[5] Yet, members of cities are all free adults, who see themselves as equal to all the others. One who willingly defers to his father will not necessarily defer *politically* to all people of his father's age.[6] In political life, as opposed to life in a village or a feudal monarchy, he would demand his share of rule in return for being ruled. And no free man would willingly submit to slavery. "It is thus reciprocal equality that preserves cities."[7] Although he admits that giving each man one art, creating a permanent aristocracy or kingship, might be more effective for some aims, Aristotle shows that if all are "equal in their nature," all must share the benefits and burdens of office.[8] Both here and in a later passage,[9] he admits that although such sharing would create defective rule because the rulers are not uniformly wise, rotation of offices is not defective politically.

Aristotle suggests by his criticisms of the *Republic* that self-sufficiency and stable diversity are more properly political aims for the lawgiver than either perfect harmony or doing justice to the better men. Surely the better men suffer when they are ruled by the worse, but for the sake of stability those who believe themselves equal, and for the sake of justice those who are in some important sense equal, must be allowed to share in rule. Widespread satisfaction with the regime due to equal treatment of roughly equal citizens is a political good, for "the good of each thing is surely what preserves it."[10]

That a city is also not really like a man seems obvious, yet it must be stated because the *Republic* seems to depend on the opposite assumption. Aristotle has indeed argued that a city is analogous to a living organism, insofar as it stands toward a citizen as the whole body to a hand. Each part of the city performs its function for the support of the whole. Again, however, Aristotle insists that that analogy cannot be stretched as far as Socrates takes it. For one human being to obey another as the body or the hand "obeys" the soul is not politics, but slavery.[11]

Politics differs from the monarchy of the household; it is a partnership of equals ruled by the participation of the members and not controlled by a person of obvious superiority. Politics also differs from the despotism of the household, in which servants are ruled as if they were not fully human, without the capacity to exercise judgment. Finally, politics takes place among a larger and more diverse group of people than the relationship between husband and wife. With many free persons contributing to the sufficiency and happiness of the whole, the city achieves a more complete end than the household—an end associated with the virtue of justice. Such an achievement has its costs: the city must contend with the danger of instability and factional conflict among those who see themselves as (at least) equals and desire honor from all of their fellows.

The activity of politics is also distinguished from the activity within a person's soul. Its requisite diversity and equality of status among the members rules out the possibility of its ever achieving the harmonious hierarchy of Socrates' philosophic soul, in which the rational part always rules the appetites and spiritedness always serves the just end. Aristotle suggests that in a political situation, the human beings who represent the appetites and spiritedness demand their due—sometimes more than their due, calculated by another standard—and cannot safely be denied some rewards and honors.[12]

MAGNESIA: PLATO'S PRACTICAL REPUBLIC

In discussing Plato's *Laws*, Aristotle associates the "political" life of a community with relations toward foreign regions, as opposed to isolation. All regimes must defend themselves against enemies, but "political" cities also must take care to "use for war the arms that are useful not only on its own territory, but in foreign regions as well."[13] A crucial part of the political city's life consists in the formidable use of the army for defense as well as the willingness to engage in offensive measures. Though this mention of political life is not associated immediately with the republic as a specific regime, it begins to narrow the limits within which a regime can be strictly described as political. It excludes settlements that are purposely established in so isolated a position as to be able to lead a private life of internal perfection. The political regime must act in the world and be prepared to enter into militarily enforced relations with others.[14]

These criteria of "political" regimes are soon related to the regime of the *Laws* through Aristotle's association of polities/republics with a dominant class that reveres military virtue: "The organization of the [Magnesian] regime as a whole is intended to be neither democracy nor oligarchy, but the one midway between them which is called a polity; for it is based on those who bear heavy arms."[15] The cultivation of military virtue to the detriment of all others is an error in legislation, but the military art is an essential one for a *political* order and cannot be ignored. To put those who are capable of practicing military arts in a position of power in the city surely elevates the status of this virtue in the regime. Aristotle points out, however, that the Athenian Stranger's proposal to support five thousand warriors (and their wives and attendants) in idleness is not economically feasible.[16] Though military virtue must be honored, soldiers will have to perform other productive services for the city as well.

The Athenian Stranger is next taken to task for his definition of the optimum amount of property for a Magnesian citizen: "as much as is needed to live with moderation."[17] Aristotle does not abandon the pursuit of moderation, but he recognizes a parallel criterion for the good political life, generosity. The political regime must support liberal moderation, or the avoidance of both luxury and penury by the practice of two quite accessible virtues concerned with property.[18] In contrast to very wealthy citizens who make grand public expenditures, the best citizen—a person of more moderate means—will perhaps not contribute so lavishly to the grandeur of his city but will be both able and willing to share his sufficient possessions with friends. At this point the republic is a good regime associated with certain virtues, but not all virtues, and perhaps not the grandest.

Aristotle acknowledges that Magnesia may be "the most attainable[19] of all the regimes for cities," but it does not surpass "more aristocratic" regimes in its excellence, "for one might well praise that of the Spartans more, or some other that is more aristocratic."[20] Aristotle says it claims to be a mixture of democracy and tyranny,[21] and that either these are not regimes at all or they are the worst of regimes. Rather, according to Aristotle, Magnesia actually mixes democracy and oligarchy, like Aristotle's republic, but tends to favor oligarchy.

Having identified Magnesia as most closely resembling a republic, Aristotle proceeds to criticize it as, in Books IV and V, he will criticize other cities that fall short of the *politeia*'s goals and tend to emulate either democracy or oligarchy excessively.[22] He cites the encouragements for the wealthy to participate in offices and elections and the lack of such encouragements for poorer citizens—a dangerous situation, because the elections turn out to favor a relative few who are willing to form coalitions.[23]

The examination of the regime of the *Laws* yields a number of criteria for a political regime and, specifically, a republic. Aristotle insists on the importance of military preparedness and involvement in foreign regions, of liberal moderation and moderate liberality, and of the judicious balance of democratic and oligarchic institutions, particularly in electoral arrangements. He also attends closely to the property distribution of this city. Care must be taken—by whom, it is not obvious—to ensure that important divisions of property will not decay over generations into great wealth for some and great poverty for most.[24] Aristotle's account of Magnesia concludes by pointing to Book IV for further discussion of the republic: "That a regime of this sort should not be constituted out of democracy and monarchy, then, is evident from these things and from what will be said later, when the investigation turns to this sort of regime."[25]

IMPROVING REAL-WORLD, HIGHLY RESPECTED REGIMES

After discussing the regimes and the reform proposals of people not engaged in politics,[26] Aristotle turns to the often-praised actual regimes of Sparta, Crete, and Carthage. These regimes test political theories in practice, showing "whether some aspect of the legislation is fine or not with respect to the best arrangement." They also demonstrate conflicts among the purposes or weaknesses in the intentions or the practices of statesmen and legislators; that is, they show "whether {some aspect of the legislation} is opposed to the basic premise and the manner [of organization] of the regime they actually have."[27] Aristotle thus warns that he will evaluate these regimes according to two standards: the simply best "arrangement" and "the basic premise"[28] of each regime.

Aristotle separates his consideration of these regimes into discrete sections, but his frequent comparisons suggest that they have much in common. "These three regimes . . . are very close to one another in a sense, and at the same time very different from the others."[29] In addition to the fact that the Spartan regime is said to have been based on the laws of Crete, they each represent better or worse answers to the same questions or political problems.[30] In his comments on property arrangements, Aristotle shows one common defect to be the tendency toward oligarchy, more or less explicitly honoring the accumulation of individual wealth. Other aspects of these regimes that Aristotle considers include the provision of leisure for the citizens, the defense of the city, the offices necessary for a good regime, and the virtues the regime will foster. None of these regimes presents a fully adequate solution to these political problems, but each is praised as fine in one way or another: the three "are justly held in high repute."[31] It is necessary to ask what justifies these good reputations for regimes that are not the best.[32]

SPARTA: MODERATED PROPERTY AND EDUCATION FOR THE FUTURE

The discussion of the Lacedaemonian regime makes no direct reference to a republic, though Aristotle holds it up to the standards of that regime in Book IV and compares it to Crete and Carthage in the next sections, where he associates the latter regimes explicitly with a republic.[33] The lawgiver's intention seems to have been to create the best regime simply, that is, the assumptions Aristotle mentions as underlying the Lacedaemonian regime resemble those of the *Republic*'s regime and in some ways those of the regime of *Politics* VII and VIII. Yet when Sparta is shown to have failed to make good on these intentions, its arrangement of offices is held up to the less exalted standards Aristotle associates with the republic. He shows Spartan practice to be "opposed to the basic premise . . . of the regime they actually have" in various ways. Its lawgiver is said to have desired the city to be hardy and not licentious and to be strong militarily (neither extraordinary nor despicable political goals), and he is assumed to have wanted to provide leisure for the citizens "from the necessary things" and to discourage greed—more lofty aims.[34] Aristotle claims that "the legislator"[35] failed to make the arrangements needed to educate and habituate the citizens to the ends he sought, yet Aristotle's suggestions for reform do not aim at the regime the Legislator evidently sought.

In Aristotle's view, the founder and lawgivers of Sparta did not understand the delicate relationship between education for citizenship and the institutional arrangements for the restraint of the citizens from vice. As Aristotle argues during his criticism of the regime Socrates builds in the *Republic*, while institutional restraints may be important supplemental devices for encouraging virtue, they can never substitute for education in and habituation to good action, and sometimes they can positively detract from such an education.[36] The *Republic*'s communal arrangement of property aimed to create an artificial friendship among the guardians and between the guardians and the working classes.[37] For Aristotle also, friendship and the virtues that flow from it are a prime concern. Genuine friendship, he argues, requires private property in order to provide opportunities for generosity toward friends and for the pleasure of having possessions to offer to a friend. If it forces all to share everything, if it creates "too much of a unity,"[38] the regime discourages both friendship and virtue:

> It is odd that one who plans to introduce education and who holds that it is through this that the city will be excellent should suppose it can be

corrected by things of that sort {communal property, women, and children},
and not by habits, philosophy, and laws, just as the legislator in Sparta and
Crete made common what is connected with property by means of common
messes. (*Politics* II.5.1263b37–1264a1)

A regime much more fitting to free people and to the free man's quintessential
virtue, liberality, would result from an arrangement of private property put to
common use.[39] The laws cannot banish depravity, the true cause of contentious
behavior. The laws must be concerned with educating souls even to mitigate
human wickedness. If they succeed with the latter, enforced communism of
property becomes superfluous at best.[40]

Similarly, in *Politics* II.9 Aristotle argues that the Spartan lawgivers have
done more harm than good with a number of their well-intentioned institutions. The helots are a troublesome and disruptive solution to the need
for leisure;[41] the failure to discipline the women provides a source of laxness
and luxury, rather than supporting hardiness and disdain for extravagance;[42]
the excessive emphasis on soldiering then leaves these self-indulgent persons
essentially in charge of the city much of the time.[43] Only after these three
considerations does Aristotle take up the "naturally first" question, concerning
the division of property and the arrangements for the family.

Sparta's once-careful equalization of property has declined by Aristotle's
time into great disparities of wealth and maldistribution of land. Together
with the general license of the women, the failure to oversee the marriages of
heiresses and the donation and bequest of land has undermined the intended
equalities. Though Aristotle emphatically dismisses the communism of women
and property in his criticism of the *Republic*, he nonetheless recognizes that
any public regulation of property is ineluctably tied to the public regulation of
marriages.[44] The concentration of land also leaves Sparta vulnerable to attack—
the inefficient distribution cannot indefinitely support a sufficient armed force.
Aristotle may assume in these criticisms that Sparta was intended to be the
best regime (with its leisured ruling class, strict citizen training in the regime's
understanding of virtue, and careful division of communal property) and
any inadequacies in the maintenance of that standard condemn it to failure.
Yet this failure also illuminates a danger for a lawgiver aiming to institute a
republic: military virtue is both practically necessary and the virtue that a
large number of citizens can reasonably practice, but it is not sufficient as the
prime focus and aim of the political regime. Economic concerns, traditionally
and perhaps naturally disdained by warriors,[45] must claim the attention not
only of the original lawgiver, but of citizens throughout the life of the regime.

According to Plutarch, Lycurgus left Sparta having insisted that the Lacedaemonians take an oath not to change the laws of his founding until he

returned. He then committed suicide. Plutarch praises the regime he left behind as a philosophical city that endured for five hundred years.[46] Aristotle, evaluating the regime at closer historical range, might agree that the lawgiver had philosophical aspirations, and he later praises the attitude implied in Lycurgus' actions, that is, government by laws rather than by human discretion. Real cities, however, cannot be ruled entirely by static law. Into the founding the lawgiver must build principles for modifying the laws when necessary and for ongoing oversight of the education of each generation so that future citizens will make the changes necessary (and only those necessary) to sustain the regime.

The regime of the Lacedaemonians fails also in its arrangement of offices, yet Aristotle is more forgiving in his analysis of these deficiencies. The board of overseers, the ephorate, is a popular office, prone to bribery, and too influential in the government. Rather than providing a balance against tyrannical tendencies in the dual kingship, the ephors became tyrannical in their own right: "Because the office is overly great—like a tyranny, in fact—even the kings were compelled to try to become popular with them; this has done added harm to the regime, for from an aristocracy, it has become a democracy."[47] Instituting the board of overseers was, however, not simply a mistake, for its existence quiets the people with a share in the regime, and thus it provides one support characteristic of a republican regime. If the popular element causes the regime to become unbalanced, tending toward an unmixed democracy, it will risk offending the few wealthy or aristocratic citizens and breaking the first law of politics: "If a regime is going to be preserved, all the parts of the city must wish it to exist and continue on the same basis."[48] As long as the popular branch remains proportionate to the other elements of the regime, however, the people should have a share, Aristotle argues. There is no argument for the justice of their claim—indeed, it is quite plainly asserted that they do not merit their office either for their virtue or for their capacities to rule for the good of the city:

> Although they are of an average sort, they have authority in the most important [judicial] decisions. Hence it would be better if they judged not at discretion but in accordance with written rules and the laws. Also the comportment of the overseers does not agree with the inclination of the city: it is overly lax, though in other respects the city goes to excess in the direction of harshness. (*Politics* II.9.1270b27–33)

There are only two grounds for granting the many a share. One is that they will make trouble if they have no share—they will not wish the regime preserved—a striking instance of political extortion to which Aristotle assents. The political imperative to preserve the regime through the common wish of all the inhabitants seems to outweigh the higher aim of distributive justice. The other reason is that the kings and the senate were becoming tyrannical and a balance against their influence was necessary. In this case, the (undeserving) citizens gain a share for the sake of the common good because the hereditary kingships and the education of Spartiates failed to produce virtuous rulers. The problem is not that Sparta's lawmakers stooped to low political considerations when creating the ephorate, but that they did so unwisely and unsuccessfully in response to another failure, that of the education of the Kings and the full citizens.

Thus, the Kings, supposedly descended from Heracles, and the venerable Senate do not escape scathing criticism. The Senate was meant to be an aristocratic element of this mixed regime, due to the senators' election and their status as elders, yet Aristotle sees the senators as senile, improperly educated, self-promoting bribe-takers. As a cure for their dangerous oligarchic propensities, Aristotle suggests that they be audited. He is reluctant to give the job to the ephors, for they already hold too much discretionary power in the regime, but, all other things being equal, they would be his choice.[49] That such an expedient—that the representatives of the many inspect and control the few—even enters the discussion as a plausible arrangement indicates again that Aristotle is not arguing for the reform of Sparta into the simply best regime, but is attempting to raise it to the level of a political regime with a fair chance at survival, a republic. His suggestion would not make the so-called aristocrats or the many into excellent men, but would balance the democratic elements of the city against the oligarchic elements to create a more stable regime.

On the other hand, Aristotle criticizes the senators' self-nomination using an aristocratic principle, that "one who merits the office should rule whether he wishes to or not."[50] This appearance of aristocracy may be deceptive, however. Aristotle speculates that "the legislator" must have wanted to promote ambition in the citizens when he instituted the practice. The argument against self-nomination is not solely that it may not select the best rulers, but also that "most voluntary acts of injustice among human beings result from ambition or greed."[51] Ambition in moderation is a virtue, not a vice,[52] and a moderate amount of it would be useful in a citizen of a republic. Yet any city, however defective in other respects, must want to discourage "voluntary acts of injustice." Aristotle could be using the standard of the republic, just as much as that of an aristocracy, in this warning against fostering excessive ambition among the city's "best men."[53]

Aristotle's commentary on the regime of the Lacedaemonians seems to aim much more toward the *Laws'* Magnesia than toward true aristocracy. To balance Sparta's oligarchic tendencies, Aristotle has praised the ephorate, while recommending that it be less corrupt and tyrannical, and he also praises the democratic institution of common meals, recommending it be so reformed that the poor could share in it as well as the rich. On the other hand, the grave error of the lawgiver in the presupposition of the Spartan regime stands as a warning to the founder of a republic, the regime that depends on those who bear heavy arms and possess a certain military virtue:

> The entire organization of the laws is with a view to a part of virtue—warlike virtue. . . . Yet while they preserved themselves as long as they were at war, they came to ruin when they were ruling an empire through not knowing how to be at leisure, and because there is no training among them that has more authority than the training for war. (*Politics* II.9.1271b2–7)

If the citizen body does not practice virtues other than courage, strength, and military cunning, it will believe that not the opportunities to practice the peaceful virtues, but merely the spoils and glory of war, are the ends for which they fight. "This error is no slight one. They consider that the good things men generally fight over are . . . better than virtue, which is not fine."[54] The citizens, not knowing the arts of peace and leisure, among them the art of politics, pursue only wealth and luxury when they return home—and they pursue them not in spite of, but as a result of, their rigorous training in military discipline and self-denial.[55] While giving full recognition to the need for military prowess in any political regime, Aristotle warns that it cannot be the exclusive preoccupation of the lawgivers or the citizens. Even if the armed class rules and is justified in doing so primarily on the ground of its military virtue, the regime must cultivate in its members and respect other virtues for times of peace.[56]

The only aspects of Sparta's way of life that escape strong criticism are essentially democratic. The *political* benefits of the principle of mixing a democratic element into an oligarchic regime become clear. These benefits remind of the lower rather than the exalted side of human life in common, of the power of numbers and self-love over virtue.[57] Sparta's experience serves as a warning to all founders and legislators. Assuming that at least the original lawgiver to whom Aristotle refers is Lycurgus and that Plutarch's profile of Lycurgus holds some water, the best intentions, thoughtful study of foreign governments, fairly sophisticated psychological analysis, and the most careful attention to minute details of everyday life will not prevent decline from lofty goals that will need to be addressed by future lawmakers. Moreover, to minimize inevitable unintended consequences in any adjustments, continuing attention to the distribution of property and to the liberal education of all citizens will be required in a Spartan republic.

CRETE: THE RULE OF LAW PLUS REAL POWER TO THE PEOPLE

The regime characteristic of Cretan cities, though it accomplishes some aims more fittingly, is not vastly superior to Sparta. Aristotle describes it as "less fully finished" or "less fully articulated."[58] Its common mess is more democratic in effect and thus more successful than Sparta's, for "everyone—women, children, and men—receives sustenance from the treasury." Aristotle calls the lawgiver "clever" or "philosophic"[59] in his understanding of the need to create a "beneficial" scarcity of food, and at the same time to control population growth by the encouragement of homosexuality and the segregation of the women.[60] As a whole, the provision for sustenance is kept in proportion to the population and does not invite the dissolution of virtue or foreign invasion that Aristotle envisions for Sparta.[61]

In the negative column, the Cretan orderers (*kosmoi*), whose powers correspond to those of the Spartan ephors, fall short of providing the political advantages of the ephors. Rather than being elected from all the people, and thus encouraging the many to wish the regime to continue, the orderers are elected from certain families and are then eligible to rise into the Council (the more evidently oligarchic body). Due to their quasi-democratic selection and status, the orderers are as little beneficial to the regime in their virtue or abilities as the ephors, and due to their oligarchic source, they are less beneficial in their political effect. Further, their opportunities to do harm are augmented by their assumption of leadership in war after the overthrow of the kingship. Moreover, the people's opportunities to defend themselves or to influence political decisions are limited to a virtually powerless assembly.[62]

This regime, like that of Sparta, is said to invite corruption because certain officials are not audited and are allowed to judge matters at their discretion and not according to laws.[63] Though there may be less corruption in Crete—there are said to be fewer instances of bribery here than in Sparta—this circumstance is not due to the orderers' virtue but to a fortuitous lack of offers. The insularity of Crete saves it from a common type of foreign influence to which the lawgivers failed to attend.[64]

Cretan cities are described as having succeeded where Sparta failed in the provision of leisure for the citizens by the use of serfs, the "*perioikoi.*" Again, this success does not reflect the wisdom of the Cretan lawgivers, however. It is instead attributed to a fear of their own serfs that surrounding cities do not ally with the Cretans' *perioikoi* to overthrow the regime. A certain international balance of terror holds between masters and servants in and around Crete, whereas Sparta's helots are not similarly deterred from frequent revolts.[65] The peacefulness of their serfs is attributed to the facts that Crete is protected by the sea and had not, since the time of Minos, pursued an imperial policy that would offend other cities and spur on those who could aid a serf rebellion.[66]

The lowest form of stability obtains in Cretan cities, a stability said twice to be "unsafe."[67] Aside from the uneasy calm among the serfs, the many keep quiet and do not revolt. This state of affairs does not indicate a "fine arrangement," because the officials rule "in accordance with human wish" and not "in accordance with law." The source of stability is not "political" but dynastic—rule by force. That is, the people do not share in rule, as political rule strictly speaking requires, and they are not empowered to expel the orderers once they are elected. This powerlessness would not be a reproach if this regime were a genuine aristocracy; the majority of the people would not be able to vote for just anyone nor to vote out incumbent officials. The Cretan regime is not, however, a genuine aristocracy, but an oligarchy, in which the members of certain families are assured offices whether they deserve them or not, and in which apparently many of the powerful families engage in factional warfare with each other and cause frequent civil disorder, even the dissolution of the government.[68] Such a situation is the very definition of political instability. When a defective regime is "not political," that is, it neglects to include the ordinary inhabitants in some functions, a dangerous situation results. The dynasties may succeed for a time in overpowering the many, but a dissatisfied majority, in addition to their rivalries with each other, will constantly threaten their ruling position.

In the course of making this point, Aristotle observes that Crete's "arrangement" has some elements of a republic, but actually is "rule of the powerful" (literally, dynasty[69]), which is, as Aristotle later describes it, the worst form of oligarchy: "when son succeeds father . . . and not law but the officials rule. This is the counterpart among oligarchies to tyranny among monarchies."[70] Also:

> If {those who own property} tighten it by being fewer and having larger properties, the third advance in oligarchy occurs—that where the offices are in their own hands, in accordance with a law requiring that the deceased be succeeded by their sons. When they tighten it excessively with respect to their properties and in the extent of their friendships, this sort of rule of the powerful is close to monarchy, and human beings rule rather than the law. This is the fourth kind of oligarchy, the counterpart to the final kind of democracy. (*Politics* IV.6.1293a26–34)

Generally speaking, the regime is the political entity: it embodies the laws, the arrangements of offices, and the way of life of the citizens of a city. In short, it is the whole in which politics takes place. Aristotle names the regime in which the majority rules for the common good "*politeia*," the name that names all regimes. This ambiguous name creates some problems for translation and interpretation.[71] In this case, the perspectives behind the two uses of the term are not mutually exclusive. If the Cretan regime is strongly dynastic, it is neither a republic (*politeia*) nor, in Aristotle's strict sense, a regime (*politeia*). If it is strongly dynastic, it is not rule of the many for the sake of the common good and it is not truly political life; order is maintained by force, not by the rule of law, persuasion, and education.

The first translation is supported by the immediate context, in that Aristotle goes on to describe the common disputes among the ruling families, supported by friends and followers, disputes that effectively dissolve the political order. Such a state of affairs can hardly be considered a regime—it is civil war. An examination of the broader context of the passage supports the second interpretation as well: The Cretan way of life has an indubitable democratic element: the arrangements for common meals in which all participate. The orderers' office, for which the people do vote, if not freely, represents a superficial attempt to involve the many in their government. If this office has become corrupt and the Council, which draws its members from the orderers, has carried its powers far beyond the intent of the lawgiver, then the Cretan cities may be said to have declined into dynasty from an older, more republican, regime. This decline may be related to Aristotle's earlier characterization of the regime as less fully articulated than Sparta. The lawgiver clearly tried to involve the people but may have lacked the political wisdom or historical examples to help to carry this intent into practice.

At any rate, both interpretations present apt points in preparation for Aristotle's argument in favor of the republic as the political regime par excellence. Either Aristotle distinguishes the regime (the political entity) from other sorts of social orderings, such as tyranny and its plural form, extreme dynasty, and thereby adds to his description of politics as a distinct human enterprise, or he distinguishes the *politeia* as a particular regime from unmixed oligarchy, and thus begins his demonstration of the superiority of the republic to one of the more common regimes, oligarchy.

CARTHAGE: ROTATING OFFICES AMONG THE LESS WEALTHY

In introducing the consideration of Carthage, Aristotle declares that "many of their arrangements are finely handled" and makes some general remarks on "a well-organized *politeia*." Apparently these criteria apply to Carthage: "The people[72] voluntarily acquiesce in the arrangement . . . there has never been factional conflict[73] worth mentioning, or a tyrant."[74] Any regime (here again Aristotle excludes tyranny from that category) must have general acquiescence, and not constant factional battling, in order to carry on its governance and way of life. This statement gives the political entity at least two essential characteristics: it is something internally peaceful and its citizens are not enslaved, but rather are willing to be ruled by its arrangements. Whereas Crete quite obviously fails these tests, Sparta comes closer to fulfilling these criteria, and as Aristotle will argue, Carthage even closer.

The Carthaginian common "messes are similar to" those of the Spartans, which is not praise, but its offices are generally better ordered. Its version of the ephors (the Hundred and Four) and its kings and senate are superior, principally because they are elected to office on the basis of merit, not heredity (in the case of the kings) or age (in the case of the senators), nor are they selected by chance from just any people, as Aristotle implies is the case with the Spartan ephors. After this introduction, Aristotle dismisses the possibility that Carthage, or either of the other actual regimes, has achieved the simply best regime. Carthage is grouped with Sparta and Crete in their common deviations from the best regime. Carthage, however, deviates uniquely from "the basic premise[75] of aristocracy and polity." Unlike Sparta and Crete, Carthage is not predominantly oligarchic. Rather, "some features incline toward rule of the people, others toward oligarchy."[76] If it is not the best, at least it represents a more balanced mixture of the elements of these two common regimes, along with some elements of aristocracy. A well-balanced mixture will be the *sine qua non* of a republic; a well-balanced mixture with the addition of an attention to virtue will be characteristic of the republic "through the middling element." To reveal further qualities of a strictly political form of government, it is necessary to discern Carthage's especially "political" characteristics and to ask what is done well and what may need to be improved.

All proposals, save those on which the senate and kings agree, must be submitted to the people for ratification or rejection. The democratic element of the regime exists not merely for the sake of appearances, therefore. The people may speak against, present their own opinions on, and come to an independent decision concerning these proposals, as well as others voluntarily submitted to them. Representing the opposite element of the regime are the "Committees of Five, which have authority in many great matters." Self-selection, the power to elect to "the greatest office," and the influence of their members even when outside of office render these bodies oligarchic. There are even aspects of aristocracy in the Carthaginian practices of election (vs. the use of the lot) and of not paying the officials, and in the arrangements for trials. Because many hold that "rulers ought not to be elected on the basis of desert alone but also on the basis of wealth" in order that the rulers be at leisure, the election practices are not simply aristocratic, but also oligarchic, "particularly in the case of the greatest offices, kings and generals."[77]

Aristotle initially criticizes these mixed priorities: if he wants the best men to rule, the legislator must take care that the men of virtue be able to be at leisure, not assume that the leisured are all virtuous. Officials receive no pay for their duties in order to prevent them from entering office for the profit, and yet this practice ensures that only the wealthy can afford to serve the regime—the same method used to discourage corruption may in fact encourage it by barring the virtuous from taking office, as Aristotle assumes that the good are not necessarily rich. In effect, the "greatest offices . . . can be bought." The argument that this effect is harmful accords with the principles of aristocracy, but not with those of oligarchy. "This law makes wealth something more honored than virtue, and the city as a whole greedy."[78] Aristotle is less concerned here with the mix of oligarchy and democracy than with setting a standard for a regime with some admixture of aristocracy, one in which the authoritative element will influence the whole citizen body to follow a beneficial opinion.[79]

In contrast to this aristocratic criticism, Aristotle next comments on a Carthaginian institution that is not popular enough: it is considered beneficial to bestow multiple offices on one man. Without providing the Carthaginian argument for such an opinion, Aristotle deprecates the practice on two grounds: "One work is best accomplished by one" and it is "more political . . . and more popular"[80] to have more persons in offices. "The legislator should . . . not command the same person to play the flute and cut leather."[81] The famous Socratic injunction that one man have only one art in the best regime might be taken to be a model for this argument, yet Aristotle attacked this aspect of the *Republic*, arguing that it is more salutary for the political partnership among equals that offices rotate, that "shoemakers and carpenters change places rather than the same persons always being shoemakers and carpenters."[82] Aristotle agrees that where the differences are quite discernible specialization is preferable. As in the account of Sparta, Aristotle here again says that "those capable of ruling best should rule,"[83] rather than allowing the rulers to be chosen on the basis of a less relevant standard, such as wealth. Where, however, "all are equal in their nature, and where it is at the same time just for all to have a share in ruling," that is, where all deserve office roughly equally, political power should rotate among the citizens. When one returns to ruling, he may not occupy the same office. This alternation of ruling and being ruled is not inconsistent with the more minimal suggestion here that one person perform one art *at a time*: in both contexts Aristotle is arguing for the more "political" arrangement among equals; in the earlier case, political is distinguished from hierarchic and aristocratic, here, from exclusive and oligarchic. In both cases, he advocates the arrangement that will involve more persons in the offices of the regime and will accustom more people to the ways of both ruling and being ruled, as both are required in many important occupations, for example, the military and sailing.[84]

The Carthaginians could thus remedy the exclusivity of their offices fairly easily. Other tendencies to oligarchy are balanced by a fortunate upward mobility in society: "a part of the people is always becoming wealthy through being sent out to the cities" of their empire. The danger that the poor will revolt is doubly cured by sending them away and by making them less poor. Yet, "if some mischance were to occur," perhaps if the empire were to fall, Aristotle warns, "there is no medicine that will restore quiet through the laws."[85] Whether his suggestions for broader political participation and for the reward of virtue over wealth are meant to be that medicine is not clear, but they might ameliorate this major defect in domestic arrangements.

Thus, in Carthage, as in Sparta and Crete, the majority of Aristotle's criticisms center on the problem of keeping the many satisfied and preventing a revolt. Though Carthage receives more praise than the others and is twice associated with aristocracy, the regime proves to be too oligarchic in its mixture of elements even for a well-mixed republic, and Aristotle fears for its future on this account. To improve the regime into either an aristocracy or a true republic would require both the alteration of some institutions and the education of the citizens' political opinions so that wealth would not be honored above either virtue or the claims of the free majority.

MAKING RESPECTED REGIMES MORE RESPECTABLE

The concluding chapter of Book II discusses legislators, including Solon (most prominently) and Lycurgus, and sparks consideration of the role of the lawgiver in establishing the best regime. Some commentators suggest that the three highly praised regimes ultimately failed because their lawgivers did not go the whole way toward the theoretically best, but it seems to follow from Aristotle's arguments that he sees these famous lawgivers as aiming too high for the citizen body or circumstances available to them. There are indications that, if they had aimed more consciously at a well-mixed republic, they would have served their cities better. The "first function of the lawgiver and true politician" is indeed "to establish and maintain the best constitution," but that best constitution for real lawgivers in real cities is not the one that "one would pray for above all, with external things providing no impediment," but rather "the best that circumstances allow."[86] While the *science* of politics practiced by philosophers includes contemplation of the simply best regime, the *art* of politics seems to be a different activity: one that encompasses knowing what the best regime might be theoretically, but also acting upon practical knowledge of a given populace and its circumstances. Every city is "impeded" by external circumstances; no regime can actually come to be "according to" a philosopher's "prayers."

Aristotle is arguing that some qualities of human nature can be foreseen, but how those qualities will interact with each other and with the surrounding circumstances is not simply predictable. In the course of her comprehensive interpretation of Aristotle's *Politics*, Mary Nichols argues that Aristotle's view is that overall the lawgivers of Sparta, Crete, and Carthage "were not comprehensive enough."[87] As she points out, they started down paths of economic, family, and educational regulation, but did not anticipate the many consequences that their regulations could produce.[88] She sees Aristotle exhorting subsequent statesmen to "a further exertion of reason" to correct their regimes for these purposes. If Aristotle judged that these three cities could realistically succeed in achieving the simply best regime, such an exhortation would be required. He is advising those cities, however, as he advises "most cities and men" in Books IV through VI, to embrace the republic as the best *political* regime, that is, to embrace both the mixed institutional arrangements that favor none of the parts of the city (not even the highly virtuous) over other parts and the moderate policies that a middling element will favor. Rather than attempt to anticipate the unpredictable or to educate a populace not suited to the highest virtue, the prudent legislator sets up a balance of power between wealthy and poor (which also means between virtuous and vicious, between educated and merely literate, even between wealth and poverty themselves) and allows the citizen body to respond to problems as they arise in the course of political life.

Using the criticisms of Sparta, Crete, and Carthage as part of his argument that Aristotle is trying to work through the difference, and yet the unavoidable connection, between political theory and political practice, Michael Davis observes that all three regimes are shown to have an idea, and not a bad idea, about the best way to organize a city, but all three work or do not work because of a collision with reality that proves their theories ultimately false. Lycurgus' laws aim at manliness and moderation and result in the dominance of women and licentiousness. Despite its unnamed lawgiver's intentions,[89] Crete seems to have stumbled accidentally upon a way to enforce moderation and harmony by being an island and short on rations, but in Aristotle's day, Crete is nonetheless falling prey to invasion.[90] The legislators of Carthage note correctly that wealthy men are in a better position to be virtuous, but by using wealth as a criterion for office, they succeed only in encouraging oligarchy rather than aristocracy. All three regimes muddle through, but not for the reasons their legislators intended.[91]

By no means does Aristotle take up a comprehensive analysis of Solon's Athens as a regime held in high repute by political thinkers, though he allows that "some . . . suppose him to have been an excellent legislator." He mentions Solon and Lycurgus as "craftsmen" of "both laws and regimes" in the last chapter of Book II, but not Solon's regime as an excellent regime.[92] Solon's appears to be a cautionary tale for legislators with more modest goals, those who wish to bring about a moderate, mixed regime out of an oligarchy: just as it is difficult to hit the mean between extremes that is the working definition of ethical virtue in the *Nicomachean Ethics*, it is difficult to introduce just the right amount of popular influence in a regime to balance out the excesses of an oligarchy. It is somewhat unclear whether Aristotle blames Solon or later statesmen for augmenting the people's power to a dangerous extent and failing to anticipate how the people would react to a combination of political power with their newfound military influence,[93] but Solon seems to escape the harshest of the criticism and to be praised for trying to guard the regime from acquiring enemies while using franchise restrictions to keep the least-worthy out of the important offices.[94]

As Aristotle will argue in Book III, politics is neither merely an economic nor essentially a military relationship, although the political order must attend to the sufficiency of goods to support the lives of its citizens and to the defense of the city from external enemies. Sparta fails in two ways with its education. First, it focuses so much on military virtue that it ignores the virtues of peace, so that Sparta's internal politics is characterized by corruption and the tyranny of the majority. Second, it takes the cluster of military virtues to such an extreme that an ordinary person cannot live up to its standards—someone who is reasonable, accommodating to all parties, self-reliant, and only moderately ambitious would likely fail on Lycurgus' training field. Spartans were taught to revere only the perfect soldier perfectly devoted to his city, but the education actually produced some (though not enough) very good warriors, and those devoted to hoarding wealth.

The first two books of the *Politics* supply a number of insights into Aristotle's understanding of the activity of politics and the arrangements proper to political life. He distinguishes standards according to which a political regime is to be judged excellent from standards for judging the best regime "according to prayer." He introduces a standard for a stable and decent regime, and that standard is applied to the regimes of Sparta, Crete, and Carthage in suggestions for their improvement. The citizens of the simply best regime may be held to the exacting expectations of full virtue, but the simply best regime and this virtue are apolitical in an important respect: their essential aims lie beyond politics. Insofar as Lycurgus expected extraordinary virtue (moderation and justice flowing from military perfection) to spring from his foundations and flourish in a real city, he doomed his regime to fail. Thus, "the best" becomes the enemy of "the best political" regime.

If a human being is by nature a political animal, a being whose perfection lies in some significant part in its political participation, then the best political regime, the best situation in which human beings rule and are ruled in turn for the sake of a good life of attainable virtue, is both a worthy subject of thoughtful speculation and the most valuable aim of active political founders and legislators. The virtue attainable by ordinary, decent human beings, the citizen obligations manageable by people who are not usually at leisure, and the level of deliberation achievable by these moderately virtuous citizens all point to the republic, indeed toward the republic based on the middling element that Aristotle will elaborate in Book IV.

Aristotle, who had the luxury of thinking about and expanding the whole range of knowledge of his day, could compose the *Politics* with a variety of goals: not only to define the activity of politics and the regime(s) most conducive to it, but also to speculate on the best regime and its requirements. There is no indication in the *Politics* that Aristotle expects his speculative best regime to come to be in the world—no indication, for instance, that he considered it possible to overcome the vices that destroy all regimes. Surely political rulers can learn from the past and from the experience of other cities, but as Aristotle's best regime shows, the best education cannot even aim to produce a city of philosophers; at best, it can aim to produce a ruling class with temperate military virtues and sophisticated artistic taste. Moreover, the most carefully constructed system of oversight cannot deter all bad actions or keep the necessary evil of a slave class under control.

Though Sparta, Crete, and Carthage aimed at becoming aristocracies, Aristotle praises them for the aspects that would make them republics. In the present day, real communities with aspirations to aristocracy, that is, with elections based upon merit and with governments attempting to hold a high moral ground in both international and domestic policy, should take Aristotle's practical political advice to heart. No political order, no order that respects the freedom and the equal claims of all its citizens can control all the chance events or the human choices that would need to be controlled in order to predict the long-range effects of their policies. Moreover, a regime that controls education and the actions of citizens to such an extent that it can guarantee full virtue is not actually producing virtue, which is a matter of reasoned choice. The best solution is not to aim so high in the first place—the best *political* regime is not the best that can be imagined, but the best that can be accomplished among free and equal people, people practicing politics. Aristotle's reasoning leads to a system in which the claims and the powers of the major social/economic classes are balanced against each other and in which the middle class will be inclined and empowered to keep those claims in balance. Aiming higher does not improve the situation; it is more likely to be detrimental to the individual citizens and to the regime as a whole.

2

CITIZENS, RULERS, AND THE LAW
ARISTOTLE ON POLITICAL AUTHORITY

Aristotle's insights into politics as a distinct and authoritative human activity lead into descriptions of the regime labeled "polity" or "republic" and form the basis of the evaluation of this good regime ruled by a large number of citizens. In turn, the accounts of the republic deepen further Aristotle's teaching concerning political life. He elaborates the sense in which "political" is his standard against which a human community that does not produce—that does not even try to produce—an aristocracy of "outstanding" virtue can be said to be the best. Aristotle's assessment of the defects found in the most common regimes and, on the other hand, the political contributions of which "a certain kind" of citizens is capable anticipate some of the remarkable aspects of Aristotle's praise of the middle class and its republic.

THE REPUBLIC: THE GOOD REGIME RULED BY MANY

Following the section on citizenship in Book III, which concludes with the centrality of the particular regime in defining and evaluating citizenship,[1] Aristotle outlines the variety of regimes and their distinguishing characteristics. The remainder of the *Politics* is structured to elaborate on the six fundamental regime types and their subtypes, assessing each for justice and durability. Of all of these regimes, those called "political" in the strict sense, that is, democracies, oligarchies, certain aristocracies, and republics, are the most relevant to an account of Aristotle's best political regime. When these regimes are not in a corrupt condition, human beings are ruled in a political manner, that is, rulership rotates among the members of the citizen body, however broadly or narrowly that membership is defined.

In his famous chart of the six basic regimes, Aristotle describes the republic as the regime in which "the multitude governs with a view to the common advantage."[2] An important factor in determining the character of a regime is the sort of person admitted to citizenship. Here, the regime is identified with the citizen body or governing body,[3] and the citizen body of the republic consists of those who possess heavy arms and practice military virtue. The standards against which the goodness of both the regime and the citizen body are judged are the requirements of political life, as distinct from other human activities.

Cities exist, Aristotle reminds his audience here, because human beings are naturally political, that is, there is a powerful urge to come together in relationships of rulers and ruled for the sake of mutual assistance in the support of life and the good life, and for the sake of simply living with other human beings.[4] The latter reason, friendship, which is discussed more extensively in the *Nicomachean Ethics*, is even an essential part of the best human life.[5] Neither gaining help nor friendship, however, provides the necessary inducement for a citizen to be devoted to a *particular* regime ordering his city. Although politics is natural to human beings, good citizenship in a particular regime must be defined and cultivated, and it is defined and cultivated differently in different regimes. Political cities, and a republic in particular, must pay careful attention to citizen education because of the large citizen body.

The purpose of city life is mutual assistance for life and the good life, so the types of regimes are first divided into the just and the defective according to whether they aim at such mutual assistance—the common good—or at the benefit of the ruler(s) alone. Only the rule of a master over slaves is properly aimed at the advantage of the ruler intentionally and that of the ruled only accidentally.[6] One may imagine a large number of slavish people properly ruled by one simply superior master, but this arrangement, classic tyranny, would not constitute a city, according to Aristotle's definition. The slaves would contribute to the good life of their superior, and the despot might, for his own benefit, act to preserve the lives of his subjects, but the latter could never participate in the good human life, and they are clearly neither equal to their master nor free. No *polis*, no political life, is possible without a "community of free persons," and no good political life is possible without attention to the good of all involved.[7]

Where political life *is* possible, that is, where a populace is free (in the sense of being capable of some self-mastery or the deliberate choice among actions[8]), no one should rule but for the benefit of the common. The form that such rule takes "naturally" is alternation of office among essentially equal citizens.[9] In recognition of the fact that no one among them has an outstanding capability to order the affairs of everyone else, the citizens of a political regime in the strict sense take turns caring for the common advantage and allowing others to do so.[10] Even while holding office, one must act as if one were one of the ruled, obeying the law and taking no special advantages from the position. Since the city exists for the pursuit of life and the good life in common, ruling and being ruled should be viewed as equally necessary parts of a common effort. Aristotle avoids the argument that political rule should be understood as exclusively for the benefit of the ruled. Rather, he distinguishes politics from the rule of the father over the household. A paternalistic attitude encourages a feeling of superiority rather than equality, and could lead to demands for a higher reward from office. Further, no one would take political office willingly if its onerous tasks produced no benefit for the ruler.[11] If wages were the only benefit, people would seek office only for personal profit. It must be made clear that political rule lies between paternalism and despotism, that, in a well-ordered community, the ruler benefits as much as, but not greatly more than, one of the ruled.

According to Aristotle, the fact that people actually seek office avidly and far out of proportion to this willingness merely to take turns ruling and being ruled indicates that fifth-century regimes are corrupt: they do not understand politics and do not fulfill its proper potential. The predominant oligarchies and democracies encourage people to serve in office primarily or exclusively for their own advantage, by rewarding rulers with wealth or much discretionary power.[12] While the practical threat of excessive paternalism in politics was small, most cities in Aristotle's time were ruled despotically, by his definition:

> Previously, as accords with nature, they claimed to merit doing public service by turns and having someone look to their good, just as when ruling previously they looked to his advantage. Now, however, because of the benefits to be derived from common things and from office, they wish to rule continuously, as if they were sick persons who were always made healthy by ruling; at any rate, these would perhaps pursue office in a similar fashion. It is evident, then, that those regimes which look to the common advantage are correct regimes according to what is unqualifiedly just, while those which look only to the advantage of the rulers are errant, and are all deviations from the correct regimes; for they involve mastery, but the city is a community of free persons. (*Politics* III.6.1279a11–22)

Actual cities are full of people of a despotic bent, who believe that they are "sick" unless they are ruling.[13] Tyrants or masters rule almost exclusively for the sake of bodily desire. Keeping in mind Aristotle's chastisement of Phaleas, that "no one becomes a tyrant in order to get in out of the cold,"[14] the satisfaction of material desires, including honor and power for its own sake or to satisfy more desires, is the aim of a despot's relationship with his subjects or slaves. Indeed, there is little more a ruler could expect to gain from those he views as vastly inferior servants. Politics is, however, aimed at another end and relationship, the good life, understood as being beyond mere life and its material concomitants. A central flaw in most cities is the failure to recognize just this distinguishing characteristic of politics. Oligarchy and democracy can be political, they can seek a common good, if properly moderated, but, on the basis of their principles, they tend to become tyrannical in precisely this sense.[15]

With this distinction between good and bad regimes in mind, Aristotle lists the six fundamental types of rule. Among the good, the rule of one is kingship, of few aristocracy, and of many a republic (polity); the corresponding corrupt regimes are called tyranny, oligarchy, and democracy. Very quickly the distinctions are shown not to depend on number so much as on other qualities in the ruling body: oligarchy is rule by the wealthy who happen usually to be few; democracy, by the poor who are usually many.[16] Both here and in the later descriptions of the republic, it is clear that what distinguishes this regime from true aristocracy is not solely the number of the rulers, but also the type of virtue they exemplify:

> When the multitude governs with a view to the common advantage, it is called by the term common to all regimes, polity [*politeia*]. This happens reasonably. It is possible for one or a few to be outstanding in virtue, but where more are concerned it is difficult for them to be proficient with a view to virtue as a whole, but some level of proficiency is possible particularly regarding military virtue, as this arises in a multitude; hence in this regime the warrior element is the most authoritative, and it is those possessing heavy arms who take part in it. (*Politics* III.7.1279a38–b5)

Genuine aristocrats acquire and practice "virtue as a whole," while the citizens of a republic can only achieve a level and type of virtue available to a multitude. Here this virtue is denominated military.[17] To earn its status as a good regime versus the despotic regimes just described, a republic must empower rulers who are concerned with the common good, who cultivate some virtue in the citizens, and who are willing to give up office and be ruled by others.

Having condemned as defective the two most prevalent forms of government, oligarchy and democracy, Aristotle must explain why so many cities and peoples have adopted these corrupt regimes. Even the widely touted Athenian democracy is defective. Democrats are, he says, correct in their principle that justice is equality, and the recognition of this idea will prove vital to a political regime. Oligarchs, however, are also correct that justice is inequality. Neither is completely correct, because each is unwilling to admit the partial truth of the other's claim:

> For all fasten on a certain sort of justice, but proceed only to a certain point, and do not speak of the whole of justice in its authoritative sense. For example, justice is held to be equality, and it is, but for equals and not for all; and inequality is held to be just and is indeed, but for unequals and not for all; but they disregard this element of persons and judge badly. . . . They judge badly with respect to what concerns themselves, but also because both, by speaking to a point of a kind of justice, consider themselves to be speaking of justice simply. (*Politics* III.9.1280a9–15, 21–23)

The poor believe that their equality in freedom is the only criterion of worth, and thus that all free citizens are entitled to equal political influence. The rich believe that their inequality in wealth renders them superior in all respects. As Aristotle suggests here, neither party can be trusted to give a just answer. Insofar as human beings must make the determinations of justice in any real-world case, all justice is tainted with self-love.[18] The political truth about justice—not an abstract notion, but justice as it applies to actual persons and actual regimes—lies somewhere between the claims of the oligarch and the democrat, in a place that cannot be determined a priori.

The fundamental error of both these most common political types is not only that they enter politics for their own gain, but that they take material possessions or the lack of them to be the prime factor of political life. If this belief were true, the political regime would be merely a joint stock company. One's birth in a certain place or from citizen parents would be irrelevant, and the only political debate would concern the way to divide the profits. Neither is the regime an alliance for the prevention of theft and the promotion of fair trade, that is, the minimum material requirements for the maintenance of life. Aristotle asserts, rather, that political associations exist "not only for the sake of living but rather primarily for the sake of living well" and that their citizens share "in happiness or in living in accordance with intentional choice," not merely in a common storehouse of property.[19] The democrats and oligarchs must be credited to the extent that a city cannot exist without both a free multitude and wealth; "whoever takes thought for good governance, however, gives careful attention to political virtue and vice."[20]

One might be tempted to make the same criticism of a republic, as it has been described to this point, as Aristotle makes of democracy and oligarchy, for "in this regime the warrior element is the most authoritative, and it is those possessing heavy arms who take part in it."[21] Aristotle needs to explain why it is good political practice to reward with exclusive political power those who provide only one, albeit a necessary, material benefit to the city, the wherewithal for its defense. Just as Aristotle suggests that the truth about political justice lies somewhere between the claims of the oligarch and the democrat, he will eventually set the optimum property requirement for the good regime ruled by many between the rich and the poor, at the level necessary to own armaments. This regime is not a military junta; it is the rule of the middle class. In defense of the virtue of these middling property holders, Aristotle seems to suggest that, however unextraordinary, the self-supporting citizen-warrior displays some virtues, while a poor freeman or a very wealthy oligarch need not display any virtues to maintain his status. To define a citizen body in terms of military capacity, then, is to give some attention to political virtue.[22]

Politics is not merely an economic nor essentially a military relationship. Although the political order must attend to the sufficiency of goods and to the defense of the city, as was clear in the discussions of Carthage and Sparta, these concerns must not consume all its attention or its power. Nor is a city constituted by a mere "alliance to prevent their suffering injustice from anyone, nor for purposes of exchanges and use of one another."[23] The political relationship, though it includes economics, household management, intermarriage, and international relations as essential components, is more than any one, or even the sum, of these enterprises. A true political order must establish common offices with authority over all its members and must use these offices to take care that the citizens measure up to its standards of just and good, at least in their political capacities, that is, to attend to "political virtue and vice."[24] This attention to political virtue is grounded in friendship or affection—the truly political regime is filled not with enemies nor with indifferent allies held at bay by a peace treaty, but with those who care about the goodness of their fellows and "intentionally choose" to associate with one another.[25] Political associations are not mere alliances; they are superior to alliances in that they aim for internal sufficiency and for the virtue and justice of their members. Political life is, however, related to an alliance, and political order always exists alongside the threat of disorder, in that the multitude involved is not tied together by natural kinship nor by strong friendship, but rather is formed from an aggregation of roughly equal adults, among whom some ties must be carefully nurtured and may easily be disrupted.[26]

It is now possible to imagine some of the characteristics of a successful political community in Aristotle's eyes. Through common activities such as festivals, households and citizens demonstrate the "intentional choice" of living together and strengthen the cohesion of the whole in pursuing a good life together. Such activities contribute little to the maintenance of mere life, but rather show the community's transcendence of necessity, its desire and capacity to act freely. Aristotle also argues that genuine friendship requires private property in order to provide opportunities for liberality (the quint-essential virtue of a free human being) and for the pleasure of having one's possessions to offer to a friend. The successful political community will place its foundation in pleasurable, limited, and voluntary friendship, based on a regulated economy that sustains private property.[27]

Accordingly, citizens do not merely live together in a place, but live together "for the sake of noble actions." Democrats and oligarchs fail to see that neither descent from free ancestors nor great wealth is a guarantee that a citizen will contribute to noble action.[28] Aristotle discerns a political virtue, according to which the principles of oligarchy and democracy are deficient precisely because they do not aspire to all that politics can achieve. The fact that a citizen has a "function" means that there must be a virtue of citizens.[29] Aristotle adduces here another argument for the centrality of virtue to political life: political virtue or noble action is what distinguishes the full practice of true politics from the practice of subordinate parts of politics (economic activity or household management, which may call forth some virtues, but not all and not the finer ones) or from the defective practice of democracy or oligarchy.

Though Aristotle has not spelled out his concept of political virtue, he has established that any citizen virtue must be available to all citizens and should not be confused with the whole of virtue, practiced by only a few great men. Nonetheless, the modern reader is likely to be taken aback by the notion that the political order should attend to individual virtue and vice at all. The standards for political virtue are not unattainably high; thus, the actions taken by a good regime to support these standards need not be extreme. In the most political regime, the republic, public attention to virtue will rely on private attention to self-sufficiency and a moderate public spirit. Aristotle will attribute much of the excellence of the middle-class republic to its ability to provide the political support for the private pursuit of life and the good life; a significant part of this necessary support is a public standard of political virtue.

Aristotle has just denominated this attainable political virtue "military virtue." The military virtue most commonly praised is courage, but other excel-lences and qualities of soul are required of a soldier. Significantly, the ability to command others sensibly and successfully must be combined in military life with the ability and willingness to carry out the orders of one's superiors. Military life also demands the controlled spiritedness that grounds the defense of one's friends and fellow citizens. In political life, strictly speaking, Aristotle insists on both ruling and being ruled and on the distinctly different treatment of fellow citizens (with affection), allies (with justice), and all others.[30]

This section of the *Politics* introduces the republic as part of Aristotle's accounting of good regimes. A large segment of this city rules, the element with a certain virtue of ruling and being ruled in turn and of defending one's friends against one's enemies. Further, distinctly unpolitical or incompletely political ways of organizing a community are introduced and dismissed: trade agreements and the prevention of injustice are parts, but not the whole, of politics; an alliance among people who care nothing for the virtue and justice of one another is not politics; the rule of others for the sole benefit of the ruled is paternalism; and the rule of others for the sole benefit of the ruler(s) is despotism, that is, slavery writ large. The task of a successful republic is to foster political friendship among its citizens, as a result of which they will trust each other to rule and treat each other as free and equal human beings, rather than as children or subjects, customers or employees.

AUTHORITY IN A POLITICAL REGIME

Because the citizens constitute the ruling body of a regime, and because qualifications for citizenship differ among regimes, qualifications for ruling must vary accordingly. Having established some criteria for judging good citizens and good regimes, Aristotle in Chapters 10 through 13 investigates the question of good and bad candidates for holding the authority to rule. Several criteria are taken up and criticized, leaving only a few possibilities.

In describing the ruling bodies of democracy or oligarchy, Aristotle considered numbers less significant than the economic characteristics the people possess—wealth or impoverished freedom. The title of the poor to rule does not rest solely on their majority status, and their claim to be the rightful authority is attacked on the ground that when they exercise full discretion, they are apt, because of their poverty, to use their authority to confiscate the wealth of the few. Even if the most authoritative body in the city resolves on this action, and even if that body constitutes the majority of the city, this action is unjust, as it would be unjust for the wealthy few or a powerful tyrant to plunder the property of all the rest.

The injustice of mass confiscation is not based on a human right to property or any other justice inherent in the individual, but on the observation about human nature that those from whom property is taken will unite to destroy the regime, whereas justice preserves a regime: "Yet it is certainly not virtue that destroys the element possessing it, nor is justice destructive of a city; so it is clear that this law cannot be just."[31] Clearly Aristotle does not equate the just with the legal. If by definition justice does not destroy the city and, therefore, the destructive is unjust, then justice preserves the city, and that which preserves the city makes a prima facie case for being just. Justice, including the justice of a particular person's claim to rule, cannot be considered in abstraction from the political need to preserve the locus of justice, the city itself and its regime. This argument reappears in several contexts.

In the case of the defective regimes, it is not surprising that Aristotle's criticisms focus on threats to the authority of the ruling body and, thus, threats to the stability of the regime. If a ruling body takes the property of the other inhabitants or uses force as its primary method of law enforcement, the regime is unjust because it will destroy the city. In this section, the claim that the just is simply the legal (that which is resolved by the authoritative element) is associated with the claim that the just is the will of the stronger (with strength resulting from numerical superiority, wealth, or physical or military power). Aristotle rejects both definitions of justice. If the ruling body can make no other argument for its legitimacy than the fact of its being in authority or its strength to stay in power by force, a more numerous or wealthier or better-armed element of the city may threaten its overthrow. Such a threat would be just according to the principles of these regimes, while at the same time it reveals the regime's instability.

One might suggest that the flaws Aristotle has discerned in these first three candidates for political authority—the strongest, the wealthiest, and the most numerous—result from a lack of restraint on the part of the unvirtuous persons in power, and thus that only the fit and good or the respectable should be allowed to rule. Yet this alternative proves unsatisfactory as well. Unless Aristotle is still worried about the same sort of discontent, this time among the unfit and bad, it is difficult to explain why he disparages aristocracy in the way he does: "In this case, all the others are necessarily deprived of prerogatives, since they are not honored by attaining political offices. For we say that offices are honors, and when the same persons always rule the others are necessarily deprived of [these honors or] prerogatives."[32] This situation was not questioned during the discussion of citizenship—there a citizen was said to be eligible for ruling office or honors, a noncitizen not. The justice of the rule of the best for the good of the whole was also not questioned in the earlier description of aristocracy.[33] The fit and good or the respectable mentioned here might be the prudent and virtuous citizens described in the chapters on citizenship, that is, the best human beings for rule. Nonetheless, the consideration of threats to the regime takes precedence over the consideration of distributive justice, just as it did in the criticisms of Sparta, Crete, and Carthage. These threats also mitigate the claims of "the one who is most excellent of all," the king whose regime is "still more oligarchic" in its deprivation of prerogatives.[34]

Aristotle needs to explain what can be done to discourage these threats while maintaining a regime that pays some attention to political virtue.

If neither those who can restrain their desires for gain nor those who cannot should rule, and neither those who claim rule on the basis of ethical merit nor those who take power because of their strength, perhaps the law should rule. This suggestion, familiar to students of modern democracy, is unsatisfactory if left unqualified. The law could easily be drafted to favor the inordinate desires of one group or to dishonor a large element of the city. What is wrong with all the candidates for authority mentioned—the poor, the wealthy, the tyrant, the respectable, and the "most excellent"—is not that they have desires, nor that they will attempt to gratify those desires; these are flaws that a written law might correct. What is wrong is that they strive for exclusivity in their gratifications. All of these schemes are too "oligarchic," and this flaw cannot be remedied simply by the institution of the rule of law as opposed to the rule of men, for the law could simply enshrine those oligarchic tendencies. Although Aristotle will soon argue that the rule of law is generally safer than rule by even the best human being, laws can be unjust. If it is not simply obvious to all that a law radically redistributing goods or political honors is "bad and unjust," it is surely obvious that many will consider it so. All regimes—not only those literally or nominally resting on a principle of equality, but also those resting on commonly accepted standards of inequality—are advised in this chapter to consider the claims of the excluded. Even those who do not measure up to a regime's standards may have at least a partial claim to consideration.

The only ruling body whose claims Aristotle does not disparage in this results-based argument is that of the republic, consisting of the multitude possessing arms and displaying some military virtue. A regime that distributes honors and offices among the greatest number and, because of its citizens' virtues, restrains its desires for exclusive gratification, a regime that deprives no one of honor arbitrarily or by force, will have a better chance of maintaining stability. Aristotle will defend the claims of the majority with some ardor, stating perhaps all that can be said in general for an unspecified multitude of admittedly not-excellent persons.[35]

THE EXCELLENCE OF "A CERTAIN KIND OF MULTITUDE"

In defending political power in the hands of the majority, Aristotle begins with the collective virtue of many who are individually undistinguished: if there are enough citizens, their virtues taken as a whole could exceed that of one or a few outstanding human beings. Such a successful concatenation of partial virtues, resulting in the whole being greater than the sum of its parts, would require extraordinarily good fortune (remember that Aristotle has just implied that military virtue is the sole class of virtues generally found in a multitude), or extraordinarily careful coordination of the plethora of individual contributions. Only in unusual circumstances does one actually find, as a democratic voice asserts, that "dinners contributed by many" are "better than those equipped from a single expenditure," or that "the many are also better judges of the works of music and of the poets."[36] If these maxims are true, they are true in a popular sense, and not so much so on an educated level.[37] Quantity cannot be so easily converted to quality in these cases—perhaps even less easily in a political situation. Only with the aid of one overarching ruling principle, if at all, can many feet, hands, senses, characters, and minds be combined into one excellent human being, just as only with the skill and genius of a great artist can the beautiful aspects of various people be combined into one flawless portrait, more beautiful than any existent person.[38] An oligarchic or aristocratic voice, referring emphatically to the similarity between some multitudes and beasts, introduces a strong doubt at this point that every people and every multitude could achieve this collective virtue. Aristotle seems then to sum up this debate, saying that "nothing prevents what was said from being true of a certain kind of multitude."[39]

It is clear that most democracies, resting solely on the equality in freedom and strength in numbers of the poor, will be defective in Aristotle's eyes. Yet, he holds out the possibility that a well-regulated and well-trained multitude could form an admirable, even virtuous regime. Since no virtue is simply natural to a human being, training in good habits will be required in any good regime.[40] The consideration of what habits are crucially necessary to a decent regime remains to be addressed, but Aristotle does not rule out the possibility of answering the question.[41]

If it is possible that a well-ordered free multitude could competently participate in the governing of a good regime, perhaps the many free people without "any claim at all deriving from virtue" should have authority in "the greatest offices."[42] The many must be given some prerogatives in order to retain them as friends of the regime, Aristotle reiterates, yet the offices with the greatest discretionary power require a greater-than-average capacity for just and prudent decision-making. Since deliberation and judging were earlier made the minimum requirements of a citizen, perhaps a deliberative assembly and popular juries are the most appropriate offices for the undistinguished citizens to share, places in which they would vote for and evaluate the higher officials, but make no decisions individually.[43] "For all of them when joined together have an adequate perception and, once mixed with those who are better, bring benefit to cities, just as impure sustenance mixed with the pure makes the whole more useful than the small amount of the latter, but each separately is incomplete with respect to judging."[44]

If this plan were adopted, the unvirtuous citizens would join in decisions concerning who should rule them while having no experience of high office themselves. Recalling his arguments against Socrates, Aristotle suggests that, if politics were an art similar to medicine, a citizen would need considerable knowledge of the art—for example, the delicacies of a statesman's dilemmas, and the intricacies of judging among various ends and means to those ends—in order to determine who would make an excellent ruler or whether a given ruler had performed well. It does not suffice to judge a doctor on the basis of curing or failing to cure a particular patient, for the circumstances of medical cases are so varied. One who is skilled in medicine, or at least one who has some knowledge of the art, is required for an adequate judgment of a doctor. It is not clear that the same is true of judging political rulers. The experience of ruling gained by participation in assemblies or juries may be sufficient to certify the many to judge the few.

If politics were an art more akin to architecture than to medicine, then the ruled citizen could adequately judge whether the officials perform properly and fulfill the city's needs, even if he could not rule alone, just as one can choose an architect on the basis of previous success and then judge a new house without being skilled enough to design a better one. This analogy seems to indicate that there is something about politics that is intelligible to free people as free people, that is, "provided the multitude is not overly slavish."[45] If human beings are by nature political animals, they can evaluate the capabilities and weaknesses of individual candidates and rulers without extensive knowledge of an obscure science. If they are not "slavish," they can stand up to the unfit candidates and choose the more fit. There may be hope for a good regime in which a popular element plays a large role. That role might, however, be restricted to the choice and audit of rulers, and not extend to deliberation over complex political issues.[46]

Aristotle appears to take the architecture analogy as adequate, giving some credence to the capabilities of the many, but then he rehearses an aristocrat's challenge, the "absurdity" of allowing the low to judge and to choose among the high—thus, "to have authority over greater matters than the respectable"— and implies an oligarch's complaint, that the poor are favored over the wealthy in the assemblies and courts.[47] Aristotle insists that the wealthy admit, however, that the aggregate assessment of the poor will usually exceed that of the oligarchs. Claims made solely on the ground of riches will not hold up. It is also no less likely that the individual merit of a common citizen will never be decisive in an assembly or jury. Unlike the holders of magistracies or generalships, the members of a deliberative body need not make prudential judgments alone or in emergency situations, so that each member requires only a part of the ruling virtues, not "the whole of virtue": "neither the juror nor the councilman nor the assemblyman acts as ruler, but the court, the council and the people, and each individual is only a part of these things."[48] In a jury, for instance, it will not be necessary that an overarching principle harmonize the virtues of the various jurors.[49] Each contributes his knowledge and judgment to a common deliberation by which a decision is reached. Aristotle proves to have faith—or to wish to instill in the many a belief[50]—that deliberations among the common people will not simply sink to the level of the lowest common denominator. "So the multitude justly has authority over greater things, for the people, the council, and the court are made up of many persons."[51] The claim of the many to some authority has some merit.

In any case, the section concludes, well-enacted laws—minimally, those based on the good and stable regimes[52]—should rule whenever possible, and the ruling body should be authoritative only in specific judgments about which general laws necessarily lack sufficient precision. This conclusion could be deceptive in implying that it is only in rare cases that people will be required to make these judgments, while surely the stuff of daily political life is almost nothing but decisions about how and when and to whom the law applies. Even if the laws are not defective by reason of favoring one class to the detriment of another, they are phrased generally and must always be interpreted by some-one in authority, so that the problem of whom to trust with that authority remains. Though Aristotle has valiantly defended the capacities of "a certain multitude" to exercise political power under the guidance of some law, he has not yet been forthcoming on the characteristics of that multitude.

The two succeeding chapters continue the theme of the proper candidate for higher political authority: the sort of person who deserves to be honored with a political office more demanding than the assembly or the jury and the sort who will be "safe" in fulfilling such an office. Chapter 12 opens as follows:

> Since in all the sciences and arts the end is some good, it is the greatest and primary good in that which is the most authoritative of all; this is the politi-cal capacity. The political good is justice, and this is the common advantage. Justice is held by all to be a certain equality, and up to a certain point they agree with the discourses based on philosophy in which ethics has been discussed; for they assert that justice is a certain thing for certain persons, and should be equal for equal persons. But equality in what sort of things and inequality in what sort of things—this should not be overlooked. For this involves a question, and political philosophy. (*Politics* III.12.1282b15–23)

Aristotle's new argument about political authority begins with a curious summary. The first sentence is, though not acknowledged as such, a restatement of the first two chapters of the *Nicomachean Ethics*, the work that is, traditionally and judging from internal evidence, taken to be Part I of Aristotle's study of politics. The second and third sentences restate the argument that precedes this one in Book III, and refer explicitly to the *Ethics*. As has been clear since the distinctions between good and bad regimes, human excellence is essential to Aristotle's definition of a good political order. Here again, however, Aristotle does not aim citizens at the highest understanding of virtue or the simply good, but rather at the political good, as the most *authoritative* or politically powerful. In pointing to the *Ethics*, therefore, Aristotle does not point to the end of that work, where he discusses the private pleasures, above all friendship and philosophy, but to its beginning. In general, the political good, which is related to the virtues of the gentleman, not the philosopher, is the subject of the first five books of the *Ethics*, culminating in the account of justice in Book V. The political good is the common good—not the individual's good for its own sake, which is the object of the simply highest life—and the common good is justice.[53]

Aristotle assumes that all contenders would agree with the general statement that those with greater preeminence should receive greater honor. There is much disagreement, however, concerning the sort of preeminence to be rewarded with *political* honors. Superiority in complexion or height or some other physical characteristic is dismissed as irrelevant to politics, but it is less clear which characteristics are relevant.[54] Aristotle's "philosophic" confrontation of the problem of distribution of office and political honors uses an analogy to flute-playing.[55] The judge gives the best flute to the best flute-player, not the better-born or better-looking flute-player. No other distribution is fair to both the flautists and the audience. The practice of the political "art" requires an instrument, the title to rule in a city's regime, and the better instrument will produce a better result when used by an excellent statesman. Surely office should be the prize only of those who will perform well in politics and should be awarded only on the basis of excellences appropriate to political action. According to this analogy, the most important questions for those who must make political choices are what constitutes a good performance and what qualities of character it requires.

If politics were simply a performance art, like flute-playing, one would expect some disagreements among connoisseurs about the best practitioner of the art, but regimes might reasonably aim to distribute political honors according to the level of skill in politics as determined by respected judges experienced in the art or in observing its practice. This analogy returns the argument to the earlier comparison between medicine and politics that suggested that only the knower can judge the actor. Because, however, the best political actor requires prudence above all in order to contribute to the good of the regime, and prudence is a virtue and a knowledge that eludes precise definition and is impossible to display fully outside of ruling office,[56] there are great disagreements, among regimes and sometimes among citizens of the same regime, about who, among those who are not holding office at the moment, has the potential to fulfill the requirements of a good political ruler:

> In political matters too it is reasonable for them not to dispute over offices on the basis of every inequality. . . . The dispute necessarily occurs in respect to those things that constitute a city. It is reasonable, therefore, that the well born, the free and the wealthy lay claim to honor. For there must be both free persons and those paying an assessment, since a city cannot consist wholly of those who are poor, any more than of slaves; yet if these things are needed, so also, it is clear, are the virtue of justice and military [or political[57]] virtue. It is not possible for a city to be administered without these things. But whereas without the former elements there cannot be a city, without the latter one cannot be finely administered. (*Politics* III.12.1283a11–12, 15–23)[58]

Since "honors" in the political realm usually entail ruling power or influence, that is, a title to exercise the qualities for which they are awarded, it is particularly crucial to establish the most sound criteria for determining what sort of person will be most likely to exhibit justice and military or political virtue in ruling office. In addition to the earlier warnings concerning the difficulty of knowing who would be the best judge of a good political ruler, Aristotle is aware that the award of a fine flute to a flute-player who turns out not to be worthy does not occasion the extensive ramifications of an award of political power to one who misuses the office. He addresses not simply the bare administration of a city, but its fine administration.

Aristotle rehearses the common opinions about the "things that constitute a city" in which a ruler must excel. Some say the ruler must be ethically virtuous in all respects, or wealthy, or of noble birth, and some argue that it is sufficient that the ruler merely not be a slave. Freedom and some wealth are absolutely required; these attributes will be characteristic of the republic's citizenry. Freeman status, wealth, justice, and military (or political) capacity are all supported by brief arguments as necessary to political order. These four characteristics must be found in the citizen body in order to keep the *polis* in being, but may not all be required in the ruler. Aristotle mentions good birth; why it might be beneficial is explained only later.[59] It remains unclear which of these characteristics, or which combination, best produces the best political ruler.

Aristotle next adds to his list education and virtue (other than the virtue of justice[60]) as having "above all . . . a just claim in the dispute," particularly when not only life but a good life is sought for the city.[61] However tenuous their claims, the rich say they control the territory and are generally trustworthy;[62] the old families claim to perpetuate a certain nobility;[63] the just claim to contribute "the virtue characteristic of communities"; and the free multitude taken together claim to promote most of these benefits at one time or another.[64] A debate follows, however, in which many of these seven titles to rule are called into question. Each may hold some just claim, but many have limits. In addition to repeating some arguments for the multitude against the few or the one, Aristotle shows how free birth, wealth, virtue, good birth, or strength might be a fleeting title to rule: each might by its own logic require the ruler—whether one, few, or many—empowered on its basis to surrender rule to another group of citizens or to an outstanding person whenever the latter is shown to be superior with regard to the criterion.[65] Further, a generally applicable defense for aristocracy, that it is the best rule by the best men, may prove its downfall, because in some cities the best may be too few to administer the offices, necessitating a change of regime to a republic.

Aristotle addresses the situation of a city that contains some virtuous, some wealthy, some well-born, and a multitude of free persons. When natural or historical circumstances have created a heterogeneous population and when none of the principles of justice based on their various merits can decide among the claims of each group to rule, it is not easy to determine who should gain the greatest authority.[66] Ultimately "political philosophy" seems to bring us to a political judgment. Political judgment, an exercise not of philosophical wisdom, but of the highest practical prudence, discerning the ends that the regime should seek, will decide what is best for the city as a whole. Aristotle's philosophizing lays out the possibilities and hints at their ramifications, but refuses to decide on a general rule for all regimes.

Granted, the city needs wealth and it needs free people. The presence of inhabitants of widely differing characters—principally of rich and poor, but also of hereditary nobility and educated aristocrats—is bound to bring on disputes that philosophy cannot resolve. A carefully reasoned argument is not likely to satisfy the poor or the rich that they should be disenfranchised on the ground of their lack of virtue or prudence. Aristotle previously warned that political claims can be stubbornly irrational and still, indeed therefore, dangerous to political order.

The regime's founder, confronted with a heterogeneous populace—and what founder is not?—will have to decide upon the principle that will define the ruling body on the ground of the advantage of the whole city and of the common good. Only rather vague rules of thumb concerning the "most correct laws" are available: "correctness must be taken to mean 'in an equal spirit': what is [enacted] in an equal spirit is correct with a view both to the advantage of the city as a whole and to the common [advantage] of the citizens."[67] Since the definition of a citizen differs with regimes, the decision on the regime to be instituted is the only authoritative determinant of the qualifications for rule, but the recognition of a certain equality among the citizens is required in a good political regime.

On the other hand, the claims to rule based on education, justice as a specific virtue, and the military or political art are not subjected to the extreme criticism that Aristotle uses on the other claims. These attributes may be so necessary as to be implied in all claims to rule. Insofar as these attributes belong to all claims to rule because all claims imply the ability to maintain the city and manage it well, perhaps they are made safe from the formal criticism (that some may appear who possess these qualities to a greater degree than those in power and thus threaten the regime). Indeed, if all inhabitants were educated in the principles revered by the regime and exercised fairness in dealings with others and military or political virtue aimed at the common good, the regime would be more easily governed and the common life enhanced. These attributes may not constitute a particular claim, but be ancillary to all.

The question then becomes what other attribute is most conducive to justice and military or political virtue in a citizen. It seems to be the only other attribute that is not attacked, education. Education is discussed at length in the *Politics* only in connection with the simply best regime, the regime that relies heavily on it to justify its authority and to attain the good life for its citizens. Education in the regime of the Philosopher's prayers aims to teach the full citizens both to rule well and to be good human beings, so that both the city and the citizens are happy. Any less rigorous education could fail to produce fully virtuous citizens, and thus provides an unreliable basis for the claim to rule in an imperfect city. Thus, Aristotle implicitly points to one solution of this perennial problem of politics, a solution embodied in the simply best regime, but stops short of recommending it as a general solution for all regimes. If the citizens are incapable of the highly trained virtues, the legislator must decide which element among his less gifted citizens to honor and to put in office in order to benefit the whole city. In *Politics* V, education turns out to be crucial to the preservation of political regimes, but an education suited specifically to the regime and not for the highest human virtues.

To put the last nail in the coffin of the analogy of politics to flute-playing, the last chapters of Book III follow out the logic of the assumption that politics is an art practiced best by the simply best human being, that is, the true king.

In Book IV Aristotle will abandon the approach of "political philosophy" that passes lightly over the not-fully rational claims of the not-fully virtuous. The community life of the political animal is a much more complicated phenomenon than this approach can encompass.

KINGLY RULE VS. THE RULE OF LAW

In contradistinction to the good citizen, the one or the few so outstanding in virtue as to surpass all others considered collectively

> can no longer be regarded as a part of the city. For they will be done injustice if it is claimed they merit equal things in spite of being so unequal in virtue and political capacity; for such a person would likely be like a god among human beings. From this it is clear that legislation must necessarily have to do with those who are equal both in family and capacity, and that for the other sort of person there is no law—they themselves are law. (*Politics* III.13.1284a9–14)

Aristotle could not make it any clearer that politics, the cooperative life of a city based on equality in ruling and being ruled in turn, is an activity distinct from the actions of the outstandingly virtuous person. While politics is associated with obedience to law, such a person is law in himself; the absolute king governs his own and others' actions on the basis of standards beyond the reach of ungodlike human beings. This sort of person is such a grave threat to the stability of democracies, tyrannies, and oligarchies that ostracism for the sake of preserving the regime is a politically just, if not a simply just, practice. This person is done injustice by any political regime—a regime based on the rotation of ruling offices that forces him to be ruled by inferiors—"as if they should claim to merit ruling over Zeus by splitting the offices."[68]

Aristotle takes up the only regime in which such a person should participate: a permanent, absolute kingship. An absolute monarchy of the most virtuous is not the best regime "according to prayer" as outlined in Books VII and VIII,[69] but like the aristocracy of the best-educated, it is comparable to household management: it is not politics, and thus is rejected in a populace of roughly similar and equal citizens.[70] Aristotle seems to accept certain objections to absolute monarchy based on the insecurity of rule by one who is superior to the laws or who rules without laws, one who is empowered to judge in all matters.[71] It seems that the appearance of such an absolute superior, who would be put in complete authority by general acclamation, would be even more rare than the appearance of a group of virtuous gentlemen such as are necessary for the simply best regime, and Aristotle does not even "pray" that it would happen.[72]

In the course of Aristotle's "investigation" of kingship, an irrepressible anti-monarchist seems to speak in defense of the rule of law. The manner in which Aristotle presents the defense of the rule of law is central to his picture of politics. One of the crucial characteristics of the middling regimes Aristotle will defend in Book IV is their reliance on the laws to rule whenever possible. "The rule of law" cannot be simply opposed to "the rule of men": laws cannot rule without the actions and decisions of human beings. This debate concerns the degree to which the person in power acts only within the law's bounds or is free to act beyond or without law.

The archetype of kingship places significant prerogative in the king's hands; it is rule by one and one only. The actions of this person then determine whether he remains a king, ruling for the sake of the common good and over willing subjects, or becomes a tyrant, ruling for his own benefit over unwilling subjects. Though monarchy always resembles household management, a king exercises rule similar to the management of the free members of a household, a tyranny similar to the mastery of slaves.[73]

Having narrowed the field of investigation to the king with authority in all things, the *pambasileus*, Aristotle turns to the debate with the adherent of subordinating the ruler to law. The first argument of the defender of monarchy is based on the problem of general laws that was mentioned earlier, that the best law is not always just when applied to particular circumstances. The wise monarch is needed to see the equity in such a circumstance and to exercise his power to do justice on the basis of a standard above the imperfect laws. The anti-monarchist replies that unless the ruler judges in accordance with the general principles of the law, not using principles held to be above the law and potentially affected by the ruler's passions, he acts unjustly. This argument asserts that the law, in some sense, governs even the acts of a judge in modifying the law to fit specific circumstances. "The law educates especially for this, and hands over what remains [undetermined by law itself] to be judged and administered 'by the most just decision' of the rulers." Indeed, the regime could make a *law* that judges must make exceptions in line with the intention of the law "on the basis of their experience."[74] Aristotle's first comment on this debate comes down on the side of law, but only on the side of just law, and leaves open the question of the goodness of kingship in certain circumstances: "That the ruler must necessarily be a legislator, then, and that laws must exist, is clear; but they must not be authoritative insofar as they deviate [from what is right], though in other matters they should be authoritative. But as regards the things that law is unable to judge either generally or well, should the one best person rule, or all?"[75]

At this point, the anti-monarchist repeats Aristotle's argument for the capacities for judgment and the relative incorruptibility and equanimity of a free multitude of individually imperfect citizens generally guided by law. Having posited the existence of such a multitude, the anti-monarchist concludes that the larger number would be more incorruptible. The monarchist responds by pointing out the potential for factional conflict within a multitude and its impossibility in one ruler. Aristotle again changes this argument by creating a middle ground: he speaks of a multitude of rulers who are all good. Such a regime would be an aristocracy, and Aristotle seems to advance the opinion that aristocracy is superior to kingship for a city—that is, for a community larger than a village—if all the rulers are indeed good. Either the danger of faction is not a significant consideration for Aristotle, a view not borne out in the rest of the *Politics*, or he is assuming that aristocrats are less likely to indulge in such conflicts, perhaps because of the earlier assumption that the defensible multitude will consist of respecters of the law. This part of the argument turns out to beg the question of the effectiveness of the rule of law in order to address in another way the question of the status of kingship as a regime.

After taking up the considerations of monarchic succession and bodyguards, the debaters continue their argument about the rule of law versus the rule of one person with the anti-monarchist's view that, among peoples similar in their "natures" or in their "souls," it is natural and just that they rule and are ruled in turn: no one person among equals deserves to rule in all matters. Up to this point, the argument is the same as that which Aristotle adduced in his own name when speaking of strictly political arrangements.[76] This argument can be extended to provide a support for the rule of law: if one agrees that the arrangements for rotation of office are laws and that these arrangements are superior to the arrangement in which one man rules permanently and in all matters, then the rule of law is superior to the rule of a king. Aristotle would agree that the city in which no obviously superior person stands above the crowd would not be a city fit for kingship. Among equals in wisdom and virtue, the laws are better guardians of justice than the souls of imperfect human beings. The case of the truly superior ruler, however, is untouched by this argument.

It may be that the law-versus-men debate rests on false assumptions. First, the anti-monarchist relies on a gross oversimplification to assume that selfish interests and passions taint only human deliberation, while established law is the voice of "intellect without appetite." As Aristotle has pointed out, laws can be framed with passionate or unjust purposes, and those entrusted with their application, despite the method of their selection or their number, can be upright, but they may also be corrupted. The monarchist's mistake, on the other hand, is embodied in the analogy, already rejected by Aristotle, between politics and medicine. The monarchist uses this analogy to argue that political rulers, like doctors, must deviate from accepted practice when the situation of the patient requires innovations. The analogy breaks down thus:

> For {doctors} do not act against reason on account of affection, but earn their pay by making the sick healthy; but those in political offices are accustomed to acting in many matters with a view to spite or favor. In any case, if doctors were suspected of being persuaded by a person's enemies to do away with him for profit, he would be more inclined to seek treatment from written [rules]. Moreover, doctors bring in other doctors for themselves when they are sick . . . the assumption being that they are unable to judge what is true on account of judging both in their own case and while they are in a state of suffering. (*Politics* III.16.1287a35–b4)

While a doctor's passions are usually unlikely to lead him to act in a way contrary to the interests of the patient, the political ruler is always subject to great temptations to bend the common good to his own purposes. A doctor's interest in maintaining his good reputation coincides with healing the sick, while the political man's interests do not always coincide with the good of the community. In addition, when a doctor's passions may sway his judgment, he is likely to ask another doctor's advice, while a political actor's interests are very often involved in the interpretation of a law, and if he is the only judge, his decision is likely to be prejudiced.

Though it would be difficult simply to satisfy monarchists and anti-monarchists with one form of government, it may be possible to imagine a regime that would satisfy the *arguments* of both sides in this particular debate. Such a regime would be based on well-enacted laws, but would provide latitude for their correction in particular circumstances, while not placing all power in the hands of an easily corrupted individual. Though it is difficult to determine Aristotle's final position on the rule of law, he has raised several objections to its superiority and apparently answered them. While holding out the possibility that there exists a multitude that would justly be ruled by a monarch, he reiterates the necessity that among equal and similar persons, political rule or the rotation of offices is appropriate. Such rule has been and will again be associated closely with the rule of law, modified by the need for judgments of equity in some cases, versus the complete prerogative of a human ruler.

THE POLITICAL MULTITUDE

A passage very late in Book III prepares for the account to come in Book IV and sums up the previous mentions of the republic thus:

> We must first determine what it is that is apt for kingship, what is aristocratic, and what is political. What is apt for kingship, then, is a multitude of such a sort that it accords with its nature to support a family that is preeminent in virtue relative to political leadership; an aristocratic multitude is one of such a sort that it accords with its nature to support a multitude capable of being ruled in accordance with the rule that belongs to free persons by those whose virtue makes them expert leaders relative to political rule; and a political multitude is one in which there arises in accordance with its nature a military multitude capable of ruling and being ruled in accordance with a law distributing offices on the basis of merit to those who are well off. (*Politics* III.17.1288a7–15)

If "well off" here means possessed of the wherewithal to own heavy arms and thus to participate in the military,[77] or if it means possessed of the moderate level of wealth found among the middling element of society, rather than great luxury, this passage can be harmonized with the accounts of republics elsewhere in the *Politics*. It clearly separates kingship and genuine aristocracy from the republic on the grounds that the former require preeminent virtue or expertise in leadership.[78] This account suggests that the republic will be a popular regime in some sense, depending on a large multitude, but not simply popular, since it recognizes the usefulness of a certain wealth for the material health and education for the psychic health of the regime. Thus the republic is a popular regime that is not so exclusive as the democracies Aristotle will deprecate in Books IV through VI; it does not offend those with some property.

In sum, in the establishment of political authority, the legislator confronts at least two grave difficulties. First, such authority is an honor; therefore, it should be given to citizens with merit, which means the legislator must determine which merit is the most worthy of reward in relation to the good of the city. Second, such authority is a title to rule; therefore, it should be given only to those who will display political prudence in office, which seems to require the legislator to determine in advance the characteristics of that person or from what part of the city officeholders should be chosen. To complicate the matter further, the legislator's decision will have to take into account the character of the inhabitants and the necessity of maintaining stability, that is, staving off the formation of enemies to the regime. If a just and safe authority is not established by the laws, the will of the stronger will prevail or, in other words, the officers of the regime will be in authority without any other claim to merit it than their superior numbers, wealth, or strength, and will generally try to aggrandize themselves on these bases. If a wholly virtuous person or group is placed in power but is incapable of staving off the claims of the common people to honors, the regime will collapse under the weight of popular discontent. Depending on the circumstances, the legislator may choose to honor either one outstanding person, a small group of virtuous people, or "a certain multitude" with a collective virtue that renders the whole greater than the sum of its parts. Once in office, the authority should, in most cases, rule by laws that take into account the desires and deserts of all inhabitants, even those excluded from high office. Many of these requirements for decent and safe political authority will appear in the republic, and Aristotle will put forward the middle class as the one most trustworthy class to produce citizens to serve in political office.[79]

3

THE BEST REGIME
ARISTOTLE'S MIDDLE-CLASS REPUBLIC

When Aristotle describes the regime best for most cities and human beings and the regime most available to most cities, he is describing the regime best suited to free and roughly equal people. As he will demonstrate in Book IV, while most cities have some form of democracy or oligarchy, neither of these regimes recognizes in principle the need to unify all the inhabitants in support of the regime, and thus the need to acknowledge the freedom (in the form of participation) of those who are not admitted to the highest offices. These most common regimes are defective. Only a republic, especially the republic based on the middle class, mixes well the consideration due to all kinds of people capable of some self-mastery: the rich, the poor, the well-born, the virtuous, and the "middling element." In other words, it makes citizens of all who could make a contribution to the good of the city, and rules in such a manner that all are satisfied and desire no other regime.

A ROADMAP TO THE BEST POLITICAL REGIME

Aristotle begins Book IV with a review of what is expected of the expert in politics,[1] one who wishes to call the enterprise an art or science. Not only must political science speak of the simply best regime under the best circumstances; it must also speak of the regimes suited to imperfect cities and imperfect human beings and the best regime to which most cities can aspire with attainable reforms. Political science is a science of the whole of governance. The descriptions of the simply best regime and of all the partially and wholly defective regimes "belong to the same science" and "neither the one that is superior simply nor the one that is the best that circumstances allow should be overlooked by the good legislator and the political ruler in the true sense."[2] In some fashion, the legislator and political actor must keep both the simply best and the practicably best regimes in mind.

Aristotle clearly suggests that knowledge of the best aristocratic regime, however unlikely if not impossible it is, influences the establishment, rule, and preservation of the more practicable regimes. There are few close parallels between the aristocratic rule of the simply best regime and the actual or possible forms of democracy, oligarchy, or republic Aristotle describes.[3] The republic has one large factor in common with the best aristocracy: its defense relies on an understanding of the defense of the simply best. Aristotle uses propositions concerning the human good adduced in his ethical discourses to support only two regimes, rule by virtuous and cultured warrior-gentlemen and rule by decent middle-class owners of heavy arms. The founder or reformer of fundamental laws must decide whether his material—the population, land, resources, and character of the people—is suited to the regime of true virtue or to a way of life based on another standard. Book IV generally argues for the highest practicable standard for most cities, but the founder of this regime must know the entire *Politics*, so to speak. To succeed, this lawgiver must have the intellectual virtue Aristotle does not expect in ordinary citizens, for example, knowing that his regime is not the best simply, while simultaneously defending it. This lawgiver must not confuse this task with that of the founder of the simply best regime, and the citizens probably should not be reminded of a standard of educated virtue that they will never attain collectively. For this reason, Aristotle discusses the more attainable virtues of the "regime of the middling sort," showing how to give these crucial citizens a defensible partisanship for their regime.

After this defense of the republic, the mood of the argument changes to an apparently analytic account of comparative institutional arrangements. It becomes clear in this section (IV.14–16) that Aristotle is presenting what a modern political scientist might call the empirical evidence for his claims that the republic is a practicable goal for most ordinary cities and that its standards are implicit, if rarely achieved, in the most common regimes, oligarchy and democracy.

In Book IV the Aristotelian republic emerges in some detail: the regime that shares ruling and being ruled among roughly equal and free human beings and remains a community in which "the part of the city that wants the regime to continue must be superior."[4] Indeed, in the best republic there exist no "parts of the city generally {that} would wish to have another regime."[5]

THE POLITICAL SCIENTIST AS PERSONAL TRAINER OF CITIZENS AND REGIMES

Aristotle distinguishes his tasks as a student of politics. Indeed, he defines political science, a new field of inquiry different from Socrates' political philosophy in its utility for political actors and from the orators' sophistry in its impartiality and concern for justice and virtue. Likening the political scientist to the gymnastic trainer, Aristotle compares this knowledge to the knowledge of various types of bodies and their needs, and he compares this task to that of the advisor who helps people train their bodies to the perfection of which they are capable.[6] Therefore, in addition to seeking (1) the simply best regime or the best regime in existence, the preoccupation of many of Aristotle's predecessors,[7] the student of the "complete" science of politics must, in order to be "useful," seek (2) the best regime possible under given circumstances, (3) the regimes "based on a presupposition," that is, governed by a partisan principle of justice that may assume it is the best simply or the best possible, but is neither, and (4) "the regime that is most fitting for all cities."[8] With prudence one must also decide which laws fit which regime.[9] At the end of Chapter 2, Aristotle lays out his plan to look into these less-than-the-best regimes and adds to the list another task, which will occupy Book V: understanding how all regimes may be destroyed and thus, what is necessary to preserve them.[10]

It is clear from this introduction that Books IV and V are meant to be of use to founders, legislators, and reformers, that is, to the most consequential political actors. The significance of the establishment, perpetuation, or improvement of a regime is demonstrated by the latest definition of the regime: "an arrangement in cities connected with the offices, establishing the manner in which they have been distributed, what the authoritative element of the regime is, and what the end of the community is in each case."[11] The regime does no less than determine the ultimate reason for its citizens' living and acting together. Depending in large part both on the types and distribution of offices and on the segment of the population given the most authority, the regime will serve, for instance, a democracy's, an oligarchy's, or a republic's purposes and the citizen will be trained, persuaded, or forced to act in ways supporting the ends of the particular regime. Insofar as those ends are persuasive or the means effectively enforced, this citizen will be a good citizen, and the regime will be peaceful. On the other hand, insofar as the ends benefit only a class of individuals holding perpetual ruling office, or become whims and lose their character as established ends, the regime dissolves. It can no longer be called a regime in the strict sense. The founder, lawgiver, or reformer would do well, therefore, to learn from the political scientist, the one who studies all the varieties, which regime will best suit the particular city and people.

Aristotle suggested first that the distinction among regimes rests on the number in the ruling body and on the intent of that body to pursue the common good or its own benefit. He then modified this position to emphasize the characteristics of the ruling body rather than its size. After reiterating and elaborating on some of the earlier argument, Aristotle here claims that the variety of the regimes is caused by the variety of parts within the city, and the variety of ways in which the parts can be combined. Twice he divides the parts of a city. The dominance of one or a combination of these parts is responsible for the varieties of regimes and of the species of these regimes. Such dominance emphasizes different plausible distinctions and likenesses among human beings and thus among their regimes.[12]

In the process of discussing the parts of the city and the way in which they underlie the various genera of regimes, Aristotle provides an example of his political science. The first division of parts may seem quite familiar to a contemporary student of political science; the second may not. The first method of distinguishing the parts also turns out to be unsatisfactory and prompts the use of the second.

The first set of divisions treats all parts as merely parts. This method of analysis seems familiar today because of its democratic tendency to treat all demographic identities alike, as well as its "socioeconomic" emphasis.[13] According to this analysis, the fundamental distinctions fall among households, categorized as rich, poor, or middling. The rich and poor are subdivided into the armed and the unarmed; the poor, into the farming, marketing, and vulgar; the rich, according to the various measures of wealth, family, and virtue.[14] Aristotle has already presented examples of the dominance of one or a few households over others: hereditary kingship, as in Sparta, or dynastic oligarchy, as in Crete. The preeminence of one economic class will create, in general, an oligarchy, a democracy or a republic. When its possession of arms, its occupation, or the objects of its expenditures further distinguish the dominant economic group, Aristotle sees different species of these regimes.

In harmony with the unhierarchic nature of this list, Aristotle soon notes that, rather than being simply at odds with each other, democracy and oligarchy have in their various species a number of correspondences. The more moderated forms of each, for example, have more in common with each other than with the immoderate forms of their own genera. The moderate oligarchy and the moderate democracy are so similar in their social or economic characteristics that they point toward a kind of republic, whereas the extreme forms of each tend toward tyranny of some sort.[15] Oligarchy and democracy come together at a central point, as do a republic and aristocracy, in what is to be called a "well-mixed regime" or the "regime through the middle."[16] Aristotle resumes his hierarchical analysis, arguing "it is truer and better to distinguish as we have, and say that one or two are finely constituted and the others deviations from them."[17] Apparently, aristocracy and the republic are more "finely constituted"; contrary to common opinion, oligarchy and democracy are merely deviations from those regimes.[18] The attempt to treat all regimes as equal has failed: it is misleading to suggest that all types of rule are equally fundamental. Aristotle embarks on another account, using judgments of better and worse.[19]

The second list of parts views the city more as an organic whole whose life depends on certain necessities. Like an animal, the city needs to be able to sense its environment, to take in sustenance and put it to use, and to act or move. Unlike the first analysis of parts, this account lends itself more readily to hierarchical judgments: it is possible to discuss which parts of an organic whole make the most significant contributions to its existence and its perfection. Because of the superiority of the good life to mere life and of the soul to the body, despite the fact that the mouth and the digestive system are crucial to existence, the parts that contribute to knowledge and that allow the whole to act are superior.[20] The farmers and the artisans cannot be ignored, but their place in the city is subordinate to that of the political and military actors.

Having introduced this organic metaphor, Aristotle lists the necessary parts in any city: farmers, artisans, merchants, laborers, and warriors provide the city's food, implements, imported goods, labor, and independent status. He argues that this list of the absolutely necessary elements is more adequate than that of Socrates' "healthy" city, a city without warriors. Whereas Socrates suggests that war only occurs when the self-restrained city indulges desires for luxuries, and therefore needs more land and expands into the territory of its neighbors,[21] Aristotle argues that warriors are necessary from the beginning to keep any city free of invaders, who would reduce it to slavery. The military virtues of a republican citizen take on essential status.

Another important part, serving less a brute necessity than a human urge for a peaceful social life, is "someone who assigns and judges what is just."[22] Aristotle now raises the warrior element to the level of this political element: these parts are "more a part of cities" than the farming and laboring elements (though the same people could, contra Socrates, both farm and bear arms or farm and serve in the assembly), because the former serve the soul more than the body. In addition to protecting needed land, the warriors serve the soul's spirited urge for independence; those who deliberate and judge provide and support the city's understanding of justice and the good life. Aristotle also lists the propertied and the magistrates as needed elements of city life, but he does not explicitly classify them as serving either the soul or the body. The various combinations of elements that could form the dominant part of the city are the causes of the various genera and species of regimes.

Just as there are two accounts of the parts of the city, there are two lists of the types of democracy and oligarchy. Interestingly, each list is ordered hierarchically, from the best type to the worst. In democracies, the worse are those including greater numbers in the ruling body; in oligarchies, smaller numbers. In both cases, the worst is the one in which the ruling body accords complete discretionary power to itself. Each time, the types are described from a differing viewpoint, which may explain why the number of types is inconstant, for in certain respects dissimilar species of the same regime may look quite similar.

The first taxonomy of regimes rests on the regime's definition of equality and the formal requirements for citizenship (property assessments and descent from the proper ancestors, primarily). The second list of democracies distinguishes the types on the basis of the source of the citizens' livelihood, which is more in keeping with the second account of the parts of a city. The key to the characters of the regimes in the second list is not so much the type of work the citizens perform, however, as the quantity of leisure time available to them.[23]

The best democracy in the first list

> is that which is particularly said to be based on equality. The law in this sort of democracy asserts that there is equality when the poor are no more preeminent than the well off, and neither have authority, but they both are similar. For if freedom indeed exists particularly in a democracy, as some conceive to be the case, as well as equality, this would particularly happen where all share in the regime as far as possible in similar fashion. But since the people are a majority, and what is resolved by the majority is authoritative, this will necessarily be a democracy. (*Politics* IV.4.1291b31–38)

Several aspects of this description deserve notice. First, the best democracy's citizen body consists of all people of free birth, which is to say that the rich are included as well as the poor and all are treated as equals based on the fact that they are all non-slaves. Second, freedom implies that all *participate*; participation is an essential attribute of a citizen's function. Third, in cases in which the interests of the poor conflict with those of the rich, the former will predominate in a democracy on account of numbers. These cases need not monopolize all political debate, but they are likely to be the most important. Because these economic disputes could undermine the political equality of the rich to the poor, it is crucial to ensure that the fundamental freedom and equality of the citizens be respected and all subordinate decrees and decisions be made on their basis.

The importance of holding some principles as fundamental is not mentioned here until the fifth type of democracy is distinguished from the third and fourth for its lawlessness. Explicitly in the first, third, and fourth democracies, and implicitly in the second, "law rules," while in the most extreme form "the multitude has authority and not the law."[24] Supplementing the earlier account of the rule of law, Aristotle elaborates its importance in a democracy here and more emphatically in the second list of democracy's types. While it is at least arguable that an extremely good human being could maintain an absolute kingship without degenerating into tyranny, it is not plausible that the many could ever be trusted with absolute power. "When decrees rather than law are authoritative," "popular leaders [*demagogoi*]" are brought to the political fore.[25] The all-powerful multitude places all of its prerogative in the one who flatters its hopes and sways its opinion, just as a tyrant hands over the execution of his decrees to a favorite. Using its flatterer as its instrument, the multitude, like a tyrant, wields unrestrained despotic power over equals and superiors. As he later says of tyranny, Aristotle here suggests that democracy by decree is not a regime, for "where the laws do not rule there is no regime."[26] While democracy is one form of regime, the most extreme democracy is no longer a political order because general principles do not govern a united people.

The second list of democracies uses the categories Aristotle adduced in his organic account of the parts of cities. The best-governed on this list is the one in which "the farming element and that possessing a moderate amount of property have authority over the regime." For lack of leisure, due to the necessity that the citizens work for their livelihoods, there are relatively few assemblies of the citizens and "they put the law in charge."[27] From this viewpoint, this type could encompass the first two democracies in the first list; that is, both the type based on the equality and freedom of rich and poor and that predicated on a low property requirement. In such a city, the farmers and the working owners of moderate property would be likely to predominate; they will have interests in common as self-supporting citizens, distinct from the interests of the very rich and the very poor, and they could outweigh either extreme when combined with the other extreme. Here are the beginnings of a "middling element" emerging out of a regime based initially on the poor.

It is interesting that Aristotle considers it possible that the best democracy of the second list be confused with an oligarchy: "In general, it is oligarchic when it is not open to all [actually to take part in office in spite of being full citizens], but that it should be open to them {those who do not meet the property requirements} to be at leisure is impossible unless there are reve-nues."[28] One characteristic of a good republic is that some might describe it as a democracy, some as oligarchy. In contrast, as the list proceeds to the more defective democracies, democracies that could not be confused with oligarchies, the ruling elements include greater numbers of poor people whose income is derived from public revenues.[29] They have almost infinite leisure time and are in this respect similar to wealthier oligarchs.

In a like manner, the first mentioned in both lists of oligarchies is a rather moderate regime ruled by law and admitting to full citizenship all who possess the required amount of property. The predominant group of citizens is composed, again, of those owning a moderate amount of property, so that they have not the leisure for constant political participation, that is, "a larger number of persons owns property, but in lesser amounts and not overly much." Therefore, "they will necessarily claim to merit having the law rule for them, rather than ruling themselves."[30] Though in this oligarchy the middle class rules due to the exclusion of the poor, the result is similar to that of the moderate democracies.[31] The type dominated by middling property owners and farmers is the least tyrannical of both the democratic and the oligarchic regimes, that is, of the regimes that Aristotle considers defective precisely because of their tendency to grow tyrannical.

As Aristotle makes clear later, a tyranny is most a tyranny when it is exer-cised over unwilling subjects for the tyrant's advantage. The subjects are most justifiably unwilling when they equal or surpass their tyrant in political virtue. The more democratic democracies and the more oligarchic oligarchies fulfill these tyrannous criteria by subjecting the noncitizen class merely on the basis of individual property and without consideration for the qualities in which the subjects may be the equals or betters of the regime.[32] It is just such a tyranny of the rich or the poor that the republic is postulated to correct. It will treat all free persons as equal in their freedom, favoring neither wealthy nor poor, neither well-born nor freedman, neither the highly educated and virtuous nor the vulgar, by giving full power to none of these groups. Its distribution of offices and honors is meant to offend none and to rest on virtues attainable by a majority.

ARISTOTLE'S BEST POLITICAL REGIME: THE MIDDLE-CLASS REPUBLIC

The moderated species of the two common defective regimes resemble each other more than they resemble the most extreme forms of their own genera, and they approach the most accessible good regime, the republic, in important respects.[33] As democratic cities become more democratic or oligarchic cities more oligarchic they tend to exclude increasing portions of the inhabitants from full citizenship and thus to become less political; they operate less as associations of ruling and being ruled among free persons treated as free.

The regime whose name names all regimes, the *politeia*, is the political arrangement par excellence.[34] As the name indicates, Aristotle associates all that supports political life with this type of association. Though other forms of government may produce a superior way of life for some of the inhabitants, it is their exclusion of large numbers of free persons from participation in ruling that marks them as inferior in this crucial respect: they are not political in the strict sense, characterized by ruling and being ruled among free and roughly equal persons. The polity/republic maintains its unity politically, achieves its justice politically, and defines citizen virtue politically. *Politics* IV, Chapters 7 to 9 and 11 to 13, describe the republic in such a manner.

Aristotle admits that the regime he calls the republic "has not often existed,"[35] though he has suggested in the accounts of Sparta and Carthage that some regimes commonly classed in other categories have approached the characteristics of republic in some aspects.[36] Unlike both Socrates' regime of the philosopher-king and Aristotle's simply best regime, this way of life has existed somewhere and could appear again. Its description is not so much a "prayer" as those of the perfect cities are.[37] This regime could be formed out of a number of existing imperfect regimes and would be an improvement over the more common oligarchy or democracy.

The republic is a good regime, despite being a mixture of the defective regimes of oligarchy and democracy.[38] This mixture is, at any rate, Aristotle's first and simple definition. After this statement, Aristotle rehearses and critiques two commonly held views about the republic.[39] First, "it is customary . . . to call polities those sorts that tend toward democracy, and those tending more toward oligarchy, aristocracies."[40] Indeed, regimes based on wealth are apt to view *themselves* as aristocratic on the assumption that descent from a prominent family and wealth entail a good education and a tendency to be just. In fact, of course, they do not. In one of Aristotle's choice moments of tongue in cheek, he states that "those who are well off are held to possess already the things for the sake of which the unjust commit injustice; this is why they are referred to as gentlemen and notables."[41] For this reason, a regime containing an admixture of oligarchy cannot generally aspire to the title of aristocracy.[42]

Some would argue that a republic could not be a good regime, since it is not identical with aristocracy: "It is held to be impossible for a city to have good governance if it is run not aristocratically but by the base, and similarly, for one that does not have good governance to be aristocratically run." Without reference to his earlier arguments in favor of the political skills of the multitude taken together, Aristotle's reply to this second common misconception is to distinguish again the best simply from the best relative to the material at hand. Most cities are not capable of true aristocracy. For most cities, therefore, "good governance" consists in enacting and enforcing obedience to "the laws that are the best of those possible for them."[43]

Aristocracy is *the* good regime relative to a body of citizens with virtue, who are also free and usually wealthy, whereas a republic is *the* good regime for those of some wealth and freedom who are not extraordinarily virtuous. This distinction represents a further interpretation of the initial criterion of a good regime, that it attend to the general welfare and not merely its own advantage. The regime that ignores the capacities of its citizens is unlikely to legislate for the general good. The closing line of this section admits the close proximity of republics and aristocracies, while reiterating that they are different.[44] The republic is a regime concerned with the best for the city while modifying the aristocratic notion of what constitutes the best. The excellence of a republic lies not so much in the virtue of its citizens individually as in its balance. This balance tends to support a collective virtue that supplements the less impressive virtues of ordinary individuals. If the regime would not be improved by favoring the rich, it would likewise be taken out of balance by favoring the poor and leaning too far toward democracy.[45] When excellence pure and simple is unavailable and excellent leisured citizens are not available in a quantity needed for true aristocracy, the moderation of an inferior regime's defects and the equilibrium of its citizens' lesser virtues become the bases of truly political life. The political animal's good life is tied to these tempered expectations.

Having established theoretically the republic's accessibility and superiority to democracy and oligarchy, Aristotle outlines the institutional characteristics of the regime not merely for purposes of analysis, but also to demonstrate how a democracy or oligarchy could be changed into a republic. The criticisms of Magnesia, Sparta, Crete, and Carthage rested heavily on the practicability of a decent republic. Now Aristotle will discuss how such a republic is to be established and maintained.

First, a republic must be a mixture. Mixtures of democracy and oligarchy can be achieved in at least three ways, but most important is to insure that it "be possible for the same polity to be spoken of as either a democracy or an oligarchy. . . . The mean too is of this sort: each of the extremes is revealed in it."[46] To create a republic from democracy, one must adopt some oligarchic measures to balance out favoritism to the *demos* and make the rich equal to the poor in influence and honors. The effect is similar to that of the most moderate democracy, the one based on freedom and equality, or the most moderate oligarchy.[47]

Aristotle draws distinctions among the measures available to oligarchies and democracies to become republics, but all aim at the mean between the arrangements characteristic of the two defective regimes. Pay the poor to sit on the jury and fine the wealthy who fail to participate; set the property assessment required for citizenship at a moderate level; use a mixture of election and lottery to choose officials. The mean is a shorthand expression for a politics that favors neither the very wealthy nor the very poor.

The second major characteristic of a republic is its stability. The regime "should be preserved through itself, not from outside." Of course, any healthy regime requires stability, which is the reason Aristotle devotes all of Book V to the preservation of all sorts of regimes from sedition and dissolution. A republic, however, rises above the lowest requirement for stability, that "those wishing its preservation are a majority," to the condition in which "none of the parts of the city generally would wish to have another regime."[48] A republic is not properly so called when its adherents merely outweigh its detractors; all the major parts of the city must be sufficiently satisfied with the regime not even to desire a fundamental reform. This satisfaction is, by definition, impossible for a tyranny, in which one person rules over "unwilling" subjects. Moreover, as long as a city is ruled by one or a few persons of preeminent virtue, as in a true kingship or aristocracy or what modern Americans call meritocracy, a large part of the city is likely to be dissatisfied with its lack of power or influence.[49]

It might be argued that the republic is an inferior regime from the Aristotelian point of view on the ground that its purpose is not to distribute honor to the most virtuous nor to form the citizens according to the best human life. Rather its purpose could be considered merely to achieve stability. This section of Book IV demonstrates, however, that stability is not to be purchased at the cost of tyrannical measures, but to be earned by satisfying all the major parts of the city.

Before taking up the "regime of the middle," in what appears as a housekeeping measure, Chapter 10 gives a very brief description of the varieties of tyranny, "that it may have its part in the inquiry."[50] Discussing tyranny in the midst of describing the most political regime serves as a vivid reminder that, although "we placed it too among the regimes," it is hardly to be dignified with that title. Unlike the compromises of wealth and power in the republic or even in many democracies and oligarchies, a tyranny, however moderated in its appearance, is fundamentally enslavement—the assertion of one person's appetites over a mass of people who do not consider him their rightful ruler. Surrounding the account of what is least a regime are two accounts of the quintessential regime, the regime called "regime."

Aside from providing a stark and instructive contrast to the republic, this short section divides the two accounts of the republic in a significant manner. Before this chapter, almost any mixture of oligarchy and democracy constitutes a *politeia*, while following it Aristotle speaks of a specific type, the *"politeia* through the middling elements" or the republic based on the middle class. It is possible that tyranny appears here to suggest a potential defect in the simple republic. A regime in which authority is distributed evenly between the rich and the poor, or the few and the many, may suffer from either aimlessness or powerlessness. That all the parts of the city are "satisfied" with the regime is not incompatible with temporizing in particular cases. In any given situation, the mixed regime may be unable to resolve on a course of action or to enforce a resolution, if one of the two factions strongly disagrees. Whatever may be said against its arbitrariness and injustice, the tyrannical regime does not experience this perennial *political* problem, termed today "polarization." Rather, whatever the tyrant resolves and whatever his bodyguards and armed forces can enforce is law: even in the two "kingly" tyrannies, which are based on law, "the rule {is} characteristic of a master and in accordance with their {the tyrants'} own will," but in unmitigated tyranny, the tyrant "rules in an unchallenged fashion" over unwilling persons.[51] What a republic mixing the two most common defective regimes needs— what politics per se requires—is a locus of authority, an element of decisiveness, both for the sake of stability and for the sake of accomplishing political acts. In the next section, Aristotle describes the *politeia* through the middle class, the republic in which the middling element arbitrates between the ordinarily warring factions and holds up its principles as those of the regime.

Chapters 11 to 13 defend in detail Aristotle's republic, the "regime through the middle," as the best regime "for most cities and most human beings." Here the significance of Aristotle's sustained attention to such issues as the essential characteristics of the activity of politics and the place of the aspirations for justice and domestic peace within that activity becomes clear.

There is some room for dispute as to whether the republic of Chapters 11 through 13 is meant to be a regime distinct from the polity listed among the original six fundamental types and discussed in Chapters 7 through 9. Inasmuch as both are highly recommended by Aristotle for similar reasons and they have much in common, it seems most useful to view the *politeia* of the middle class as a species of the genus republic. It is a particular way to mix oligarchic and democratic elements in a stable and just regime.[52]

The middle regime satisfies uniquely the requirement that the republic take account of riches and poverty without outstanding virtue, by mixing riches and poverty in the same persons, so to speak, in a combination that produces a certain moderate virtue. Aristotle praises at some length the man of moderate means for his moderate habits. This praise is more enthusiastic than that earlier given to the *demos*. It seems to be the description of that "certain multitude" that Aristotle posited could rule as well as the few in key respects. At any rate, Aristotle accords to the middle class a more unambiguous talent for maintaining reasonable and stable relationships and a willingness to rule untyrannically and to be ruled unslavishly.

VIRTUE AND THE MIDDLE CLASS

The argument that the republic based on the middle class is the best regime for most cities and most human beings explicitly rests upon certain of Aristotle's principles of virtue: "If . . . the happy life is one in accordance with virtue and unimpeded, and . . . virtue is a mean, then the middling sort of life[53] is best—the mean that is capable of being attained by each sort of individual. These same defining principles must also define virtue and vice in the case of a city and a regime; for the regime is the way of life of a city."[54] This doctrine of the mean is based upon the argument found in the *Ethics* that the mean is the key to analyzing ethical (as opposed to intellectual) virtue. The citizens of a republic must exhibit some virtue in order to justify Aristotle's distinction between this regime and the democracies and oligarchies it corrects. The earlier account of republics assumes that military virtue is the one virtue (or cluster of virtues) attainable by the majority. In a political regime, public aspirations for the citizens do not take their bearings from "virtue as a whole." The lawgiver and political leaders must emphasize that the citizens are capable of acting for the common good, but the definition of public virtue cannot be so fine as to place it beyond the reach of the large number of citizens.

If, as Aristotle suggests here, the virtues of a human being's way of life and the city's way of life (its regime) should be the same, it might be appropriate that these citizens be trained to moderation in all respects, for their regime is the embodiment of political moderation, steering a course to avoid extreme democracy, extreme oligarchy, or tyranny in any form. Aristotle seems to make a further suggestion, however: these moderate property holders are temperate by the nature of their social and economic position, not so much by an education that tries to create a "second nature,"[55] and thus the lawgiver can expect them to impart a certain temperate character to any regime they control.

There are a number of remarkable aspects to this argument. In contradiction to the *Ethics*, the mean that defines virtue here is "capable of being attained by each sort of individual," while the Nicomachean mean is an extreme of virtue and only a mean with respect to the more easily practiced vices that oppose it.[56] The *Ethics* clearly argues not that virtue lies in a mean where anyone can fulfill its requirements, but that the attainment of ethical excellence through exercising the mean of each virtue—for example, the "right" courage, which is neither reckless nor excessively cautious—is the province of a very few who may take pride in its consistent practice.

Also in contradiction to a number of passages in the *Ethics*, Aristotle argues here for a moderate fortune, as opposed to great wealth, as the soundest basis for the best way of life. As he quickly reiterates, "Since . . . it is agreed that what is moderate and middling is best, it is evident that in the case of the goods of fortune as well a middling possession is the best of all."[57] On the other hand, some virtuous actions described in the *Ethics*—for example, acts of magnanimity and magnificence—require more than a modest fortune. According to the *Ethics*, the virtuous man needs external goods, and sometimes a great amount of them, both to afford the leisure to practice all the virtues and to support his acts of liberality,[58] magnificence, and reciprocal justice.[59] Though those of moderate means are self-sufficient, they have neither great wealth nor much leisure time.

Third, it is a strange suggestion that a middling amount of property is the primary factor in citizen virtue, considering Aristotle's argument against Phaleas of Chalcedon: "Yet even if one were to arrange a moderate level of property for all, it would not help {stop factional conflicts}. For one ought to level desires sooner than property; but this is impossible for those not adequately educated by the laws."[60] Surely this regime must educate the middling citizens in some sense to actualize the potential of their economic position.[61] It is possible that Phaleas fails in his pacification scheme because he does not retain a wealthy class that could absorb those with immoderate desires without disturbing the political stability of a large middling ruling class. The American founding generation points to the difference between a formerly poor person who gains wealth by a redistribution of the goods of the rich and the middling property holder who procures his self-sustaining status through his own efforts. Self-reliance is one of the virtues of the middle class that Aristotle will praise.

In order to take up these three problems it is necessary first to examine the virtues Aristotle attributes to the middling class to discover their political significance. Having identified virtue with the mean, Aristotle makes four claims in favor of "means" generally found in middling property holders. (1) The passions of the middle class are more ruled by reason so that they are inclined neither to the arrogance of the rich, strong, and well-born nor to the malice of the poor, weak, and dishonored, both of which tend to produce injustice. Possessing neither too much nor too little of the "goods of fortune" allows and perhaps encourages one to control the passions and to be more reasonable.[62]

(2) The middling type has the right degree of ambition with respect to political office, that is, this person neither wants it too much nor shuns it. Middle-class citizens must attend to private affairs, primarily the provision of

daily needs, to such a degree that they do not desire great political responsibilities, while, on the other hand, they are sufficiently dependent on a smoothly running regime to be willing to serve in offices occasionally. Thus, they are willing and able to rule and to be ruled in turn: the quintessential political characteristic. The very strong, very wealthy, and very influential are so accustomed to luxury and mastery that they "neither wish to be ruled nor know how to be," while the poor, weak, and humble tend to be slavish and lacking in the qualities of either a responsible citizen or a ruler/statesman.[63] Aristotle reiterates here his crucial point that cities ruled exclusively by the rich or the poor usually become despotisms with a master-slave relationship among the inhabitants. The very rich with no other redeeming qualities tend to want to tyrannize; the very poor, wanting influence but not familiar with the arts of rule, give up their power to tyrannical demagogues, who promise to serve their desires: "What comes into being, then, is a city not of free persons but of slaves and masters, the ones consumed by envy, the others by contempt."[64] Free political arrangements are closely tied to a dominant class of citizens roughly equal among themselves.

Political partnership in the strict sense, that is, among free men, requires a sort of friendship among equal and similar persons.[65] Envy and contempt are politically undesirable. Aristotle asserts that (3) people of moderate means have much in common to encourage friendship among themselves. It is also possible that there will exist members of this class who have interests in common with either the rich or the poor. Aristotle concludes that since the *polis* "wishes[66] . . . to be made up of equal and similar persons to the extent possible," and since the "middling elements" are most in this condition, the *polis* is "by nature constituted" of middling citizens. If the ruling body need only be "equal and similar" to itself, democracy or oligarchy would fulfill this requirement. Clearly Aristotle is claiming more: the middling property holders are somehow "equal and similar," thus potential friends, to others in the city as well. The strictly political regime, the one suited to the *polis* as an association of equal and free human beings, is ruled by the "middling element."[67]

The moderate amount of property to which he has repeatedly referred is roughly defined by Aristotle's next praise of the middle class: (4) they have enough not to be envious of the rich and not so much as to fear the envy or thievery of the poor. They "preserve themselves."[68] Just as the best size for a city's wealth is defined as large enough for the community to defend and support itself without continual expansionist war, while not so great as to invite invasion,[69] the best amount of property for an individual is that required for self-sufficiency without stimulating a craving for luxury or exciting envy. Very wealthy people are no more self-sufficient than very poor people, the ones generally lacking the necessary moderation with regard to desire, the others the means to subsist.[70] This point amplifies the earlier one that great wealth and great poverty both contribute to injustice.[71]

In this list, there is no obvious mention of courage or other military virtues. Aristotle does, however, continue to associate the middling class and the dominant class in the best republic with the possession of armaments.[72] It is possible that his argument for a moderate amount of property is linked to the ownership of arms in two ways: first, the status of hoplite is a shorthand way of indicating that one is wealthy enough to equip himself with heavy arms, though not so wealthy as to support horses and cavalry weapons.[73] Second, middle class citizens "preserve themselves" in the sense that they do not rely on mercenaries, expensive weaponry, or vast numbers, but can take up arms to defend their city and way of life.[74]

Rational control of the passions, moderate ambition, friendliness, and self-sufficiency receive praise as qualities of the soul in the *Ethics*, though only the second is called a virtue.[75] Nowhere does Aristotle claim for his citizens of moderate means a general possession of the ruling prudence described in *Politics* III and the *Ethics*.[76] These men of moderate means do, however, display citizen virtues. Though they are not the pure ethical virtues performed only for the sake of the nobility of the deed and the perfection of one's soul, they must be admirable. Aristotle makes a point of redefining virtue here in order to encompass the characteristics he associates with middling property. Each of these virtues is politically salutary; each seems to be related to justice, not in an abstract sense, but in the practice of real cities. Each tends either to discourage unjust deeds or to encourage the fair treatment of fellow citizens. These qualities are not, then, mere expedients for keeping the rabble in line, but the foundations of a political order strictly so called, justice and equal treatment of the equally deserving. This political order then provides a basis for a good life, though not by raising the citizen's eyes beyond the generally attainable to full human virtue.[77]

PRACTICING MIDDLE-CLASS VIRTUE FOSTERS POLITICAL LIFE

The praise of the middling element in Book IV, echoing earlier suggestions for the improvement of "the mode that prevails now," culminates in a quotation of the "prayer of Phocylides . . . : 'Many things are best for the middling; I would be of the middling sort in the city.'" From the point of view of the individual inhabitant, the best place to be in a city is in the middle. Aristotle proceeds then to the conclusions that "the political community that depends on the middling sort is best . . . , and that those cities are capable of being well governed in which the middling element is numerous."[78] Aristotle assumes that the rich *and* the poor will always be with us, but their influence in the regime should be tempered by the reasonable middle class—the not grasping, not excessively ambitious, not despotic, not slavish, not contentious, and not dependent citizenry. Aristotle puts his somewhat faint praise more positively when he argues that the more of these natural "arbitrators" there are, the more peaceful and stable the republic, both in its government and its way of life.[79] If he is faint in his praise of the men, he is effusive in praise of the regime they tend to create: "Thus it is the greatest good fortune for those who are engaged in politics to have a middling and sufficient property, because where some possess very many things and others nothing, either rule of the people in its extreme form must come into being, or unmixed oligarchy, or—as a result of both of these excesses—tyranny."[80]

As Aristotle reiterates the parallel between the good of the community and the good of its inhabitants, he also elides the praise of the middling regime with that of the middling person. Chapter 11 is both an exhortation to the lawmaker to include a large middling element in the regime and an exhortation to citizens of a republic to appreciate the benefits of middling status. The citizens must feel the importance of self-control and reasonableness to their essential role as arbitrators in the never-ending disputes of free politics in order to support the long-term existence of the middle class, which in turn supports the long-term existence of the republic. Though Phocylides' encomium of the middling type of person may border on propaganda, Aristotle seems to use that tactic in its non-pejorative sense of propagating right opinion. Becoming rich has its attractions, but the sensible middling citizen understands its pitfalls as well. The best regime for most cities and most human beings relies on an appreciation *in* the middling citizen of his middling virtues.

It is somewhat unclear how and to what extent this regime pays active attention to the nurture of citizen virtue. On one hand, the passage just quoted might lead one to believe that Aristotle relies on chance, "good fortune," to provide the right sort of citizen body for the best practice of politics. On the other hand, a republic, whose aim is to achieve political stability and a certain justice through harmony and satisfaction in all parts of the regime, must be concerned not only with the political balance of power between actual or potential factions, but also with the character of the people holding and desiring political influence. As Book III argued, a good political order could be ruled by a multitude *if* it were "well-ordered."

The virtue of the middling element is praised enthusiastically for its suitability to a political regime strictly defined and to "those engaged in politics." This regime is Aristotle's answer to the question, "What regime is best and what way of life is best for most cities and most human beings, . . . a way of life which it is possible for most to participate in, and a regime in which most cities can share?"[81] If one is concerned with most of mankind, and with a partnership in which decent human beings, who attend to private affairs most of the time, can practice the virtues to which they can reasonably aspire, then this republic of the middle element is the best. The regime provides opportunities for ruling and being ruled in turn; that is, for citizen education in the form of public action for the common good, the only sure route to political virtue, while not demanding extraordinary expenditures of money or leisure time.

Both the justice and the stability attained by a republic should be able to withstand chance, the hard times or crises that are brought on by domestic strife, warfare, and economic decline. They do not rely on extraordinary circumstances, so they should be able to weather changes. The moderately temperate citizen does not expect perfection and is, therefore, not likely either to abandon the city in despair in a crisis or to exploit a crisis situation to make radical improvements in the regime. He will muddle through and restore his life to an even keel. If the middling element can manage to hold sway in the regime, then the individuals' attempts to right their lives will aggregate into a restoration of normalcy in the republic.

The regime Aristotle calls the republic "has not often existed." Davis ingeniously explains Aristotle's reason for this fact: no regime understands itself as a republic, though many may actually be classifiable as such.[82] Because there is a broad range of possible ways of achieving its characteristic mixture, a republic is a regime that could be formed out of a number of existing imperfect regimes and would be an improvement over the common oligarchies or democracies that fill the world—as well as over those rare regimes that aspire to aristocracy, though they fail—while the inhabitants might continue to think of their regime in the terms they used before the reforms.

Thinking in terms of politically practicable citizen virtue, then, Aristotle's takeaway message is clear: the extensive education necessary to underwrite the simply best regime relies on the confluence of many unlikely conditions. Real republics, insofar as they successfully establish a way of life, are educational in the way they operate—they institutionalize the tendency toward moderation that the middling citizen ordinarily displays—but they cannot be expected to oversee every aspect of a citizen's life, to habituate everyone to make the right choices under every circumstance. The founders of real republics, which means in most cases the reformers of failing regimes, can choose institutions that counteract the sources of failure (usually excesses coincident with the type of the existing regime) and point the regime toward a republic. Since (1) a republic is a mixture of regimes that an observer or participant might identify as any of its constituent regimes (or none of them) and (2) stuff happens—foreign invasion, plague, famine—and people react to shelter themselves or to take advantage of chance events, a republic's citizens must be habituated to appreciate and therefore maintain this balanced mixture in the future. The laws and the political culture must guide the middling citizen to appreciate the reasonable self-control his economic and social status encourages.

In a republic based on a simple mixture of the rich and the poor, a citizen whose party or class holds a political advantage will need to give up that advantage to keep the regime in balance—not a very likely outcome short of class warfare. Hence the need for the dominance of the middle class, a party that will feel no disadvantage from throwing its weight into the opposite scale when one party has gained too much political power. The great advantage of the virtues associated with middle-class citizens is that they do not require rigorous training. Aristotle sees the virtues accruing "by nature" to people who find themselves in the middle socially, economically, politically, even morally. Unlike many opinion leaders of the American founding generation, Aristotle does not explicitly warn that the citizens' upbringing will need to instill a broad appreciation of their middling political institutions and the temperate ethic of their regime.

In the modern age, it is not at all obvious why it is useful to examine Aristotle's arguments concerning the virtues of the middle class and its regime. Modern political thinking warns that the attempt to define and impose citizen virtues leads to divisiveness and disunity. Late modernity has also "discovered" the relativity of all "values." The latter discovery seemed to follow from the first insight—one that Aristotle could also have made. He did not, however, draw the late-modern conclusion—that it is best for the political order to leave the question of virtue or the good life wholly to private definition. The paradoxes inherent in Aristotle's praise of middle-class virtues, however, pave the road into the relevance of his political regime to our way of life.

The virtues Aristotle praises are not the noblest ethical virtues. They are the qualities of character that tend to make citizens peaceful and moderately public spirited. If these qualities exist simultaneously, they support politics as Aristotle defines it: ruling and being ruled among free and roughly equal people. Such political life, in turn, sets a standard to which a citizen must make some effort to aspire, but such aspirations should create no dangerous divisions among roughly equal persons. It is simply good for human beings to live in accordance with a definable and decent standard, and in the case of the vast majority of human beings, the highest standard to which they can reasonably be held is good citizenship in a good regime. It becomes the legislator's responsibility to encourage a respect for these virtues in both the middling element that is to practice them and in the higher and lower classes that are to submit to the middle class' arbitration.[83] Framing the middling virtues in terms that recall the gentlemanly virtues of the *Ethics* may be intended to persuade the more finely educated in the regime not simply to spurn the middle class; emphasizing repeatedly the accessibility of the middling virtues might be intended to encourage the poorer citizens not to resent them, but perhaps to emulate them.

Thus, the citizen virtue of a middling republic does not create grand *individuals* worthy of great honor but rather good citizens who, when considered as a whole, sustain a *regime* worthy of emulation. The laws of a middling republic provide an education by example for acts of good citizenship, while leaving the population free for private pursuits—a similarity to modern liberal arrangements. His students should not be quick to condemn the individual virtues Aristotle expects from these people, because he mentions some revered founders and statesmen as coming from the middle class. Solon, Lycurgus, and Charondas are examples of the "middling" type Aristotle has in mind,[84] and they performed the essential political act of lawgiving. Lycurgus' Sparta and Solon's Athens exhibit some moderate characteristics. Whether or not these founders intended to create republics, they did use some republican "devices"— their real-world effects are what Aristotle emphasizes. He argues in *Politics* II that Solon's democratic reforms were intended to prevent the predominance of the most vulgar;[85] Lycurgus' regime mixed an aristocracy elected "from all by all the citizens" with the preexisting dual monarchy. Not much is known of Charondas, but Aristotle claims his city, Catana, employed the device "used in polities" by which the rich are fined more than the poor for nonattendance at the law court.[86] Thus, it seems, all three whom Aristotle portrays as men of moderate means can be credited with political initiatives using some of the principles of the republic. They were not great kings (if Plutarch's sources are creditable, Lycurgus actively turned down a king's crown) nor the most virtuous philosophers imaginable, but at least Solon and Lycurgus exercised legislative prudence, which Aristotle praises very highly in the *Ethics*,[87] and they created moderated regimes out of corrupt oligarchies.

Nichols discusses the middle-class polity, pointing out that Aristotle even "speaks as if it were simply best."[88] She emphasizes Aristotle's remarks about the capacity of the middling element to befriend members of both the upper and lower classes and thus to support a harmonious life. Although an accommodating attitude is a good start, more is needed to achieve the goal Aristotle lays out for the political regime per se: stability through fairness to all parties. The middling citizen is also reasonable, willing both to rule and to be ruled, attentive enough to wealth to take care of himself and "his own" but not so much as to become arrogant or envious. As Sparta's and Carthage's political problems seem to grow out of an intention to encourage the most virtuous to rule—an intention that produced its opposite, the rule of the merely wealthy and corrupt—both cities would do well to cultivate a middle class that could bridge the gap between rich and poor and, more importantly, between high aspirations for individual virtue and the inescapable bad tendencies of human nature. Throughout her book, Nichols stresses the need for statesmen who know what is at stake in maintaining the balance of democratic vs. oligarchic institutions and can explain the relation of each part of the city to the whole regime. While Aristotle sees the advantage of such a person's being available to a republic, and perhaps he is expecting someone with such an understanding to emerge from among his students to initiate reform in the direction of a republican regime, if most cities populated with most human beings have to rely consistently on a statesman's training and persuasive capacities, most republics will be doomed. It is an important indication of the political utility of middle-class virtues that the middling element in Athens and Sparta produced a Solon and a Lycurgus—according to Aristotle—but it obviously did not happen often.

Reasoning from Aristotle's presentation of Sparta, Crete, and Carthage, it is clear that the statesmanship a political order *usually* needs is not that embodied in a Lycurgus or a Solon, or a Lincoln or a Churchill. In reasonable deliberations over day-to-day matters, some political horse trading will usually serve the purpose. The middling elements of the city will have the virtues that are normally associated with their middling status: reasonableness, lack of arrogance and malice, moderate ambition, willingness to rule *and to be ruled* as free people are ruled, friendliness, self-reliance.

MIDDLE-CLASS POLITICS AND POLITICAL JUSTICE

Generally, then, the middling sort make good citizens, if not completely good human beings, and their regime produces a peaceful and stable city. Aristotle explains how this lasting peace is maintained. If the middle class is large enough to counterbalance either extreme class when added to the other, its "natural" temperance will incline it to act against measures that threaten to transform the regime from a republic into either democracy or oligarchy.[89] Further, since the moderates have more in common with either extreme than the extremes have with each other, the rich and poor are unlikely to band together against the middle. Neither extreme will trust the other to rule and they will never reach a better accommodation of their desires than that afforded by the moderates. Even more stable is the republic in which the moderate party is larger than both extremes added together, but Aristotle does not hold out much hope that such good conditions will arise. Regimes, especially in large cities, in which the middling element is numerous, provide Aristotle with the empirical evidence that his regime through the middling sort is the most free of faction and conflict over what the regime should be. In other words, the republic is most apt to satisfy the key requirement of a republic, that no element of the city desires another regime.

Unfortunately, in Aristotle's mind, it is a matter of chance, "the greatest good fortune," that a large middle class should spring up in a city.[90] He presents no suggestions for encouraging its growth. He does, however, seem to expect chance to be on the side of republics, as opposed to true aristocracies, judging from the first lines of Chapter 11: "What regime is best . . . for most cities and most human beings?"[91] Aristotle is quite clear that the republic "through the middle citizens" is meant to be possible and "best," if only the city has a sizeable middle class, while the simply best regime is beyond the reach of almost all cities for a great variety of reasons.[92]

Aristotle's most emphatic claim, "that the middling sort {of regime} is best is evident," is supported by the argument that it is least subject to factional conflicts and "splits over the regimes."[93] The prime criterion of the politically best is stability. The best practical regime must not teeter always on the brink of revolution or civil war. It seems that Aristotle is ignoring the criteria of virtue and justice, which he elsewhere cast as prime concerns of political actors. Later, when describing the method by which a lawgiver should decide what regime and what type of that regime suits the city best, Aristotle counsels that regardless of the regime, the middling sort should always be included in the citizen body. The property requirements, whether primarily democratic, aristocratic, or oligarchic, should extend high or low enough to include the middle element, in order to ensure "a lasting polity {or regime}."[94] Again, the justification is the discouragement of factional arguments between the rich and poor. Again, what happened to justice?

A principle of justice stands behind all of these arguments for the stability of a republic. Because this portion of the *Politics* discusses the regimes available to cities without inhabitants of great virtue, Aristotle has already modified his standards. With that proviso, the issue of justice is precisely the distribution of offices and honors according to the "equality and similarity" of the citizens. If all the citizens are roughly equal in virtue, a regime that assumes they are equal and treats them all as free to participate in the city's decisions and to attend to their private lives as well is the most just, even according to the criteria Aristotle uses in discussing his simply best regime in Book VII: "Among similar persons nobility and justice are found in ruling and being ruled in turn, for this is something equal and similar: to assign what is not equal to equal persons and what is not similar to similar persons is contrary to nature, and nothing contrary to nature is noble."[95] The middling republic, then, will be the most stable regime because it will not irritate the poor or the rich by imposing on them and aggrandizing itself. It will be the most stable, because it is the most just.[96] The wealthy and the needy agree that it is the most just regime *possible* precisely because each refuses to be ruled by the other, and each considers the moderate regime more just than any available alternative:[97]

> Where the multitude of middling persons predominates either over both of the extremities together or over one alone, there a lasting polity is capable of existing. For there is no reason to fear that the wealthy and the poor will come to an agreement against them: neither will want to be the slaves of the other, and if they seek a regime in which they will have more in common, they will find none other than this. They would not put up with ruling in turn on account of their distrust toward one another. The most trustworthy person everywhere is the arbitrator; but the middling person is a sort of arbitrator. (*Politics* IV.12.1296b39–1297a6)

The middling element of the city will exact justice both in the cases of its fellow middling citizens, because of its natural temperance, and in the cases of the rich and the poor, because of its natural position as arbitrator. It is this character as arbitrator that makes Solon a successful lawgiver, and perhaps accounts for Lycurgus' success as well.[98] Insofar as they were successful, they balanced the claims of the poor against those of the rich, taking into account the justice of allowing the less virtuous citizens to participate in the political life of their cities along with the more virtuous. Beyond these acts of justice, the middling republic should not require the common devices used against the *demos* to diminish their influence in the regime. If the middle class remains large enough to balance out in practice any extreme measure of the poor to the detriment of the rest of the city, it should not need to create permanent institutions to deprive the poor of all power. Although "a polity should be made up only of those possessing [heavy] arms," it should also arrange the property qualifications so that "those sharing in the regime [are] more numerous than those not sharing."[99] For instance, since the lawmaker cannot be certain of the virtue of those holding office in the republic, it is best to include the poor in the regime so that they are not later treated arrogantly or unjustly. Aristotle appears to be advocating some institutional arrangements to restrain future parties in power from injustice against opponents.[100]

On the other hand, Aristotle does not fall prey to the criticism he leveled against the *Republic*'s Socrates. In Book II Aristotle insisted that the laws and the regime teach citizens to restrain their desires and contentions by training them in virtue, and not try to restrain any vicious tendencies merely by force or by enslaving the ruling class to oppressive institutions. Whereas this polity does not attend actively to the education in virtue described in Books VII and

VIII, it no less crucially rests on the useful and not-ignoble virtues of the middle element. Aristotle's description of the principle of political regimes implies that the regime must give its citizens a healthy sense of their responsibility to maintain stable and just relations among the classes and to ensure that no one party desires any other regime. It exhorts them to the virtue of which they are all capable, that is, the temperance that they are inclined to cherish in any case.

Institutional Adjustments for the Political Regime

A brief examination of Chapters 14 through 16 of Book IV reveals that Aristotle wishes to transmit some specific practical advice for the improvement of defective regimes—especially democracy and oligarchy. This advice reiterates that at least the republic, if not the republic through the middle element, is accessible to and beneficial for the most common regimes in existence. Again much emphasis is placed on the moderation of politics and the sharing of authority, especially through the methods of distribution of and election to office.

In matters of deliberation, such as "war and peace, alliances and their dissolution, laws, [judicial cases carrying penalties of] death or exile or confiscation, and the choosing and auditing of officials,"[101] a republic is characterized by mixed arrangements. Both a republic and an aristocracy combine giving authority to all in some matters and to a certain group in others. What distinguishes the republic is apparently that it mixes deliberators chosen by election with those chosen by lot to decide on the same matters, whereas aristocracies apparently would give some decisions to the elect and others to a body chosen at random.[102] Since a democracy chooses primarily by lot and tends to refer all matters to all, while an oligarchy chooses primarily by election from a preselected group and refers most decisions to a few, the mixture of these principles, obliterating any favoritism toward either the rich or the poor and tending to favor a larger segment of the city while still being somewhat selective, is characteristic of republican government.

Aristotle makes some pointed suggestions for reformers regarding the superior forms of oligarchy and democracy. He repeats the conditions for a "political oligarchy" that were mentioned in Chapter 6, that the property requirement be moderate and open to a large number, and that the regime be law governed.[103] In approaching a republic, this regime contrasts both with the potential injustice of self-elected oligarchies and the certain dangers of lawless dynasty. Oligarchies should allow the people some voice in deliberations, however limited by the oligarchs, or should give them a veto power. This oligarchic arrangement is said to be the opposite of the practice in republics,[104] but it would have the desired effect of maintaining a community of a sort between the rich and the poor.

Democracies are also advised to moderate their extreme popular tendencies. Moderate democracies avoid the measures that empower only the poor. As in the republic, when the notables deliberate with the people, their work will be improved. All the parts of the city should be represented in the deliberative body, another measure reminiscent of the republic's concern to satisfy all citizens and to discourage sedition or radical reform.[105]

Clearly, according to Aristotle, both democracies and oligarchies are improved by becoming more like polities in regard to the constitution and workings of the deliberative body in the regime. If they do not become *simply* more just, they will certainly be *perceived* as more fair by the parties who are not ordinarily accommodated by that type of regime. Similarly, the magistracies (or "offices to which are assigned both deliberation and judgment concerning certain matters and command, but particularly the latter"[106]) and the adjudicative powers should be distributed in such a way as not to offend the rich in a democracy or the poor in an oligarchy. The complex and confusing account of the election of officers redoubles the thrust of previous remarks on republics: there are more or less "political" forms of all four political regimes.

In oligarchies and certain oligarchic polities, for example, some citizens choose the officers from a selected group or from the whole citizen body either by election or by lot. In democracies and certain democratic polities, all choose from all by election or by lot. Between these possibilities is the republic, which mixes the use of elections with the use of the lot, uses a mixture of bodies of citizens eligible for offices, and mixes the size of the electoral body, sometimes enfranchising all and sometimes only some of the citizens. Although election is essentially aristocratic, the lot democratic, and the restricted franchise and restricted eligibility oligarchic or aristocratic, the republic uses all these devices to gain the benefits of each method while balancing the influence each may give to a certain party or part of the city.

This section of *Politics* IV treats of the three parts of any regime, the deliberators or legislators, the officials or executives, and the judges, and what "the excellent lawgiver" must know regarding the fine condition of each, because "as long as these are in a fine condition, the regime is necessarily in a fine condition."[107] After the listing of the kinds of offices found in each part of most regimes and the kinds peculiar to certain regimes, the predominant issues in the discussions of each part are clearly the selection process and the eligibility requirements for each type of office. No practical advice is given, for instance, regarding the types of legislative procedures to follow, the best methods of law enforcement, or the structure of the judicial bodies.[108] Rather, if the republic's rule of selection is followed, so that no major part of the city can complain of having no access to the powerful positions, "the regime is necessarily in a fine condition." Aristotle implies that without such political principles no regime can last or remain peaceful.[109]

THE DEFENSE OF THE MIDDLING REPUBLIC

According to Aristotle, the type of person likely to be the best citizen of a decent, stable political regime in practice is one of moderate means. Though this regime does not achieve the highest justice, the whole of virtue, it achieves political justice, avoids injustice better than most regimes, and satisfies its citizens of all types that they could not achieve greater justice in another arrangement. The middle-class citizen avoids vice better than the rich or the poor and satisfies a modest standard of reasonableness and decency. With Lycurgus and Solon as models and with some training in legislative prudence, one who has had the experience of being ruled in a free and fair regime could be an excellent leader for the establishment of new examples of the best regime for most cities and most human beings.

In the practical arrangements for ruling, the principle of moderating the claims of rich and poor and of oligarchs and democrats takes the form of opening offices to all parts and potential factions in the city and thus of offering to all in an orderly fashion some opportunity to influence the deliberations, official acts, and judicial decisions of the regime. Each city should moderate its actions through balance among the parts or, better yet, by the ascendancy of the most temperate chosen by the less temperate as the most trustworthy arbitrators.

The concession made by the republic to the freedom of action of all non-slaves is a just act. To treat free human beings as if they are incapable of making decisions for themselves that will affect their futures and the future of the city is simply unjust. The best regime in practice will free its less-than-fully virtuous citizens to participate in their city's future.

Once Aristotle shows the sense in which he associates political justice with political stability and with the treatment of free people as equal in respect of their freedom and capacity for political contribution, the account of the minimal republic, the mixture of oligarchy and democracy, and the special republic through the middle elements seems to proceed naturally. Aristotle shows how political justice demands that a *polis* be ruled by a stable regime and how political stability, in turn, demands that the regime give credence to the various claims to authority by various parts of the city. A regime that takes this stable justice and this just stability as its primary aims will empower the most reasonable, free-minded, friendly, self-supporting, moderately public-spirited citizens it can find. Aristotle recommends the middling property holders, without recommending a reduction or augmentation of all property to the middling level. The rich should not be greatly deprived of their advantages, nor the poor unexpectedly relieved of their cares, but both should be so satisfied with their treatment as not to want to seize complete political power.

In Aristotle's eyes, one of the most favorable assessments is that there exist no parts in the middle-class republic that desire the regime to change.[110] It is the most stable political regime. Whereas democracy offends the wealthy or noble few, oligarchy the freeborn many, aristocracy the not-sufficiently virtuous, kingship the unappreciated virtuous, and tyranny almost everyone, the best polity maintains a unity among the people. It does so politically—not by artificially inducing a family or household atmosphere among unrelated people, but by treating all free and roughly equal people as free and equal. It defines its justice politically—not as distributive justice for a mostly unattainable excellence, but as the accommodation of the consideration due to free human beings. Finally, it conceives of citizen virtue politically—not as the excellence of the philosopher blended with the nobility of a great king nor even as the leisured "culture" of educated gentlemen, but as those characteristics of soul, particularly the appreciation of the value of mediocrity, that lead to a reasonable and moderate attitude toward ruling, the willingness to be ruled and to rule in turn, friendliness toward one's fellow citizens, and the ability to provide for one's own wants without excess and without envy.[111]

Writers among the Federalists and Anti-Federalists alike were keenly aware of the threat that instability poses to any regime and to a democratic regime especially. The American founding generation famously saw, as Aristotle stresses, that no regime without "domestic tranquility" can possibly "establish justice, promote the general welfare," or "secure the blessings of liberty." The founding period is also replete with writings that suggest concern for "political virtue and vice," though those aspects tend to be overlooked. Observing certain unchanging characteristics of human nature, the founding generation thought about the varieties of ways of life and education that constrain the most disruptive tendencies in predictable ways. In the process of developing a constitution that would work more effectively than the Articles of Confederation and that would stand the test of a broad franchise and popular pressure—a republic—the founders tried to promote in the citizens an attachment to the national union and to the principles at its foundation; the citizens needed to believe that their form of government, albeit new, was not only "their own" but "lovable." These ruminations—insights on the middling character of the dominant class of Americans, the citizen virtues a republic requires, and the necessity of citizen education—parallel Aristotle's arguments in revealing ways.

Part II

THE AMERICAN FOUNDERS' REPUBLIC

4

"Happy Mediocrity"
AMERICA'S MIDDLE CLASS

[We] have been sent into life, at a time when the greatest law-givers of antiquity would have wished to have lived. How few of the human race have ever enjoyed an opportunity of making an election of government more than of air, soil, or climate, for themselves or their children. When! Before the present epocha, had three millions of people full power and a fair opportunity to form and establish the wisest and happiest government that human wisdom can contrive?

• John Adams, "Thoughts on Government," 1776[1]

The Athenian democratic regime is commonly named the first democracy. Though saying much—both positive and negative—about democracy as a specific regime, the whole of the *Politics* reveals more about the meaning of politics per se. The phenomenon of democratic Athens is, however, crucial for that revelation. The essence of politics—the balanced combination of freedom and equality—becomes visible for Aristotle's inspection and analysis only after successful democratic argument had disclosed the serious claims of the majority of human beings. Only after a practical alternative to the dominance of kings and tyrants, aristocrats and plutocrats had made an effective case (backed by a willingness and an ability to fight for it) did human beings become open to politics in Aristotle's strict sense. Historically, the reality of democracy introduced the world to the possibility of politics.

There is a historical parallel between Aristotle's project to describe and defend politics, which results in praise of the middle-class republic, and the project of the American founding generation from the 1770s to the 1790s.

The American revolution and the ratification of the Constitution together constituted both a practical attempt to make an effective governing order that rests on both equality and liberty, and an experiment in the improved science of politics. Both the Federalists and Anti-Federalists rejected the monarchies and tyrannies of the day in favor of a fresh look at a republic in which free and equal citizens would take turns ruling and being ruled. Though the process of grafting liberal institutions onto an existing monarchy had been going on in England for a long time, America was a frontier where new institutions could be created with much more leeway for experimentation. Using this freedom, the American founding generation created not pure democracy with its inherent dangers, but a governing structure combining elements of democracy with what they called "aristocracy" and Aristotle would call "oligarchy" to form a stable and practically more fair way of life. They did what Aristotle advises reformers of corrupt regimes to do—they emphasized what was salvageable from their English antecedents and balanced oligarchic with more democratic institutions.[2]

Many of the founding generation use their historical and philosophical educations to think about the optimal form of government for the new American nation. John Adams attempts to further the edification of his countrymen by condensing and analyzing the writings of all past thinkers on good government and the experience of past republics in his three-volume work, *A Defence of the Constitutions of Government of the United States of America*.[3] He spends quite a large portion of this work in analyzing Aristotle's *Politics* and, to make a very long story short, argues that Aristotle was "very wise" in his doctrine on the middle-class republic and the sort of person who makes a good citizen.[4] Exploring the ways in which the American founding generation created a republic similar to the Philosopher's republic, appreciating many of the same political requirements for a good citizen in a good political order, illuminates both the prudence of the framers and the responsibilities they bestowed upon succeeding generations.

Two prime factors make the modern liberal state praiseworthy in Aristotelian terms: political stability and an understanding of justice as fairness to all parts of the society. What modern liberal citizens clearly have in common with the polity's citizens is both a widespread opinion that one should pay some attention to politics and a widespread disinclination to do so. Modern Americans, like Aristotle's middling element, know they *should* participate in elections and they *should* serve on the jury, but when the moment arrives, many think of something they would rather be doing. Thanks to the economies of scale of modern agriculture, most Americans are not farmers, but a life spent largely providing for oneself and one's family still tempers political enthusiasm.

Technically the system allows citizens to take turns ruling and being ruled, and many in the "middling class" do serve in social leadership positions, but in practice most citizens do not even aspire to, let alone take, ruling political office. Aristotle would observe that human nature has not changed: moderns debate the advantageous and disadvantageous, the just and the unjust, and (sometimes quite large) groups will be caught up by the flattery of a demagogue or the charisma of an extraordinary leader. Modern citizens can be tempted to go to extremes in the pursuit of an abstract notion of justice or in support of one man, but the weakness in every argument and any hero's feet of clay are difficult to conceal for very long, so it is unusual for an established liberal state to fluctuate widely between extreme democracy and extreme oligarchy or to undergo frequent revolutions.

The American founders imagined a middle class in some significant senses parallel to the one Aristotle recommends to a republican founder or reformer. An examination of a range of actors in and commentators upon the founding demonstrates that "the people," the "establishers" of the Constitution and the wellspring of authority for the regime, were expected to be predominantly neither very wealthy nor unable to support themselves, but rather self-reliant farmers, merchants, and artisans or, perhaps, doctors and lawyers. Opinions differed on the specific virtues these citizens would display, but not upon the expectation that they would practice politically useful self-control. Opinions differed upon the sorts of livelihood that would produce the best examples of good citizenship, but not much on the sorts that would produce the worst. Though some, most notably John Adams and Melancton Smith, spoke repeatedly and explicitly of the "middle," while other writers did not, it is likely that the latter did not view their ideal citizens in terms of a middling position because the middling element was so dominant in late eighteenth-century America. The typical American might have occupied a more perceptible middle class in a European setting between clearly defined aristocrats and peasants, but such classes were minuscule in the United States. Judging from the way opinion leaders spoke, the opportunities and the resources widely available made it so possible to move from straitened circumstances into a more comfortable, self-reliant position as to discourage thinking of impoverished citizens as occupying a fixed stratum as it would have been understood in the old world.[5]

Adams, the "Citizen of New Jersey," and Benjamin Franklin all describe an American middle class, distinct from the poor and the rich, and observe a correlation between moderate property ownership and crucial citizenship qualities, such as independence, industriousness, obedience to law, and the common sense to choose able representatives.

JOHN ADAMS CONFRONTS ARISTOTLE ON THE MIDDLE CLASS

The prime example of a founder with an appreciation for Aristotle's praise of the middle class is John Adams in his exhaustive study of the "History of the Principal Republics in the World."[6] Adams takes as his foil a 1778 letter by Anne Robert Jacques Turgot, which examines critically the state constitutions adopted immediately after American independence. Turgot's criticisms target many aspects of those constitutions: the attempts to prevent the participation of clergy in some state governments but also the requirements in some states of a profession of Christianity for officeholders; the centralization of laws and administration of local matters in state governments; the failure to declare the separate rights of landowners versus non-proprietors; and the lack of uniformity in taxation and commercial regulation throughout the Union (which should act according to "the sacred principle of commercial freedom"). He sees the Union insufficiently unified in "laws, customs, and opinions," making the states unequal in strength and "progress." He decries the lack of a standing national army in addition to militias, where "the attributes of a good citizen" are combined with "those of a soldier and militia-man." Adams is correct that under this array of criticisms lies Turgot's fundamental belief in small-scale direct democracy: individual (property-owning) citizens should be actively participating in the assembly that governs them; therefore, most legislation that affects them should be made close enough to home that they may attend without threatening their private affairs, and all power, legislative and executive, should be exercised by these local assemblies.[7] The most concise summation of Adams' criticism of Turgot: dangerous nonsense.[8] Most famously and most consistently, Adams insists on representation rather than direct democracy and on separation of powers, including an independent executive with veto power and a bicameral legislature.

ADAMS CONFRONTS ARISTOTLE'S *POLITICS*

The argument of Letter III from the third volume of *A Defence of the Constitutions* reveals most clearly Adams' love-hate relationship with Aristotle's political teachings. In brief, Adams reviles the argument for exclusive aristocracy drawn from *Politics* VII and VIII, but embraces quite passionately Aristotle's praise of the middle class and the regime in which it predominates drawn from *Politics* IV.

Like the *Politics*, Adams' letter examining parts of the *Politics* in detail begins with a general observation on studying political things: unlike most sciences, the "science of legislation" has failed to define its terms consistently, fueling speculation "like merchants with false weights, artificial credit, or base money."[9] These similes imply a remediable failure of definition, a failure growing from motives of self-aggrandizement rather than from an unavoidable imprecision in studying human society, as Aristotle might put it.[10] Without consistent term, that is, without surmounting this flaw in the understanding of politics created by the self-interest of its students and teachers, a people will never unite in a peaceful and just society. "Superstition, prejudice, habit and passions" attach to different words or different understandings of words as long as those terms remain malleable in the hands of the greedy "merchants" of political power.[11]

"King" is Adams' first example of an ill-defined term that distorts political understanding, but his prime case of misleading political terminology is the cluster "republic, commonwealth, and popular state."[12] One use of the term "republic" derives from its Latin roots as a general term to denote "public affairs," as Aristotle uses the term *politeia* to refer to any political order—the form of a *polis*. Some "define a republic to be a government of more than one," which excludes only despotism.[13] A narrower, but still too broad, definition includes "only aristocracies and democracies and mixtures of these, without any distinct executive power." This category may be consistent with one of Aristotle's uses of the term, as Adams understands him.[14]

> The third form of good government, not having a proper name, was called by the Greeks *politia*, and by the Latins *respublica*, a name common to every species of government. *This is the dominion of the multitude, viz. of the whole body of the city, composed of all sorts of citizens, rich and poor, nobles and plebeians, wise and foolish, which is also called a popular government.* (Adams [1794, III.171], emphasis Adams')

Adams endorses a yet more precise, "more rational" definition as "the true, and only true definition of a republic": "only a government, in which all men, rich and poor, magistrates and subjects, officers and people, masters and servants, the first citizens and the last, are equally subject to the laws."[15] For Adams, then, it is less significant that all citizens in a republic have political power than that all citizens be subject to the same law. Here Adams joins Aristotle, who categorizes democracies and oligarchies as the best of their kind when they are ruled by law and the worst when ruled by the mutable desires of the powerful.

Working from his interpretation of the Roman *res publica* as "a government, in which the property of the people predominated and governed," Adams approves the government in which the property of everyone is protected, because it "implies liberty" more generally, arguing that "property cannot be secure, unless the man be at liberty to acquire, use, or part with it, at his discretion, and unless he have his personal liberty of life and limb, motion and rest, for that purpose." For Adams, "the people" in this formulation means not the majority, but quite literally everyone who owns any property. Similarly, Aristotle associates a stable and just polity with the ascendancy of moderate property holders and the fair treatment of all under law, and he recommends a low property requirement for citizenship in order to enlarge the middle class.

Turgot and Marchamont Nedham, another foil for Adams' political disputations, argue that a "republic" is not determined by the commonwealth of property, but by the interests and rights of the individual people. Adams tags their definition of republic as "democracy, or rather a representative democracy," and as lacking in historical authority. By implication theirs is one of the false and self-interested definitions. These new republicans insist that the republic must be governed by a single representative assembly invested with all the legislative, executive, and judicial power.[16]

Rather puzzlingly, Adams suggests that the many "English and French writers," despite their "mathematical precision, the most classical purity, and extensive learning," have adopted their understanding of a republic uncritically from "the grave sentiments of Portenari and Aristotle," which Adams quotes at length at this point in his argument.[17] Portenari quotes two passages from *Politics* VII where Aristotle describes the regime "for which one would pray," though those passages do not "employ the words republic, commonwealth, and popular state." That Adams quotes these passages and then shows that they conflict with parallel passages in *Politics* IV that do refer to Aristotle's middle-class republic is instructive for an analysis of the relationship between Aristotle's and Adams' recommendations to statesmen.

> We may say with the philosopher, that six things are so necessary to a city, that without them it cannot stand. 1. The first is provisions . . . 2. The second is clothes, habitations, houses, and other things . . . 3. The third is arms, which are necessary to defend the city from its enemies, and to repress the boldness of those who rebel against the laws. 4. The fourth is money . . . 5. The fifth is the care of divine worship. 6. The sixth is the administration of justice, and the government of the people. For the first are necessary, cultivators of the land; for the second, artificers; for the third, soldiers; for the fourth, merchants and capitalists [*sic*]; for the fifth, priests; for the sixth, judges and magistrates. Seven sorts of men, therefore, are necessary to a city: husbandmen, artificers, soldiers, merchants, rich men, priests, and judges [Aristotle, *Politics* VII.8].—But, according to the same philosopher [*Politics* VII.9], as in the body natural not all those things, without which it is never found, are parts of it, but only instruments subservient to some uses, as in animals, the horns, the nails, the hair, so not all those seven sorts of men are parts of the city; but some of them, namely, the husbandmen,

the artificers, and the merchants, are only instruments useful to civil life, as is thus demonstrated. (Adams [1794, III.161–62])

Adams notices that, in the context of the regime "constituted for felicity . . . reposed in the operations of virtue and chiefly in the exertions of wisdom and prudence," that is, the simply best regime, not everyone qualifies as a citizen, despite significant material contributions to the city's welfare.[18] Aristotle indeed argues that these workers are like instruments in the service of the citizens' pursuit of happiness; they take no citizen roles. For Aristotle, in Book VII as well as in Book IV (Chapter 3), all these human elements are necessary to any self-sufficient city. What differentiates regimes are the various ways the inhabitants are distributed among these functions, for example, whether farmers or artisans could also be judges or soldiers, which depends upon the assumptions of the lawgiver concerning the capacity for virtue in the populace, the material circumstances available, and the aims they can reasonably seek in common.

Adams is incensed that Aristotle could praise the virtues of the middling element of society as he does in Book IV, while arguing that the regime of Books VII and VIII could be considered good when it does not include in the citizen body those in the middling class. Here is Adams (translating Portenari) quoting "the wisest sentiments of Aristotle" in *Politics* IV.11:

The middle state is most compliant to reason. Those who are very beautiful, or strong, or noble, or rich, or, on the contrary, those who are very poor, weak, or mean, with difficulty obey reason. The former are capricious and flagitious; the latter, rascally and mean; the crimes of each arising from their different excesses. Those who excel in riches, friends, and influence, are not willing to submit to command or law; this begins at home, where they are brought up too delicately, when boys, to obey their preceptors. The constant want of what the rich enjoy makes the poor too mean; the poor know not how to command, but are in the habit of being commanded, too often as slaves. The rich know not how to submit to any command; nor do they know how to rule over freemen, or to command others, but despotically. A city composed only of the rich and the poor, consists but of masters and slaves, not freemen; where one party despise, and the other hate; where there is no possibility of friendship, or political community, which supposes affection. It is the genius of a free city to be composed, as much as possible, of equals; and equality will be best preserved when the greatest part of the inhabitants are in the middle state. These will be best assured of safety as well as equality; they will not covet nor steal, as the poor do, what belongs to the rich; nor will what they have be coveted or stolen; without plotting against any one, or having any one plot against them, they will live free from danger. (Adams [1794, III.166])[19]

The virtues that Aristotle ascribes to the middling element, that he sees as predominating in his most political regime, and that Adams approves are (1) being "compliant to reason," (2) being "willing to submit to command or law," but "know[ing] how to rule over freemen," (3) "not covet[ing] nor steal[ing] . . . ; nor . . . [having its property] be coveted or stolen," (4) not "plot[ting] against any one, or hav[ing] any one plot against them," and (5) being "least liable to . . . seditions and insurrections." Adams defends "husbandmen, merchants, and tradesmen," so long as they are self-supporting, as entitled to "the rank and rights of citizens."[20]

Adams is not, however, blinded by their just "rank and rights" or their characteristic qualities into thinking that the middling people would always make good political rulers. Unlike Aristotle's citing of Solon's and Lycurgus' middle-class backgrounds, Adams does not mention great republican lawgivers who came from the middle class, although he might himself qualify, given his participation in writing the Declaration of Independence and his drafting of the Massachusetts Constitution. While Aristotle could have been stretching a point for rhetorical purposes, Adams does not flatter the middling citizens: they are not, for the most part, going to be the representatives in the national assembly, but rather the electors of those representatives:

> These, or at least those of them who have acquired property enough to be exempt from daily dependence on others, are the real middling people, and generally as honest and independent as any; these, however, it must be confessed, are too inattentive to public and national affairs, and too apt to submit to oppression. When they have been provoked beyond all bearing, they have aimed at demolishing the government, and when they have done that, they have sunk into their usual inattention, and left others to erect a new one as rude and ill-modelled as the former. A representative assembly, elected by them, is the only way in which they can act in concert; but they have always allowed themselves to be cheated by false, imperfect, partial, and inadequate representations of themselves, and have never had their full and proper share of power in a state. (Adams [1794, III.168])

Nonetheless, the middling majority deserves a full voice in choosing its governors. Adams groups Turgot and Nedham with all previous political theorists as affirming aristocracy. The long passage from *Politics* VII disenfranchising the agrarian, manufacturing, and commercial elements of society evinces

> not only the grave sentiments of Portenari and of Aristotle, but it is the doctrine almost of the whole earth, and of all mankind: not only every despotism, empire, monarchy, in Asia, Africa, and Europe, but every aristocratical republic, has adopted it in all its latitude. . . . There is no doctrine

and no fact, which goes so far as this towards forfeiting to the human species the character of rational creatures. (Adams [1794, III.163])

Aristotle, who defines humanity in the *Politics* by its capacity for reason,[21] could express such apparently contradictory views because he was talking about regimes established in widely different circumstances: the regime "one would pray for" strives for a highly cultivated aristocratic citizen body, but it is dependent upon so many contingencies whose confluence is so unlikely that it is truly utopian, while the republic of the middle class rests on more attainable, homely virtues so that it is available to "most cities and men" as political animals. On one hand, the aristocratic republic would not include the uncultured in its ruling class, but harsh, perhaps unjust, measures would be necessary to maintain stability in such an exclusive regime and, more important for Adams, the noncitizens "amazing[ly]" would surrender their humanity to be protected like sheep by shepherds, who ultimately "devour the lambs, the wool, and the flesh."[22] A true republic for Adams, like Aristotle's polity of the middling element, on the other hand, would include in its ruling body citizens exhibiting a wider, though moderate, range of wealth, education, occupation, and political ambition. Aristotle explicitly includes the agrarian element in the moderate republic.[23]

On the basis of his observation of the behavior of the American colonists, Adams suggests that the American states should establish constitutions in which the middling property holders have "their full and proper share," which means they have appropriate influence over the election of representatives, which, in turn, will produce a fuller representation of their interests to prevent their being oppressed. A community in which the farmers, merchants, and artisans do not "have any voice or share in the government of the state, or in the choice or appointment of any who have," is unjust, because it is incompatible with human rationality.

> Until this wicked position, which is worse than the slavery of the ancient republics, or modern West Indies, shall be held up to the derision and contempt, the execration and horror, of mankind, it will be to little purpose to talk or write about liberty. This doctrine of Aristotle is the more extraordinary, as it seems to be inconsistent with his great and common principles, "that a happy life must arise from a course of virtue; that virtue consists in a medium; and that the middle life is the happiest." (Adams [1794, III.165])[24]

Adams seems to blame Aristotle for creating a world that accepts the argument for an aristocracy that behaves like shepherds to sheep who accept their protection only to be devoured in the end. The ultimate indignity of this aristocratic tyranny is that it triggers the *philosophes'* embrace of a single democratic assembly. The difference between Adams and those he critiques lies in the disparate definitions of a republic that they see as the only alternative to this tyranny. Adams defends the capacity of any owner of "small property, by which he may be supposed to have a judgement and will of his own, instead of depending for his daily bread on some patron or master, [a]s a sufficient judge of the qualifications of a person to represent him in the legislature." Unlike Turgot, Adams believes that most such citizens should not become that representative, but at least the small property holder's interests will have to be taken into account by the representative "whom he most esteems, and loves best, for his knowledge, integrity, and benevolence," the one whom he has participated in choosing "by elections, frequently repeated."[25] Adams chooses a representative assembly, not a direct democracy. Further, he vehemently argues against Turgot's insistence that the assembly be the sole authority. Other institutions—an oligarchic senate and a separate executive—must check even a republican assembly.

Adams does make an exception in favor of certain small property holders: "The moral equality that Nature has unalterably established among men gives these [husbandmen, merchants, and mechanics . . . of the most splendid geniuses, the most active and benevolent dispositions, and the most undaunted bravery] an undoubted right to have every road opened to them for advancement in life and in power." The farmers, craftsmen, and traders will know who, within their social and economic sphere, are worthy of being "brought forward upon the stage, where they may exert all their faculties, and enjoy all the honors, offices and commands . . . of which they are capable."[26]

Rather than blame Aristotle for the oppression committed by almost every known government in world history, perhaps Adams should blame influential (and self-interested) "merchants" of political ideas for using an aristocratic gloss to cover brute domination rather than instituting the more equitable and stable, but also less exploitable, middle-class republic that Aristotle outlines in association with his praise of the middling citizen. That Aristotle argues it is "best for most cities and men" has not, prior to 1787, made this republic attractive to the most ambitious men, apparently. Adams seems to think that the American states' constitutions belong in the class of governments that promise more liberty through more protection of individual rights as well as (except in the case of Pennsylvania) a popular assembly checked by a senate and an independent executive. He also strives to ensure that the citizens of those states continue to appreciate their neither wealthy nor poor situation, to obey the property laws as the grounds of their liberty, and to support this balanced governmental system.

A central part of the passage Adams quotes from Aristotle could easily be the slogan of Adams' proposed republic: "It is the genius of a free city to be composed, as much as possible, of equals; and equality will be best preserved when the greatest part of the inhabitants are in the middle state." As much as this reliance on equality in freedom resonates with America's declared political principles, Adams' further quotation from "the wisest sentiments of Aristotle"—the latter's ultimate praise of the regime in which the middling element predominates—anticipates one of the "innovations" of the modern science of politics claimed in Federalist 10 and 14: a larger republic is a more stable republic, even though a large territory is not a sufficient safeguard of political stability. As Adams' translation of Aristotle puts it, "The middle state is best, as being least liable to those seditions and insurrections which disturb the community; and for the same reason extensive governments are least liable to these inconveniences: for there those in the middle state are very numerous."[27] The extension of the country and the growth of the populace is only beneficial if the middle class also grows and remains the dominant class in the political arena. For Aristotle and Adams, this government will be more stable because the middle class is not factious in itself and can build bridges to the wealthy and the poor, so that even the latter's factious tendencies do not become dangerous. Adams agrees with Publius' conclusion that an extensive republic will be less prone to the violence of faction, but for a different reason. While Publius pictures multiple factions vying with each other at the state level and in the private sphere, thereby negating or diluting each other's political influence prior to entering the national legislature, Adams relies on the self-restraint and public spirit, that is, the virtue, of the dominant middle class to keep factional conflict at bay both inside and outside the government.

The farmers, merchants, and craftsmen who have attained self-reliance constitute for Adams "the real middling people." Despite his assertion earlier that this rank of life can produce some men of impressive public virtue, exerting their faculties and enjoying honors on the public stage, Adams remains convinced that most in this class are "always" "inattentive to public affairs, and too patient under oppression." The tendency of the middle class to attend more to private than to public affairs is generally a positive quality, making them least liable to sedition and insurrection. It seems a good republic will require them to attend to public affairs when they choose representatives at those "frequent elections," but to return to private life between times. Adams, like Jefferson in the Declaration of Independence,[28] is here treading the fine line between exhorting the populace to vigilance against tyranny (and the duty to throw it off) and singing the praises of a republic whose peaceful protection of property relies on a people who usually pay little attention to politics. Adams' concluding remarks in the last letter of the *Defence*, dated December 26, 1787, flesh out his reconciliation of his arguments with both the "wisest sentiments of Aristotle" and the shape of the newly proposed American Constitution:

> Happiness, whether in despotism or democracy, whether in slavery or liberty, can never be found without virtue. The best republics will be virtuous, and have been so; but we may hazard a conjecture, that the virtues have been the effect of the well-ordered constitution, rather than the cause: and perhaps it would be impossible to prove, that a republic cannot exist even among high-waymen, by setting one rogue to watch another, and the knaves themselves may, in time, be made honest men by the struggle. (Adams [1794, III.505])

Adams sees Aristotle's point about the virtues of the middling class, and like the Philosopher, he associates happiness with virtue. Even if aristocracy and kingship are the regimes most associated with virtue in its most brilliant forms, the well-constructed republic that models moderation will teach its citizens the middling virtues and is likely, therefore, to produce happiness more broadly spread through the community. Though Adams argues that climate and soil do not "decide the characters and political institutions of nations" and implies that the regime does not inevitably fix the destiny of all the inhabitants—virtue and happiness are possible within "despotism or democracy, . . . in slavery or liberty"—nonetheless the "well-ordered constitution" promotes virtue and not vice versa. The founder cannot simply focus on the creation of virtuous citizens and then let them govern themselves without restraint, as the advocates of rule through a single all-powerful assembly argued.[29] In what seems to be an endorsement of the "Report of the Convention at Philadelphia of the 17th of September 1787," Adams takes his argument quite far: republican virtue can be learned within the right constitution—even dishonest men may become honest from the experience of the struggle among three evenly matched powers in a government of laws. In earlier parts of the *Defence*, Adams insists on balancing three powers because everyone is always concerned with interest over virtue.[30] Those powers are usually delineated along class lines: royalty, nobility, commoners. He quotes Aristotle's argument that the best polity has a middling class large enough to balance out both rich and poor. Later in the same book of the *Politics*, Aristotle distinguishes the three aspects of ruling: the legislative, the executive, and the judicial. Under the circumstances of the American states prior to the Constitutional Convention, Adams, however, falls back on Montesquieu's tripartite division of the people, the nobility, and the king, which for Adams form the bases of the assembly, the council, and the governorship.[31] When he does so, he retains the social characteristics of each branch, insofar as he expects the assembly to be a house of commons, the council to be a senate that represents the wealthier and the more educated citizens, and the executive to be an arbiter with veto power to balance the influence of the other two.[32] For Adams, the rule of law in this balanced system takes account of both the virtue of the citizens and the vice of ambitious politicians. The representatives of the virtuous middle class will look to their own interests in the House and will need to be balanced by the senators representing the wealthy, and this (inherently unstable) bipolar balance will need to be policed by a third, equally powerful executive, serving the purpose Aristotle associated with the middle class. Adams' middle-class republic is peaceful because its majority party exhibits political virtue and is not interested in revolution. The middling citizen's common sense and honesty play against the sometimes impractical talents and knowledge of the wealthy, his interests as a property owner neither poor nor rich will be represented in one branch of the legislature, and his status as a rational being will be acknowledged in his right to vote for his representative.

THE CITIZEN OF NEW JERSEY: THE MIDDLE CLASS
DESERVES REPRESENTATION IN GOVERNMENT

Though Adams gives the most extended analysis and praise of the role of the middling class in a successful republic, others in the early years of the Union were taking up the defense of the non-aristocratic, yet independent, citizen. The self-styled "Citizen of New Jersey" in his essay, written shortly after the United States had declared its independence, first appears to disapprove of certain states' governments in which "an aristocratical idea" has predominated. He criticizes the New Jersey charter's property requirements for holding legislative office. He asks, "Why should these be made qualifications? Are not many, who have not these qualifications, as fit to serve their country in . . . these capacities, as any that are worth the money?"[33]

It appears that the Citizen might launch into a diatribe favoring an abolition of all property requirements. He is sympathetic, however, with the concern that legislators be independent. As Adams argues in more detail, the problem is not that a legislator might be dependent upon the electorate—that is the point of elections in a republic. It is, rather, that he should not be financially dependent on some wealthier person who will exercise excessive influence over his opinions, and perhaps that he should not be dependent on the income from elective office to such a degree that he will seek it as if he would otherwise starve.[34] In good republican fashion, however, the Citizen responds to a high property qualification: "According to my observation, many who are not worth so much, are of more independant spirits, and will not be so soon biassed by the prospect of gain, as those in general who are much richer than themselves."[35] The complaint is not that there is a property qualification for holding office, but that it is too high—higher than the qualification for voters.[36] A higher bar creates two problems: First, the judgment of the wealthy, despite or perhaps because of their riches, is more likely to be affected by the desire for more wealth than that of the moderate property holder. Second, if only the rich may hold legislative office, then they should rule over (and collect taxes from) only the rich. In a better arrangement, the electors should indeed choose as their lawmakers people who are independent, but they should be able to choose from the full array of citizens, or else "the poor, and those in moderate circumstances, ought to be entirely excused from bearing any part of the burden of a government, from the honors of which they are wholly excluded." There may be men of moderate circumstances who are independent, yet not possessed of estates worth 500 to 1000 pounds, that is, middle-class citizens who are comfortable enough not to be tempted by bribes nor to be on the lookout for "gain" from office, while also not so subject to the arrogance of the rich as to "think it is their right" to govern. This Citizen of New Jersey thus observes the political significance of citizens "in moderate circumstances" in categories similar to Aristotle's "middling element": (1) if they are not accorded the honors of office, they will (rightfully) resist paying taxes and obeying laws they have no part in making, and (2) if they are eligible for elective office, they are more likely to be trustworthy as legislators than either the poor or the more wealthy.

BENJAMIN FRANKLIN: THE HAPPY MEDIOCRITY OF AMERICA

Benjamin Franklin develops the theme of the practical benefits of moderate wealth in his inimitable tongue-in-cheek style. In 1782, as the war for independence is winding down and the American states are looking for potential immigrants to help in turning the land's abundant resources into prosperity, Franklin writes an open letter to those who might wish "to remove to America." He describes the American economic system as dominated by "a general happy mediocrity": "There are few great Proprietors of the Soil, and few Tenants; most People cultivate their own Lands, or follow some Handicraft or Merchandise; very few rich enough to live idly upon their Rents or Incomes."[37] Self-supporting farmers, artisans, and merchants dominate the economic landscape and to good effect. If one wishes to become fabulously wealthy, America is not the place to do it, through either the accumulation of a grand estate or the exploitation of a government office. Most of the states, he claims, follow Pennsylvania's rule that public office should not be salaried at an attractive rate, lest it attract only officeholders who seek profit. "As every Freeman, to preserve his Independence, (if he has not a sufficient Estate) ought to have some

Profession, Calling, Trade, or Farm, whereby he may honestly subsist, there can be no Necessity for, nor Use in, establishing Offices of Profit," Franklin quotes from the Pennsylvania constitution.[38] It is not so much that Franklin expects that if it pays very little, the state automatically gets honest officers, but rather that the state will be forced to employ only those who have "some Profession, Calling, Trade, or Farm, whereby he may honestly subsist," that is, those who are self-reliant to begin with. The goal is to encourage, even to honor, the middling element of society: "The Husbandman is in honor there, and even the Mechanic, because their Employments are useful. The People have a saying, that God Almighty is himself a Mechanic, the greatest in the Universe; and he is respected and admired more for the Variety, Ingenuity, and Utility of his Handiworks, than for the antiquity of his Family."[39]

Though passages in this letter border on parody,[40] and the whole smacks more of a warning to those who would not be welcome in America than an appeal to those who would, there is a basic truth at the core of Franklin's argument: a large class of citizens of moderate property, a class that must and does work to subsist in comfort, discourages both the idleness that can be found in wealthier households and the dependency that plagues the poor. Such a society will not produce vaunted men of virtue admired by all, but the ordinary virtue of the average citizen will thrive: "Industry and constant Employment are great preservatives of the Morals and Virtue of a Nation."[41] Franklin writes his appeal to potential immigrants from a situation Aristotle did not know how to create: in America in 1782 there is no titled nobility to resent a regime that does not award aristocratic honors or to resist a broad distribution of land, plus there is abundant land for the industrious and frugal poor to become self-sufficient, and for the self-sufficient to continue in that state.

Franklin mentions virtues he sees preserved by the middling way of life. In association with America's mediocrity of wealth, there are honest self-subsistence (the opposite of "Dependance and Servility"), usefulness, perhaps the capacity to admire variety and ingenuity in the practical arts, industry, religion, and religious toleration or the "mutual Forbearance and Kindness with which the different Sects treat each other."[42] Of course, honest self-subsistence, usefulness, and industry could all be aspects of the same quality. In another writing published around the time the Constitution began taking effect, Franklin suggests a further attribute of property holding, one that is not augmented by large holdings: the wisdom necessary to make an elector.[43] In sum, honest and independent citizens "respect" and "honor" honesty and independence and can be expected to select honest and independent representatives to serve in public office for reasons other than personal profit. A society dominated by these independent-yet-not-rich people will be well governed and open to economic and religious freedom.

THOMAS JEFFERSON, JAMES MADISON, AND CHARLES PINCKNEY: WIDESPREAD BUT NOT LARGE LANDHOLDING

In a letter to James Madison in 1785, Thomas Jefferson, observing the social and economic woes of the poor in France, reveals his hopes for the future in America. Though he suggests that an equal division of property would be an ideal situation, he also knows it is impractical. In addition to allowing property to be divided among a family's children and suggesting a progressive scheme of taxation, and in light of what is likely to be practicable, Jefferson modifies the Lockean labor theory of ownership to suggest what he considers a reasonable accommodation: let the industrious accumulate property, but take steps to prevent large numbers of citizens from becoming propertyless. Only if they cannot be provided with "honest work" will the country be forced to allow tenant farming, that is, the propertyless who find an uncultivated piece of land should be allowed to cultivate it, "paying a moderate rent." In sum, public policy should take as its maxim that the landed middle class makes the best citizens: "The small landholders are the most precious part of a state."[44]

In reply to Jefferson's lessons in the value of free government and small landholdings, Madison posits an additional source of the "comfort" of America's inhabitants: the small size of the population in comparison to the extent of the country. Anticipating Malthus' argument in *An Essay on the Principle of Population*, Madison posits that "a certain degree of misery seems inseparable from a high degree of populousness."[45] He worries about the proper means to "dispose" excess population:

> No problem in political Oeconomy has appeared to me more puzzling than that which relates to the most proper distribution of the inhabitants of a Country fully peopled. Let the lands be shared among them ever so wisely, & let them be supplied with labourers ever so plentifully; as there must be a great surplus of subsistence, there will also remain a great surplus of inhabitants, a greater by far than will be employed in cloathing both themselves & those who feed them, and in administering to both, every other necessary & even comfort of life. What is to be done with this surplus? (James Madison to Thomas Jefferson, 19 June 1786)[46]

It becomes clear later in this letter that, as with Malthus, Madison's concern is not how a society will afford to supply the wants of the poor (there is "a great surplus of subsistence"), but rather how certain types of work, as well as idleness, threaten individual virtue. He evidences the concern, common to many of his contemporaries, that in the process of establishing a republic in a new land, they not neglect the essential connection between the success of a republic and the virtue of its citizens. Republican arrangements in a prospering economy are a double-edged sword: they both encourage and rely upon citizen virtue and, in the long term, undermine individual virtue. Jefferson shows his concern with that problem in his proposal for an education system for Virginia,[47] as well as in the letter to Madison that prompted Madison's response. Though he claims not to be writing a "dissertation," Madison enjoins Jefferson to consider that the responses to poverty that states had at that time been considering would threaten citizen virtue:

> Hitherto we have seen them [the "surplus of inhabitants"] distributed into Manufacturers of superfluities, idle proprietors of productive funds, domestics, soldiers, merchants, mariners, and a few other less numerous classes. All these classes notwithstanding have been found insufficient to absorb the redundant members of a populous society; and yet a reduction of most of those classes enters into the very reform which appears so necessary & desireable. From a more equal partition of property, must result a greater simplicity of manners, consequently a less consumption of manufactured superfluities, and a less proportion of idle proprietors & domestics. From a juster Government must result less need of soldiers either for defence agst. dangers from without or disturbances from within. The number of merchants must be inconsiderable under any modification of Society; and that of Mariners will depend more on geographical position, than on the plan of legislation. (Madison to Jefferson, 19 June 1786)

Unpacking the assumptions behind Madison's argument reveals two prominent points that he takes for granted. First, the state or local governments—those at the time that would have controlled the distribution of land and the employments of citizens—should be engaged in "desireable reform" of society to encourage simple lifestyles that require work. In Madison's mind, a republic is peopled with good citizens who are good human beings and generally of moderate means, so Jefferson's insistence on abolishing primogeniture is sound policy, but more needs to be done to prevent prosperous middle-class citizens from striving for and achieving an upper-class lifestyle. Second, free government surely allows the citizens to choose their occupations, those in which their natural talents may be fully realized, but certain occupations are inherently dangerous to virtue and, even if useful, not "desireable." Even if there is a large class of people who work for a living and maintain a certain level of comfort for themselves, there will be some inhabitants whose work to support the economy—such as domestic service, the sale of "superfluities," seafaring, and soldiering—is dangerous to their own virtue. To put the problem in more modern terms, Madison posits that full employment is impossible, but even if the economy achieves something close to it, it cannot avoid producing (1) an underclass not unlike those Jefferson derides in France, (2) unhealthy, danger-ous, morally questionable work for only a portion of that class to perform, and (3) some in the middle class who find luxury and idleness a tempting goal. Madison and Jefferson tie the citizen virtue necessary to a republic to the economic circumstances of the citizen body and, more specifically, to an industrious middle class.[48] Madison adds the worrisome threats beyond the idle poor to be expected from those who work in the production and sale of luxuries and those whose employment depends on war or domestic instability.

Though much has been written about certain founders' fear of giving political power to the propertyless and risking "the danger of the levilling spirit,"[49] which may explain to some extent their insistence on protections for the right to property, not enough has been noticed about the fear of the rich. Such an Anti-Federalist as "Brutus" quotes Montesquieu on the immodera-tion of the wealthy: "In a large republic there are men of large fortunes, and consequently of less moderation; there are trusts too great to be placed in any single subject; he has interest of his own; he soon begins to think that he may be happy, great and glorious, by oppressing his fellow citizens; and that he may raise himself to grandeur on the ruins of his country."[50] Further, the soon-to-be-quintessential Federalist, Madison, suggests that a luxurious lifestyle is dangerous to the virtue of both the rich man and those whose labor serves his luxury. This argument parallels Aristotle's praise of the middle class: Aristotle praises those of moderate means in contrast to the wealthy as well as the poor, but he also praises certain occupations, such as farming, over others that do not leave their practitioners the modest amount of leisure time and wealth to support moderate attention to politics and some military virtue.[51] Aristotle and Madison might both recommend that the citizens not rely on serving in a standing army for their daily bread. Aristotle speaks positively of the military virtues in a citizen of a republic, likely referring to a moderately wealthy farmer who is prepared to take up arms for his city if necessary, while Madison does not refer to them here, but does appreciate the virtues a part-time militia member would develop.[52]

In describing the need for a senate in the new constitution, Charles Pinck-ney reveals his perception of "the people" of the United States to his fellow delegates to the Constitutional Convention. It is clear that he includes in this term all free men, rich, poor, and in between, and declares each to have a right "to the same protection and security." He observes that America is singular in using few "distinctions of fortune or of rank." In line with Aristotle's recom-mendations, Pinckney is pleased to see that there are property qualifications for voting and officeholding, but that they are low enough to disqualify only the truly dependent. The vast majority of Americans will enjoy the right of self-government, which is the right either to be eligible for elective office or to vote for those who are. Further, Pinckney, like Jefferson and Madison, suggests the continued dominance of those of middling wealth and their way of life. Those who may be disqualified by inadequate wealth today may take advantage of ample uncultivated lands and use their own efforts to rectify their condition:

> The genius of the people, their mediocrity of situation and the prospects which are afforded their industry . . . are unfavorable to the rapid distinction of ranks. The destruction of the right of primogeniture and the equal division of the property of Intestates will also have an effect to preserve this mediocrity: for laws invariably affect the manners of a people. (Charles Pinckney, 25 June 1787)[53]

As he observes that a large amount of uncultivated territory will prevent the increase of a potentially discontented class of paupers, Pinckney encourages his fellow lawgivers to use a political "device," a bicameral legislature, just as Aristotle recommended devices to create the atmosphere in which a large middle class will hold the most sway in the political order. America's unused land is a crucial "means of preserving that equality of condition which so eminently distinguishes us," an equality clearly meant to reside neither in luxury nor in mere subsistence, but in "mediocrity." Introducing a second legislative body viewed as the "upper house" will not corrupt American politics as it did that of Greek republics or Rome, because wealth will be spread broadly, and manners by which most people will divide inheritances among their children will be adopted as primogeniture is discountenanced, so as to make a "class of nobles" unlikely to arise.

Pinckney closely associates the republican goals of the American founders, "civil and religious liberty," with a large middle element and very small classes of wealthy and impoverished. When he speaks of the "three classes" in the United States, indeed, they are not the rich, the poor, and the middle, but the three types of occupations/ways of life that produce moderate incomes: professional, commercial, and landed. These three he sees not in conflict, but in a state of mutual dependence, which means, because they are equal in political power, "after all there is . . . but one great & equal body of citizens composing the inhabitants of this Country among whom there are no distinctions of rank, and very few or none of fortune." Positing this characteristic of the people, Pinckney proceeds, as Aristotle advised, to ask "what kind of Government is best suited to them."[54] In brief, it is not the British model. In his opening speech at the South Carolina Ratifying Convention, Pinckney reiterates his assessment of the widespread "mediocrity of fortune," and then elaborates on the corresponding ways of life:

> The greater part of the people are employed in cultivating their own lands; the rest in handicraft and commerce. They are frugal in their manner of living. Plain tables, clothing, and furniture, prevail in their houses, and expensive appearances are avoided. Among the landed interest . . . there are few of them rich, and few of them very poor; nor . . .—while the means of subsistence are so much within every man's power—are those dangerous distinctions of fortune to be expected which at present prevail in other countries.
>
> The people of the Union may be classed as follows: Commercial men, who will be of consequence or not, in the political scale, as commerce may be made an object of the attention of government.
>
> . . . Another class is that of professional men, who, from their education and pursuits, must ever have a considerable influence, while your government retains the republican principle, and its affairs are agitated in assemblies of the people.
>
> The third, with whom I will connect the mechanical, as generally attached to them, are the landed interest—the owners and cultivators of the soil—the men attached to the truest interests of their country from those motives which always bind and secure the affections of the nation. In these consists the great body of the people; and here rests, and I hope ever will continue, all the authority of the government. . . .
>
> These classes compose the people of the Union; and, fortunately . . . they may be said in a great measure to be connected with and dependent upon each other.
>
> . . . I . . . conclude that mediocrity of fortune is a leading feature in our national character; that most of the causes which lead to destructions of fortune among other nations being removed, and causes of equality existing with us which are not to be found among them, we may with safety assert that the great body of national wealth is nearly equally in the hands of the people, among whom there are few dangerously rich or few miserably poor; that we may congratulate ourselves with living under the blessings of a mild and equal government, which knows no distinctions but those of merits or talents—under a government whose honors and offices are equally open to the exertions of all her citizens, and which adopts virtue and worth for her own, wheresoever she can find them. (Pinckney, South Carolina Ratifying Convention, 14 May 1788)[55]

Farmers and artisans, as well as merchants and landowners, observe the republican rule of moderation in Pinckney's America. Without sumptuary laws, the people practice temperate living by choice. The greatest political power, he argues, does and should continue to lie with the merchants, the professional men, and the landed farming interest (in which he includes those who make the implements farmers use). The mutual dependence of these groups coupled with their "mediocrity of fortune" creates the "mild and equal government" led by those of merit and talent (not by the "dangerously rich") chosen by a broad franchise.

Jefferson, Madison, and Pinckney enlarge upon the economic underpinnings of a free republic—the need to keep the rich and poor classes small and to elevate the desirability and accessibility of the life of self-supporting, moderate wealth—though Madison worries about the sustainability of this arrangement. That Pinckney is ready to "congratulate" his political community for adopting the correct government, a meritocratic republic, suggests that he may not feel Madison's anxiety that development of the commercial and manufacturing sectors along with increasing prosperity for some could threaten the well-balanced "mediocrity of fortune" of their day and thus the political equality that allows "merit and talent" to prevail in the "assemblies of the people." If old distinctions of birth and social rank are discarded and differences of wealth lose significance in a state of relative equality, Pinckney, like Jefferson, predicts that merit and talent will become the sole distinguishing characteristics of leadership.

MELANCTON SMITH AND FEDERAL FARMER:
A SUBSTANTIAL YEOMANRY OF BETTER MORALS

Speaking against adoption of the new constitution in the New York Ratifying Convention in 1788, Melancton Smith appears to have been (though he surely was not) reading from Aristotle's *Politics*. More likely he was influenced by John Adams' Aristotelian argument[56] when he describes the characteristics of a "middling class" in America, which he distinguishes from what he calls the "natural aristocracy":[57] "The author of nature has bestowed on some greater capacities than on others—birth, education, talents and wealth, [which] create distinctions among men as visible and of as much influence as titles, stars and garters." In contrast, as in Pinckney's vision, Smith's middling class is "used to walk in the plain and frugal paths of life." Unlike the aristocrat, the middling citizen will be "sensible" of the expectations that a national legislator live a "high" life and, therefore, will not be inclined to seek the office. Although "the same passions and prejudices govern all men," Smith argues that the "substantial yeomanry" of the country will be more likely to control them for their own comfortable self-preservation and this restraint will redound to the common good of the community: "The circumstances in which men are placed in a great measure give a cast to the human character." Because of their economic circumstances, members of this class have less temptation—they are inclined by habit and the company with whom they associate, to set bounds to their passions and appetites—if this is not sufficient, the want of means to gratify them will be a restraint—they are obliged to employ their time in their respective callings—hence the substantial yeomanry of the country are more temperate, of better morals and less ambition than the great. (Melancton Smith, New York Ratifying Convention, 21 June 1788)[58]

Smith agrees with Aristotle that the wealthy have trouble understanding the habits and manners of the less wealthy. As Smith puts it, though they may have no animus against those with less wealth, they have "no difficulty in paying their taxes, and therefore do not feel public burthens: Besides if they govern, they will enjoy the emoluments of the government. The middling class from their frugal habits, and feeling themselves the public burdens, will be careful how they increase them."

Although Aristotle suggests that a larger city will have the greater chance of having a sufficiently large middle class to outweigh the unjust schemes of either the rich or the poor, he was, of course, speaking of communities on a much smaller scale than the modern state. When Smith despairs that the new United States is too large to allow the middle class to have much influence in the federal government, he is worried that the proposed constitutional arrangement of offices provides too few seats in the House to give an opportunity for the middle class to participate, despite its greater size relative to the upper class. Since, in any society, the most educated and prominent citizens will be chosen first, and the first Congress under the Constitution would have only ninety-one members chosen from three million inhabitants, the wealthiest and the scions of the most prominent families—even if their numbers are small relative to the whole population—would predictably fill all the seats. As if capitalizing on Publius' observation in the Federalist papers that the expansion of the size of a representative legislature must be limited in order "to avoid the confusion and intemperance of a multitude,"[59] Smith argues that, at a certain point, the extended size of the republic becomes a detriment, rather than an encouragement, to the political influence of the middling class. For Adams, that the elected officials must be found choiceworthy by the largest segment of the electorate, the middle class, is enough to make elections reliable. For Smith, it is necessary that, in addition to offices filled by the "natural aristocracy," some offices—perhaps a majority—be available to the middle class, so that they can balance out the dangerous tendencies of, indeed "controul," the wealthy:

But I may be asked, would you exclude the first class in the community, from any share in legislation?[60] I answer by no means—they would be more dangerous out of power than in it—they would be factious—discontented and constantly disturbing the government—it would also be unjust—they have their liberties to protect as well as others—and the largest share of property. But my idea is, that the Constitution should be so framed as to admit this class, together with a sufficient number of the middling class to controul them. You will then combine the abilities and honesty of the community—a proper degree of information, and a disposition to pursue the public good. A representative body, composed *principally* of respectable yeomanry is the best possible security to liberty.—When the interest of this part of the community is pursued, the public good is pursued; because the body of every nation consists of this class. And because the interest of both the rich and the poor are involved in that of the middling class. No burden can be laid on the poor, but what will sensibly affect the middling class. Any law rendering property insecure, would be injurious to them.—When therefore this class in society pursue their own interest, they promote that of the public, for it is involved in it. (Smith [1788])[61]

Note how Smith "defends" the justice of including the wealthy in the legislature in much the same way Aristotle defends including the poorly educated or the less virtuous: before he admits that it would be unjust not to allow them to protect "their liberties" and not to acknowledge their property holdings, he observes that they will make trouble if they are not included. As for Aristotle, the middling class balances the politically dangerous, oligarchic tendencies of the wealthy. While the aristocrats bring "abilities" and "information" to the legislative table, the middling class brings "honesty" and a "disposition to pursue the public good."

Smith argues, further, that the knowledge and "discernment" of the middling citizen is as necessary to good legislation as the education of the privileged, if not more so, and such knowledge and discernment are not attainable from "abstruse" theories:

The knowledge necessary for the representatives of a free people, not only comprehends extensive political and commercial information, such as is acquired by men of refined education, who have leisure to attain to high degrees of improvement, but it should also comprehend that kind of acquaintance with the common concerns and occupations of the people, which men of the middling class of life are in general much better competent to, than those of a superior class. To understand the true commercial interests of a country, not only requires just ideas of the general commerce of the world, but also, and *principally*, a knowledge of the productions of your own country and their value, what your soil is capable of producing, the nature of your manufactures, and the capacity of the country to increase both.

> To exercise the power of laying taxes, duties and excises with discretion, requires something more than acquaintance with the abstruse parts of the system of finance. It calls for a knowledge of the circumstances and ability of the people in general, a discernment how the burdens imposed will bear upon the different classes. (Smith [1788])[62]

Smith, in a fashion reminiscent of Aristotle's paean to the middling, argues that the interests of the middle are equivalent to the interests of the whole community: they constitute the "body" of the nation. They feel the pain of policies that harm either the poor or the wealthy; they defend the interests of all, because their interest is "involved in" the interest of the whole community.

Defending the related position common among Anti-Federalists that the proposed House of Representatives will be too small to be truly representative, Federal Farmer observes that

> gentlemen of the law, divinity, physic, &c. probably form about a fourth part of the people; yet their political influence, perhaps, is equal to that of all the other descriptions of men; if we may judge from the appointments to Congress, the legal characters will often, in a small representation, be the majority; but the more the representatives are encreased, the more of the farmers, merchants, &c. will be found to be brought into the government. (Federal Farmer 7 [31 December 1787])[63]

Congress should be larger, in other words, in order to make space for these men of less economic and social influence to exercise their due political influence. How quaint it appears today to expect there could ever be so many offices that there would not be enough lawyers to fill a majority of them! A glut of lawyer-candidates poses a problem for the Farmer if, unlike in Pinckney's America, legal professionals move out of the middle and into the wealthy class.

Like Aristotle, Smith and the Federal Farmer do not see the middle class becoming politically useful without some institutional tinkering. Aristotle proposes, for instance, defining the minimum property requirements low enough to include the maximum number of competent citizens, while Smith and the Farmer want to make the House of Representatives large enough that there will not be enough rich men or "legal characters" to fill a majority of the seats. John Adams even proposes that the Senate be viewed as the place to ostracize the wealthy so that the House may be left to the less wealthy—he argues that if there is only one legislative body, even one open to moderate property holders, the wealthy will dominate it; therefore, there must be a Senate for the wealthy, so that the House can offer a platform for "simple honesty and plain sense."[64]

Federal Farmer argues in his seventh letter that the middle-class way of life is so "happy," and its benefits to the nation's virtue so significant, that it must be the concern of the national government to support its members. Lacking Pinckney's self-congratulatory attitude, he observes that, as the country begins with so few "oppressed with riches or wants," much care must be taken to keep it that way, in order to preserve the happiness available to middle-class citizens. If they remain in the middle, they will remain good citizens and the lawmakers they choose to represent them will make good laws. His description of the alternative created by insufficient influence in elections—the predominance of the rich or the poor producing "national depravity" and a master/slave relationship—could have been taken right out of Aristotle:

> In fixing this branch [the House of Representatives], the situation of the people must be surveyed, and the number of representatives and forms of election apportioned to that situation. When we find a numerous people settled in a fertile and extensive country, possessing equality, and few or none of them oppressed with riches or wants, it ought to be the anxious care of the constitution and laws, to arrest them from national depravity, and to preserve them in their happy condition. A virtuous people make just laws, and good laws tend to preserve unchanged a virtuous people. A virtuous and happy people by laws uncongenial to their characters, may easily be gradually changed into servile and depraved creatures. Where the people, or their representatives, make the laws, it is probable they will generally be fitted to the national character and circumstances, unless the representation be partial, and the imperfect substitute of the people. However, the people may be electors, if the representation be so formed as to give one or more of the natural classes of men in the society an undue ascendency over the others, it is imperfect; the former will gradually become masters, and the latter slaves. (Federal Farmer 7 [31 December 1787])[65]

In light of Aristotle's association of a middling element with "letting the laws rule" and a peaceful and stable regime, Federal Farmer's connection between a virtuous people and making laws that "arrest them from national depravity, and . . . preserve them in their happy condition" deserves attention. He posits that, if the legislature is truly representative, lawmakers chosen by "the people" will make laws appropriate for their nation, but he fears that some arrangements may not successfully transmit the people's virtue into the lawmaking process. If one of the "natural classes," the rich or the poor, takes predominant power, the legislators will "gradually become masters" over the opposite party's slaves. Here the Farmer makes the accurate representation of the middle class in the legislature the fulcrum on which the republic succeeds or fails to reach the proper balance. Aristotle did not have the extensive theory of representation that the modern science of politics develops, but Federal Farmer's understanding of the importance of actually representing the interests and the virtues of the middle class fits neatly into the Aristotelian republic's governing principles. The Farmer is not willing to assume, as Aristotle seems to do, that the large middle class will be able to keep control over its assembly in the hands of officeholders who practice their moderate, public-spirited, fair-minded virtues. He worries that the middling voter may become inclined to select the "natural aristocracy" rather than his own fellows as his representatives and not to appreciate the need for honesty and the middling virtues—at least when there are not very many legislative seats to be filled. As Aristotle hinted, it is the founders' job to instruct statesmen and the statesman's job to instruct the middling elements to appreciate the necessity and desirability of middling virtues and not to bestow greater honor on the more splendid life of the wealthy. Unmixed rule of the most talented and expensively educated does not produce a good government for most cities and human beings.

During the period of ratification, the Federal Farmer sees the two smaller but more active parties dominating the debate:

> One party is composed of little insurgents, men in debt, who want no law, and who want a share of the property of others; these are called levellers, Shayites, etc. The other party is composed of a few, but more dangerous men, with their servile dependents; these avariciously grasp at all power and property; you may discover in all the actions of these men, an evident dislike to free and equal government, and they will go systematically to work to change, essentially, the forms of government in this country; these are called aristocrats, M[onarch]ites [?], etc. etc. Between these two parties is the weight of the community; the men of middling property, men not in debt on the one hand, and men, on the other, content with republican governments, and not aiming at immense fortunes, offices, and power. (Federal Farmer 5 [13 October 1787])[66]

Here is a problem that Federal Farmer discerns and Aristotle, who speaks of single lawgivers rather than constitutional conventions, did not: middling property holders do not appreciate the danger that the rich and the poor pose in the crucial process of founding a republic. They are, perhaps, too "content with republican governments," seeing that representation suits their way of life, and too moderate in their ambitions to combat the avaricious forces of the other parties. At a time of fundamental decision-making such as ratification represents, the middling class is not sufficiently alarmed to rouse it to resist the partisan rhetoric that is sweeping the country to accept the new constitution unreflectively.

THE POLITICAL BENEFITS OF A MIDDLE CLASS PER SE

John Adams quotes Aristotle's enumeration and explanation of the middle class' virtues without cavil or question, using them to bludgeon all who have excluded farmers, artisans, and merchants from political influence in the name of aristocracy. Previous republics have failed because the legislative assemblies in them were "false, imperfect, partial, and inadequate representations" of "the real middling people," who have therefore "never had their full and proper share of power in a state."[67] A variety of other writers on and participants in the Revolution and the drafting and ratification of the Constitution observe the crucial role that the neither-rich-nor-poor play in a stable republic. They make various proposals to continue and to expand that role: bring property requirements for both voting and officeholding down to include the middle class; discourage those who desire more than a modest competence from immigrating to America; write laws to encourage many to hold moderate property rather than a few to accumulate vast estates; encourage the moderately wealthy professional, commercial, and agricultural classes to appreciate their interdependence rather than to strive to outdo each other; ensure that the common sense and practical experience of the self-reliant middle class are reflected in the legislature.

Not merely the superiority of a moderate self-supporting lifestyle, but the conscious appreciation of that superiority is a theme that runs in the background of many of these arguments. The regime's support of middle-class political power is expected to foster a widespread rejection of idle wealth and indulgent lifestyles. Even if one selects a better-educated or more politically talented fellow citizen for public office, one should expect the representative to advance the interests of the middling majority (as the true interests of the community and the best of the populace) not that of the merely wealthy, false *aristoi*.[68] If the society is not conscious of a middling element, the electoral choice becomes rich and privileged vs. poor and ignorant. No republic can survive with only those choices. In Smith, there is a hint of Aristotle's criticism of Sparta, Crete, and Carthage: striving for unrealistic virtue in a republic tends to degenerate into excessive respect for wealth—the shorthand indicator of families who pay attention to their children's upbringing and are ambitious for public honor.

Though most are not statesmen by nature, the middling members of society exhibit behaviors that make them both deserving of political recognition and capable of choosing the statesmen who will deliberate and decide upon the laws that all must obey. Equality of political rights among all citizens will promote the elevation of the broad interests of society as reflected best in the middle class, rather than the admiration and emulation of wealth and family name.

It remains to examine the specific middle-class virtues that some in the founding generation thought to reside in the economic and political middle naturally or by second nature, but also the arguments of those who expected that a significant effort would be required to instill those character traits and an adequate appreciation of them *as* virtues in successive generations. As Aristotle has shown, the task of the founder of a regime includes making an assessment of the capacity for virtue in the populace, the material circumstances available, and therefore, the aims the citizenry can reasonably seek in common. America's founding generation assessed the material circumstances as ample for a wide distribution of moderate self-reliance, though some anticipated a limit to the population size that even the rich lands of the continent could support. What capacity for virtue did they see and what was the basis for their judgment that it would also be a widespread characteristic that could support free, popular government? In what sense did the new regime support the propagation of the social customs and opinions or the education that would carry that capacity to fulfillment?

5

CITIZEN VIRTUE
"SIMPLE MANNERS" AMONG THE
"LABORIOUS AND SAVING"

All sober enquiries after truth, ancient and modern, Pagan and Christian, have declared that the happiness of man, as well as his dignity consists in virtue. Confucius, Zoroaster, Socrates, Mahomet, not to mention authorities really sacred, have agreed in this. If there is a form of government then, whose principle and foundation is virtue, will not every sober man acknowledge it better calculated to promote the general happiness than any other form?

• John Adams, "Thoughts on Government," 1776

The Constitutional Convention aimed to create a national government capable of collecting taxes for the support of national objects, defending the United States against external enemies and internal disruptions, and promoting interstate and foreign commerce. The problems the new United States experienced under the Articles of Confederation were condensed into the perception, shared by those who would later be termed Federalists as well as those who would become Anti-Federalists, that the central authority, the United States in Congress assembled, was not strong enough to carry out the tasks expected of it. The hotly debated questions, then, were how much power had to be ceded to the central government and how the exercise of that power could be made "safe" for a federation dedicated to liberty. From an alliance of fiercely independent entities, the framing of the Constitution began a process of making a nation, but a nation with inhabitants holding dual citizenship in both the Union and their individual states. Taken for granted was the need to secure the ongoing cooperation of the people. Without citizen allegiance to the national union, the whole project would collapse—a "popular" government cannot enforce its laws at the muzzle of a musket—but the best methods of securing the allegiance of three million people of differing backgrounds, practicing different faiths, living in widely disparate climates, and pursuing differing means of living were not obvious.

This debate concerning the character of the Union under a new charter has broad implications for two classes of issues: for the top-down mechanics of the governmental structure—the separation of powers and the internal checks to keep them separated—and for the bottom-up attachment of the people to the new order. A discussion of the virtues expected of the average American embraces primarily the latter cluster of concerns. For some, primarily Federalists, the structure of the government according to the improved science of politics should attract reasoned, self-interested acceptance. For others, both Federalists and Anti-Federalists, a more intense moral and emotional citizen attachment to the principles of, and the laws produced by, the government—a belief in the justice of republican liberty and equality entwined with a sincere love of country—is required to create and sustain a large republic.

Both the Federalists and the Anti-Federalists associated republican government in the older sense with state-level politics, where liberty properly understood promotes virtue and virtue supports free government. As John Adams writes in 1776 in reference to crafting new state constitutions in light of independence,

> All speculative politicians will agree, that the happiness of society is the end of government, as all Divines and moral Philosophers will agree that the happiness of the individual is the end of man. From this principle it will follow, that the form of government, which communicates ease, comfort, security, or in one word happiness to the greatest number of persons, and in the greatest degree, is the best. (Adams [1776])

Because "the foundation of every government is some principle or passion in the minds of the people," the republic, whose principle is citizen virtue, is the best form of government, according to Adams. Not only does a republic encourage virtue in the citizenry, but annual elections for government offices also will teach the officials "the great political virtues of humility, patience, and moderation, without which every man in power becomes a ravenous beast of prey." Adams toys with the idea of sumptuary laws, though he knows they are considered laughable, because "the happiness of the people might be greatly promoted by them, and a revenue saved sufficient to carry on this war forever. Frugality is a great revenue, besides curing us of vanities, levities and fopperies which are real antidotes to all great, manly and warlike virtues."

Virtue imposed by law, in the form of limiting property to a certain moderate level, is both good for a citizen's soul and beneficial to the public purse. Adams knows free people will resist such an imposition, but only because they tend to interpret their liberty too licentiously.

The many dismissive references to state politics in the Federalist Papers suggest those thirteen communities in 1787 were already too large for direct participation and their "representative" legislatures were characterized by factious contentions because they had already grown beyond any possibility of homogeneity. The Union was always too big for a homogeneous community seeking a comprehensive common good. The built-in, deep divisions of interest, worldview, and religion among a far-flung populace necessitated a new sort of republic, based upon an improved understanding of government predicated upon free and equal citizens.[1] The Federalists thought it possible to establish a limited, though flexible, national government, that is, a republic to legislate only on matters common to all the states and all the people. The Anti-Federalists distrusted anything more ambitious than an alliance for strictly enumerated purposes. They saw even the common interest in foreign affairs as a tenuous bond, anticipating contention over tariffs and trade, and over the defense of border areas versus less threatened areas (and therefore the need for a standing army), for example. Using pre-1787 understandings, "Centinel" argues that if a republic requires rough equality, broad participation, and a virtuous populace (which in turn requires a consensus on certain moral questions), then it is impossible to have a republic at the national level.[2] To argue that it is achievable, Publius in Federalist 39 defines "republic" as claiming the title for any government in which "the persons administering it be appointed, either directly or indirectly, by the people; and that they hold their tenures . . . during pleasure for a limited period or during good behavior."[3] "Love of country" and "citizen virtue" have disappeared, not to mention the private virtues of humility, patience, moderation, frugality. For the Anti-Federalists, popular input at the ballot box was necessary, but not nearly sufficient. They argued that, if lawmaking and enforcement rely upon the conflict of nation vs. state, state vs. state, branch vs. branch (at two levels), ambitious politician vs. ambitious politician, faction vs. faction—rely, in short, upon conflict, obstacles, and delay to ensure that all major actions of government will require compromise, it may foster a certain practical self-restraint, but it is not likely to cultivate other "republican virtues," such as frugality and public spirit.

According to Publius, the new American government will test whether mutually imposed restraint is enough to keep government officials' actions under control, or "safe," to use the era's terminology. Publius appears to reject the Aristotelian advice that a successful republic requires attention to citizen virtue. Other writings by Federalists, as well as Madison's remarks at the Virginia Ratification Convention, however, show that they, as much as the Anti-Federalists, saw the success of the government as resting upon certain virtues in the populace. For example, a strong Federalist, Jeremiah Atwater, president of Middlebury College, argues in 1801 that, because the republic relies upon public opinion favorable to obedience to law, rather than upon force, to control universal human selfishness, citizens must have a faith in their representative system comparable to, and reinforced by, the faith of a devout Christian in God. To obey freely the laws that a republic makes, the citizen must believe that the system works. Further, voters must choose to reward only the virtuous with public office. He mentions many of the middle-class virtues—sobriety, industry, simplicity of manners, honesty, love of justice among roughly equal farmers—taught by families, schools, seminaries, and public opinion, as grounded on this dual faith.[4]

Many supporters of the Constitution seem to have been relying fundamentally, though often without Atwater's explicitness, on the foundations within each state's republic, including the states' agriculture-based and free-market economies, and the pressure they consequently felt to eschew luxury (and therefore debt) in favor of frugal self-support, to educate one's children to serve the community as well as to be able to support their own families, and to cultivate enough ambition to be willing to take turns in local offices while being willing to relinquish political roles to others. Perhaps the founding generation was broadly characterized by these virtues. It is reasonable to ask whether the expectation that each generation replicate the virtues of its ancestors with no explicit national support was well founded. In a sense, when the Federalists left the control of education and the administration of people and things to the states and their localities, they practiced the laissez-faire attitude over what recent commentators call family values or personal moral choices that some then and many now would argue was prudent in the economic realm. It is fair to ask whether "to each his (or her) own" has proven to be prudent in the realm of political virtue. Are the writings and speeches of these opinion leaders of the founding era sufficient to fulfill Aristotle's role in his model republic—as cheerleaders for the virtues associated with life in the middle?

Aristotle argues that there is a fundamental difference between a political order and an alliance for purposes of trade and mutual protection.[5] The Articles of Confederation set up an alliance, essentially a treaty among states that allowed them to retain most of their sovereignty, surrendering only what was necessary for the prosecution of the war for independence and the maintenance of the boundaries of each state. The delegates, not "representatives," to Congress maintained the closest possible ties to their sponsoring states, and each state's sovereignty was recognized both in word and in the mechanics of Congress' operation—the equality of the states in all votes, the supermajority required for most important decisions, and the unanimity required for any alterations to the Articles. The Constitution, as it emerged in Philadelphia in the summer of 1787, leapt from alliance to regime, according to Aristotle's categories. It created a governing organization empowered to act upon the citizens directly, the governors receiving their positions of authority from the people, sometimes through the agency of the state governments but sometimes directly. It not only gave hints in its preamble of the broad objects to which it would be devoted, but also bestowed upon Congress eighteen powers, many of them new, plus the "necessary and proper" clause implying at least a choice of means and possibly an expandable interpretation of those powers. While the Federalist Papers argued that the United States would remain a federal system, recognizing the utility and authority of the states, Publius also argued that this constitution created a nation with interests distinguishable from those of the entities of which it was composed.[6]

With the assumption of governing powers—with the creation of a political community strictly speaking; that is, one based upon the liberty and equality of the citizen body—Aristotle argues, go both "offices common to all" and taking "thought that the others should be of a certain quality, or that none of those coming under the compacts should be unjust or depraved in any way."[7] With a political community, in other words, comes the necessity to care about the virtue and vice of the citizens, the necessity of a moral whole. A political community exists not only for the sake of physical protection or for trade and "use of one another," but also for the sake of "living well . . . [sharing] in happiness or in living in accordance with intentional choice" as free human beings, as Aristotle puts it, or "the pursuit of happiness," in American terms. As these latter words in the Declaration of Independence suggest, the American founders recognized this need for mutual moral concern, though they had various, often guarded, ways of expressing it.[8]

The character traits that Aristotle ascribes to and praises in the middling element are being "compliant to reason"; being "willing to submit to command or law," but "know[ing] how to rule over freemen"; "not covet[ing] nor steal[ing] . . . ; nor . . . [having its property] be coveted or stolen"; not "plot[ting] against any one, or hav[ing] any one plot against them"; being "least liable to . . . seditions and insurrections." John Adams defends "husbandmen, merchants, and tradesmen," so long as they are self-supporting, as entitled to "the rank and rights of citizens,"[9] because they occupy a middling position in the republic and can be expected to practice these virtues. There were other leading voices among the founding generation expressing the importance of moral consensus to support a proper understanding of liberty and equality and proposing methods to perpetuate that consensus consistent with that liberty and equality.

Like Aristotle, these authors associate certain traits of character that support a free government with a middling economic and social position. As long as conditions support a large proportion of the populace in a self-reliant, comfortable, but not very wealthy way of life, the republic should flourish. If, or when, those middling property holders or their heirs become wealthy enough to eschew industriousness and frugality, or if the propertyless become a dominant voting bloc, the republic faces a fundamental challenge. What are the virtues of a republican citizen, and what makes them essential?

THE INDUSTRIOUS, MODERATE, AND FRUGAL CITIZEN

Work, not abundant leisure or government provision, grounds the republic, according to some founders. As long as Americans stay the hardworking, self-supporting course and choose wise and moral representatives, the Union will remain a republic and not strive for empire, which rests on licentious desires and ends in tyranny. For Oliver Ellsworth, John Dickinson, and Noah Webster, the life associated with moderate property supports all citizen virtues and the right to property supports all other rights.

OLIVER ELLSWORTH: THE "VIRTUOUS, INDUSTRIOUS, AND ECONOMICAL"

Constitutional framer Oliver Ellsworth of Connecticut, writing "to the Landholders and Farmers" under the pseudonym "A Landholder," demands religious liberty at the same time as expecting the civil power (the state and local authorities) to "punish gross immoralities and impieties," such as "drunkenness, profane swearing, blasphemy, and professed atheism."[10] For him, as for others of his era,[11] religious freedom does not extend to irreligion or disrespect for religion, nor does a demand for free religious exercise imply condoning the loss of the self-control that he associates with piety. Defending the Constitution in March of 1788 against the Anti-Federalists' persistent insistence upon changes prior to ratification, Ellsworth tries to put their concern for citizen virtue into perspective: "It is good government which secures the fruits of industry and virtue; but the best system of government cannot produce general happiness unless the people are virtuous, industrious and economical." He agrees with the Anti-Federalists' concern to sustain citizen virtue for the sake of the republic, but he divorces the "system" of government from the task.

Ellsworth dilates upon the potential for profit from various agricultural pursuits, but all in the context of the "just regulation" of wealth acquired by industriousness, the fundamental virtue that supports "the moral virtue of the world":

> Industry may be encouraged by good laws—wealth may be protected by civil regulations; but we are not to depend on these to create it for us, while we are indolent and luxurious. Industry is most favourable to the moral virtue of the world, it is therefore wisely ordered by the Author of Nature, that the blessings of this world should be acquired by our own application in some business useful to society; so that we have no reason to expect any climate or soil will be found, or any age take place, in which plenty and wealth will be spontaneously produced. ([Ellsworth] [1787])[12]

It is not wealth, but the virtue of industriousness that produces wealth as well as all the other virtues, upon which the republic relies. Ellsworth argues that the republic will remain uncorrupted as long as Americans are industrious, and Americans will remain industrious because no one can survive without working.

JOHN DICKINSON: SIMPLE MANNERS ARE "APPLES OF GOLD IN PICTURES OF SILVER"

John Dickinson, writing as "Fabius" in early 1788 (after his home states, Delaware and Pennsylvania, had voted to ratify the Constitution), argues in defense of the document he actively participated in composing. Fabius' seventh letter addresses the relationship among citizen virtue, the virtue and wisdom of government officials, and the success of the Union. Responding to Anti-Federalist predictions, he argues that American liberty will not be destroyed by "conspiracies of federal officers," but only by "the *licentiousness* of the people, and *turbulent temper* of some of the states."[13] The people, as individuals or collected in communities, are the greatest threat to the new government. His first step in avoiding the loss of liberty is to beg God for protection and to enjoin Americans to strive to use God-given reason to fulfill God's purposes.

Fabius postpones discussing popular license and concentrates first on the historical lessons of "misbehavior of . . . constituent parts acting separately, or in partial confederacies" against a union of "truly democratical republics."[14] A combination of liberty and equality must be the foundation of, and energy must characterize, the central government, so that it may "counteract for the common welfare, the designs hatched by selfishness in separate councils." He envisions a free and equal populace working together actively on the national level against state-level or regional parochialism. It turns out that the key to success in overcoming this second threat to the Union, disunity, lies in the first area of potential danger, citizen virtue. Harkening to the experience of the ancient Greeks, he asserts that without "wisdom and virtue enough to manage their affairs with as much prudence and affection of one for another" as the members of the Achaean League, federal officials may not legislate in the interests of the whole nation. Dickinson faintly praises the American "temper"—it "seems to be acknowledged equal to that of any nation in the world"—but he doubts that temper is enough. Americans' innate or customary self-control may fail to resist the temptations of luxury. He prays:

> May simplicity be the characteristic feature of their manners, which, inlaid with their other virtues and their forms of government, may then indeed be compared, in the Eastern stile, to "apples of gold in pictures of silver." Thus will they long . . . escape the contagion of luxury—that motley issue of innocence debauched by folly, and the lineal predecessor of tyranny, prolific of guilt and wretchedness. . . . Our wants are sources of happiness: our irregular desires, of misery. The abuse of prosperity is rebellion against Heaven; and succeeds accordingly. ([Dickinson] [1788])[15]

Dickinson already observes the beginnings of decay in middling temperance as a result of the seductions of the foolish in the midst of prosperity—at least the other temptation to be feared in a republic, the "thirst for empire," seems not to have taken root as of 1788.

In his eighth letter, Fabius attacks the Anti-Federalists' claim that a large and diverse country has never been ruled by a single government except under a despot. Like Publius in the Federalist Papers, Dickinson points out that the scheme of government proposed for this confederacy is unprecedented. In 1788 it is impossible to predict the Constitution's future on the basis of past experience. Moreover, it is carefully constructed and balanced to produce representation for both the "sovereignties and people of all the states," a controlled executive, an independent judiciary, distributed authority over the armed forces, provision for revenue, and direct authority over individual citizens. In the midst of this list of the Constitution's unique arrangements lies an observation about the unique character of the social whole: this is a people "so drawn together by religion, blood, language, manners and customs, undisturbed by former feuds or prejudices" as has not been seen before. One of the integral means of maintaining republican, and staving off despotic, government will be a populace unified by no less than five bonds, of which at least three have moral content: religion, manners, and customs.

For Dickinson, the Constitution sets up the best means to achieve "equal freedom and common prosperity," to prevent the "corruption of manners" and to spur "the improvements that endear or adorn life." In short, it is the form best suited to the nature of man. Unlike a machine that would go of itself, however, the "seeds of liberty" that Fabius sees in this Constitution require perpetual cultivation. They "will indeed demand continual attention, unceasing diligence, and frequent conflict with difficulties; but to object against the benefits offered to us by our Creator, by excepting to the terms annexed, is a crime to be equalled only by its folly." These benefits—freedom, prosperity, uncorrupted manners, and improved conditions of life—are worth the "unceasing" effort of a people unified by a common moral heritage. That unity takes various efforts: new generations raised "to defend their own happiness, and ready to relieve the misery of others"; a navy "formidable, but only to the unjust"; sufficient revenue and affluent, but not debased, commerce; and peace, plenty, and the proper use of international power.[16] The onus seems to lie on the citizens themselves to practice their customary habits, to pass them on to their children, and to use these standards when they choose representatives—licentiousness in the populace will be the primary cause of the downfall of the republic.

In his concluding comparison between the British and the new American constitutions, Dickinson argues that the only way that the new government will become a despotism is "after a general corruption of manners," at which time it will be a matter of course. The system relies on "a virtuous and sensible people" choosing "men of wisdom and integrity" to represent them, men who either maintain their wisdom and integrity in office or are replaced at the next election. He suggests that human nature will prefer certainty to uncertainty and "things safe and honorable" to "things perilous and infamous." Treacherous conspirators will, therefore, be few and easily discovered.[17]

Despite, or perhaps because of, this paucity of serious malefactors, the effort to keep the citizens alert to the danger and resistant to its temptations must be "unceasing." In sum, he prays, "may our national character be—an animated moderation, that seeks only its own and will not be satisfied with less."[18] The citizens of virtue and sense, wisdom and integrity associated with simplicity of manners need to be educated to see what is the safe and honorable, versus the perilous and infamous, course to securing what is their due.[19] The expression "animated moderation" is reminiscent of Aristotle's propaganda campaign: "Many things are best for the middling; I would be of the middling sort in the city." The country will become more powerful and more wealthy, but middle-class ways must remain the most attractive and admirable. We need not fret for lack of wise candidates, but we may worry that the electorate will not vote them into office. The key is to prepare the people for the appropriate wielding of their new power—for the sake of the improvement of the nation's happiness, rooted in self-restraint; not for the sake of empire, rooted in corrupt selfishness.

NOAH WEBSTER: "THE LABORIOUS AND SAVING"

Noah Webster, evaluating the results of the Constitutional Convention, lists the benefits of property rights for all and no entail (which is what he means by "an equal distribution of property"): first, that they protect freedom and, second, that America will produce no landed aristocracy, which fosters "family influence" over a "large territory." Instead, "the laborious and saving, who are generally the best citizens, will possess each his share of property and power, and thus the balance of wealth and power will continue where it is, in the body of the people."[20] In Webster's vision of the future, property broadly distributed will be used to defend the "inferior" rights of "liberty of the press, trial by jury, the Habeas Corpus writ, even Magna Charta itself." Property ownership will, however, need the auxiliary supports of the electoral franchise and education to remain the bulwark of freedom.

"Equal distribution" does not signify a national office overseeing all property ownership. It refers to a system of free acquisition and use of property, including the freedom to split it up among one's children, plus the opportunity to support oneself by one's own labor, producing no very rich and no very poor citizens. That is, it means what Aristotle means by a predominant middling element. Webster argues that these middling property holders, like Aristotle's, will expend enough attention upon picking worthy officials/representatives that they may return to their private pursuits and not spend all the time between elections jealously watching the government. Aristotle seems to see a natural check upon personal political ambitions in the life of a middling property holder—the middling class does not itself tend toward hegemony over the other classes, but rather is content to tend its own garden. Webster addresses the concern of the Anti-Federalists—who also appreciate the virtues of the not-overly rich—that once elected, the members of the national House and Senate will succumb to hitherto-concealed ambitions. Webster assumes that the property-holding electors will choose well and should, then, rest easy for a while.

> Why should we choose the best men in the state to represent us in Congress, and the moment they are elected arm ourselves against them as against tyrants and robbers? Do we not, in this conduct, act the part of a man, who, as soon as he has married a woman of unsuspected chastity, locks her up in a dungeon? Is there any spell or charm, that instantly changes a delegate to Congress from an honest man into a knave—a tyrant? ([Webster] [1787])[21]

In Webster's mind and in contrast to Montesquieu, whom he derides, virtue cannot alone serve the purpose of protecting liberty, because it is unreliable. But, unlike the Anti-Federalists, he does not see an individual's virtue as threatened by taking up public office. Rather, he seems to expect it to blossom reliably in moderate property holders. Property ownership is the only consistent foundation for popular liberty: "An equality of property, with a necessity of alienation, constantly operating to destroy combinations of powerful families, is the very soul of a republic. While this continues, the people will inevitably possess both power and freedom; when this is lost, power departs, liberty expires, and a commonwealth will inevitably assume some other form."[22]

Webster highlights property's relation to liberty: all other liberties are inferior to the "general distribution of real property among every class of people." Unlike the Lockeans, he looks not to the individual property holder to defend his rights, including his life and freedom, against another individual or a state that threatens to encroach, but to the liberty to distribute property freely among one's children and thus the tendency of the whole economy to be characterized by holders of some property, neither too large nor too small. When property is distributed so as to promote a predominance of middling property holders, "the body of the people" (i.e., the middling class as a whole) will defend the "principles of freedom," "liberty of the press, trial by jury, the Habeas Corpus writ." The greatest threat to a republican government, then, is not an aristocratic, out-of-touch government, or the development of wide disparities of wealth per se, but the reduction in relative size of the class of moderate property holders, which will cause a change in the character of the electorate and its attachment to republican liberty and will ultimately undermine the republican regime.

Property widely diffused is the main engine of free government, but property is supported in this function by two further factors. First, education, by which Webster means what is later called "civics," that is, "knowledge of the rights of men and the principles of government" working with the "keen sense of liberty and a watchful jealousy," keeps the people vigilant. Second, the right of popular election defends property "from assault, and guards it from the slow and imperceptible approaches of corruption."[23] Notice that the voter, or the husband in Webster's simile, is justified in "watchful jealousy," if not in completely controlling his selected "delegate" to Congress.

In a long footnote to his Fourth of July oration of 1802, correcting failures to understand the "doctrine . . . of political *equality*," Webster, probably reflecting upon the Jeffersonian "revolution of 1800," questions the reliance upon a widening electorate to choose representatives well. His confidence in the middling property owners' holding the majority and choosing representatives who govern sensibly seems shaken. While he still supports equality of property rights enthusiastically, he challenges the argument for equal suffrage for non-property holders, which, he argues, results in *inequality* of property rights. Sounding a bit like John Adams, Webster observes that people acting "from their unbiassed sentiments" will usually choose qualified candidates out of a "natural respect for age, experience, superior wisdom, virtue and talents." If so, democratic selection of representatives could work. Two problems arise, however. First, though many (of the propertyless?) acknowledge that they are not themselves qualified to take important offices, they claim equal rights to choose who *is* qualified, in effect claiming, unjustly, a right to "equal influence in government." Webster's second and "main" objection to equal suffrage, however, relates to an observation voiced by Publius in Federalist 10: by far most of the "objects of government" involve property laws.[24] An equal right of suffrage gives "those who have *little* and those who have *no* property . . . the power of making regulations respecting the property of others . . . that is, an equal right to control the property with those who own it." Thus, equal suffrage becomes the basis of disproportionate power between property owners and the propertyless.[25] The ordinary common sense of a large proportion of the electorate will be corrupted by property (or rather lack-of-property) interests, resulting in improper choices of legislators and magistrates.

Moreover, Webster sharply criticizes two Anti-Federalist talking points that had survived the ratification debates: first, Brutus' and Federal Farmer's assertion of a popular right to "instruct" legislators and second, the description of government officials as "servants of the people, and accountable to them," a view that survives more or less unscathed to this day. Insofar as both locutions tend to "degrade all authority, to bring the laws and the officers of government in to contempt, and to encourage discontent, faction and insurrection," they are dangerous to political order.[26] That excessively jealous husband returns. Webster later makes the observation that the combination of too-frequent elections and small electoral districts, rather than improving the performance of legislators, "makes [offices] an object of desire only to worthless and incompetent men" and "subdues the firmness of mind which is a primary quality in a public officer"; it "even lays snares for his integrity."[27] As Aristotle argued, more democracy at the ballot box is not good for the quality of democratic government. For Webster, the trend fosters a decline in both the quality of the representatives' decision-making in office and in their moral standards. Excessive public attention to the accountability of legislators threatens the lawmaker's integrity; representation becomes pandering. Proper firmness will succumb to popular demands, and this degradation will set up a feedback loop in which the public, seeing its success, will increase its demands and become ever more discontented and factious.

In the long run, the greatest danger that Webster sees in popular election seems to be the growth of the power of government that it occasions. While "the open advocate of a strong government is subject to popular odium," the demagogue who has captured the confidence of the people by "pretending to patriotism" seduces the people into surrendering power, which he then wields "like a giant."[28] For Webster, a strong supporter of the Constitution, the interplay between education and moral judgment, on one hand, and property rights and political power, on the other, creates a dangerous prospect for the United States. He fears for the future because the electorate will fail to recognize and reward "age, experience, superior wisdom, virtue and talents," creating a powerful lawmaking body favoring the propertyless over the moderate property holder and not restrained by moral integrity. The concern that the citizen virtues he associates with the middle class will be threatened if the middle class does not retain a clear understanding of its own importance to the success of a republic fuels Webster's education proposals examined in the next chapter.

THE REPUBLICAN ELECTORATE

The people must employ virtue and intelligence to select representatives who can be trusted to do their duty. The correct understanding and practice of liberty as entailing moral self-control is crucial to republican government. Madison and Wilson do not expect aristocratic virtue in the American electorate, but they do insist that more modest virtues will be exhibited in selecting and monitoring elected officials and, in turn, in the process of their selection of administrators.

James Madison: "If There Be Not Virtue among Us, We Are in a Wretched Situation"

Madison's remarks at the Virginia Ratifying Convention indicate a conviction that virtue in the citizenry is required for a successful republic:

> I consider it reasonable to conclude, that [the national legislators] will as readily do their duty, as deviate from it: Nor do I go on the grounds . . . that we are to place unlimited confidence in them, and expect nothing but the most exalted integrity and sublime virtue. But I go on this great republican principle, that the people will have virtue and intelligence to select men of virtue and wisdom. Is there no virtue among us? If there be not, we are in a wretched situation. No theoretical checks—no form of government can render us secure. To suppose that any form of government will secure liberty

or happiness without any virtue in the people, is a chimerical idea. If there be sufficient virtue and intelligence in the community, it will be exercised in the selection of these men. So that we do not depend on their virtue, or put confidence in our rulers, but in the people who are to choose them. (James Madison, Virginia Ratifying Convention, 20 June 1788)[29]

Madison's point is that, if there is capacity and inclination among the citizens to choose their representatives well, to look for wisdom and virtue in the candidates, then confidence in the governing officials is warranted. He claims not to rely upon virtue in the elect or upon "checks" that he, writing as Publius, claimed the framers built into the structure of the government so much as upon "virtue and intelligence" in the electors.

Months after the publication in Federalist Papers 10 and 51 of the arguments for the extended republic and its consequent multiplication of conflicting factions, Madison defended his position in favor of a "well-regulated republican government" at the Virginia Ratifying Convention, elaborating on the meaning of "well-regulated." He speaks of the "bands of government," which, if "relaxed," allow "confusion" to arise, by which he means confusion about the expectations of citizen behavior, leading to anarchy and despotism. Inhabitants of "every state," both native-born and immigrants, are betraying "dissipation and licentiousness," which Madison sees as further encouragement to "establish a republican organization."[30] America's republican organization is meant to combat this moral decline that is, historically, a tendency of all republican government. Madison's first response in this battle is to underscore "responsibility" in the representatives chosen by the people: to allow them only short terms and to remove all but an age qualification for office. Voters will have the broadest possible array of candidates from whom to choose when qualifications such as a certain amount of property or a certain degree of education are removed. It remains puzzling how this feature of the Constitution will produce "a well-regulated" rather than a "relaxed" republic, unless Madison is assuming virtue and good judgment in the electors.

JAMES WILSON: THE DUTIES INCUMBENT UPON LIBERTY

Delivering an oration on July 4, 1788, James Wilson, another active framer and promoter of the Constitution, celebrates ratification by sufficient states to put it into operation. His theme is liberty's blessings. When a republic is at peace, agriculture, manufactures, and commerce flourish with liberty under good government. Together farmers, artisans, and merchants, John Adams' triumvirate of middling virtue, ensure "plenty, convenience, and elegance."[31] "Where there is no security for property, there is no encouragement for industry.

Without industry, the richer the soil the more it abounds with weeds." Like Ellsworth and Fabius, Wilson argues that for the individual, as for the country, prosperity without the need for occupation breeds vice. "The industrious village, the busy city, the crowded port—all these are the gifts of liberty," Wilson observes, but he soon adds that these gifts require attention, both to maintain them and to maintain the liberty to enjoy them.[32]

"In a serene mind the SCIENCES and the VIRTUES love to dwell. But can the mind of a man be serene when the property, liberty and subsistence of himself, and of those, for whom he feels more than he feels for himself, depends [*sic*] on a tyrant's nod?" Identifying science and virtue with the accomplished man, Wilson argues that the new government will support a society in which people perform their duties and promote their happiness in this world and for the next. It will require exertion: "The constitution and our manners must mutually support and be supported." Certain virtues and manners "both *justify* and *adorn*" the Constitution.[33]

Wilson lauds the traditional republican virtues of frugality, temperance, and industry, plus attachment to liberty and to the Constitution. Prosperity can cause a great republic, such as Rome's, to succumb to luxury and dissipation, while "idleness is the nurse of villains." As the sciences, so the arts "flourish all together"—for the sake of the strength of the whole nation, each member seeks his own interest by hard work and a moderate use of the products of that labor. If the profits of labor are viewed as solely one's own to spend, and the virtues of frugality and temperance are not practiced, the Constitution will not be "justified" and the freedom it produces will turn to licentiousness. Like his fellow Pennsylvanians, Benjamin Rush and John Dickinson, Wilson insists that the citizenry must hold to moral principle to live in the republic. In an extended and vivid metaphor, Wilson describes the results of a society not attached to the correct understanding of liberty and the Constitution: the false idea of liberty "steals her dress, imitates her manner, forges her signature, assumes her name." Licentiousness is the identity thief of liberty. "She" takes the honors that liberty, rightly understood, deserves, but, as destructive as she is, she is a mere cat's paw for a "dark ambition" that plans to use a licentious populace to install despotism in the place of true liberty under law.[34]

True liberty, Wilson elaborates, requires every citizen to perform "useful services" for the country, beginning with the "original movement of the people," that is, the selection of wise and good representatives, a task it is of "immense consequence" to discharge "faithfully and skillfully." These carefully selected representatives will in due course appoint wise and good officers for all parts of the administration. "No government, *even the best*, can be *happily* administered by *ignorant* or *vicious* men." The logical inference to be drawn from Madison's and Wilson's insistence on a virtuous electorate is the need for conscientious voting by all citizens. Every vote counts: "In *battle*, every *soldier* should consider the *public safety* as depending on his *single arm*. At an *election*, every *citizen* should consider the *public happiness* as depending on his *single vote*."[35] In Wilson's vision, the nation cannot rely upon the clash of factions' interests and passions to produce good governing decisions. Citizens who take the elective franchise lightly or make their voting choices on the basis of vicious motives or low interests produce a disease in the body politic that "can never be *corrected* in any *subsequent* process." Again, a licentious populace undermines the electoral process and thereby the republic, however carefully constructed.

A conscientious voter needs to have available wise and good candidates for elective office, and elected officials need a generous pool of candidates for appointive office. Both Wilson and Madison expressed concerns at the Constitutional Convention about proposed provisions to make elected legislators ineligible (even for one year) to hold appointive office following service in Congress. A person of moderate ambition, that is, the degree of ambition appropriate to republican officeholders, would not allow himself to become a candidate for Congress under these restrictions, according to Wilson, maintaining

> the impropriety of stigmatizing with the name of venality the laudable ambition of rising into the honorable offices of the Government; an ambition most likely to be felt in the early & most incorrupt period of life, & which all wise & free Govts. had deemed it sound policy, to cherish, not to check. The members of the Legislature have perhaps the hardest & least profitable task of any who engage in the service of the state. Ought this merit to be made a disqualification? (Wilson [23 June 1787])[36]

Madison joined Wilson in this concern that "the backwardness of the best citizens to engage in the legislative service gave but too great success to unfit characters." With Wilson, he claims that "the objects to be aimed at were to fill all offices with the fittest characters, & to draw the wisest & most worthy citizens into the Legislative service." If that is so, however,

> the impulse to the Legislative service, was evinced by experience to be in general too feeble with those best qualified for it. This inconveniency wd. also be more felt in the Natl. Govt. than in the State Govts as the sacrifices reqd. from the distant members wd. be much greater, and the pecuniary provisions, probably, more disproporti[on]ate. It wd. therefore be impolitic to add fresh objections to the Legislative service by an absolute disqualification of its members [after they have left Congress]. The point in question was whether this would be an objection with the most capable citizens.[37]

Arguing from experience he concluded that it would. The Legislature of Virga. would probably have been without many of its best members, if in that situation, they had been ineligible to Congs., to the Govt. & other honorable offices of the State. (Madison [June 23, 1787])[38]

For both these key Federalists, then, the whole edifice of representative government rests upon a morally responsible populace, one with both the knowledge of republican principles and the public spirit to attend to elections, on one hand, and the moderate ambition to serve the public for the sake of the public and not exclusively for personal aggrandizement, on the other.[39] Only upon the basis of these moral qualities, wedded to an attachment to the Constitution, can a system of incentives and discouragements within the Constitution work to produce lawmakers and administrators who overlook the "inconvenience" of office and serve with integrity and honor.

Another aspect of the civic-virtue debate is the question of whether a good representative acts as a mirror of his constituents' opinions and interests—what was called "fidelity" or "responsibility"—or engages in high-level deliberations with an eye to the "aggregate interest of the whole"—something like what Aristotle called prudence. The latter understanding might be implied by Federalist 10's prediction of the channeling of factions in the new government to "refine and enlarge the public views."[40] The Anti-Federalists favored the representative's fidelity to the constituents' "instructions." Brutus is one exemplar: "The manner of choice and the number [of representatives] chosen, must be such, as to possess, be disposed, and consequently qualified to declare the sentiments of the people; for if they do not know, or are not disposed to speak the sentiments of the people, the people do not govern."[41] Federal Farmer is another: "A fair and equal representation is that in which the interests, feelings, opinions and views of the people are collected, in such manner as they would be were the people all assembled." And "each order must have a share in the business of legislation actually and efficiently. It is deceiving a people to tell them they are electors, and can chuse their legislators, if they cannot, in the nature of things, chuse men from among themselves, and genuinely like themselves."[42]

In Federalist 57, Publius uses the term "virtue" in reference to a representative's job in both the sense of fidelity and the sense of prudence when addressing the Anti-Federalist objection that the Constitution as written will encourage the election of representatives from the class least likely to be in sympathy with the populace:

> The principle of [the objection] strikes at the very root of republican government.

> The aim of every political constitution is, or ought to be, first to obtain for rulers men who possess most wisdom to discern, and most virtue to pursue, the common good of the society; and in the next place, to take the most effectual precautions for keeping them virtuous whilst they continue to hold their public trust. The elective mode of obtaining rulers is the characteristic policy of republican government. The means relied on in this form of government for preventing their degeneracy are numerous and various. The most effectual one, is such a limitation of the term of appointments as will maintain a proper responsibility to the people. . . .
>
> Who are to be the electors of the federal representatives? Not the rich, more than the poor; not the learned, more than the ignorant; not the haughty heirs of distinguished names, more than the humble sons of obscurity and unpropitious fortune. The electors are to be the great body of the people of the United States. (Hamilton et al. [2000, 57.365–66])

These chosen legislators must be kept on the straight and narrow path of good behavior in office, away from the path of favoring themselves or a single class. Publius' famous solution to this problem presages Madison's Virginia Convention remarks, to the effect that virtue in the populace will maintain virtue in the elected officials:

> [The solution is] the genius of the whole system; the nature of just and constitutional laws; and above all, the vigilant and manly spirit which actuates the people of America, a spirit which nourishes freedom, and in return is nourished by it. If this spirit shall ever be so far debased as to tolerate a law not obligatory on the legislature, as well as on the people, the people will be prepared to tolerate any thing but liberty.
>
> Such will be the relation between the House of Representatives and their constituents. Duty, gratitude, interest, ambition itself, are the chords [*sic*] by which they will be bound to fidelity and sympathy with the great mass of the people. . . . Are they not the genuine and the characteristic means by which republican government provides for the liberty and happiness of the people? (Hamilton et al. [2000, 57.368])[43]

Publius thus suggests a reliance on some virtues in the legislator, duty and gratitude as well as a proper ambition, to render the electors' virtues effective. In order to remain free, the "vigilant and manly" citizens must pay attention to the moral fiber of the person they elect (both before and after the election). If his own moral scruples fail to restrain him, the representative behaves well in office for the sake of self-interest fueled by the reasonable ambition to be returned to office by those vigilant and manly voters.

Webster and Madison, highly influential founders who surely intended to extend their influence into the future as the republic stood up on its own feet, saw citizens with their property rights secure displaying the virtues necessary to perpetuate the civil society that protects those rights. Despite their repeated reference to the danger of passionate factional politics, these Enlightenment thinkers assume a prodigious capacity of the rational part of human nature. When they speak most optimistically about the future, they seem, like Aristotle, to associate a moderately prosperous society with a class displaying the middle-class virtues of reasonableness and restraint of the passions. Given the tendencies of a prosperous economy to produce ever-increasing wealth for some and jobs only the desperate would fill for others, neither man seems wholly sanguine about the long term.

The virtues or "manners" mentioned during the ratification period and at the end of the Federalist era as especially important to a flourishing republic echo Aristotle's encomium of the life lived in the middle. As Adams' translation expresses Aristotle's argument, the middling citizen is compliant to reason, as opposed to "capricious and flagitious" or "rascally and mean," which suggests a rational restraint of the passions but also generosity in the use of property. The Americans cite temperance and sobriety, frugality and liberality, plus a disinclination to be bribed, as virtues to be expected from the industrious citizen who must live within moderate means. Aristotle also associates obedience to reason with ruling and being ruled among free men, that is, with the willingness to obey law and the ability to command others. The founding generation speaks similarly of the citizen's duty to pay attention to the virtue and wisdom of candidates, but also understands that the laws that their representatives make are to be obeyed as if the voter made them himself. Various writers speak, like Aristotle, of the proper ambition to serve the community rather than to feather one's own nest—the willingness to take office among those who are best suited to it and the gratitude they feel toward those who elect them. A good citizen who is not holding office expresses a "vigilant and manly spirit" when he holds not only his governors, but also himself, accountable to the principles of free self-government. Liberty is law-governed; license is anarchy.

Like Aristotle, the American writers speak of the virtue of friendliness toward other classes and toward fellow citizens generally in their praise of honesty, simple manners, "zeal for the public good," and "affection for fellow citizens." Aristotle argues that the republic with a large middle class will be most inclined to sustain the principle of equality at the root of this "good" form of rule by the many, just as so many of the Americans saw great hope for their republic as long as there remained a rough equality in terms of land and opportunity for the majority to be self-supporting. Overall, citizens need to trust each other rather than engage in class warfare fueled by envy or arrogance, to resist breaking the Union into competing regions, and to cooperate based upon an "animated moderation."

While many of the middling virtues may grow best in the soil of civil society, it is doubtful that they may all be left to that sphere. Industry and frugality may accrue almost automatically to a farmer or artisan who must earn a living without inherited wealth or position; sobriety, liberality, honesty, and simple manners are best engrained within a family neither rich nor destitute; honest speech, a freely self-restrained way of life, affection for fellow citizens, and responsibility in voting and other community services can be encouraged by a village or small town of people learning by experience that their interests are best served by cooperation. The wisdom and intelligence that Atwater, Dickinson, Madison, Wilson, and Webster claim to be necessary in citizens and officials, however, probably require some support from the political arena itself. Atwater calls for republican virtues to be taught not only by families and public opinion, but also by schools and seminaries. Dickinson claims citizens need both wisdom and virtue, both prudence and mutual affection to choose well-educated legislators and to support the laws without succumbing to the "contagion of luxury" that can infect the foolish. For Madison, the people need both "virtue and intelligence" to select legislators of "virtue and wisdom." Wilson insists the good citizen choose his representatives "skillfully," because "ignorant or vicious" administrators will undermine "the public happiness." In order to rest somewhat more easily after the election, citizens must be wise enough to understand the crucial importance of the middle class and to select trustworthy representatives at the ballot box—those of "age, experience, superior wisdom, virtue and talents" who will promote the true interests of the moderate middle class. Like Madison's and Wilson's morally responsible citizens, using knowledge of republican principles to select respectable and intelligent representatives and exercising vigilance to keep them faithful and sympathetic to their constituents, Webster's future Americans will do their duty to keep themselves free, but they will be most likely to do so only on the basis of a republican education. That citizens are free to hold property and to divide it among their children and that the middling property holders are the largest class in society are Webster's fundamental safeguards of the republic. Those property-holding citizens, however, must vote and vote prudently in order to guard their property rights and, consequently, their other rights from government corruption and the growth of its power. They will need education to know and to appreciate their rights and the principles of republican government.

A cluster of citizen qualities several American writers mention is an understanding of the doctrine of rights and an appreciation of the struggle to protect them that produced the state and national constitutions. They anticipate that attachment to their states and to the Union will diminish with the passionate fervor of the revolution and founding eras. They see the need to attach passions to the rational principles and arguments that make republican government choiceworthy. Self-government, at both the individual and the community levels, requires sustained effort, and in the modern world, where the acknowledgement of human rationality has released humanity from blind obedience, that sustained effort must be rationally defensible and appealing. Even if the people will inevitably fall into habits and communities into customs, they must be the right habits and customs—they must be chosen freely. The choice is not free, Aristotle would remind them, unless they are chosen for the right reasons. The Revolution's passionate attachment to rationality has indeed proven difficult to sustain. Already in 1838, the young Abraham Lincoln sees it fading with the result that the fundamental, rationally obvious connection between "we make the laws" and "we should obey the laws"—Atwater's "fervent faith in the representative system"—has been lost to view, and mob rule is taking its place.

The delicate balance between watchful jealousy and locking one's wife in a dungeon; the proper amount of ambition to serve the public, taking no advantages for oneself and letting others have their turns; the self-control to work industriously to support a family in modest comfort but not to aspire to luxury; the responsibility to take care of one's own in a society of equals and yet to practice liberality in helping others in need—these are not character traits that develop on their own. For instance, only an ambition somewhat tamed—not that of Caesar—may be controlled by institutional checks and balances. Various educational systems proposed during the founding era saw the necessity to reconcile the development of the rational faculty to think for oneself with a founding faith in republican principles and the truth of inalienable individual rights.

6

Securing America's Future

MORAL EDUCATION IN A MIDDLE-CLASS REPUBLIC

Like Aristotle, many thinkers during the American founding era observed that a large middling class of citizens acting according to principles of self-restraint and public spirit would have a salutary effect upon a government based upon the freedom and equality of its participants. The middle class is politically useful because it enjoys a moderate lifestyle and can be expected to obey the laws its representatives, who rely upon their votes and taxes, write. A variety of suggestions were made as to the sorts of training or education that each generation of citizens would need in order to perpetuate both the appeal of the middling way of life with its attendant virtues and republican political institutions. The large middle class can only provide the ballast and balance that a successful republic needs if each new generation resists the temptation to climb into a more luxurious social position and the chosen leaders of the political institutions resist the lure of becoming an oligarchy. The American system of selection has always relied on the votes of the people, ever more broadly conceived. Voters need to be encouraged to choose the best citizens for office, and they need to understand what "the best" means in a republic. Aristotle argues that certain characteristics mark the middling citizen—reasonableness, friendliness, capacity for ruling and being ruled, self-reliance—and he expects those characteristics to be reflected in a republic's political debate and decision-making through the balancing and arbitration roles he delineates for the middle class. The Americans want to take advantage of the inbred temperance of the middling class but also the improved science of politics (and economics) to bring knowledge to bear on governing. It becomes necessary, then, to foster an education that places the right emphasis among multiple goals: moral development, competence in a trade or profession, and knowledge of the political and social world.

THE "NATURAL ARISTOCRACY" CONTROVERSY

Some leaders of the founding generation, mostly associated with the Anti-Federalist position, speak as if ruling offices should rotate frequently among a large citizen body, each citizen taking a turn at rule and returning to private life at the end of a short term, assuming that little more than common sense, respect for the community's manners and mores, and ordinary experience will be required for political decisions. Others, mostly Federalists, anticipate an ever-widening array of sciences and arts, some familiarity with which will be needed to make political decisions. Those who take official roles in the new national government would be required to travel far and take account of issues foreign to their constituents' interests. What qualities these new officials need, in terms of both educational accomplishment and moral astuteness, are left open to be determined by the voters. What voters need to know and what the voters should expect in a candidate for office will affect the vision of citizen education for the new republic.

The majority of voters will live in the middle class. The virtues they practice must be widely considered respectable, that is, to be characteristics not only deserving of respect in daily life, but also deserving of protection by the government and laws. The most prominent citizens, chosen for their wisdom and public spirit to hold national office and administer national laws, might very well believe what Aristotle knew—that the middle class' virtues are not the most impressive. These rulers must, however, understand that the republic's stability is based on equality. Public honor, such as the award of powerful office, must be bestowed with the knowledge that it is temporary (ruling and being ruled rotate). Furthermore, from those who are most talented the greatest deference to others' rights is expected.

Into this delicately balanced situation, the concept of a natural aristocracy was introduced. The most famous propounder of the concept is Thomas Jefferson, who argues repeatedly and vehemently for a public education program that would support his understanding of the only justifiable aristocracy, composed of the virtuous and talented, "which nature has wisely provided for the direction of the interests of society, & scattered with equal hand through all it's [*sic*] conditions."[1] Jefferson distinguishes the natural aristocracy from the pseudo-aristocrats or what Aristotle would call oligarchs or dynastic rulers, holding power on the basis of mere wealth or good birth. When neither talent nor good character is required to secure influence, the result redounds to the detriment of society. The natural aristocrat may appear in any class, born with these talents, but he must be raised to cultivate his talents and develop his virtue, so that he deserves to hold political power for the benefit of society and not merely for himself. The best young persons will be drawn from any and all classes of society to be educated for these leadership roles.[2]

Jefferson sees the need to put the best and the brightest in office and sees no threat to the self-evident truth he so eloquently posited as the basis of the united efforts of the states of America—that all men are created equal in rights—when the less talented and less virtuous hold only lower offices. As long as political promotion rests solely upon these "natural," meaning politically salutary, distinctions of talent and virtue, and not upon false and politically detrimental distinctions of wealth and family, a republic can thrive.

Yet it is interesting to consider Jefferson's detailed description of a certain Mr. Pendleton in a debate over the abolition of the fee-tail in Virginia. Because it complements his vision of a society of roughly equal property holders, Jefferson declares that this policy "was deemed essential to a well ordered republic." Then he describes Pendleton's talents and virtues in poetic triplets:

> . . . the ablest man in debate I have ever met with. . . . He was cool, smooth and persuasive; his language flowing, chaste & embellished, his conceptions quick, acute and full of resource; never vanquished; for if he lost the main battle, he returned upon you, and regained so much of it as to make it a drawn one, by dexterous manoeuvres, skirmishes in detail, and the recovery of small advantages which, little singly, were important altogether. You never knew when you were clear of him, but were harassed by his perseverance until the patience was worn down of all who had less of it than himself. Add to this that he was one of the most virtuous & benevolent of men, the kindest friend, the most amiable & pleasant of companions, which ensured a favorable reception to whatever came from him. (Thomas Jefferson, *Autobiography*)[3]

If Pendleton, who was "born to a poor family and a widowed mother . . . a bright young man . . . received little in the way of formal education, was apprenticed to . . . the Clerk of Court of Caroline County, at age thirteen, and began practicing law at age twenty,"[4] is not an exemplar of Jefferson's natural aristocrat, it is hard to imagine who is. Yet Jefferson portrays this man, of "low birth" but extraordinary talent and virtue, as his chief opponent, succeeding in proposing an amendment that would dilute the effect of Jefferson's republican bill. It is clearly a challenge for Jefferson's political thought that a natural aristocrat will not always favor what Jefferson deems "republican" measures. Pendleton is "zealously attached to ancient establishments," that is, anti-republican policies, despite the fact that it was America's republican principles that allowed him to rise to political prominence. The talented and virtuous are to make up the natural aristocracy of the future, but perhaps the content of the education they receive in Jefferson's schools is more significant than their natural "talents." Despite the apparent oxymoron, the natural aristocrat is the product of a man-made educational system. The molding of the gifted into the right kind of republican governors is crucial.

In contrast, the Anti-Federalist leader Melancton Smith does not trust the men he groups into the "natural aristocracy": the citizens of "birth, education, talents and wealth" who have been honored with political prominence by their fellow citizens.[5] Whether they come from lower or higher economic echelons, once in positions of influence, the educated and talented no less than the merely wealthy or well-born come to behave like the hereditary and/ or moneyed aristocracy of the world left behind in Europe. In Smith's mind, those who live in the middle class, though perhaps of less stellar virtue and less expensive education, are the heart of the republic because their economic circumstances allow them to pursue their class interests, and their class interests are compatible with those of all classes.

Hamilton ridicules Smith's definition of a rising aristocracy in America: "all governors of states, members of Congress, chief magistrates and all officers of the militia. This description, I presume to say, is ridiculous. . . . Does the new government render a rich man more eligible than a poor one? No. It requires no such qualification. It is bottomed on the broad and equal principle of your state constitution."[6] It is ridiculous to criticize a system that produces aristocrats through the broad franchise, with electors choosing the best from a large field of eligible candidates. Of course, election per se is a mode of choice associated with aristocracy. Yet Hamilton later admits that these new republics will eventually exhibit the same pathologies as all other attempts to govern human beings because elections will fail to select for virtue:

> Sir, if the people have it in their option, to elect their most meritorious men; is this to be considered as an objection? Shall the constitution oppose their wishes, and abridge their most invaluable privilege? While property continues to be pretty equally divided, and a considerable share of information pervades the community; the tendency of the people's suffrages, will be to elevate merit even from obscurity. As riches increase and accumulate in few hands; as luxury prevails in society; virtue will be in a greater degree considered as only a graceful appendage of wealth, and the tendency of things will be to depart from the republican standard. This is the real disposition of human nature: It is what, neither the honorable member nor myself can

correct. It is a common misfortune, that awaits our state constitution, as
well as all others. (Alexander Hamilton, New York Ratifying Convention,
21 June 1788)

While a substantial moderately wealthy class survives and all citizens are
informed, elections will probably favor the reward of merit and virtue, though
Hamilton refrains from labeling it "natural." In a land of increasing prosperity,
which Hamilton predicts and applauds, the poor and those on the way up
financially will come to revere the wealthy for their wealth.[7] While moderate
property holders predominate, the republic is safe, but they will not be able
to retain their moderate ways of life as they become rich. Eventually wealth,
once considered a shorthand indication of cultivated virtue, will substitute for
virtue. With an inevitable growth of the propensity toward luxury, the concept
of virtue will disappear from most voters' considerations in favor of wealth
pure and simple. Hamilton here admits what was apparent to John Adams in
his survey of all past republics: there is a tendency in human nature to revere
the few, to elevate some over others, and to respect wealth. Changes in social
conditions, brought about by increased prosperity, will threaten the congru-
ity between the people's wishes and wise legislation.[8] The science of politics
demonstrates for Hamilton that, as happens in every government, even in a
republic constructed according to the insights of that science, human nature
unavoidably necessitates decline.

John Adams' exhortation, in the *Defence of the Constitutions,* to establish
bicameral legislatures and a balancing of powers rests on his assessment of the
incapacity of the electorate to reward with government office only those who
display the best characters:

> Self-interest, private avidity, ambition, and avarice, will exist in every state
> of society, and under every form of government. A succession of powers
> and persons, by frequent elections, will not lessen these passions in any
> case, in a governor, senator, or representative; nor will the apprehension
> of an approaching election restrain them from indulgence if they have the
> power. . . . Of all possible forms of government, a sovereignty in one assem-
> bly, successively chosen by the people, is perhaps the best calculated to facil-
> itate the gratification of self-love, and the pursuit of the private interest of a
> few individuals; a few eminent conspicuous characters will be continued in
> their seats in the sovereign assembly, from one election to another, whatever
> changes are made in the seats around them; by superior art, address, and
> opulence, by more splendid birth, reputations, and connections, they will
> be able to intrigue with the people and their leaders, out of doors, until they
> worm out most of their opposers, and introduce their friends; to this end,
> they will bestow all offices, contracts, privileges in commerce, and other

emoluments, on the latter and their connections, and throw every vexation and disappointment in the way of the former, until they establish such a system of hopes and fears throughout the state, as shall enable them to carry a majority in every fresh election of the house. (Adams [1794, III.283–84])

Though Jefferson and Adams thought themselves on opposing sides of the debate concerning the meaning and significance of "natural aristocracy"— society fostering naturally talented individuals versus human nature producing natural classes—they were in agreement upon one crucial point: republican community needs educated and morally upright governors. The alternative is a corrupt, false "aristocracy," or what Aristotle calls oligarchy. Whatever representation means in a republic, it is not intended to facilitate the poorly educated or the morally weak selecting people like themselves to represent them in national deliberations. These citizens cannot be trusted, untutored, to choose fit candidates from among those of superior rhetorical skills.[9] Unless provision is made—through either universal moral schooling or viewing one house of a bicameral legislature as reserved for the wealthy (and, therefore, better educated)—majority rule will mean the rule of those who are unfit for the job.

Smith's "natural aristocracy" includes the talented and the educated, whom Jefferson praises and upon whom Hamilton relies, as well as the merely wealthy and the well-born. Smith sees what John Adams also notes, that even in largely republican America, old-fashioned aristocracy is developing: in some communities, wealth and political influence have already begun to be passed down in certain families and *that process*—the accumulation of respect paid to wealth and family prominence—is somehow natural to human societies. Virtue and talent are not reliably passed from parent to child,[10] but Smith expects that the wealth and influence acquired by the naturally talented and the well-educated will. A hereditary aristocracy no longer tied to talents and virtue will develop as long as a democratic society reposes its hopes in aristocrats, ever floating to the top of society, being elected to leadership positions. Rather than emphasize the excellence of a few, Smith argues for the appreciation of the larger class of "the substantial yeomanry." Once the naturally talented start living the "high life" of the politically powerful, they will lose touch with the interests of the middle and poor classes from which they arose.

In the debates at the New York Ratifying Convention, in the context of the clash between Smith's challenge to the ascendancy of an aristocracy in American politics and Alexander Hamilton's response, Chancellor Livingston dilates at length on his view of the American aristocracy.[11] This long extract from that speech reveals that Livingston does not even imagine the existence of a middling class, and when given the choice between the imperfectly virtuous rich and educated, on one hand, and the imperfectly virtuous poor and uneducated, on the other, the voters' obligation is obvious:

The honorable gentleman from Duchess [Mr. Smith] . . . has pointed his artillery against the rich and the great. I am not interested in defending rich men: but what does he mean by telling us that the rich are vicious and intemperate? . . . If he will look round among the rich men of his acquaintance, I fancy he will find them as honest and virtuous as any class in the community. He says the rich are unfeeling; I believe they are less so than the poor; for it seems to me probable that those who are most occupied by their own cares and distresses have the least sympathy with the distresses of others. The sympathy of the poor is generally selfish, that of the rich a more disinterested emotion.

The gentleman further observes, that ambition is peculiarly the vice of the wealthy. But have not all classes of men their objects of ambition? . . . The great offices in the state are beyond the view of the poor and ignorant man: he will therefore contemplate an humbler office as the highest alluring object of ambition; he . . . will equally sacrifice to the attainment of his wishes the duty he owes to his friends or to the public. But, says the gentleman, the rich will be always brought forward; they will exclusively enjoy the suffrages of the people. For my own part, I believe that, if two men of equal abilities set out together in life, one rich, the other of small fortune, the latter will generally take the lead in your government. The rich are ever objects of envy; and this, more or less, operates as a bar to their advancement. . . .

The gentleman, sensible of the weakness of this reasoning, is obliged to fortify it by having recourse to the phantom aristocracy. I have heard much of this. I always considered it as the bugbear of the party. We are told that, in every country, there is a natural aristocracy, and that this aristocracy consists of the rich and the great: nay, the gentleman goes further, and ranks in this class of men the wise, the learned, and those eminent for their talents or great virtues. Does a man possess the confidence of his fellow-citizens for having done them important services? He is an *aristocrat*. Has he great integrity? Such a man will be greatly trusted: he is an aristocrat. Indeed, to determine that one is an aristocrat, we need only be assured he is a man of merit. But I hope we have many such. I hope, sir, we are all aristocrats. So sensible am I of that gentleman's talents, integrity, and virtue, that we might at once hail him the first of the nobles, the very prince of the Senate. But whom, in the name of common sense, will we have to represent us? Not the rich, for they are sheer aristocrats. Not the learned, the wise, the virtuous, for they are all aristocrats. Whom then? Why, those who are not virtuous; those who are not wise; those who are not learned: these are the men to whom alone we can trust our liberties. He says further, we ought not to choose these aristocrats, because the people will not have confidence in them; that is, the people will not have confidence in those who best deserve and most possess their confidence. He would have his government composed of other classes of men: where will we find them? Why, he must go out into the highways, and pick up the rogue and the robber; he must go to the hedges and ditches, and bring in the poor, the blind, and the lame. As the gentleman has thus settled the definition of aristocracy, I trust that no man will think it a term of reproach; for who among us would not be wise? Who would not be virtuous? Who would not be above want? How, again, would he have us to guard against aristocracy? Clearly by doubling the representation, and sending twelve aristocrats instead of six. The truth is, in these republican governments, we know no such ideal distinctions. We are all equally aristocrats. Offices, emoluments, honors, are open to all. (Chancellor Livingston, New York Ratifying Convention, 23 June 1788)[12]

Implicit in Smith's argument is the retort that Livingston falls into the very trap of which Smith warns New York. Livingston sees what Aristotle saw in the poor: a lack of sympathy with those who have more. He fails to see what Aristotle and Smith observe, that the very wealthy suffer from the same myopia when contemplating the challenges of the less wealthy. The greater sympathy Livingston attributes to the rich, Smith (channeling Aristotle) associates with the middle—those who partake a little of both wealth and poverty and can see the world through both lenses. On the other hand, Livingston posits wealth as a hindrance to political success, due to the envy of the non-rich. He takes for granted that the public will choose the wise and the virtuous over the merely rich men who are neither, because inheritors of great wealth are the objects of envy, not admiration. Smith insists that a truly republican government must both distinguish the class of "small fortune" that Livingston absorbs into the upper class (e.g., "I hope, sir, we are all aristocrats") and appreciate the middle class, per se. When a republic forgets the political ballast and the characteristic virtues supplied by the middling element—neglects to see and cultivate the middle as a class and as a class whose distinct interests are most compatible with the interests of all—the project of self-government will fail.

Smith's republic may need the talents and knowledge of well-educated citizens, but it must also appreciate the common sense of the ordinary yeomen and provide opportunities for the latter's political virtues to influence lawmaking. The men of talent who don't grow too rich and the virtuous who strive for self-sufficiency through self-restraint, keeping the middling virtues as touchstones, would occupy Smith's middling class of substantial yeomen. Though Smith struggles to describe the institutional arrangements that would foster and sustain such a class—that would keep the middle in the middle and its way of life dominant—he clearly argues for their necessity. As he sees the natural progression of society without such arrangements, either the rich or the poor will come to mastery and enslave the rest.

EDUCATION AS CENTRAL TO A REPUBLICAN REGIME

Given the consensus that the republic's electoral process is meant to choose "men who possess more attractive merit and the most diffusive and established characters"[13] from a wide field, the national union apparently needs to pay some attention to discerning and cultivating the talents and virtues of each generation of voters and candidates. Robert Coram, a "strong Anti-Federalist during the ratification period" and editor of the Wilmington *Gazette*,[14] provides an illuminating bridge between the arguments for encouraging virtue through promoting a strong middle class and those for specific educational plans that targeted young citizens' moral characteristics and patriotic devotion. To his "Political Inquiries" of 1791, he adds a proposal for a national education curriculum intended to produce good citizens of the new republic through job training.

Coram argues that truly free government, suited to the nature of man, requires teaching all the citizens how to make a living. "Are ye aware, legislators, that in making knowledge necessary to the subsistence of your subjects, ye are in duty bound to secure to them the means of acquiring it?"[15] Historically, when "civilizations" drew men away from hand-to-mouth existence, they educated only a few, who exploited the many and produced only oppression in various forms.[16] Free government requires that society educate everyone in public schools, free to all, in the three Rs plus sciences, "natural history, mechanics and husbandry," and compel parents and guardians to apprentice their children in the arts (trades or professions), so that all citizens are able to support themselves. The resulting independence will produce a double benefit: discouraging the growth of classes of the dominating rich and oppressed poor and enabling "the subject to know the obligations he is under to government" and to be informed of public affairs.[17] Without speaking of a middle class, Coram advocates a national program that would produce the self-reliant neither-rich-nor-poor farmers and artisans a free republic requires.

In contrast to some Federalist education reformers such as Benjamin Rush and Nicholas Collin, Coram insists that "no modes of faith, systems of manners, or foreign or dead languages should be taught in those schools." He invokes "the Deity" as approving government schools that instruct the young in only those subjects "necessary to obtain a knowledge of the obligations of society." As the schools aim to produce republican citizens, the only rewards for good work should be praise—never medals, which only inflame competition and a desire to acquire the prize, rather than to excel in good work. Independence and self-reliance—the capacity to claim one's rights and perform the duties of citizenship—are the fundamental qualities of both a happy human being and a free citizen:

> Let it not be said . . . that the descendants of an Eastern nation, landed in this Western world, attacked the defenseless natives and "divorced them in anguish, from the bosom of their country," only to establish narrow and unequitable policies, such as the governments of our forefathers were.
>
> But let us, since so much evil has been done, endeavor that some good many [sic] come of it. . . . Let us begin by perfecting the system of education as the proper foundation whereon to erect a temple to liberty and to establish a wise, equitable, and durable policy, that our country may become indeed an asylum to the distressed of every clime—the abode of liberty, peace, virtue, and happiness—a land on which the Deity may deign to look down with approbation—and whose government may last till time shall be no more! (Coram [1791])[18]

Keeping the more attainable virtues in view, a variety of early Americans gave serious thought to education appropriate to the republican citizen, one who must balance the private pursuit of happiness with duties to sustain the political order that makes that pursuit possible. Various writers link education with moral habituation to citizen duty, often emphasizing the challenges to the middling virtues created by rising prosperity; Alexander Hamilton was skeptical of virtue's success in the long run and suggests a way to rely on vice that may put off the inevitable decline.

BENJAMIN FRANKLIN: "THE BEAUTY AND USEFULNESS OF VIRTUE" . . .
AND "THE FIRST PRINCIPLES OF SOUND POLITICKS . . . FIX'D IN THE
MINDS" OF "YOUTH IN PENSILVANIA"

In a collection of "Proposals Relating to the Education of Youth in Pensilvania," published long before he became involved with separating from Britain, Benjamin Franklin expounds multiple benefits from the teaching of history in a school system not provided by the government, but established by a civil association. From a well-organized study of the human past come knowledge of geography and chronology; understanding of "antient customs, religious and civil"; appreciation of the effects of both oral and written rhetoric, and demonstration of the "Necessity of a Publick Religion from its usefulness to the Publick; the Advantage of a Religious Character among private Persons; the Mischiefs of Superstition, etc. and the Excellency of the CHRISTIAN RELIGION above all others antient and modern."[19] In the midst of this list Franklin speaks of the opportunities that teaching history affords for "making continual Observations" on the benefits to the individual of practicing moral virtues: "Temperance, Order, Frugality, Industry, Perseverance, *etc. etc.* Indeed the general natural Tendency of Reading good History must be, to fix in the Minds of Youth deep Impressions of the Beauty and Usefulness of Virtue of all Kinds, Publick Spirit, Fortitude, *etc.*" Only after these many personal advantages does Franklin approach the more obviously political lessons of history: the young need to learn that government is to protect "Men and their Properties" as well as to encourage an individual's industry. History teaches "the Advantages of *Liberty*, Mischiefs of *Licentiousness*, Benefits arising from good Laws and a due Execution of Justice, *etc.*" History is more than names and dates, it is the means by which "the First Principles of Sound *Politicks* [may] be fix'd in the Minds of Youth."

Within the catalog of history's lessons, Franklin also places the opportunity to debate "Questions of Right and Wrong, Justice and Injustice," that is, to engage in the quintessential activity that makes human beings political animals according to Aristotle. In the pursuit of victory in debate—whether with or without prizes, he does not specify—students willingly learn "the Use of *Logic*" and the art of rhetoric from "Grotius, Puffendorff," and their kind.[20] Capitalizing upon the competitiveness of young people, Franklin expects that they will relish perfecting their skills through the study of the best.

The engrossing study of "Great Men whose Lives and Actions they read in History" will stimulate students to learn the Latin and Greek languages for the sake of the beauty, wisdom, longevity, pleasure, and universality of their literature. Though no foreign languages should be compulsory, they should be available for those interested in entering professions for which they are useful. Thus Franklin combines the traditional lures of liberal learning with the commercial inducements of a modern society. Like the later appreciators of the political utility of a moderately wealthy lifestyle, Franklin combines his enthusiasm for political history with a persuasive account of studying natural history for its usefulness to preserving health, commercial history for its entertainment value and utility "for all," plus "Mechanical Philosophy" or "the Principles of that Art by which weak Men perform such Wonders, Labour is sav'd, Manufactures expedited, *etc., etc.*" A commercial and manufacturing republic, benefiting not merely the few, but "Mankind, one's Country, Friends and Family," rests upon educating the youth not only in business practices and technology, but also in personal virtue, "Publick Spirit," "a Publick Religion," liberty, and "good Laws and a due Execution of Justice."[21]

In Franklin's academy,

> The Idea of what is *true Merit*, should also be often presented to Youth, explain'd and impress'd on their Minds, as consisting in an *Inclination* join'd with an *Ability* to serve Mankind, one's Country, Friends and Family, which

Ability is (with the Blessing of God) to be acquir'd or greatly encreas'd by *true Learning*; and should indeed be the great *Aim* and *End* of all Learning. (Franklin [1749], emphasis Franklin's)

In Franklin's Pennsylvania, education aims to produce industrious and capable citizens, not only aware of how their government came to be, but also morally trained to govern themselves in liberty—distinguished from license—and practiced in carrying their habits and the "Publick Religion" into the public square for the sake of a common good.

SAMUEL ADAMS AND THE WORCESTER SPECULATOR: MASSACHUSETTS' PUBLIC EDUCATION IN THE PRINCIPLES OF MORALITY

As the Revolution builds steam, ardent patriot Samuel Adams writes to James Warren of his concern that Massachusetts towns with established schools are dismissing the schoolmasters to divert funds to what is now called the defense budget.[22] His attachment to education becomes typical—many of this generation saw publicly provided education as essential primarily because of its salutary effect on morals. When very few citizens are eligible to participate in or to influence government, it is assumed that those few will be educated in the habits and knowledge necessary for statesmanship. Whether wholly successful or not, the task of educating a small ruling class is considered manageable and is supported by tradition and the wealth of the class itself. Americans expected that their new governments would be based on the informed consent of the whole people and that the people would not consent to be excluded from political decisions. However "the people" is defined, it includes many more than previous regimes included. For Adams, public education serves the moral purpose of making republican government possible: that purpose is to "diffuse among the Individuals of the Community the Principles of Morality, so essentially necessary to the Preservation of publick Liberty."

In this letter, Adams first describes these essential principles of morality negatively, as the opposites of "corruption, dishonesty to one's Country, Luxury and Extravagance." Public liberty relies on citizens with the moral fiber to resist bribery, to speak honestly on public matters, and not to spend too much money. For Adams, these self-restraints do not occur in the human soul by nature, nor are they reliably implanted by economic circumstances alone. They must be taught. In addition to these "political virtues," Adams quotes an unnamed source on the wisdom of inculcating the private virtues as well: "There is a Connection between Vices as well as Virtues and one opens the Door for the Entrance of another." For Adams, the connection that often eludes later politicians and their apologists was perfectly clear—one who is not virtuous in private life "very soon will be void of all Regard for his Country." Adams takes for granted that public education must inculcate "the Principles of Virtue" and keep "the moral Sense alive," and that it is the duty of the (state) government to encourage the dual and entwined goals of diffusing knowledge and preserving virtue in order to keep the republic afloat: "When People are universally ignorant, and debauchd in their Manners, they will sink under their own Weight without the Aid of foreign Invaders." Moral decay is as large a threat as foreign invasion and perhaps a more likely one.

At times the writings of the founding era seem to take for granted that any increase in knowledge, any acquisition of science, will improve the capacity of the citizenry to govern itself, as Adams links ignorance and debauchery. What Adams actually assumes is the infusion of all schooling with moral lessons. During the ratification debates, "The Worcester Speculator," writing in the *Worcester Magazine*, illuminates this assumption while posing quite bluntly a dilemma Massachusetts faced:

> Perhaps there is not a people on earth better instructed than the inhabitants of this state: but our state of refinement is the most unfavorable to political tranquility—did we know more, we might govern ourselves—did we know less, we should be governed by others. If America would flourish as a republick, she need only attend to the education of her youth. Learning is the paladium of her rights—as this flourishes her greatness will encrease. (Worcester Speculator 6 [October 1787])[23]

In his mind, learning implies "refinement," which implies the suppression of individual self-interest: "Where learning prevails in a community, liberality of sentiment, and zeal for the public good are the grand characteristics of the people." He elaborates on the imperative to transmit moral appreciation of republican principles from generation to generation: "Learning expands the heart, and is the sure basis of a republican government. . . . Should we neglect the education of our children—should we transmit to them our rights and possessions, *without teaching them their value*, they would soon become a prey to internal usurpers, or invite the attention of a foreign power."[24]

Like many of this era, the Speculator sees prosperity spreading ever more widely across American society. He anticipates a future in which Americans will associate their individual rights only with the protection of their property and forget the principles that justify that association. A "foreign power" might well offer the protection of property in exchange for submission to its political will. An "internal usurper" might pay for his elevation above the many with a promise of more prosperity. Every citizen needs education in "the principles of civil liberty, the constitution of his country, and the rights of mankind in general," but also in the value of the principles and their fundamental law. The Speculator's quotation of a verse that concludes that "Fair Education . . . makes us angels while we're here below" elevates his expectations of education quite impressively. For the claim that "a republick . . . need only attend to the education of her youth" to make sense in this context, the Worcester Speculator must assume that publicly supported education, while spreading general knowledge and advancing prosperity, will also instill a moral appreciation of the value of the citizen's rights and the duty to protect the constitution that guards them.

The Worcester Speculator spells out the danger that various writers in this era foresaw: future citizens of the republic would benefit from the economic and political freedom their institutions protect, but they would fail to use those benefits in a manner consistent with continued liberty because they would not appreciate the individual behavior that makes them defensible. Schooling appears to him to be the only substitute for the first-hand experiences of oppression, the struggle for independence, and the public deliberations concerning the Constitution that implanted the moral habits of his generation. All the writers of the founding period here examined assume that lessons in history will impress the young with the excellence of the American republic. For Franklin, Adams, and the Worcester Speculator, those lessons, extolling homely virtues, republican principles, and the rights of man, aim to produce explicitly moral results: personal virtue, "Publick Spirit," "a Publick Religion," "liberality of sentiment," "the moral sense," and appreciation of the value of those principles and rights.

Alexander Hamilton: Rich Men's Vices Probably Favor "the Prosperity of the State"

In contrast to those emphasizing the need to restrain self-interest, Hamilton argues in the New York Ratifying Convention that consulting self-interest will preserve the republican character of the new government as well as (or better than) ethical training: it will keep the representative in line with the wishes of his constituents, because he is "dependent on the will of the people, and . . . it cannot be his interest to oppose their wishes. . . . In the general course of things, the popular views and even prejudices will direct the actions of the rulers."[25] Unlike Noah Webster, he does not consider this interplay of popular will and the legislator's actions dangerous. Hamilton charges the Anti-Federalists with a simplistic understanding of political ambition: a representative will either be prone to corruption or have a sense of duty to his constituents. For Hamilton, these attitudes are equally unlikely to occur in pure form, while the politically useful, more temperate ambition for reelection will usually predominate and render the representative sympathetic to the interests of his district. Though Hamilton admits that this attention to public opinion and local interests will not always produce the optimal outcome, that there are times "when it may be necessary and proper to disregard the opinions which the majority of the people have formed," he apparently considers the argument sufficient to refute that of Melancton Smith speaking for devices to ensure more representation for middling citizens' opinions and interests.

Later in the same speech, in response to Smith's insistence that the House be made larger immediately and grow faster than it is likely to grow under Article I, Section 2, Hamilton argues against the necessity of electing a representative from every walk of life to the national legislature. Questions of commerce and taxation require not personal acquaintance with each employment, but only "information . . . open to every intelligent enquirer."[26] It is not the moral virtue or personal experience of the life of the average citizen, but rather intellectual virtue that will assure a congressman's competence to make commerce regulations and tax laws. What the American people as a whole needs is not Smith's "large" collection of middling citizens experienced in working in the private sector and habituated to frugality and the appreciation of industry, but a "few" masters of the "science of taxation."[27] Education, for Hamilton, therefore, need not focus on moral edification so much as "enlightening" wonks to produce "perfect policy":

> In free republics . . . the will of the people makes the essential principle of the government; and the laws which control the community, receive their tone and spirit from the public wishes. It is the fortunate situation of our country, that the minds of the people are exceedingly enlightened and refined: Here then we may expect the laws to be proportionably agreeable to the standard of perfect policy; and the wisdom of public measures to consist with the most intimate conformity between the views of the representative and his constituent. (Hamilton [21 June 1788])

America is "fortunate" to have a population suitably educated (i.e., "enlightened and refined"), but it is worrisome if the perpetuation of this level of education, and thus of the republican "principle of government," relies upon fortune alone. Hamilton's sanguinity about the conformity of public wishes to wise measures, especially when he has himself mentioned the occasional need to ignore the people's wishes to achieve good legislation, seems ill advised. He soon makes clear that he is quite aware that this luck cannot last.

Hamilton brings in virtue, but through the back door. He attributes to Smith an assumption that higher education promotes "wickedness." Hamilton himself assumes that the prosperous will make efforts to educate their children and that the better-educated will become prosperous, so Smith's distrust of a government made up of a new aristocracy of the prosperous and ambitious boils down to a distrust of the education of this class:

> It is a harsh doctrine, that men grow wicked in proportion as they improve and enlighten their minds. Experience has by no means justified us in the supposition, that there is more virtue in one class of men than in another. Look through the rich and the poor of the community; the learned and the ignorant. Where does virtue predominate? The difference indeed consists, not in the quantity but kind of vices, which are incident to the various classes; and here the advantage of character belongs to the wealthy. Their vices are probably more favorable to the prosperity of the state, than those of the indigent; and partake less of moral depravity. (Hamilton [21 June 1788])[28]

Unlike Robert Coram and Benjamin Franklin, Samuel Adams and the Worcester Speculator, Hamilton is not claiming that education will increase the quantity, so to speak, of morals in the community, but only that the better educated will be or become wealthy and that the vices of the wealthy are more socially advantageous than those of the poor. That advantage consists in a combination of an increase in the community's prosperity and a decrease in "moral depravity." As with the trait of self-interestedness, certain vices can become allies to good government. In a world where everyone is flawed, it is necessary to distinguish between the useful and the less useful vices. In direct contrast to Samuel Adams, therefore, Hamilton argues that vice in general does not open doors to politically harmful vices in particular, but rather that certain vices can serve as a politically salutary barrier to the harmful ones. In the context of a speech deriding the notion of the rise of a dangerous aristocracy in the new Congress, Hamilton both approves the tendency of republican citizens to choose the best among themselves as their governors, and reassures us that, when the best—the better-educated—are no longer very admirable, they will still be safe, as long as the republic can stave off the voters' complete confounding of wealth per se with political virtue.

EXTENDED EDUCATION PROPOSALS

James Madison sees trouble ahead for the republic in the form of laborers who never move into the middle class or practice citizen virtues, while Hamilton locates the cause of inevitable decline in an increasingly prosperous populace that begins to revere wealth rather than merit. In both cases, the middle class shrinks and its beneficial influence over politics decreases proportionally. As Sheehan and McDowell summarize the writings of the "other Federalists" on "popular government and civic virtue":

The need for ethical and religious instruction in the polity was widely felt and frequently spoken of, though as a whole the Federalists did not draw a detailed roadmap for the journey of moral education in the United States. Instead, they tended to speak to their fellow citizens in generalities, almost in matter-of-fact tones, about the need for and the benefits that would derive from religion, education, good statesmanship, and law. (Sheehan and McDowell [1998, 313])[29]

Noah Webster provides one of these more general reminders of the importance of education, in addition to rough equality of property, to citizen virtue,[30] but he also spent much of his life promoting various education reforms for the sake of making good citizens. Thomas Jefferson (who refused to be labeled Federalist or Anti-Federalist) and the strong supporters of the Constitution Benjamin Rush and Nicholas Collin (Collin calling himself "a Foreign Spectator") all speak very specifically on republican education and its moral ramifications.

Noah Webster: Educating "Honest Men," not "Dupes of . . . Artful Men"

Among those concerned about the people's capacity to choose competent and virtuous leaders, Noah Webster in 1790 dilates on a potential downside of independent, self-reliant citizens enjoying "an equality of condition," namely that they can be duped by the wily. Occupying a dominant class characterized by moderate property holding and the need to work for one's living supports, but does not guarantee, the qualities of character that a republic requires. A native of Connecticut, Webster uses the New England states as his exemplar of the consequences of equality of condition. Equality makes New Englanders "mild and condescending" toward anyone who convinces them of his friendship, which produces the politically salutary effect of an openness to persuasion. Their independence makes them "irritable and obstinate in resisting force and oppression," which makes them wary of laws that tend toward despotism. These useful attitudes can lead men astray, however. An ambitious politician need only hide all pretensions to superiority of wealth or education in order to "coax them into hiz views."[31] While a few honest voters pay close attention to the characters of candidates and officeholders, the vast majority make political decisions based on superficial assessments and, therefore, resent any candidate with distinction—anyone who, in Webster's mind, might be especially fit to hold government office. Webster assumes that those who are not wealthy will resent both wealth and superior education,[32] rather than consider them qualifications for political office. Webster's "people" have not been well trained to separate the sheep, the talented and virtuous, from the goats, the merely wealthy or the canny orators. Rather, he observes that many among the electorate

> become the dupes of a set of artful men, who, with small talents for business and no regard for the public interest, are always familiar with every class of peeple, slyly hinting something to the disadvantage of great and honest men, and pretending to be frends to the public welfare. The peeple are thus guverned at times by the most unqualified men among them. If a man wil shake hands with every one he meets, attend church constantly, and assume a goodly countenance; if he wil not swear or play cards, he may arrive to the first offices in the guvernment, without one single talent for the proper discharge of hiz duty; he may even defraud the public revenu and be accused of it on the most indubitable evidence, yet by laying hiz hand on hiz brest, casting hiz eyes to heaven, and calling God to witness hiz innocence, he may wipe away the popular suspicions, and be a fairer candidate for preferment than before hiz accusation. . . . Government suffers a material injury from this turn of mind; and were it not for a few men who are boldly honest, and indefatigable in detecting impositions on the public, the guvernment of theze states would always be, az it often iz, in the hands of the weakest, or wickedest of the citizens. (Webster [February 1790])

Note that these artful men are the "weekest" and "wickedest" candidates for office because of several factors, mostly matters of character: holding small talent for business, (despite some pretense) having no regard for the public interest, behaving familiarly with every class, campaigning by hinting at the bad qualities of "great and honest men," trading on an appearance of virtue burnished by pious disclaimers of wrongdoing. Webster's independent and self-reliant voters will not naturally be suspicious of those who are not worthy of their trust. He saw the need for an education system to produce in people of honest, public-spirited ambition both the political savvy necessary to a republic's electorate and the qualifications to rule.

Though Webster sees America in 1790 as supplied with hardy, literate citizens willing and able to perform their citizen duties, he foresees a day when economic circumstances will move the society away from rough equality and self-reliance: the family farm will decline and manufacturing rise. The majority of the people will no longer own land and will lose the independence it confers. The types of jobs a growing, non-farming middle class will perform will weaken their capacity to be good citizens.[33] He worries that educational attainments will become too concentrated in a small class, and that the militias will not survive without men practiced in bearing arms for hunting. He asks rhetorically,

Wil not poor peeple multiply, and the possessions of real estates be diminished in number, and increased in size? Must not a great proportion of our
citizens becum manufacturers and thus looz the bodies and the spirit of
soldiers? While the mass of knowlege wil be increesed by discuveries and
experience, wil it not be confined to fewer men? In short, wil not our forests
be levelled, or confined to a few proprietors? and when our peeple ceese to
hunt, will not the body of them neglect the use of arms?[34] Theze are questions
of magnitude; but the present generation can answer them only in prospect
and speculation. At any rate, the genius of every guvernment must addapt
itself to the peculiar state and spirit of the peeple who compose the state,
and when the Americans looz the principles of a free guvernment, it follows
that they will speedily looz the form. Such a change would, az in Rome, be
ascribed to bad men; but it is more rational to ascribe it to an imperceptible
progress of corruption, or thoze insensible changes which steel into the best
constitutions of government. (Webster [February 1790])

Like most of his contemporaries thinking about education, Webster,
writing in the same year that he delivered the previous "remarks," believes
education necessarily has "an inseparable connection with morals and a consequential influence upon the peace and happiness of a society."[35] Some of the
"errors" he finds schools commonly making indicate the moral goals Webster
hopes American education could achieve when producing generations of future
citizens. Like Coram, he wants public schools to concentrate on subjects and
methods of learning useful to the large number of "merchants, mechanics,
and farmers"; therefore, he emphasizes English grammar and composition over
the dead languages. Also like Coram, he would not employ the Bible to teach
reading, but unlike Coram, Webster sees public schools using the Bible "as
a system of religion and morality." He does not oppose its use so much as its
overuse, which could "weaken the influence of its precepts upon the heart,"
as surgeons and soldiers become insensitive to blood and death.[36]

Because the "common schools" must offer the education all citizens need,
the curriculum should always begin with reading and writing the native
tongue, arithmetic, and some mathematics, that is, "the sciences necessary
for every man." In "country schools," all should read "practical husbandry."
No one can, however, learn everything, so, in addition to teachers training
in specialized areas, students preparing for different careers will take different courses of study, some followed by apprenticeships. After acquiring the
basics, proto-merchants, for example, might learn other "living languages"
while young, then study "chronology . . . geography, mathematics, history, the
general regulations of commercial nations, principles of advance in trade, of

insurance, and . . . the general principles of government"—all by the age of sixteen. Then they would be ready to apprentice in commerce.[37]

In response to what he calls "the principal defect in our plan of education in America," Webster pays extended attention to finding good teachers for the common schools as well as academies, reflecting the importance of training young people in moral habits while they are impressionable. "The *virtues* of men are of more consequence to society than their *abilities*, and for this reason the *heart* should be cultivated with more assiduity than the *head*." A teacher should, indeed, master the subject taught, but also be "most prudent, accomplished, agreeable, and respectable," in order to encourage the students to apply themselves to their studies. He calls for strict discipline at home and in school, suggesting that if parents were less indulgent—not allowing "licentious behavior" and appeals from one parent to the other—schools could spare the rod somewhat. Employing teachers whom the students esteem and therefore strive to obey and please could further reduce the necessity for corporal punishment: "Whenever . . . pupils cease to respect their teacher, he should be instantly dismissed."[38]

Interspersed with these injunctions to common schools, Webster makes several jabs at college-level education. With regard to the development of good behavior, though it is more possible to acquire polished manners in the city, Webster advises founders of colleges to place young students in country villages away from "dissipation" and "bad examples." He prioritizes the formation of moral and intellectual habits—"goodness of heart" and "principle in the mind." Greater knowledge of the world and its corruptions is advisable only later. Submission to the authority of "age and superior wisdom" would be the beneficial by-product of living with "decent families," rather than in dormitories, while studying at "literary institutions."[39]

Regarding curriculum, one problem with "liberal education" in 1790, using English universities for models, is that it produces graduates with a mere smattering of all the sciences, too old for apprenticeships and untrained for work, that is, gentlemen with no habits for business:

> Why should a merchant trouble himself with the rules of Greek and Roman syntax or a planter puzzle his head with conic sections? Life is too short to acquire, and the mind of man too feeble to contain, the whole circle of sciences. The greatest genius on earth, not even a Bacon, can be a perfect master of *every* branch, but any moderate genius may by suitable application, be perfect in any *one* branch. (Webster [1790])[40]

Beginning the second part of this essay, Webster reiterates the intimate connection between good student behavior that fosters order and learning on one hand, and the ethical qualities of a citizen on the other: "With respect to morals and civil society . . . the effects of education are so certain and extensive that it behooves every parent and guardian to be particularly attentive to the characters of the men whose province it is to form the minds of youth." Nothing less than the efficacy of "making laws" and of "preaching the gospel" is determined by the formation of young minds "for good men, and useful citizens." Obedience to law and attention to moral principle are habits that must be inculcated early to prevent the acquisition of the habits of disregarding law and morality. Parents who abide ill-mannered, clownish, or profligate teachers must not be paying sufficient attention or must "fear . . . expense." "Laws can only check the public effects of vicious principles but can never reach the principles themselves."[41]

Webster cites Montesquieu to support his injunction not to teach oratory from Demosthenes and Cicero, but rather to concentrate historical studies closer to home—"every child in America" should learn useful ideas from America's experience, and the most useful idea is the admiration of America's political order and virtuous citizens: "As soon as he opens his lips, he should rehearse the history of his own country. He should lisp the praise of liberty and of those illustrious heroes and statesmen who have wrought a revolution in her favor." History, geography, and principles of federal and provincial governments enlighten nascent citizens to the interests of their homeland and "assist in forming attachments" to their country while "enlarging the understanding."[42]

Though Webster speaks of the education of girls as designed "not to raise them above their station," that station is crucially important: habituating the very young to "sentiments of virtue, propriety, and dignity." To produce mothers with "just sentiments and enlarged understandings" and women who influence men to good behavior, girls must learn speaking and writing English, arithmetic, geography, and *belles lettres*. Beyond her schooling, an American woman should read *The Spectator* and similar journals and only novels that draw a favorable picture of the social virtues.[43] In the same vein as his criticism of "sending boys to Europe for an education," Webster's view of girls' tutelage in "music, drawing, and dancing" is colored by social and political utility. Better to focus young people's attention on subjects that prepare for good citizenship and playing necessary roles in the economies of the household and the state.

The moral development of American education parallels the political maturation of the nation as a whole. Ultimately Webster wants to inspire this new nation's citizens of all ages to grow up, to develop a new and independent character as self-confident and free: "Americans, unshackle your minds and act like independent beings. You have been children long enough, subject to the control and subservient to the interest of a haughty parent. You have . . . an empire to raise and support by your exertions and a national character to establish and extend by your wisdom and virtues."[44] Webster understands what Aristotle taught, that an agglomeration of people—an alliance or a trade compact—becomes a political association only when the members live together "in accordance with intentional choice," taking thought that their fellows be of a certain character, which requires the regime to "attend to political virtue and vice." As Aristotle puts it in concluding his discussion of the factors that discourage faction and encourage stability,

> The greatest of all the things that have been mentioned with a view to making regimes lasting—though it is now slighted by all—is education relative to the regimes. For there is no benefit in the most beneficial laws . . . if they are not going to be habituated and educated in the regime—if the laws are popular, in a popular spirit, if oligarchic, in an oligarchic spirit. If lack of self-control exists in the case of an individual, it exists also in the case of a city. But to be educated relative to the regime is not to do the things that oligarchs or those who want democracy enjoy, but rather the things by which the former will be able to run an oligarchy and the latter to have a regime that is run democratically. At present, however, in oligarchies the sons of the rulers live luxuriously, while those of the poor undergo exercise and labor, so that they are both more inclined to attempt subversion and more capable of it. . . . In democracies [where freedom and equality involve doing whatever one wants] everyone lives as he wants and "toward whatever [end he happens] to crave" as Euripides says. But this is a poor thing. To live with a view to the regime should not be supposed to be slavery, but preservation. (*Politics* V.9.1310a12–26, 31–39)

In the last book of the *Politics*, Aristotle begins his account of the education appropriate to the simply best regime with a general observation of the importance of education in all regimes: "One should educate with a view to each sort [of regime], for the character that is proper to each sort of regime both customarily safeguards the regime and establishes it at the beginning—the democratic character a democracy, for example, or the oligarchic an oligarchy; and the better character is always a cause of a better regime."[45]

THOMAS JEFFERSON: RAKING "GENIUSSES . . . FROM THE RUBBISH" IN VIRGINIA

In his attempt to explicate an education scheme appropriate to America's republic in the pre-Constitution *Notes on Virginia*, Jefferson writes that manufacturing and commercial occupations degrade the soul along with the body:

> We have an immensity of land courting the industry of the husbandman. Is it best then that all our citizens should be employed in its improvement, or that one half should be called off from that to exercise manufactures and handicraft arts for the other? Those who labour in the earth are the chosen people of God, if ever he had a chosen people, whose breasts he has made his peculiar deposit for substantial and genuine virtue. It is the focus in which he keeps alive that sacred fire, which otherwise might escape from the face of the earth. Corruption of morals in the mass of cultivators is a phaenomenon of which no age nor nation has furnished an example. It is the mark set on those, who not looking up to heaven, to their own soil and industry, as does the husbandman, for their subsistance, depend for it on the casualties and caprice of customers. Dependance begets subservience and venality, suffocates the germ of virtue, and prepares fit tools for the designs of ambition. (Jefferson [1954, XIX])

Jefferson opines that honest farmers should not "be called off" to work in "manufactures and handicraft arts." He does not elaborate upon a method of discouraging such a call, nor does he address Webster's later concern that the drift toward manufacturing and away from the countryside is inevitable, but he advocates discouraging it nonetheless. Dependence on "heaven, their own soil and industry" does not beget "subservience and venality," but dependence upon the "casualties and caprice of customers" does. For Jefferson, even the best-laid educational plan is unlikely to prevent this low self-worth and moral decay, unless it can also teach the youth not to abandon the farm for the city.[46] Without an agricultural majority, the voting public will decline into vice and become followers of ambitious demagogues. As for Aristotle's primarily agricultural middling citizens, self-reliance and genuine virtue are crucial for Jefferson's republic, but he seems to associate these good qualities with ultimate reliance upon "heaven" or perhaps "Nature's God," as he phrases it in the Declaration. Aristotle associates middling virtue with the need to attend to private affairs and not to meddle too much in public issues, as well as a social position that encourages empathy with the rich and the poor and a capacity to compromise—Aristotle does not reject the marketplace and artisan labor, as long as it supports a middling lifestyle. Viewed from the industrial and post-industrial America of the twenty-first century, the predominance of yeoman farmers appears hopelessly out of reach, unless one can imagine small businessmen, entrepreneurs, and workers who take pride in their work and their place in society, rather than succumbing to subservience and venality (or, for that matter, to jealousy of the wealthy).

During the war for independence, Jefferson had proposed to the Virginia House of Delegates his Bill for the More General Diffusion of Knowledge, arguing in its preamble that even a well-ordered republic, such as Virginia, can degenerate into tyranny under the influence of ill-intentioned leaders. Community-supported education is essential for producing citizens who will recognize and defeat "ambition in all its forms."[47] Beyond reading, writing, and arithmetic, Jefferson outlines comprehensive instruction in previous republics, that is, "Grecian, Roman, English, and American history" taught to "all the free children, male and female," with the clear purpose to illuminate the errors and vices of previous "ages and countries." When properly schooled in others' mistakes, a virtuous people will not be apt to make them again.[48]

At his proposed grammar schools, the best students promoted from the lower schools learn Latin and Greek, English grammar, geography, and "the higher part of numerical arithmetick."[49] As Jefferson elaborates his proposed education reform in his *Notes on Virginia,* the best of these young men were to go on to college, one from each grammar school each year supported by public funds, and the rest were to be ready to become teachers in the lower schools.

> By this means twenty of the best geniusses will be raked from the rubbish annually, and be instructed, at the public expence, so far as the grammar schools go. At the end of six years instruction, one half are to be discontinued (from among whom the grammar schools will probably be supplied with future masters); and the other half, who are to be chosen for the superiority of their parts and disposition, are to be sent and continued three years in the study of such sciences as they shall chuse, at William and Mary college. (Jefferson [1954, XIV.146–49])

About half of those who succeed at the middle level of schooling will become the teachers of the lower and middle levels of school and about half will be promoted to university education, where they will specialize their studies according to their talents and interests. The members of Jefferson's natural aristocracy, at birth "endowed with genius and virtue," require "liberal education" so that they may be trusted with guarding "the sacred deposit of the rights and liberties of their fellow citizens."

Thus, from the most highly educated, both those whose families have supported them and those who have been supported by the public, are to be chosen the leaders of the republic. "By that part of our plan which prescribes the selection of the youths of genius from among the classes of the poor, we hope to avail the state of those talents which nature has sown as liberally among the poor as the rich, but which perish without use, if not sought for and cultivated." To the end of producing "wise and honest" legislators and administrators of the laws, the most accomplished and promising, those "whom nature hath fitly formed and disposed to become useful instruments for the public," are to be educated at university to such a level that electors are not forced to choose their governors from among the merely wealthy or well-born.[50] Those who are not so talented or virtuous will not be promoted to the higher levels of education if their families cannot pay for it, but they will learn self-government appropriate to their station in society by carrying out some from a long list of ward-level duties: "the care of their poor, their roads, police, elections, the nomination of jurors, administration of justice in small cases, elementary exercises of militia . . ." Living in a well-ordered republican community is part of the education of a republican citizen in the art of selecting "the veritable *aristoi* for the trusts of government."[51]

To the extent that the study of history is provided for all citizens, even "the rubbish" with only the lowest levels of schooling, to enlighten them to the dangers of excessive ambition and the means of preventing its ascendency, this is an education steeped in a conception of public virtue. For Jefferson as for Webster, the chosen representatives of the people must exhibit and practice virtue, but so must the voters, when they resist the wiles of ambitious men, and so must all the inhabitants, who are to fulfill public duties close to home and respect the laws their representatives make. Insofar as advancement on Jefferson's publicly funded track requires both genius and virtue, "superiority" of both "parts" and "disposition," the system runs on an assumption that all the educational disciplines both advance and are supported by moral virtue.

Jefferson posits a dual purpose—freedom and happiness—for his public education scheme: "The general objects of this law are to provide an education adapted to the years, to the capacity, and the condition of every one, and directed to their freedom and happiness."[52] Citizens, equal in rights, will differ in at least three ways: in age, in natural abilities, and in social and economic position in society. Some will have been educated by fathers who previously displayed "the capacity" or enjoyed favorable socioeconomic conditions, but the republican society Jefferson envisions must provide both public encouragement and financial support for the education of those not born into optimal conditions. He assumes the wealthy will educate their children; the less wealthy may wish it, but not be able to afford it. In Jefferson's school system, education will continue to be viewed as a distinguishing characteristic, but not, as in the past, because it signifies wealth and good breeding; rather, because it perfects the excellence of the talented and virtuous and enhances "freedom and happiness" for all. Once all have passed through the system up to their appropriate levels, its benefits will become obvious to all. This atmosphere then encourages the political results Jefferson wants: the less well-educated, the less talented and virtuous will appreciate the better-educated and be able to distinguish the more talented and virtuous in order to elect them to governing offices, and to vote out any talented officeholder who displays excess ambition after his election. To guard his own liberty (his rights), every citizen must learn from the past "to judge of the future."[53] It is not enough for some wise leaders to know some history and political science and thereby to guide citizen opinion—each must know and use that knowledge for himself.

Jefferson excludes biblical studies from his curriculum. Like a good student of the Enlightenment, he expects educated people to construct their own morality, but within some broadly republican limits. He claims that his education system would instill

> the first elements of morality . . . such as, when further developed as their judgments advance in strength, may teach them how to work out their own greatest happiness, by shewing them that it does not depend on the condition of life in which chance has placed them, but is always the result of a good conscience, good health, occupation, and freedom in all just pursuits. (Jefferson [1954, XIV.147])[54]

It is the business of public education, organized at the state level but controlled at the local level, to teach all citizens these basic moral underpinnings of happiness. Jefferson here spells out what he undoubtedly had in mind in 1776 when he told mankind that "we" hold that all men have an inalienable right to pursue happiness: all have a right to make of their chance circumstances what they will by just pursuits. The greatest happiness one can expect is the result of a conscientious combination of good health, work, and freedom.[55]

Jefferson thought to preclude the "progress of corruption" Webster also conjures in a future of greater prosperity and a decline in the influence of the middle class by providing the people at large with enough education to allow them to see through excessive and misplaced ambition, but his educational scheme was not adopted in Virginia, let alone in other states. He expresses his continuing faith in the progress of knowledge and the potential for American education in his famous 1813 letter to John Adams, in which he decries the results, but not the effort, of the French people to overcome their false aristocracy. Their failure was the fault of

> the mobs of the cities, . . . debased by ignorance, poverty and vice, [that] could not be restrained to rational action. but the world will recover from the panic of this first catastrophe. science is progressive, an[d] talents and enterprize on the alert. resort may be had to the people of the country, a more governable power from their principles & subordination; and rank, and birth, and tinsel-aristocracy will finally shrink into insignificance, even there. (Jefferson to Adams, 28 October 1813, NAFO)

His prediction of an eventual good outcome in France is based on his assessment of success in America: "It suffices for us, if the moral & physical condition of our own citizens qualifies them to select the able and good for the direction of their government, with a recurrence of elections at such short periods as will enable them to displace an unfaithful servant before the mischief he meditates may be irremediable."

In that letter to Adams, Jefferson reinforces the conclusions he drew earlier in the outlines of his proposed education system:

> The law for religious freedom, which made a part of this system, having put down the aristocracy of the clergy, and restored to the citizen the freedom of the mind, and those of entails and descents nurturing an equality of condition among them, this on Education would have raised the mass of the people to the high ground of moral respectability necessary to their own safety, and to orderly government; and would have compleated the great object of qualifying them to select the veritable *aristoi*, for the trusts of government, to the exclusion of the Pseudalists: and the same Theognis who has furnished the epigraphs of your two letters assures us that "Ουδεμιαν πω, Κυρν', αγαθοι πολιν ωλεσαν ανδρες [*sic*] [Curnis, good men have never harmed any city]." (Jefferson to Adams, 28 October 1813, NAFO)

Along with the moral lessons inhering in the study of history, Jefferson assumes that the citizens who receive the primary level of education will absorb a respect for learning and the moral elevation it produces in the true aristocrat, and a disrespect for wealth unaccompanied by virtue found in the false aristocrat. Here is the "high ground of moral respectability": that each citizen is capable of protecting his own liberty ("safety") within a popular government because each can recognize virtue as well as the lack of it in candidates and in government officials. Though Jefferson does not suggest that every citizen will attain, or even aspire to, the highest prudential judgment about the ends of the regime, each elector will need to judge whether a given candidate for office is fit to serve the purposes of that office in a free society, not by virtue of wealth or family connections, but by virtue of his virtue. This capacity for judgment, including enough historical perspective to defeat the ambitious, is synonymous with "moral respectability."

In his first inaugural address, Jefferson reminds the country of the equal rights of all, whether situated in the majority or the minority after an election. He makes clear the association of the right to the property acquired by our own industry and the right to the "honor and confidence from our fellow-citizens" won by action with a "benign religion," which inculcates "honesty, truth, temperance, gratitude and the love of man," and "acknowledg[es] and ador[es] an overruling providence"[56] Government exists to "restrain men from injuring one another" and, while not taxing them too much, to "leave them otherwise free." Government is, however, a mere part of the conditions of social happiness; it is necessary to close "the circle of our felicities." Our rights, our morals, and the favorable dispensations of providence are equally essential.

Jefferson here goes beyond the educational schemes of his younger days to posit a "benign religion" that makes feasible both the regime in which any citizen may accumulate wealth and a way of life in which the wealthy are not automatically given all political power, all while citizens guard "the sacred deposit of the rights and liberties of their fellow citizens." Phrased in a traditional tone, "acknowledging and adoring an overruling providence," this benign religion supports some of Aristotle's middle-class virtues—moderate living and friendliness to others, the Speculator's gratitude and Webster's and Franklin's honesty, but also the enlightenment ideals of truth and the love of humanity. In Jefferson's republic, citizens practice a multifaceted virtue: to adore an overruling providence, to have faith in the power of human knowledge, and to love mankind all at the same time.

Jefferson (like other founders) saw the citizens of the new republic as "the ultimate guardians of their own liberty."[57] This guardianship is not merely an individual's attention to his rights and interests, but the fulfillment of a duty to the free community. If eligible voters do not clearly judge the actions and designs of men, they will not be able to defeat "ambition under every disguise it may assume." It is not enough for a successful republic that the people vote, or that they vote to protect their own interests, or even that, through voting, they foster allegiance to the government—all important goals. The people must exercise judgment in their voting. Most obviously, Jefferson refers to corruption's entering the public sphere through bribery, but more subtly, ambitious men can disguise their ambitions as aimed at the public welfare (or more insidiously, as aimed at a voter's individual or group welfare) and dupe a historically illiterate public into electing them. Once in office, if the people do not remain vigilant over the government, the "cunning" and "wicked" will exploit every human weakness in the institutions. Jefferson sees the improvement of the public's minds "to a certain degree" as an essential requirement of this shared responsibility of vigilance.

Among those "other Federalists," as Sheehan and McDowell term them, who pay extended attention to the virtue needed in a republic and provide some indications of how it is to be fostered over time, some, like Noah Webster, believe a republic needs the sort of citizen virtue that is summed up in patriotism and zeal to maintain the Union.[58] "A Foreign Spectator" (Nicholas Collin) combines instilling patriotism with training in moral habits. Collin also discourses on the association between the "facility of subsisting by very moderate industry," which makes one independent, in contrast to those who depend upon "Negro slavery," which creates "habits of pride, dominion and severity."[59] Middling status in a free society is a start toward avoiding certain vices, but requires devotion to a rational government with the energy to enforce its laws to keep its liberty from becoming license. As with the Worcester Speculator, the Foreign Spectator insists upon teaching the next generation patriotic sentiments as well as moral habits to stave off licentiousness. For most, some effort of moral education is required. Among the most detailed is Benjamin Rush's education proposal, encompassing religious teachings, patriotism for one's state and nation, and a broad array of sciences related to political and social liberty.

BENJAMIN RUSH: WITHOUT RELIGION, NO VIRTUE; WITHOUT VIRTUE, NO LIBERTY

A fervent patriot of the American revolution in "forms of government . . . principles, morals, and manners," physician, and teacher of medicine, Benjamin Rush made a speech "to the People of the United States" in Philadelphia in January 1787 encouraging support for anticipated changes and proposing certain amendments to the Articles of Confederation. Not only should Congress' powers of coercion and regulating commerce be strengthened, but the states' power to issue currency should be removed and the legislature should become bicameral, among other improvements. Rush takes time in his exhortation to propose Congress appropriate $125,000 to the erection of a "federal university." He sees a crying need for a central "seminary" for teaching "everything connected with government," including the "principles of commerce," all subjects "connected with defensive and offensive war," and the European discipline of "oeconomy," supported by the researches of "a traveling correspondent" who would roam through Europe and "transmit . . . all the discoveries and improvements that are made in agriculture and manufactures." He goes so far as to propose that "after a while," "offices of the united states should . . . be confined to persons who had imbibed federal and republican ideas in this university."[60] It is clear that this university will succeed only after the states have established school systems and colleges where the prospective federal students will be prepared for these capstone political and economic studies. Thus, the speech obliquely incorporates Rush's "Plan for the Establishment of Public Schools and the Diffusion of Knowledge in Pennsylvania . . ." published the previous year—a scheme that reveals much about a proto-Federalist's vision of the educational requirements of a successful republic and deserves close attention.[61]

Before outlining his plan for a public school system, Rush lists what he sees as the "advantages of learning upon mankind." Education in the arts and sciences benefits "just notions of the Deity," "just ideas of laws and government," civilized manners, agriculture, and manufacturing.[62] Learning spread widely lifts the whole populace from slavery to liberty. Rush favors advancement in all fields of learning for their political and moral benefits—understanding justice and God, and enjoying freedom, alongside improving production.

True to the priorities implied in this list, Rush advocates a single state-supported university for the study of the learned professions, "law, physic, divinity, the law of nature and nations, economy." In the "Thoughts upon the Mode of Education Proper in a Republic" appended to the "Plan," he insists that the education provided in every township's free public schools be founded upon the study of the Bible, both for learning to read and write and for inculcating at the most retentive age the Christian virtues of "humility, self denial, and brotherly kindness" and the golden rule, all of which are "useful to the republic" and "wholly inoffensive": "The only foundation for a useful education in a republic is to be laid in Religion. Without this there can be no virtue, and without virtue there can be no liberty, and liberty is the object and life of all republican governments."[63] Each township's free school becomes responsible to teach all the youth to read, write, and "do figures." Further education at county-level academies (with tuition paid by the family) includes languages to prepare the student to enter one of the state's four colleges. The colleges offer lectures in mathematics and the "higher branches of science," plus opportunities to habituate the students in "order, diligence, and decent behavior," preparing some ultimately to attend the state's university.

This insistence on the need for religious education as the basis of a repub-lican society should not be simply labeled either prejudice or proselytizing zeal. In the spirit of the Enlightenment's insistence on man's responsibility for his own moral life, Rush reasons that, if one wishes to allow, even encourage, young people to choose the religion that will form the moral center of their adult lives, the best basis for that choice is a full knowledge of at least one religion's doctrines. Further, his advocacy of the use of Christian religion for the moral education of youth, he claims, is not based upon an assumption of "the truth of the Christian revelation," but rather upon its political util-ity: "All its doctrines and precepts are calculated to promote the happiness of society and the safety and well-being of civil government."[64] He declares that any religion (even Confucianism or Islam, as long as it teaches about a "future state of rewards and punishments") is a fit basis for public education and preferable to a non-religious model. He does not ground his Pennsylvania system on one sect of Christian doctrine, but suggests that various traditions be accommodated. The state legislature should consider how to distribute the public schools such that "children of the same religious sect and nation may be educated . . . together." Localized doctrinal differences apparently pose no obstacle to a consistent moral teaching supporting a state-level republican community. Rather, the system's reliance upon a variety of schools might enhance the citizens' toleration of other religions.

Rush defends public expenditures for all levels of schooling, including public libraries for adult education, on the ground that all benefit from "the propagation of virtue and knowledge." The connection between learning and virtue is very close in Rush's mind: "Confessions of criminals show that vices are the fatal consequences of the want of proper early education." Among the foremost political/social benefits he claims already evidenced by widespread free schooling in New England (and Scotland) is the tendency to reduce the costs of other government activities. A well-educated populace results in (1) lower taxes due to three factors: increases in production in agriculture and manufacturing, improvements in transportation, and public officials who "defend us from hasty and expensive experiments in government by unfolding to us the experience and folly of past ages, and thus . . . furnish us with the true secret of lessening and discharging both of them"; (2) less crime and thus lower expenses of punishment; (3) diminished temptation to extravagance.[65] These benefits assume the easy interrelation of informational and moral teachings in the classroom, from the earliest ages through university. Education implies moral advancement. Having learned the lessons of history, the best methods of industry, and the consequences of bad behavior, a free citizen will vote wisely, work hard, obey the law and stay out of trouble, and make efforts to improve his community and his state without taxing and spending too much.

Rush's statewide school system rests on the conviction that the children of a republic descended from immigrants from many different cultures must be made "more homogeneous, and thereby fit . . . for uniform and peaceable government."[66] He goes so far as to declare as the goal of republican education the creation of "republican machines" that will fit as parts into the "great machine of government of the state."[67] Since "the people" are the government, their wills must be made compatible with each other to "produce regularity and unison in government." This uniformity apparently does not extend to the content of their worship, but it does signal Rush's desire to assure that every young citizen has been exposed to biblical moral teachings at the same time the youth's prejudices are ingrained in favor of his country and its form of government.

Rush argues against the education theories of his day that would remove the reading of the Bible from schools. He does not object to studying classical history, poetry, or ancient fables, but insists that the Bible contains the most wisdom of any book of its size for the government of states and individuals toward "acquiring happiness both here and hereafter." Citizens need to retain the lessons especially suited to a republic that he sees in Christianity: humility, self-denial, brotherly kindness, and the golden rule.[68] If the Bible is not learned in school, where it will make the longest-lasting impression, he foresees its growing irrelevance. The long-range ill effect of this irrelevance would be the Bible's use "only" in churches and eventually not even there, but only—perhaps cynically—in magistracies and courts of justice.[69]

Apparently Rush does not take for granted that the plentiful resources of America coupled with the lack of a fixed aristocracy will produce the middling virtues that are consonant with a middling level of wealth. His vision of a good school system is aimed primarily at the active encouragement of qualities of character and certain attitudes toward the likely prosperity to come including duty to God, to country, and to family, friends, and property, in that order; love of private life, but willingness to take up a public station; care for one's reputation, guarded by lawful means; defense of family honor based on "personal merit"; attention to public controversies without descending into partisan "rage and acrimony"; love of mankind, but more affection for those of one's own state and nation. Furthermore,

> above all he [the pupil] must love life and endeavor to acquire as many of its conveniences as possible by industry and economy, but he must be taught that this life "is not his own" when the safety of his country requires it. These are practicable lessons, and the history of the commonwealths of Greece and Rome show that human nature, without the aids of Christianity, has attained these degrees of perfection.[70]

Young people need to be taught that one amasses wealth for comfortable self-preservation, but also to be able to contribute to the wants and needs of one's state. "Giving back to the community" is not an afterthought in Rush's republic, but rather a main point of its economic prosperity. Interestingly, he points out that the Greeks and Romans recognized and practiced these insights without the aid of Christian teachings, so classical literature cannot be a wholly detrimental influence on the new republics. Moreover, just as he advocates the study of the Bible for its practical political effects, Rush advocates the study of Greek and Latin for their practical benefit in both the professions that rely on literary skills, such as the law or the ministry, and the commercial occupations.[71] He does not wish the learned or dead languages . . . to be reduced below their present just rank in the universities of Europe, especially as I consider an acquaintance with them as the best foundation for a correct and extensive knowledge of the language of our country. . . . The advantages of a perfect knowledge of our language to young men intended for the professions of law, physic, or divinity are too obvious to be mentioned, but in a state which boasts of the first commercial city in America, I wish to see it cultivated by young men who are intended for the counting house, for many such, I hope, will be educated in our colleges. The time is past when an academical education was thought to be unnecessary to qualify a young man for merchandise. I conceive no profession is capable of receiving more embellishments from it. (Rush [1786])[72]

Moreover, he wishes the youth to be educated in the "history of the ancient republics," as well as "the progress of liberty and tyranny in the different states of Europe." Like Jefferson, Rush sees an understanding of history as the main route toward making effective electors. Every participant in the civil society needs to be able to detect when a politician or a policy tends away from liberty and toward tyranny, and that ability grows out of a thorough knowledge of language and history guided by a devotion to the good of the community as well as oneself.

Beyond the fundamental distinction between liberty rightly understood and license, for Rush, liberty requires patriotism. A republic's citizen is profoundly free, but that freedom does not include the freedom not to appreciate his country's freedom. Liberty requires due attention to private life, but the "republican duty" to country takes priority over family and property. "Republican principles" include the beliefs that a republic is the *only* locus of durable liberty and that devotion to *one's own* republic is the only way to live freely. Rush, like others of his day, saw that "the science of government is of a progressive nature," so that it must be open to further improvement, but he does not imagine that the definition of republican liberty could ever include the freedom to reject republican liberty or to abandon its pursuit in one's own community.

In addition to these overtly patriotic lessons, good schooling for a free citizen requires singing and physical discipline, including proper diet, avoidance of spirits, work with the hands, "sleep, silence, occasional solitude, and cleanliness." Students need masters with absolute authority in order to learn "the subordination of laws and thereby qualify them for becoming good citizens of the republic." Rush, like Webster, does not approve of boarding schools, but rather counsels the benefits of the break from study afforded by relaxation at home and the improvement of manners afforded by the habits of the family.[73]

In addition to the "learned or dead languages," the remaining parts of Rush's curriculum for a "liberal or learned education" include eloquence; history and chronology; commerce and money; chemistry; the arts of war and practical legislation (since "every citizen is liable to be a soldier and a legislator"); technical improvements in agriculture, manufactures, and navigation; "the prerogatives of the federal government"; and foreign policy and comparative government. Though he takes the teaching of "the usual arts and sciences" for granted, each of the fields of study he proposes is defended as useful for political purposes, that is, for the participation of citizens in a republic (with reference to Rome as a model) and for the advancement of the "science of government." Even the study of commerce and money, in addition to "humanizing mankind" and promoting international ties, serves a politically salutary purpose: it is "the best security against the influence of hereditary monopolies of land, and therefore, the surest protection against aristocracy."[74] Chemistry and improvements in production and distribution of goods support prosperity for individuals, but also "national prosperity and independence." Outside the classroom, students are encouraged to attend county courts to witness eloquence in action, the discovery of truth, and the explication of the laws.

The qualifications for teachers, paid out of public funds, include being not only "distinguished for their abilities and knowledge," but also "grave in their manners, gentle in their tempers, exemplary in their morals, and of sound principles in religion and government."[75] As with Webster, schoolteachers are moral models; not only their behavior, but their opinions should exert a wholesome influence over their students.

Rush's argument for the education of girls in a republic is based upon the political need for the education of boys as well as the success of the republic altogether. In addition to "the usual branches of female education," the young women need to "be instructed in the principles of liberty and government, and the obligations of patriotism."[76] They will be the first teachers of their children and will have much influence over the behavior of men. They must be educated to support republican laws and the educational system lest the political system fail altogether.

Rush concludes that, though religion, liberty, and learning can each pose problems for society individually, when combined, they avert their separate dangers:

> From the combined and reciprocal influence of religion, liberty, and learning upon the morals, manners and knowledge of individuals, of these upon government, and of government upon individuals, it is impossible to measure

the degrees of happiness and perfection to which mankind may be raised. . . .
I can form no ideas of the golden age, so much celebrated by the poets,
more delightful than the contemplation of that happiness which it is now
in the power of the legislature of Pennsylvania to confer upon her citizens
by establishing proper modes and places of education in every part of the
state. (Rush [1786])[77]

Those who plan to leave all support of religion to the private realm, all education to private or very local control, will undermine the project of planting
liberty in the American psyche. Without their aids, liberty will be misunderstood and misused; the republic will fail.

Like Aristotle, Rush appreciates the need for fertile soil in which virtue
may grow. He does not share Aristotle's apparently sanguine attitude toward
the association of the middling virtues supportive of free and equal political
arrangements with middling economic and social status. Living under a
government established along republican lines is not sufficient in Rush's
mind to create republican citizens. Free people do not automatically feel
loyalty to the arrangements that protect their freedom; innocent youth given
the liberty to choose will not always choose the life best for themselves or
for their communities. He does not advocate Lycurgus' remedy against
foreign vice—Pennsylvania will and should remain open to new citizens
from varying backgrounds—but the state must take pains to form the young
as early as possible into good Pennsylvanians, good republican machines,
"to preserve our morals, manners, and government from the infection of
European vices."[78]

Time is of the essence. If these schools are not established by the state
legislature within a few years on the wave of enthusiasm generated by the
successful revolution, Rush fears they never will be. Well-educated citizens
are needed to support good education into the future. His earlier observation
returns in a new form: one must impress the young with patriotic zeal and the
habits of virtue—not only young individuals, but a young country. Just as an
older child who has not benefitted from a sound education will be harder to
teach, a state that has had a chance to become indifferent to "the safety and
happiness of ourselves and our posterity," a state in which parties may arise that
oppose educating the many for the sake of their own ambitions, a state that
receives immigrants from "the jails of Britain, Ireland, and our sister states,"
will not be so receptive to an educational plan as complete as Rush's, nor, if
it is established, will the people be receptive to its teachings.[79]

For Rush, then, a successful republican government is not simply the
expression of politics rightly understood, nor is it simply natural to human
beings left free to pursue their political natures. It is a regime no less rigorous

than any other, and it must be fostered through a combination of free and equal political arrangements and an educational system imbued with moral lessons based upon republican principles and religious belief.

NICHOLAS COLLIN: "TURBULENT," RATIONAL, SELF-CONTROLLED CITIZENS PRACTICING PUBLIC VIRTUE

Nicholas Collin, calling himself "a Foreign Spectator," penned a series of essays in a Philadelphia newspaper during the Constitutional Convention. He begins with an observation that seems oddly placed: "republican liberty" has the effect of slowing down the operation of government. Collin is a friend of republican liberty and an advocate for the coming Constitution as a way of saving the all-important Union. Yet, while not repudiating the argument that energy is indispensable for effective government, he seems complacent about the "clogged" operations of government or the temporary success of the disaffected or even of "infernal traitors."[80] Here is displayed the Foreign Spectator's method of dramatizing the potential dangers of liberty and, thus, his foremost concern: the education of the broad population in the duties of citizenship and the virtues of a peaceful life. He sees the national government's power—the union acting for the common good of all the states—as central to the success of the American project. That project is to advance the moral and political "progress" of the community, in whole and in its parts. To advance this progress, which is both natural to human beings and easily derailed, he adds to the voices of those who will approve the document that will emerge from the convention on the grounds of its "political arrangements" his arguments for a strong attachment to the Union apart from its practical effectiveness. The Foreign Spectator seems to anticipate Publius' argument in Federalist 10 and to aim his essays at a supplementary project to aid in the control of factious conflict.[81] He plans to show that only with a solid educational system and nationwide attention to certain moral standards will the number and vehemence of dangerous factions—a predictable by-product of liberty—be reduced.

Collin posits "grand" and mutually supporting "operations" of the national government necessary to the confederation's success: (1) promoting a "general disposition for order and Government"; (2) limiting the power of the union's government; (3) limiting alliances or "partial affection" among states; and (4) rendering "the Confederacy an object of general attachment." Citizen loyalty and public virtue are required for a safe and happy republic; a "small defect in either may produce critical dangers." The republic may very well fail for lack of orderly citizens with sufficient patriotism and devotion to the political whole. He asserts that human nature is difficult to govern: "Man is naturally an unruly animal, little capable of governing himself, and very averse to controul from others."[82] Collin's specific recommendations for republican education track some of the "thoughts" his fellow Pennsylvanian, Benjamin Rush, published the previous year.

The means of effecting Collin's grand governmental operations, which take up the bulk of several essays, illuminate the meaning and depth of his concern for moral guidance. One of his primary proposals is schooling provided at the public expense: "The encreasing idleness, profligacy, thieving, and robbing, among the populace of great towns, call aloud for the erection of free schools: without them Philadelphia will soon have a numerous and desperate mob."[83] This education is meant to raise the potential members of a mob above their profligate and thieving ways, but also to provide crucial moral education for higher purposes: to "qualify a people for domestic, social, and civil duties" and to prepare them "for the important functions of jurymen, magistrates, electors, legislators," that is, for ruling as well as being ruled. Prosperous towns with neither a house of worship nor a good school produce moral laxity and political folly:

> In some places we see good plantations with convenient buildings, well kept taverns, and shops with many articles of luxury; but no house of public worship, and miserable schools. Silly people may admire such improvement; for my part I lament this unequal civilization, and find ample reason for it: The owner of this fine plantation got it by cheating illiterate wretches, who did not know what they signed; another lately belonged to a spendthrift, who, because he knew no higher enjoyment, drank grog, and followed horse racing—Several likely girls have been seduced, under promise of marriage, by fellows, who are too free and independent for the bonds of matrimony; and besides cannot support a family, because they hate work, and must ride an English horse—Gentlemen of superior fortune and character, who for many years have been in civil authority, are turned out, because they are against paper money; and ignorant, knavish demagogues chosen for legisla- tors—A number of labourers play at quoits for the whole day at the taverns, running in debt for liquors, while their wives and children want bread— Numerous law-suits arise from drunken frais, malice, lying, fraud, extortion, inability and unwillingness of paying debts—executions are common, and often ruinous to whole families. ([Collin] [1787])[84]

Note that this colorful description of moral laxity begins at the top of the economic scale, with the owners of fine plantations, whose character is so badly formed that they cheat the illiterate, and proceeds through those who spend beyond their means, who hate work yet love luxury, and who know no better entertainment than liquor and horse racing. These bad habits—of the wealthy (contra Hamilton) as well as the poor—and poor education affect more than the souls of their practitioners: "illiterate wretches" are cheated of their land, girls are seduced and abandoned, "gentlemen of superior fortune and character" lose their legislative seats to demagogues, families starve, lawsuits abound, "executions are common." Without effective moral education, the social and political fabric is seriously frayed.

So, moral education is essential to sustaining a republic. Collin displays a clergyman's conviction that religious training is the best source of such an education for most people, and a clergyman's dismay at the uneven distribution of houses of worship over the settled areas of the United States, but he is quite open to making this moral education widely available through public schools. He toys with the Enlightenment idea of nondenominational preaching, though he seems to see its practical pitfalls. It appears to him possible, however, to write a how-to book incorporating all the wisdom of the world's religions that teach about an afterlife without offending any one of them—he even recommends such a syncretic effort that he saw in Europe—and then to incorporate it into the public school curriculum.

The aim of public education is to instill moral habits through teachings with teeth—the critical component is rewards and punishments for actions, but not carried out by a ubiquitous government. A truly republican government cannot impose its laws by force. The citizens are the supreme authority, so the vast majority must be so satisfied with the laws that they obey them as if they had made them themselves.[85] It is a serious challenge to know what to do about those who do not impose laws upon themselves, who do not restrain their own impulses. Such people cannot be expected to obey even good laws without threat of punishment. Only an omniscient deity can both watch those people all the time and threaten them with ultimate punishment. A republic needs the supplemental support of clearly visible consequences of bad habits and disobedience to law.

It is revealing that Collin recommends "a treatise on the whole system of natural religion and morality . . . under the title of *Dialogues between an old man and a boy of eight years*" as well as a certain catechism for its "perspicuity and universality" before he begins discussing the virtues he finds most vital to a republic:

> Some virtues are peculiarly important in a certain state of national affairs, or the circumstances of a particular county, and even township. There is an intimate connexion between the moral virtues; they defend, support and adorn each other, so that one cannot be violated without hurting the other.[86] Few men are so ill disposed as to have no good affections; most have some tender part in the heart, by which they can be led—if therefore

all the consequences of virtue and vice were clearly and pathetically pointed out to a young person; he would behold so much dignity in one virtue, beauty in another, delight in the third; he would feel the meanness, anguish, horror of the several vices; he would find the impossibility of indulging one vicious inclination, without stabbing his favourite virtue, the mistress of his heart—he must, if not of the worst clay, become a tolerable character; and if naturally good, grow excellent. Men do more frequently rush into crimes and miseries from blindness, than the impulse of a wicked heart. Many, when they awake from intoxicating passions, or behold the sparks wantonly thrown, kindle a dreadful fire; stand aghast at their woeful gilt; and unable to pluck the daggers from their hearts, plunge with despair into a dark eternity. ([Collin] [1787])[87]

He proceeds to observe that "all the good and wise in the world" believe that religion's influence on "diverse characters" provides "a most valuable security to states" against tyranny. If the consequences of virtue and vice were broadly known they would encourage good behavior. Drawing on a Socratic theme, Collin suggests that it is not wickedness, but "frequently" ignorance that leads men into "crimes and miseries."[88] Again, without being very specific, Collin associates the virtues with the affairs of the community, although different virtues may be called upon in different circumstances. In addition to the social consequences outlined above, Collin considers it a social failure of education when citizens are not taught the moral consequences of virtue (dignity, honor, beauty) and of vice (meanness, anguish, horror).

The theoretical foundation of republican government is the justice of each human being's ruling himself. As Aristotle taught, human nature is as much a universal potential as a universal fact: what makes us political animals by nature is the *logos*, the capacity for speech and reason, that provokes debate over the good and the bad, the just and the unjust. That capacity has to be developed; it arose over many generations of pre-political life before arranging rule by turns and treating all citizens as free and equal became possible. In the individual, the potential for reasoned speech, just like the capacity for moral virtue, has to be trained. The laws lay down the community's expectations for good behavior, but they cannot enforce themselves. The fundamental political role of education is not job training, though Coram, Franklin, and Webster argue its importance, but moral training that includes both citizenship and self-restraint.

The laws of a republic must be obeyed out of an informed trust in the integrity of the representative legislature. The electorate needs to be able to restrain itself—its own desires—and to detect in a potential leader the capacity for self-restraint in order to obviate the rise of a demagogue or a revolt of the Shaysite ilk. Without this widespread capacity to practice virtue and to see vice in others, plus the power to turn out legislators on a regular basis, Collin's insistence that even bad laws be obeyed makes no sense. Without a meaningful arrangement for the morally astute citizenry to make the laws itself, obedience loses its moral foundation.

Collin delivers his discussion of the moral underpinnings of a republic in the context of a defense of the Constitution. This "Foreign Spectator," actually a permanent immigrant to America since 1770, wants to prove that the efforts to strengthen the national government are necessary and that republican government and moral education are mutually reinforcing. The new constitution will need a moral foundation, and its existence will support the continuance of moral education. Like Rush, Collin makes an argument for religious belief in the populace that goes beyond making courtroom oaths believable and is based on the hard realities of human moral failings.[89] He does not argue that only the well-educated gentleman is capable of moral integrity, but rather makes a practical observation that it is even difficult for the well-off to stick to the straight and narrow.[90] Their temptations are greater because more easily indulged, but all human beings are subject to temptation. Collin's position presents a roundabout argument for middling wealth spread throughout the citizenry plus a hearty dose of fire and brimstone for all.[91]

The economic circumstances of a new country with vast resources plus moral education delivered in public schools make it possible to imagine a citizen body capable of self-restraint that will vote for necessary taxes or restrictive laws when they see the true need: "A sermon every Sunday is a powerful antidote against selfish and malicious passions,—it would often dispose people for good government better than the wisest laws, and by promoting all the civil virtues, enable them to pay taxes, and to fulfil all the duties of a good citizen."[92] The Foreign Spectator makes apt observations on the difficult road of statesmanship in a regime where the people as a whole has to be the statesman and each person the obedient citizen at the same time. While Aristotle argues that the virtues that living in the middle encourages plus the distractions from excessive political participation that middling status requires create the type of citizen who can make, or acquiesce in, the assessments of fairness the regime needs, Collin would probably consider Aristotle too sanguine about the maintenance of even the middling virtues over time without frequent reminders of the benefits of virtue and the costs of vice.

Collin combines Enlightenment concepts of "natural progress" and universal education with Protestant reminders of the fallibility of humankind. He foresees improvements in the happiness of civil society,[93] but not inevitable improvement. With bad leadership, civil society may fail to progress.

Civilization, by which he means "the rapid increase of population" and its resultant "loss of the great comforts," will encourage certain virtues: it forces people to work and thereby develop "sobriety and frugality," "assiduous, orderly and ingenious industry," competitive improvement in manufactured goods, attention to customers, punctuality and exactness in trade. He tries to fit the virtues that Aristotle, Atwater, Webster, and Melancton Smith associate with middle-class farmers into a new economic environment that rests much more significantly upon local, national, and international trade. Collin combines the arguments being made at the Constitutional Convention and soon to be made public in Federalist 10—in defense of the multiplication of interested factions—with a sociology of civil and private associations that Alexis de Tocqueville will praise in *Democracy in America*:

> The multiplicity of interests and connexions, that increases in every progressive society, and is in America quickened by a rapid population, will improve the general manners by a deeper and more frequent sense of the necessity, propriety, and advantage of an equitable, obliging, and decent conduct—men will from interest and examples learn to check rude and selfish passions; to yield, not only to the rights, but sometimes even the fancies of others; and will be easily reconciled to this self-denial, because they receive the same good treatment from others. ([Collin] [1787])[94]

The people must exert effort to make the future better than the past, and for that task, the government must provide education. Collin's happy future requires not only something like self-interest well understood—a moral teaching based on self-regarding considerations that Tocqueville saw in 1830 being delivered from American pulpits—but also a faith that the clash of multiplying interests in an ever more crowded society will make everyone less "rude and selfish" and more respectful of the rights and wishes of others. As Tocqueville points out, in such a system, people behave well toward others because they expect others will behave well toward them.[95] In schools both religious and public, they have been educated with the apparently universal golden rule—Collin claims its recognition in "Japan and America, in Lapland and Otabeite [now known as Tahiti]."[96]

For Collin, civilization means population growth, which leads to city life. Growth toward such civilization is a public good, but it carries with it inevitable complications that require a more strictly regulated way of life. In an analysis reminiscent of Book II of Plato's *Republic* and the first chapters of Aristotle's *Politics*, Collin traces the requirements of city life that would never have occurred to "a peasant from the wilder part of the country." Only in a city do lawsuits, theft, and robbery, even foreign enemies, become salient concerns. Only a citizen of a prosperous city "finds a jail the most necessary building in the city." Only living close to many others calls forth the need for "strict police," that is, regulations for the protection of "health, life, and [one's] dearest interests," and for defense against enemies that a citizens' militia cannot combat. Collin, then, concludes that the very harsh facts of city life will produce a salutary effect: citizen allegiance to a new and stronger national constitution. The "remoter counties" and "the poorest country people" may for a time resist, because they do not feel the need for extensive and powerful government, while, in addition, some of these "have, from ignorance, rude manners, and a weak sense of social dependence, dispositions very unfavorable to civil, and especially federal, government." Apparently, a better-educated, better-mannered rural population might be brought to appreciate the benefits of "strict police," but Collin also does not see these remoter parts of the country supporting schools and moral training. To make progress toward a civilized republic, Collin's argument suggests the need to ally reason with the uncorrupt portion of human nature. Political progress is a path not toward "wealth and luxury," which "brings on political diseases and final dissolution," but toward a self-perpetuating republic.[97]

In this successful republic, the people will govern themselves, but in the attenuated way produced by representation and frequent elections. As in Jefferson's educational theory, all are capable of improvement, but some will excel in education and integrity and should be elevated by election and relied upon to govern. Though a republic needs the obedience of the population to duly made law, the people should not be passive—Collin, again in agreement with Jefferson, would rather the people were "turbulent than servile." The root of the problem of a republic seems to be that liberty, properly understood, is a good in itself, but, both properly and improperly understood, can produce ill effects. Free citizens must have a skeptical attitude toward their rulers, but the legitimate freedom to dissent, if not combined with education and the moral virtue of restraint, can produce subversion: "The more ignorant and turbulent pretend, that the people have a right to disobey any disagreeable law . . . a doctrine subversive of all Government."[98] Even more care needs to be given to educating the populace in a federal arrangement, because their suspicions of the (national) representatives chosen by their (state) representatives will be even more severe:[99]

> Knowledge, prudence, temperence, industry, honor, decency, justice, benevolence—all those qualities, which enable men to govern themselves, to regard the rights of others, to respect superior merit, to love order and tranquillity, are so many excellent dispositions for civil Government. They are necessary in Republics, where the energy of Government depends on

a chearful obedience. As the people cannot be led as children, or drove as mules, the only method is, to make them rational beings. Men of reflection have the advantage, not only to see things in extensive combinations, and remote consequences, but to feel an important truth with more sensibility; because in a chain of reasoning the result does not forcibly strike the mind, except it can rapidly run through the links—doubts or slow apprehension dull the feeling. This accounts for the great difficulty of persuading thoughtless people in the greatest concerns, even when their understanding is at last convinced. ([Collin] [1787])[100]

Collin's ambitious task for the new government is to "make" the people rational, so that they need neither to be "led as children," nor to be "drove as mules." He does not argue that a reasonable populace will automatically adhere to a rationally conceived government. Though humans are rational beings, some more quickly understand and adopt reasonable arguments, while those who are brought to the conclusion slowly may not accept its truth so willingly. Suspicion, bred of slow wit as much as of ignorance, blights the growth of trust in the necessary government of men.

Further, society inevitably contains "refractory members," those of weaker morals as well as slower intellect. Collin seems to hope that they will be brought to trust willingly those with "better knowledge" of political matters, as people trust their doctors and those who sail their ships. Surely this trust in politicians is a more challenging attitude to cultivate. "Every man his own physician" or "his own ship's captain" may appear absurd to those without medical or marine training, but "every man his own governor" is at the root of the American doctrine of liberty. The task becomes to train those of slower intellect or weaker morals or persistent "doubts" to the level of reflection necessary for self-government, to the level of self-restraint of which they are capable, to a useful level of political activity rather than passivity, and yet also to an appropriate level of deference to those of quicker understanding and stronger moral fiber. Religious education is Collin's preferred means: "The fears of religion have a salutary check on many: if not on every vicious disposition: on some, if not constantly; at some periods; would it then be wise, to take off one strong chain from ungovernable beasts, and to let others quite loose on society?"[101]

The source of the qualities of character Collin associates with rational beings, "knowledge, prudence, temperence, industry, honor, decency, justice, benevolence," bears some investigation. Aristotle argues in the *Nicomachean Ethics* that the virtues of prudence, moderation, and justice are acquired only by imitation of the actions and deliberations of the prudent, moderate, and just, but, according to the *Politics*, industry (self-reliance), benevolence (friendliness), and a variety of temperance (self-restraint) appear to be the more or less automatic products of a middling station in life. For both Collin and Aristotle, all character traits are developed through interaction with others in the community—they are not simply innate, nor do they develop without encouragement and habituation. While Aristotle associated the middling virtues with middling economic status, Collin implies that the larger the ruling class, the more effort has to be put into their intellectual and moral development.

In a later letter, published just before the Convention signed the completed Constitution, in the context of arguing for the necessity of federal control of international trade, Collin discusses the relative merits of a commercial vs. an agricultural/manufacturing economy. He associates world trade with luxury and, what is worse, the desire for luxury among those who cannot afford it. Because of Americans' "overdriven spirit of trade," setbacks in the international market put some into genuine difficulty and lead others to believe that they are in difficulty. When trade is good, people become used to making much money. They begin to live in a style they cannot reasonably expect to sustain, which creates unreasonable expectations of the commercial benefits to result from the national government's "exertions." Collin hopes to exploit the credit crisis of 1787 by combining the cessation of credit with the citizens' "good sense" ultimately to suppress their "ridiculous fondness" for trinkets and to return to "common honesty . . . national integrity, honor, liberty and independency."[102]

Collin recommends the arguments of Tench Coxe, "merchant of Phila-delphia," whose observations on the American system of commerce he says are consonant with those of Adam Smith. From Coxe he draws the proper order of national priorities: first, agriculture; then manufacturing; next, internal trade, to render the first two mutually beneficial; and, fourth, foreign commerce only to procure "valuable articles really wanted."[103] The life of farming, by which he means that of "a great Virginia proprietor," is morally superior to the life of a shopkeeper, characterized by solicitude "from morn till night how to make a penny." The "evils arising from an absurd spirit of trade" take three main forms: the waste of potentially productive energy spent in "huckstering," the unsustainable proportion of buyers to sellers (only two to one!), and the decline of "generous and patriotic sentiments."[104] Jefferson would probably agree with Collin that it would be impossible for such a merchant to display "noble, generous, independent sentiments" even if he were to become wealthy enough to support such virtues. Further, it is questionable whether he would be fit to lead a brigade of militia or serve in state or national political office. Rather than set its sights on a significant share of the international market, which requires either traveling to the far reaches of the world searching "in every puddle" for exotic goods or driving workers to produce solely for export, America as a whole should view itself as the proprietor of a vast and resource-rich landed estate, primarily self-supporting and deriving its satisfaction from that fact.[105] Again, the middling virtues of frugality and self-sufficiency take center stage, and they rely not solely upon a not-too-rich and not-too-poor status, but also upon the appropriate means of self-support. Though many future Americans will occupy the middle economically, they will not be born with the same intellectual gifts, be raised in the same faith, practice the same occupations, or work in the same conditions. The potential virtues of their social station will not always be realized without considerable societal support. Like Smith's reflections in *The Wealth of Nations* and Madison's letter to Jefferson, Collin's remarks as "a Foreign Spectator" warn against certain occupations because of their threats to citizen virtue.

The "overdriven spirit of trade," put together with America's "overdriven principle of equality," creates the sense that all can have and should have whatever they desire. As Tocqueville will later argue, there is moral hazard in the combination of equality of condition and commercial society. As the Foreign Spectator puts it, "inequality of property dictates a difference in living; if people do not comply with this from principle; pride, luxury, vanity will urge them to a thousand tricks of knavery and violence, and perhaps to mutiny and open rebellion." Further,

> Great disparity of property is bad; but some must arise from the inequality of genius and industry, inheritance, and that chance, which in fact is the disposition of providence. Whatever the quantity of national wealth, the great body of a people can never be rich; an easy decent competency, is the utmost they can obtain, and should be the height of their wishes. The people of America cannot complain of poverty. . . . Every pair of hands is a competent estate—the present difficulties may easily be removed by proper federal government. America equally removed from the distress of poverty, and the danger of wealth, has obtained from all-bountiful heaven that happy lot, which Solomon in all his glory thought the most desirable. ([Collin] [1787])[106]

Beyond a certain point, greater wealth does not advance the public virtues of gratitude "to God and their country, . . . dignity, humanity, generosity and public spirit." In contrast, "a labourer, who by honest industry supports his family," with a sympathetic heart and a willingness to "act for his country, is a far greater man than a voluptuous, idle, selfish beau." The danger in America is that there are no fixed classes, so everyone may both envy and emulate the rich. If the whole populace—explicitly both the men and the women—is not taught that "wealth and show" are "glittering baubles," "not to overvalue these trifles, and at any rate to acquire them honestly," the country could be quite overrun with corruption.[107]

Collin concludes one portion of his argument with the following summary remarks on the necessity for citizen virtue:

> There can be no republican liberty, but where the great body of the people does by representatives exercise the sovereign power. A great number should therefore be qualified to rule in their turn—the far greater majority should have the knowledge and virtue of electors—the whole nation ought to have a warm zeal for liberty, integrity and courage to intimidate the boldest ambition; yet be generous enough to love and respect a good government, and to support it with their lives and fortunes. We may heartily despise those politicians, who pretend to establish a noble republican system only by a nice balance of civil powers. Can a Palladio erect a palace, that shall be the wonder of ages, with untempered mortar, soft bricks, and rotten timbers! ([Collin] [1787])[108]

In 1787 Aristotle might well have put it this way himself. The structure of government powers balanced against each other by a reliance upon interest and ambition cannot stand if the people holding those powers—the people in and out of governing office—are not morally in tune with the way of life of a republic. In Collin's eyes, the economic as well as the political circumstances of the American republic require an educational system supported by and supporting moral teachings.

THE NATIONAL NEED FOR REPUBLICAN EDUCATION

To the objections of the Anti-Federalists that the new constitution threatens the states' and local communities' capacity for republican government and thus for fostering republican virtues, the "other" Federalists posit their own understanding of the relationship between a republic and citizen virtue. As Fabius and James Wilson see it, they are mutually reinforcing. This arrangement appears to ensure that virtue will be perpetuated as long as republican institutions last, but when examined more deeply, it reveals that both those institutions and the moral qualities of citizens that support them require effort. The citizens cannot relax in the assurance that their liberties are protected automatically by the fact that the elective franchise is wide—they must be "attached to liberty" and "love the constitution."[109] Their republican government will not, by its leaving them free, ensure that they will pursue the best life for themselves or for their communities. Other factors are at work. The Anti-Federalists and John Adams are most concerned to enlarge and represent, and thereby perpetuate, the middle class. Some Federalists argue for the liberty of religion as more likely to encourage true adherence to Christian virtue than a forced establishment or a religious test for office. In any case, the end sought is not individual freedom to believe or not to believe as one wishes, but rather the most likely encouragement for virtue. Beyond support of an economic class and the "free exercise of religion," the Federalists argue for the protection of private property, which encourages industry and frugality, and the attention of citizens to the character of their chosen representatives (and for those officials they in turn choose) and to their own public spirit.

Insofar as the Federalist vision is of states as the nurturers of the citizenry and the crucibles of republican government, the provision of the necessary citizen education would demand attention at the state and local levels. The most fervent advocates of extensive education in republican principles and virtues examined here were not present at the Constitutional Convention. It is possible that those who were, and especially the authors of the Federalist Papers whose advocacy of the new document has become the standard interpretation of the intentions of the framers, take these state efforts for granted, assuming that each state will educate its own to become good citizens not only of their state, but also of the larger republic.

The founding generation was neither hyperreligious nor hyperrealist— neither moralism nor amoral self-interest alone undergirds the new system or the contemporary critiques of it, but rather a deep amalgamation of moral conviction with an appreciation of the power of self-interest. Only a concept like Tocqueville's self-interest well understood makes sense of their position. Both Federalists and Anti-Federalists speak as if they would agree with Aristotle's observations that the best regime for most cities and men is a republic— requiring ruling and being ruled in turn among equals who are free, and aimed at the good of the whole, rather than the advantage of the rulers. As with Aristotle's *Politics*, the American understanding of the political also contains a sober assessment of the biggest pitfall of politics among equals—- faction—which creates in the Federalists more attention to the balance of forces among interests and in both Federalists and Anti-Federalists a concern for moral education.

The discouragement of *stasis*, factional strife, is an extremely significant part of Aristotle's defense of the middling polity. The lesson of *Politics* V's analysis of *stasis* in a wide variety of regimes is that every practicing government should reform itself gradually in the direction of a republic and, if possible, expand the middling element's political influence. Hamilton and Madison are famous for their interpretation of the Constitution's mechanism— representation over an extensive territory—that controls factions at a level usually below physical conflict, keeping many of its effects outside of the governing bodies of the national state; but they also acknowledge that the resultant multiplying factions "may clog the administration, . . . convulse the society."[110] The Anti-Federalists do not trust such a system to keep the flood of interests and passions in a large commercial society within manageable channels because there is no explicit place in the federal system to encourage virtue, understood as either individual self-restraint or public spirit. They argue that a republic cannot rely on ambition to check ambition rather than to ally with it. John Adams argues that "the education of a great nation can never accomplish so great an end" as Plato et al. contemplate—the public virtue to support a well-tempered aristocracy. "Orders of men watching and balancing each other are the only security." His argument is based on his extensive study of history:

> Experience has ever shown that education, as well as religion, aristocracy, as well as democracy and monarchy, are singly, totally inadequate to the business of restraining the passions of men, of preserving a steady govern-ment, and protecting the lives, liberties, and properties of the people. . . . Religion, superstition, oaths, education, laws, all give way before passions, interest, and power, which can be resisted only by passions, interest, and power. (Adams [1794, I.324–25])

Adams still assumes, however, that somewhere in this system, education and religion must continually promote some approximation of aristocracy that balances the democratic and monarchic forces. He is unwilling to rely on one branch to check the power grab of another branch if the members of neither branch are capable of controlling themselves.

Though no one in this sampling of the founding generation expects American virtue will rival the highest attained in the old world, all have a picture of the kinds and qualities of attainable virtue, whether they worry about them or assume their continuance or, like Hamilton, assume they simply cannot survive over the long term. Critical to the maintenance of the republic is the perpetuation of the middling virtues, such as frugality, respect of others' property and rights, obedience to law, moderate ambition to attend to public affairs, and friendliness or benevolence. If these virtues work to make a safe and effective republican system, then the system will inspire the patriotism to sustain it into the future. If the system betrays, even celebrates, its reliance on self-interest, if citizen "virtue loses all her loveliness,"[111] that patriotism may not survive; it may turn to cynicism.

The crucial Aristotelian question for evaluating the American republic asks whether it fosters a republic's way of life. From the Anti-Federalist viewpoint, if there is no attention to the traditional republican virtues at the national level and all education and distributive decisions are taken care of at the state level, the national union can hardly be considered a republic. Formally, the new regime is both national and federal, but wholly republican, Publius argues.[112] It satisfies the minimal formal requirements proposed by Federalist 39: all offices are filled by "the great body of the people" directly or, more frequently, indirectly. The Anti-Federalists thought that nod to the authority of the people was not enough, and Noah Webster, Benjamin Rush, and Nicholas Collin show that the Federalist enthusiasm for the new constitution actually presupposes extensive moral citizen education. Their attention to the details of a republican curriculum, including employment criteria for educators, the location of schools, and salutary extracurricular activities, illustrates the depth of both their moral and their practical political considerations.

A democratic republic governed by a "natural aristocracy" (in the nonpejorative sense) implies two possibly contradictory things. A democratic regime wants (1) "the people" broadly understood to hold authority—to vote and to judge their fellow citizens in court, to maintain order and a safety net in their communities—but also (2) that they be educated to recognize the true *aristoi* in their midst and to elect them, not themselves, to higher political office. For Jefferson, political equality—equality in rights to life, to liberty, to the pursuit of happiness, to the alteration or abolition of the current government and the institution of a new government—only works if inequalities of talent and virtue are discovered, nurtured, and rewarded with governing power. To call this arrangement a "natural aristocracy" is to reveal the fact, hidden within modern democratic states everywhere, that elections are a "device" of aristocracy, not of democracy.

When Jefferson distinguishes his preferred mode of governance from pseudo-aristocracy, he is merely renaming Aristotle's categories of aristocracy and oligarchy. The renaming reminds of Aristotle's observation that what he calls a republic is sometimes thought of as a mixture of democracy and aristocracy because it pays attention to virtue while it enlarges the citizen body. Aristotle seems to conclude, however, that it is best to think of a republic as a mixture of democracy and oligarchy that produces its own, fairly humble understanding of virtue, not the noble virtues associated with aristocracy. While Jefferson lauds his yeomen as "the chosen people of God . . . whose breasts he has made his peculiar deposit for substantial and genuine virtue," he distinguishes his most talented and virtuous youth, "geniuses" raked from the "rubbish," and bestows upon them an education in sciences well beyond the ambit of the farming majority.

Aristotle's republican virtues, individual and collective—reasonableness, temperance, moderate ambition, friendliness, self-reliance, as well as political stability and fairness to all—do not include the highest political prudence, let alone wisdom, full moderation, or justice. Aristotle hints at the need for the initial lawgiver(s) and subsequent legislators to understand that the republic is the best political regime for most cities and men, but is not the simply best regime imaginable, and yet that the vast majority of citizens should not believe that there is anything better, because there is nothing better *for them.* The prospect of something better can undermine the continuance of the available excellence. The regime's institutions may need periodic tweaks to keep the middle class in ascendancy and the laws properly balanced not to favor one part of the city over another, but the average citizen's confidence in the regime as a whole should not be shaken by frequent attention to its flaws and potential upgrades, a common interest among the brightest students.

The other education schemes here considered, Franklin's, Webster's, Rush's, and Collin's, seem to be most concerned with educating each and every voter, juryman, militia member, and parent for responsible republican citizenship. Each, noting the significance of a prosperous economy produced by the industry of self-reliant working people, speaks of inculcating moral self-restraint and maintaining a standard of the life of liberty that is incompatible with licentiousness. They focus on nurturing the average citizen, including through a rigorous curriculum of the practical sciences, but only within the confines of an attachment to their particular state and the nation, and an appreciation of republican principles. Left free to pursue individual interests within such an educational framework, the "brightest" would likely rise to the top, but as long as the moral content is kept in the forefront, the "best" would be those most capable of putting those moral principles into effect. These first-among-equals would possibly be prepared for the task Aristotle associates with the fully knowledgeable political scientist: to detect needed tweaks to sustain the republic but not to undermine the principles of the regime. In such a system, the democratic principles of equality and freedom might fruitfully coexist with the aristocratic device of elections, because morally molded average citizens would be able to vote for the talented and virtuous for "the direction of the interests of society" because they would recognize both talent and virtue and would have suitable candidates from whom to choose.

Conclusion

FOR ARISTOTLE AND AMERICA, WHY THE MIDDLE CLASS MATTERS

> Much of the strength & efficiency of any Government in procuring and securing
> happiness to the people, depends, on opinion, on the general opinion of the good-
> ness of the Government, as well as of the wisdom and integrity of its Governors.
>
> • Benjamin Franklin, Constitutional Convention, 1787[1]

The Aristotelian lawgiver attempting to transform a defective regime into a sustainable republic would be quite comfortable with the preamble to the United States Constitution: "We the People of the United States, in Order to . . . establish Justice, insure domestic Tranquility, provide for the common defence, promote the general Welfare, and secure the Blessings of Liberty to ourselves and our Posterity, do ordain and establish this Constitution." Through extensive debate over the just and the unjust, the good and the bad, an entire nation establishes a fundamental law composed by a committee of prudent citizens in order to protect their liberty. The Constitution illustrates methods of mixing devices that different parts of the citizenry consider good, as Aristotle urges in a republic—the power of states as states mixed with the authority of the people as a whole, but also election mixed with appointment to office; short tenures of office mixed with longer ones; a large, more democratic house mixed with a smaller, more aristocratic senate; a single civilian commander-in-chief mixed with a congress empowered to declare and finance war and separate state militias. Politics—the experience of debating and horse-trading, drafting and redrafting, articulating principles and compromising on specifics—led the Americans to produce a republic similar in crucial ways to Aristotle's best political regime.

191

As Aristotle advises, the American founders obviously strive for rule by law rather than by human whim, insofar as the legislative branch—its powers and the structure that would constrain them—is the first focus of their attention and occupies the most specifically articulated section of the Constitution. The framers use the "supreme law" to balance democratic modes of election, terms of office, and distribution of authority with more exclusive modes to prevent a primarily popular government from drifting toward pure democracy or the unrestrained power of the people.[2] They understand the tendency of free human beings to serve their own interests before those of their fellows or the community as a whole, and the necessity to restrain the elected officials' freedom to do so, in order that America's regime might be described accurately as "the multitude governing with a view to the common advantage," Aristotle's definition of the republic or the good regime ruled by many. The long-term challenge is to satisfy Goldilocks: to sustain a regime that the poor may sometimes call oligarchy and the rich call democracy, while the middle class, the largest, sees it as just right and, most importantly, no part or party can expect a better arrangement.

So many of the Philadelphia debates and ratification struggles over this document are taken up with its structural arrangements that it is easy to overlook the underlying assumptions concerning "the People" who would live by it, that is, concerning the way of life and the moral-political virtue of the American citizen. Twentieth-century political science focuses most on the institutional checks and balances in the founders' "improved" science of politics, and surely they are vital. The founding generation also took up Aristotle's parallel concern with the moral qualities, the "manners," as they term them, of the citizens who both rule and are ruled, whose way of life characterizes the republic.

POLITICAL LIFE AS A GOOD HUMAN LIFE

Aristotle defends political life as natural to human beings, as a realization of their capacity to engage in a morally infused activity: to speak and reason together about the just and the good. Though it is not the highest activity— philosophy partakes of the divine—it may be the highest wholly human activity. In any case, politics is an activity most people can practice at one level or another and through which they can acquire and hone key character traits. Aristotle's best political order is a republic in which the citizens treat each other as political animals, that is, as equally able to rule and to be ruled in turn. The way of life that supports his order is good for its participants. A successful republic requires a large, politically and socially dominant[3] middling class practicing certain virtues. Therefore, it requires both an economic system that supports a majority of citizens in self-reliant moderate circumstances and a method of encouraging all citizens to value the middling virtues. Without the protections for equality of citizenship and the rotation of offices, but also without a middle-class majority practicing humble virtues and selecting officials by its standards, the republic will decline into either the democratic or the oligarchic service of self-love and its political life will be neither desirable nor defensible.

Likewise, the founders of the American Constitution, their supporters, and their critics understood politics as a necessary and not wholly bad human activity that requires both free and equal participants. When he quotes the middling-virtues passage from the *Politics*, John Adams insists that a founder of a republic must include in the active citizenry the "husbandmen, artificers and merchants."[4] Those whose labor and service are "necessary" will demand a voice in the city, and their voice serves an essential political purpose for both Adams' and Aristotle's middling regime: to balance the no-less but *no-more* legitimate claims of the soldiers, the wealthy, and the more impressively virtuous. For Adams, those in the middle state, or "those . . . who have acquired property enough to be exempt from daily dependence on others, are the real middling people, and generally as honest and independent as any."

REPUBLICAN STATESMANSHIP: FOUNDING AND
PRESERVING A REPUBLIC

Aristotle's criticism of Sparta suggests that into the founding the lawgiver should build principles for modifying the laws when necessary and for ongoing oversight of the education of each generation so that future citizens will make the changes (and only the changes) necessary to sustain the regime. Through his attention to Sparta, Crete, and Carthage, Aristotle suggests that, as important as the initial lawgiver is for setting the tone for the regime, he cannot take all contingencies into account in the institutions he establishes; it may be a matter of chance that future statesmen maintain the way of life or the balance in the government against the decay of original principles. Insofar as the American founding leaders speak of something like Aristotelian prudence, it seems to manifest itself in the citizens' not-extremely-taxing choice of "wise and good" men to fill political office and then their exercise of vigilance over them, as well as those officials' capacity to synthesize local knowledge of their communities with more general knowledge of the laws and economics in order to deliberate while remaining honest and public spirited. Whatever their actual capacities, the founders do not generally speak of themselves as extraordinary for their wisdom and virtue—their authority to propose a new constitution or to write either critically or in its defense is not based upon their superiority to the average good citizen, but upon their willingness to submit the results of their labors to debate and ratification by "the people." The amendment process in the Constitution, rejecting the requirement of unanimity in the Articles of Confederation, shows the founders' understanding that unpredictable adjustments will be necessary. That the process is not simple and quick shows these adjustments were not expected to be frequent, and they were to be well considered, approved by a supermajority of the citizens.

Aristotle insists that a lasting, peaceful political order requires a majority of citizens to wish the regime to continue. Adjustments of voting eligibility rules, for example, are required at the beginning of a reform project to elevate the middling element to political preeminence, but tinkering will also be required over time. In America, the yeoman farmers, self-sustaining artisans and manufacturers, and merchants of the eighteenth century are posited as "the people," the citizens whose character puts its stamp on the regime: their life is seen to be the American way of life. Citizens making their livings in these ways constitute the dominant class already, though they may not view themselves as a class. Diverse political writers and statesmen during the founding period refer to America's favorable situation in terms of abundant resources and a populace neither rich nor poor. Most hope such citizens will continue to predominate, because freedom and political equality only manifest themselves in self-government when they coexist at both the individual level as temperate self-control and the community level as citizen understanding of the system and participation, primarily in the forms of selecting and assessing officeholders and serving on juries and in the local militia. Though James Madison and Nicholas Collin, the "Foreign Spectator," evidence familiarity with the economic theories of the day and the potential social and political impact of the changes catalyzed by the free market system, they seem to hold differing levels of confidence in the capacity of the market or the government to maintain a large class of self-reliant, politically aware citizens.

Institutional Adjustments to Maintain Middle-Class Dominance

In an age when self-supporting yeomen, craftsmen, and merchants are exceedingly rare, and a middling income and its accompanying self-sustaining habits and moderate political attitudes are hard to sustain, the temptation, when problems arise, to blow the system up and see what happens becomes almost irresistible. A regime that thinks of itself as democratic in such an atmosphere is ripe for a demagogue, according to Aristotle's analysis. If the majority finds itself losing control of its regime and losing sight of an avenue to pursue happiness, the people will seek some semblance of control and invest the one they believe has the answers with all the power needed to realize his or her plans. An unrestrained multitude can use its political power to strip itself of political power.[5] Aristotle and the founders would observe that, like a war to end all war, this desperate attempt to escape political give and take will not end well for the political animal. As long as laws and procedures and countervailing ambition restrain the demagogue's impulses, there is hope that the citizen body will regain its senses and restore the political system, but that hope dwindles with every reduction in civic education and economic self-reliance. If the majority of citizens no longer knows how the system works or why it was instituted, no longer cherishes citizen virtues and votes for respectable officials, and no longer sustains itself independently, the majority will be hard pressed to make a sensible judgment about needed reforms and trustworthy reformers.

The framers wisely made amendments to the American Constitution feasible but not easy. Unlike Aristotle, the Federalists do not seem to have expected that constitutional amendments or revisions of voting laws would be needed specifically to keep the moderately wealthy and their virtues dominant, despite the fact that James Madison and Noah Webster, no less than Alexander Hamilton, anticipate that property and finance will be prominent issues for Congress. Voting requirements were left to the states to adjust as would be appropriate to local conditions. As events turned out, national changes to voting laws have moved overwhelmingly in the direction of more democracy—guaranteeing the franchise to the propertyless, women, and non-whites, who were never excluded by the national constitution but had been restricted by state laws and social pressure, and subjecting senatorial candidates to a popular vote.[6] Aristotle would appreciate the need to make political influence available to the poor, but he would not consider it a problem if middling citizens were more active voters than the poor, as long as the middle class continued to be "friendly" toward the demands of both of the smaller classes of wealthy and poor. An imbalance arises when large proportions of both middle and lower classes stop paying attention to the selection of their representatives or attending to their behavior in office. If those who actively exercise their political power in a democratic regime consistently represent only a minority of the country, they pull the republic toward the rule of the few—for Aristotle, an inherently unstable, exclusive regime. If those with political influence gain or keep it in the most common way, by the use of wealth, their success can undermine many of the republican virtues that justify the regime—sociability/civility, enterprise/industry, sobriety, and simple manners/frugality, for instance. From this line of thinking, the challenge of the twenty-first century is to attend to the rebalancing of the political order around the middle class to prevent the long-term triumph of populism, a demagogue, or the rule of unsympathetic elites.[7]

According to Aristotle, the statesmen who make and enforce a republic's laws must understand something most citizens need not: the way in which a republic is both the best and not the best regime. It is not the best one could possibly imagine—not the regime for which a philosopher with infinite resources and favorable circumstances would pray. Those who defend the government publicly cannot be distracted from their "love of the regime" by something better that could be imagined. The republic is the fairest and most stable regime that a real citizenry of non-philosophers in a real world of non-philosophic regimes can reasonably hope to attain.

It is unlikely that the deviations of contemporary America's republic from the expectations of the founders can be traced to philosopher/statesmen striving for the aristocratic regime for which Aristotle "would pray." It looks likely, however, that John Adams' deep suspicions of the philosophic demands of Turgot and Nedham (demands he associates negatively with Aristotle's aristocracy) were vindicated by the changes wrought in the nineteenth and early twentieth centuries by libertarianism, various socialisms, and progressivism, to name a few. These political theories set standards for liberty and/or equality that make the self-consciously middling virtues no longer admirable or widely defensible. Henry David Thoreau's essay on "Resistance to Civil Government" sets a standard for individual self-government, "the majority of one," that explicitly eschews obedience to a law one would not have made and strives ultimately for "no government at all."[8] Disdaining the citizen who does not subject every law or custom to the scrutiny of a philosophy seminar, as John Stuart Mill does,[9] makes it impossible to encourage peaceful obedience to law among educated citizens. Whether or not it is ever achieved, the goal of eliminating both the class of the wealthy and the class of the poor—eliminating wealth and poverty per se—creates a standard by which the virtues of the self-reliant middle class are no longer valued. The goal of Marxian society, "from each according to his ability, to each according to his need," implies equal rewards for all despite unequal talents and industriousness. Moreover, all virtues become suspect as grounded in class domination.[10] Basing *The Promise of American Life* on his definition of democracy, "a theoretically absolute popular government," including individual freedom, "but more important still . . . the freedom of a whole people to dispose of its own destiny," Herbert Croly sets the same goal for his progressive government as Aristotle's extreme democracy. Ensuring that every citizen has equal opportunities to exercise his or her rights equally,[11] a goal that animates self-described "progressive" leaders to this day, becomes "all must be enabled to do as they wish" and everything that such liberty misunderstood as license entails.

The "best" social/economic orders demanded by these philosophically devised principles of justice are the political enemies of the republic's more political good. What is viewed today as salutary transgressiveness—questioning any and all authority, social or political, customary or legislated, in order to achieve a more just (meaning more free and/or more equal) society—is actually subversive of a middling republic, as Thoreau, Mill, and Croly, no less than Marx, surely knew. The Constitution's framers anticipated and feared the easy equation of liberty with license (or "doing whatever one wants," as Aristotle puts it) and might attribute to this formula, on one hand, those self-interested politicians who let license dress up as liberty in order to foster a climate in which they will be invited to save the populace from themselves, or, on the other, the removal of all property, literacy, and residency requirements for officeholders or voters, among other arrangements that had been intended to give the stable middling citizens and their virtues dominant political influence.

CONSERVING THE MIDDLE WHILE RESISTING EXTREMES

The American founding generation carries out a revolution in an important sense: it forges a new constitution and begins the process of forging a national identity. It makes a *conservative* revolution, such as Aristotle recommends, however, using English law and a study of the institutional "devices" tried in state constitutions, plus eleven years of postcolonial experience under the Articles of Confederation, to decide what changes are feasible.[12] However unique some of its aspects at the time, the regime is not completely new—the framers have both the political culture and the moral training the colonists brought with them and good and bad historical examples to draw from. The Federalists claim to use the "improved" science of politics, a political psychology that purports to understand the self-interested motives universal in humanity and to set them in opposition in order to produce a stable order. In 1776, Adams calls the advantage the American framers hold over past founders of republics "the divine science of politics . . . the science of social happiness."[13]

Aristotle's republic is based on the rule of the many, but it cannot be allowed to become the unmixed dominance of the poor, because such a regime easily becomes a tyranny of the poor over the wealthy, even the moderately wealthy. From time to time, most of the American founders use the language of democracy interchangeably with "republic," but they understand that pure democracy would pose a danger. They describe the danger as the threat to the individual rights of those people who find themselves in the minority on controversial public issues, those whose rights to life, liberty, and property could be threatened by unfiltered majority rule.[14] On the other hand, in the attempt to protect the minority, citizens and rulers cannot allow the regime to become simply an oligarchy—an unjust regime in Aristotle's typology and synonymous with European aristocracy in the American mind. For Aristotle, the majority must feel they take part in the regime; the best polity is the one in which the group that defends the regime is larger than all of those that criticize it put together, but even the dissenting voices do not expect that a revolution will solve their problems.[15] Economic status will affect one's political position, and a successful regime must take the various economically defined factions into account to keep the peace. In the struggle to eliminate factional conflict, he criticizes Phaleas for proposing to equalize property without teaching citizen moderation of desires and *The Republic*'s Socrates for suggesting abolishing property for the ruling classes. Without approaching a concept of rights, Aristotle argues that the freeborn many must hold a significant role in the regime not solely because they will make trouble if they are ignored, but also because a certain fairness requires it. Likewise the wealthy make contributions to the whole by virtue of their wealth and they cannot be stripped of political influence without sparking a revolt, so it is both unjust and impolitic to allow the poor to hold decisive power.

Publius' essays indicate that the Federalists were inclined to hope that the national government would be peppered with "fit characters," those of "the most attractive merit and established characters." Publius speaks, for instance, as if the election of representatives would be aristocratic, in the Aristotelian sense that all choice is choice of the better while democratic selection would be random, but also admits that "enlightened statesmen will not always be at the helm." Like Aristotle he looks for practical political arrangements in which unworthy candidates are less likely to be successful practicing "the vicious arts by which elections are too often carried," not an arrangement in which there are no vicious politicians. For the Federalists, the national level is where the various interests of the larger society clash and property interests will be the most enduring source of conflict. The citizens' property will not (cannot) be precisely equal and no representative will be an unbiased judge of the just regulation, but all the various kinds and varying quantities of property will be represented, so the differences will become politically insignificant. Government will not be dominated by a few—whether wealthy oligarchs or vocal demagogues, let alone enlightened statesmen—who control the debate, but rather will be pulled to a middle ground of compromise.[16]

Later, Publius suggests that representatives and senators, legislating for this diverse republic, will be constrained by their offices to practice some of the middle class' characteristic virtues: (1) they will have to be ready to obey reason (engage in true deliberation); (2) though they will not be forced (by the non-reeligibility rules the Anti-Federalists favored) to take turns ruling and being ruled, they will be ruled by their own laws *if* the public asserts a "vigilant and manly spirit" to insist upon it; and (3) they will be self-reliant, in the sense of maintaining independence from any single source of influence, because of the proliferation of factions.[17] While predicting these results, Publius also admits a national representative will be prone to the ingratitude that characterizes all human beings and to exhibiting pride and vanity. The new science of politics teaches that good public behavior can be produced by the channeling of these vices more reliably than by relying *solely* on habituation to virtue.

MAINTAINING CITIZEN VIRTUE IN THE FACE OF PROSPERITY

A large but partially obscured challenge of the founding era, as for Aristotle, is to make mediocrity admirable. That twenty-first century Americans no longer recognize that the term has a non-pejorative sense indicates that the effort failed.[18] Mere "reasonableness," Aristotle's first quality of the middle-class citizen, is hard put to stand up to partisanship characterized by arrogance and malice. A person of moderate ambition to participate in the government of one's community makes very slow headway in the face of those who would do anything to gain political office and reap its benefits.[19] Generosity or "friend-ship" across class lines is strangled in an atmosphere so deeply rooted in the protection of self-interest and ever-expanding rights, not to mention identity-group intersectionality.[20] When military service is not expected of all citizens, excluding only true pacifists, many of the citizens who vote and take public office lose this opportunity to experience the discipline of both ruling and being ruled for the sake of a common enterprise. When "luxury" is used so appreciatively in advertising real estate, cars, watches, hotels, and even finger-nails, and not as a term of opprobrium, John Adams no less than the Federal Farmer would sigh for republican frugality and would expect comparably luxurious public spending and consequently higher taxes upon the middle class. Only when the drive to better oneself has a self-imposed limit and the routes to a better income all flow through industriousness can ambition and upward mobility be politically useful.

When asked to name the form of government the Constitution establishes, Franklin responds, "a republic, if you can keep it." A republic does not fly on autopilot. John Adams predicts in 1776 that considerable upkeep will be necessary: all state officials should face the electorate annually, not simply to turn out failures, but rather to "teach them the great political virtues of humil-ity, patience, and moderation, without which every man in power becomes a ravenous beast of prey."[21] In the same letter, he makes further suggestions for state laws that would continuously encourage the skills and virtues in the populace necessary for "the happiest governments and the best character of a great people," including

> a militia law, requiring all men, or with very few exceptions besides cases of conscience, to be provided with arms and ammunition, to be trained at certain seasons . . .
>
> Laws for the liberal education of youth, especially of the lower class of people, are so extremely wise and useful, that . . . no expense for this purpose would be thought extravagant. (Adams [1776])

It is not only the policy content of the laws that would encourage citizen excellence, but the political system built upon the principles of liberty and equality well understood:

> A constitution founded on these principles introduces knowledge among the people, and inspires them with a conscious dignity becoming freemen; a general emulation takes place, which causes good humor, sociability, good manners, and good morals to be general. That elevation of sentiment inspired by such a government, makes the common people brave and enterprising. That ambition which is inspired by it makes them sober, industrious, and frugal. You will find among them some elegance, perhaps, but more solidity; a little pleasure, but a great deal of business; some politeness, but more civility. If you compare such a country with the regions of domination, whether monarchical or aristocratical, you will fancy yourself in Arcadia or Elysium. (Adams [1776])

The combination of balanced governmental powers with empowering and educating "the people" and the "best & most virtuous" will result in a happy community. His use of "Arcadia or Elysium" as his metaphor indicates that Adams does not praise this republic as the second-best regime or the merely best commonly attainable, but the pinnacle, "the happiest government," when properly judged.

The United States had to be a republic.[22] The group whose qualities distinguish a republic must practice self-restraint in personal life and in politics: these citizens are sober, frugal, honest, and generous. Aristotle argues that the only way to transmit virtue is to instill habits early, not by talking about them, but by providing good models for the young to follow. Ellsworth, Dickinson, Madison, and Wilson all see good qualities in their contemporaries, but all fear that that virtue will not last long into the future.

Citizens left free to serve their self-interest will seek happiness, which entails, for the founders as for Aristotle, moral self-governance. No titled nobility and rigid class system or national church will favor certain inhabitants over others or close off the pursuit of the good life of any citizen. When they speak of the citizenry of the new United States, they assume a certain moral fiber and a certain public spirit.[23] Many writers took for granted the lessons of Aristotle's middle-class republic, though few other than John Adams and Thomas Jefferson[24] would have acknowledged Aristotle's influence. If the association of the good life with moral rectitude is destroyed, the regime can no longer rely on citizens' self-government and must impose law by force. Such a regime is no longer a republic.

If the citizen virtue of eighteenth-century America was produced and/or supported by the not-too-rich-nor-too-poor economic status of the vast majority of the populace, and a large and fruitful land populated with free people pursuing happiness will produce an ever more prosperous society, that virtue could decline with expanding wealth. Collin despairs of a country with no fixed classes, however just the arrangement may be, being able to discourage the populace from envying the rich and striving for a life of luxury. John Adams flirts with the suggestion of sumptuary laws to discourage the taste for luxury amid plenty, but he could see in 1776 that a popular government would not be likely to adopt them.

> Whether our countrymen have wisdom and virtue enough to submit to [sumptuary laws], I know not; but the happiness of the people might be greatly promoted by them, and a revenue saved sufficient to carry on this war forever. Frugality is a great revenue, besides curing us of vanities, levities, and fopperies, which are real antidotes to all great, manly, and warlike virtues. (Adams [1776])[25]

Madison presents a rather dire, Malthusian vision of the future, when the country is "fully populated," because poverty threatens individual virtue; certain types of labor, though crucial to the economy, are degrading to the soul; and a perpetually poor class threatens the virtue of the society as a whole.[26] Whether the class of the wealthy or the class of the poor grows larger, it may be impossible to ensure institutionally that a dominant majority of the citizenry will continue to practice the middling virtues and to be attached to the principles of self-government that make a republic function.

The Anti-Federalists predict that a central, national government with significantly enhanced powers will be taken over by a small cadre of self-styled aristocrats (what today are called career politicians and policy wonks) out of touch with "the people," so they want to keep as much authority in the states as possible. For those who resist the new constitution, the leaders of society at the state and local levels represent a middle ground between the people who cannot or will not participate meaningfully in national politics and the aristocracy in the center. For Centinel, for instance, a "true republic" (governing a single state) is populated with the "virtuous" and its property is "pretty equally divided."[27] For him, the virtuous are not a highly educated elite, but those who have absorbed their community's moral and public-spirited principles to be able to control themselves, to contribute to self-government through community decision-making, and then freely to obey the laws they participate in making. They are neither the rich, who are suspect as not self-controlled, nor the poor, who depend on others to an extent that constrains their decisions. Anti-Federalists like Centinel and Federal Farmer expect a good citizen to display the sort of accessible virtues that Aristotle associates with the middle class—ready to obey reason, able to rule and willing to be ruled in turn, self-reliant—and they saw the distant and potentially aristocratic national government as setting a standard that would undermine this way of life. The moral compass of each state would be pulled away from true north, the life of modest ambition, honesty, self-support, and frugality, toward the life of social prestige and luxury that would characterize the national ruling class. Their method of perpetuating politically essential virtues is to leave each state to nurture its own republican virtues according to local principles. At the state level, where the people can see what their governors are doing while at the same time attending to their own families, the practice of self-government through both political awareness and self-reliance will perpetuate their virtues.[28] This argument for what is now called federalism is the strongest on Aristotle's terms, but is widely ignored today.

THE ROLE OF PUBLIC EDUCATION

John Adams sees the utility and wisdom of state "laws for the liberal education of youth, especially of the lower class of people" in 1776. He is speaking of the drafting of state constitutions, so he is advocating the guarantee of publicly funded schooling in a state's highest law and he certainly intends to broaden the availability of education beyond the children of the well-to-do and the subject matter beyond vocational training. Though he is not specific about structure or curriculum, Adams is clearly associating education with building citizen character.

As a rule, the Anti-Federalists did not emphasize education schemes—certainly not on a large scale. They seem to take for granted that a thriving small republic would necessarily educate its youth in the knowledge, skills, and virtues the community values. Robert Coram is an exception to this rule; he strongly advocates publicly funded, free schooling in the three Rs plus "natural history, mechanics and husbandry," while parents would be required to apprentice their children to an art or profession. His goal is that all citizens be able to support themselves. Such independence will produce a double benefit dear to the heart of any Anti-Federalist: to discourage the growth of a dominating rich class and to enable all to inform themselves of public affairs. That is, it will produce a solid citizen body capable of keeping elected officials in line by holding them to their standards of honesty and frugality. Coram's public school is required to instruct the young, both native born and immigrant, in only those subjects "necessary to obtain a knowledge of the obligations of society," that is, supporting themselves and knowing and doing their public duties.[29]

It is incumbent upon the ardent supporters of the new constitution—of a more powerful national government taking over some responsibilities of the state governments—to show how the ordinary citizen, who is expected to provide for his family's support, will have the inclination and the role models both to attend to local and statewide affairs and to keep tabs on his or her national representatives. The Federalists argue, contra the "fears" of the Anti-Federalists, that the United States under the new constitution will be a republic, albeit a federal republic.[30] The citizens of all states, then, must feel as much a part of the national republic as of their states, and national officials must practice republican virtues while holding office and work to advance the good of the whole rather than personal profit.

Public efforts to educate the youth began shortly after ratification and persisted exclusively at the state level until the mid-twentieth century. Congress has not taken up Rush's call for a national university whose political and economic curriculum would certify candidates for national office, nor did it follow Coram in requiring all states to educate their citizens for citizenship in free schools or all parents to apprentice their children in a trade or profession. The states eventually took up some of Coram's tasks, but their initial impulses have been weakened. If the national republic is to stand for liberty as self-government, rather than license, and for equality of rights, rather than equality of possessions (or any other measure)—in other words, if it is to achieve what Aristotle deems necessary, the discouragement of the rich from arrogant luxury and the poor from pursuing whatever they might crave out of degrading desperation—those who practice the middling virtues must be the models for young citizens. Education in the principles as well as the moral outlook of the regime is imperative. It may have been unavoidable that the American dream of pursuing happiness by becoming the best you could be would decay into the dream of endless upward economic mobility.[31] It is surely difficult for a moderated understanding of liberty as self-government, including moral self-restraint, to stand up in the face of the temptations of license.

To answer the need for freely chosen patriotism and moderated ambition, Jefferson, Rush, Collin, and Webster enjoined public schools to teach not only the basics of literacy and numeracy, but also the obvious lessons of history that make the United States the model of liberty and equality for the world. Collin and Webster see education at all levels as instilling public spirit and the republican virtues through overtly moral lessons and schoolteachers worthy of emulation. Rush emphasizes that liberty requires patriotism, which is best instilled at a young age.[32]

As Aristotle puts it in concluding his discussion of the factors that discourage faction and encourage stability, "The greatest of all the things that have been mentioned with a view to making regimes lasting—though it is now slighted by all—is education relative to the regimes. . . . To live with a view to the regime should not be supposed to be slavery, but preservation."[33] In a republic, the citizens must be educated in such a way that they freely choose to "live with a view to the regime," so that, when they take some political power, the citizen-rulers will "do the things . . . by which [they] have a regime that is run" in republican fashion. A citizen of a society that prizes freedom and equality must knowingly choose to be constrained by law and not to object to some differences in wealth or social prominence for the talented and virtuous, the sober and industrious. If a successful oligarchy must keep the youth of the ruling class from indulging in luxury, and a democracy must discourage its young people from pursuing infinite desires, then the mixture of these two regimes, a republic, requires moral training to discourage both kinds of vices in all citizens, who are also potential rulers. In contrast to Hamilton's resignation toward inevitable decline and, at the other extreme, to Jefferson's famous liberty tree fertilized periodically with patriot and tyrant blood, Collin, Jefferson himself, Rush, and Webster follow Aristotle's advice that "education relative to the regime" is all-important to long-term stability. They emphasize the linkage between the virtues supportive of free political decision-making and middling economic and social status.[34]

Though twenty-first-century Americans continue to speak very highly of universal education, it is an entirely different institution today, in both process and content. Presidents, presidential candidates, and governors speak almost exclusively of the personal economic value of education—the improvement in earning potential. Even when Coram and Webster advocate a requirement to teach all citizens a skill or profession so that they may be financially independent, they stress as equally important the moral habituation that making one's own living both requires and furthers the understanding and practice of good citizenship. These thinkers would not be surprised that contemporary American society exhibits a number of the problems against which they warned their fellows. Barely a single one of the Aristotelian middling virtues or the founders' republican manners is openly revered today. The term "virtue," or even the somewhat more neutral term "manners," is barely to be found in public discourse.[35] A widespread admiration of wealth and a predilection for spending over saving might begin to explain the problems of government budgeting. The average citizen's disinclination to "get involved" in either social or political associations (beyond writing a check or an angry Facebook post) indicates a failure to instill habits of both taking turns ruling and being ruled and viewing one's fellow citizens as friends. Advocates of the universal basic income were probably not schooled in industriousness and self-reliance as central to self-government at both the personal and the political levels.

It is not clear who in the constitutional system the founders expect to notice a problem with the education of the young and to formulate curricula paying greater attention to the citizens and officeholders they produce, let alone to implement workable reforms. Most, including the four writers on education examined here, would expect the locus of education reform to be the states, not the national government, with each state striving to instill in its people a sense of national unity as well as local loyalty. A national statesman might be able to articulate the goals of such reforms, but the citizen body, in the forms of state and local agencies, must decide for itself what reform is necessary and when. Can the majority be persuaded by reason alone or out of patriotic sentiment to act contrary to its acquired habits or to what it views as its advantage? Rush argues that if a good republican school system is not established in Pennsylvania immediately (i.e., in the 1780s), the impetus will be lost. If, at this late date, the majority is no longer "middle class" in the full sense, no longer brought up to practice and admire the middle-class virtues, it will be increasingly unlikely to choose to realign the educational system with the appropriate moral and patriotic curricula in the future.

Aristotle and the founders of the Constitution enunciate what is ultimately at stake: the loss of a common standard of both political and personal virtue and the concomitant decline of a generally felt respect for the regime and one's fellow citizens—both rooted in the decline of the large and confident middling class—presage a republic, however democratic in form, on the way toward despotism, with individual leaders' whims imposed by force.[36] As political animals, human beings need to understand and practice the political virtues in order to live satisfying lives. If a large segment of society is not satisfied and does not know why, it is too easy to persuade them to give up political and moral institutions they do not understand for something new that sounds good (and seems easily and cheaply done).

HIGHER EDUCATION AND MERITOCRACY

Both Aristotle and many of the early American leaders argue that the political and moral value of the middle class in a free country needs to be appreciated by the political leaders, the expensively educated and wealthy elite, as well as the ordinary citizens. The middle class needs to understand on some level that the way it lives is the best way for a free citizen to live—best for the individual and his family, and best for a free society. All the founding leaders agree that a republican community needs educated and morally upright governors. Whatever representation means in a republic, it is not intended to facilitate the poorly educated or the morally weak selecting people like themselves to represent them in national deliberations. Many American opinion leaders, however, no longer appreciate what the founders saw: the roles a self-confident, self-restrained middle class plays in balancing opposing political poles while modeling the good life most people can aspire to live.

Beyond citizen preparation, vocational training, and basic education, Jefferson sees ever-higher education as honing certain young people's innate talents and virtue in order to provide true aristocrats "for the instruction, the trusts, and government of society."[37] Over two centuries of the American experiment in democratic republican governance provide a test case for examining Jefferson's vision. American political leaders and opinion leaders should think about how a people that thinks of itself as essentially equal can coexist with a talented subgroup that thinks of itself as deserving to be selected for all the highest ruling positions; whether the existence of such a subgroup threatens the ascendancy of the middling personal and social characteristics, virtues Aristotle and an array of American founders thought were critical to a stable republic; whether the political and social elevation of the best and the brightest has caused that group to emulate the privileged lifestyle and political attitudes of aristocracy, losing empathy with the middle and poorer classes; whether the goals of educational excellence associated with these "geniusses" (goals that seem to conflate "best" with "brightest," rather than insisting upon fulfilling two criteria) have obscured or denigrated the virtues of the middling citizen.

Self-assured "natural aristocrats" are likely to associate primarily with other aristocrats. Those who rose from the rubbish grow distant from their humble roots, and once society grows used to electing officials from the *aristoi*, the excellence of middle-class virtue—the best that politics can reasonably attain—must lose its authority. If the modest republican virtues are no longer respected as virtues, and if the many left behind by the excelling few are taught to prove their "moral respectability" by voting for their superiors, understanding that their superiority is based on their educational resumes and not on the "genuine virtue" that resides in the voters' breasts, Aristotle would predict the republic would degenerate into either an oligarchy of the amoral smart, or a democracy of the poorly educated probably clustering around a demagogic leader to assert their prerogatives against the elite. America seems in fact to be suffering under both pathologies at the moment. The current saving grace may be the persistence of a few in Congress and the bureaucracy who maintain Melancton Smith's model, those who occupy the middle class and, though perhaps of less stellar virtue and less expensive education, "keep" the republic because their experiences give them some practical wisdom in compromising extreme demands and allow them to pursue their class interests, which are compatible with those of all classes.

In the project of providing itself with appropriately talented and virtuous governors, America has gained mixed success. The nation has not adopted Jefferson's eugenics program, so there is no greater expectation today that the best and the brightest will emerge from one sector of society more than another. Wealth, family connections, and certain educational certifications still aid a portion of the nation's youth in attaining positions of political influence. Some would respond that that is to be expected, while others challenge these citizens' enjoying privileges that others do not. Talent and certain character traits (frugality and industry, perhaps, or "passion" and "commitment") also provide assistance.

Though it would be impossible to measure the relative significance of any of these factors in a given case, in the aggregate, Aristotle and the founders might be interested to view the current American meritocracy. The climate within the middle and upper classes, which assumes that everyone needs a college degree and, in some circles, post-graduate degrees, represents a threat to a stable middle class of moderate expectations. Using the rationale that everyone deserves a chance to join the top class (not the Aristotelian doctrine that life in the self-supporting middle is the best and the pursuit of greater wealth provides diminishing returns[38]), the national government provided first grants, then loan guarantees, then the loans themselves to make it possible for all to afford and all to be considered for a college education. Though the reward of achievement among the poor might warm Jefferson's heart, the creation of a new aristocracy without regard to "disposition" might not. To some significant degree, social and political influence flows to the wealthy and famous whether they deserve to rule or not, and wealth and influence accrue to those with expensive educations whether they have proven to be talented and virtuous or not. In Jefferson's scheme, public monies are concentrated on polishing gems found among those not wealthy enough to pursue polishing on their own and on providing solid but not high-flown education for the less brilliant stones. A problem arises when the society is so pervaded with democratic fervor as to insist that the highest polishing be available to all, despite talent or virtue, that all be treated as if they were "the best" as long as they say they are trying "their best." Possessing the resultant diploma becomes the equivalent of wisdom, and the virtue that should accompany the meritocrats into office is either assumed (as entailed by their right opinions) or written off as irrelevant (as long as their policies "work"). America seems to have arrived at the divorce of talent from virtue and at the point Hamilton called inevitable, where money (public or private) spent has become a substitute for excellence achieved.

• • • •

Because the founding generation saw the success of the American republic depending on the persistence of a middle class and its characteristic virtues, it confronts us with several challenging questions that deserve further study. Does a middle class that exerts salutary political, social, and moral influence still exist, and if not, can it be revived? Does America have a political system that supports the necessary moral training for free and equal citizens? Is republican virtue—however modest and unimpressive—reliably produced in an environment of unrestrained freedom or of limitless self-enrichment? Or is it necessary to teach the young and remind the old of the source of their good lives in the principles of the republic and the virtues of a good citizen?

I began this project believing that the founding generation could have learned something from studying Aristotle's middle-class republic; perhaps they could, but much less than I thought. Writers along the political spectrum from Federalist to Anti-Federalist, along the spectrum of education from Adams and Jefferson to the Federal Farmer and the Worcester Speculator, appreciate the correlation of a cluster of homely virtues practiced by middling property holders with good citizenship in a successful republic. Though Aristotle speaks of education in the moral habits and opinions that support a peaceful and fair polity, he also speaks at times as if a populace in which the middling element (economically, and in other ways) predominates can be counted on to pass on those habits and opinions. The most influential American founders—Adams, Hamilton, Madison, Washington—see citizen virtues as part of the requirements for success, but they either take their transmission for granted or, in Hamilton's case, expect that their decline is unavoidable. A few of those whose names survive, among them Jefferson, Webster, and Rush, but also some writers whose names have become obscure, for example, Coram and Collin, speak out for a much more concerted effort of state governments to make both liberal and vocational education of the broad population a top priority. Not only do they agree broadly on the need to educate an ever-widening electorate, but most agree that that education needs a thoroughly edifying content. The voters need to know their rights and the workings of the government, but also their responsibilities: not only to choose good and wise representatives and to keep an eye on their behavior in office, but also to be industrious, frugal, public spirited, and moderate, and to be ready to serve in the militia.

Human beings are, by nature, political animals. Aristotle's analysis of politics and regimes, however, suggests several reasons citizens of a republic might avoid political participation, even say they "hate politics." A major one is that they depend upon it so fundamentally. Most people do not think much about life without political order or with a nonpolitical order such as kingship or despotism—the many examples of the latter in the world are treated as pitiable, not with the attitude, "there but for the grace of our community's consensus go I." Whenever we sense our dependence on the community, when a natural or man-made disaster spurs some social disarray, for instance, we are reminded of our flaws. Our individual insufficiency and our reliance upon the cooperation of many others; the fragility of the consensus about the right and the good that underlies that cooperation; the never-ending need to debate how such broad principles apply to changing circumstances; the necessity to react effectively to bad or unjust behavior within or without the boundaries of the community—all of these enduring human qualities are distressing, maybe even embarrassing.

If political life is so important to human flourishing, we need to ask why so many citizens of free regimes today hold politicians in complete disdain. Aristotle understood why so many prefer private life to political activity—self-supporting citizens have other very important matters to attend to. He saw this willingness to let elected officials rule according to law as a stabilizing force in a popular regime.[39] It is good that many have very modest public ambitions. But then, one might conclude that each citizen should appreciate those who do take up public responsibilities rather than look down upon politicians as a class. Perhaps some citizens perceive that their elected leaders have excessive ambition, forgetting that no one should seek political office like Jason the tyrant, as if he were hungry unless he held political power,[40] or they are perpetually on the lookout for corruption, like Webster's green-eyed husband.[41] If officeholders have forgotten the good reasons for serving in office and seek only material benefits, they will not, and should not expect to, hold a citizen's respect.

Apart from expectations of public virtue, the candidates put in office by majority vote regularly fail to produce the material results the voters hope for, often for reasons beyond their control. Not infrequently, the voters, like the subjects of Amasis, begin by looking up to a golden statue, only to find out that their new leader is an artifact, produced by order of a power-hungry political "activist," out of a melted-down chamber pot.[42] Aristotle might go as far as to argue that to believe one hates politicians is not a bad thing, but rather a reflection of the truth that *overweening* ambition is a vice. It becomes a bad thing, however, if citizens believe that any ambition is suspect, if no respect attaches to those who tend to the public business while most people pursue happiness in other ways. It may easily produce cynicism, which then leads to giving up on holding public officeholders to even minimum standards of reasonableness, self-control, friendliness, and self-reliance. More insidiously, it leads to the officeholders themselves not appreciating those standards as necessary.

Aristotle's consistent attention to moral virtue has distressed modern thinkers at least since Machiavelli. For the purposes of the middling polity, however, that attention is not so foreign as it at first appears. On one hand, Aristotle stresses in this context that political virtue be attainable, so as to discourage one threat to stability posed by aristocratic exclusivity.[43] On the other hand, if the citizens understand their political order to employ no notion of individual excellence to reward people with political influence, then the choice becomes merely the deployment of numbers or money and the extreme of democracy or oligarchy becomes a more serious threat. Citizens may easily discern the ethical flaws of their elected officials, they may institutionalize mechanisms to deter unethical actions, but Aristotle teaches that they should not cynically renounce all character standards against which to judge officials. If a republic shies away from insisting upon the minimal "virtues" in the governors, a formidable restraint from the impulse to use political influence to benefit oneself and one's class alone disappears.

Then arises the perennial problem of getting the ruled to obey the officeholders when all know the latter are really no better than the former. The perks of office that remind the citizenry of their governors' temporary elevation over the rest can also be irritants and invitations to cynicism if the officeholders do not behave as expected, that is, *better* than the average voter. Aristotle comments on another persistent problem of political life: once they gain power, people are reluctant to give it up.[44] The appropriately ambitious can easily become the over-ambitious. Those whose authority is supported by titles, honors, and perquisites begin to believe their own public relations hype.

In a final piece of advice to citizens of the American republic, Aristotle might point out a failure of self-knowledge involved in their attitude of disdain toward politics. The middle class seems to have lost its appreciation for its roles as arbitrator between the demands of the rich and the poor, and as peacekeeper in the endless debate over the good and the bad, the just and the unjust. They are frustrating roles, but crucial to the ongoing human activity of politics. It may seem far easier to relinquish all decision-making to the experts, but past a certain point political decisions are not subject to scientific determination; they require instead thoughtful debate among well-disposed citizens and a willingness to submit to the decisions of a majority of one's equals.

Contemporary American political rhetoric often laments the demise of the middle class, but it seems to forget why the middle class is so important. It is not simply that a peaceful regime needs lots of citizens who are able to support their families and pay taxes to support the government. It is not all about the economy. A peaceful regime needs a predominant majority that believes a number of important tenets of republican faith: that a life lived in the middle guided by good habits fortified by modest resources is the best attainable human life; that great wealth is as morally threatening as penury; that self-control is as important in private life as we expect it to be in public officials' behavior; that compromise between legitimate interest groups begets a win-win situation rather than a betrayal of principle; that the degree of virtue and wisdom in our governors that would justify, first, closing down the use of reason to debate the good and the bad, the just and the unjust, and then, dictating life-changing choices to a whole society, is unavailable to a real-world community.

It is possible that the framers of the national Constitution took too much for granted, that they relied too heavily on an expectation that the resources of America, coupled with an effort to expunge the pseudo-aristocracy of the old world (e.g., discountenancing primogeniture), would make a middling lifestyle available to most people and then the majority would achieve it and be satisfied. In any case, they left most of the administration of people and things to the states, as they believed appropriate: within broad contours, communities should govern themselves and establish models for individual self-government. That process is itself educative. The states, as a rule, tried to educate their children and regulate commerce and public health within their borders. A variety of factors beyond their control—climate, immigration, business cycles in a newly industrialized economy, and war, to name a few—have resulted in transfers of some of the states' authority to the national government. Some authority in these matters, however, has simply been surrendered to a culture that prizes self-definition (license) over old-fashioned liberty and notions of equality that are beyond the capacity of a free society to achieve.

It is not the national government's job, for instance, to educate every child, but it is its job to foster an atmosphere in which education is sought as a self-evident good—both for modest economic advantages and its character-building capacity—and considered a component of moral development. None of the thinkers herein examined would argue that it is the government's job to put a "middle-class income" in every family's bank account. Aristotle and the American founding generation would, however, exhort the national and state governments to do all in their power to foster an economy in which most can earn a moderate income and to revive an understanding of the American dream as achieving self-reliance and making the most of that moderate income through rational self-control, generosity, moderate ambition, friendliness, and fairness. Citizens who spend their lives practicing these virtues will also expect their representatives in state and national government to exhibit them and to serve as models for future generations to emulate. In this extended sense, the middle-class republic is the best, the most peaceful and self-sustaining political regime.

ACKNOWLEDGMENTS

Memories of Michael Davis declaring, "Aristotle is an eminently sensible man," while ferreting out the humor in those dense, sometimes baffling texts, have sustained me in many a dark hour of analyzing the Philosopher since 1974 at Dickinson College. I believe Christopher Bruell is most responsible for my dropping Hegel and concentrating on Aristotle's teaching on the middle-class republic for my dissertation, which formed a significant basis for this book.

Decades of students in American politics—government, political thought, and constitutional law—at Kenyon College, the University of Houston, and Duquesne University of the Holy Spirit kept alive my fascination and deepened my engagement with the debates of the founding era first kindled by Robert Scigliano and Robert Faulkner at Boston College. I am especially grateful to the three classes of good sports who became delegates to the Constitutional Convention for reenactments made possible by the generosity of Patrick Coby and the Reacting to the Past program.

Kent Moors began my quarter-century association with the Society for Greek Political Thought and, with it, access to a network of inspiring friends who combine scholarship with teaching in the spirit of the ancients in the modern world, with a view to the betterment of souls pursuing happiness.

Joan Lapyczak, indefatigable administrative assistant to the Duquesne Political Science Department for most of my time there, provided support, both material and psychological, for my scholarship and teaching well beyond what any adjunct, visiting, or tenure-track professor could fairly expect. Knut

Kipper and Sarah Stevens were valuable research assistants when the pressure to bring Aristotle together with the Americans in a viable manuscript became undeniable.

Without the patience, guidance, and encouragement of Carey Newman, editor and tour guide extraordinaire, the ideas in my head would never have made it over the last hurdles and passed the finish line.

Annalisa Haughwout and the ladies of Curves provided moral support for writing and rewriting on days when I would rather have been doing something else. Even more important, they, like the parents at the school bus stop, the volunteers for the PTO, the WHHS Band Parents, the Stingray swimmers' families, and my many helpers during a decade of RIF book distributions, provided almost daily examples of the moral life of the middle class—generous, willing to serve their communities but not excessively ambitious, friendly, not contentious, self-controlled, and self-reliant. These women and men lead a life that deserves respect and needs preservation if the republic is to survive.

My friends at Parkway Jewish Center had faith in my ability to finish this project, even when I did not. The late Syma Levine and the often-early Diane Bloomfield, along with the whole Sisterhood, demonstrated for me the American and Jewish virtues that unify service to one's family, to one's community, and to God, as so many of the founding era hoped they would.

I am grateful to all for these inestimable contributions.

—Leslie Rubin

• • • •

At the time of Les' sudden and shocking death in October 2017, she was eagerly anticipating putting the finishing touches on her book: checking the page proofs and completing the index. I am deeply grateful for the generous and sensitive way Carey Newman, Diane Smith, and Anna Mateo Roca at Baylor University Press stepped in to do what she could not. I am similarly indebted to Matt Franck, director of the William E. and Carol G. Simon Center on Religion and the Constitution at the Witherspoon Institute, who showed himself a true friend by looking over the proofs with an editorial eye as keen as Les' own.

Many, many people miss her, but I hope there is consolation, even if of necessity bittersweet, that some of what she was at her best is preserved in this volume: her clear-minded insight into things ancient and modern, her quiet humor, and her love for her country.

—Charlie Rubin

Notes

INTRODUCTION

1 Plato, *The* Republic *of Plato*, trans. Allan Bloom (New York: Basic Books, 1991), 439e–440a. All translations of the *Republic* are taken from this text.

2 Alexander Hamilton, John Jay, and James Madison, *The Federalist: A Commentary on the Constitution of the United States*, ed. Robert Scigliano (New York: Modern Library, 2000), 9.48, 47.308.

3 Hamilton et al. (2000, 10.53).

4 Hamilton et al. (2000, 51.330–32).

5 Hamilton et al. (2000, 51.331).

6 Aristotle, *Aristotle's* Nicomachean Ethics, trans. Robert C. Bartlett and Susan D. Collins (Chicago: University of Chicago Press, 2011), II.7.1107b22–1108a3, IV.4. All translations of the *Ethics* are taken from this edition.

7 *Ho anthropos phusei politikon zoon*. Aristotle, *Aristotelis Politica*, ed. W. D. Ross (Oxford: Oxford University Press, 1957), I.2.1253a2–3. All quotations from the Greek text are taken from this edition.

8 M. I. Finley argues persuasively that a prime difficulty in studying ancient political life is that the Greeks "invented politics," so to speak, and, as a result, they were often making up its rules as they went along. Finley, *Politics in the Ancient World* (Cambridge: Cambridge University Press, 1983), 53–54.

9 Aristotle, *Politics*, trans. Carnes Lord, 2nd ed. (Chicago: University of Chicago Press, 2013), I.1.1252a7–16. Except where noted, all quotations of the *Politics* are taken from this translation. The translator's interpolations are enclosed in brackets; the present author's interpolations are enclosed in braces.

10 *Politics* I.2.1253a22–24.

11 *Politics* I.1.1252a9–18. "Science" translates *episteme*.

12 *Politics* I.2.1253a13–18.

13 This assertion is surely strange for modern readers, who live in a world so often described by its ethnic, sexual, racial, and class demographics. Aristotle sees the political association

as fundamentally different from the social, economic, or tribal relationships that subsist beneath it. A common place, effective oratory, or long-held customs may reinforce the regime's moral way of life, or possibly undermine it.

14 *Politics* I.2.1253a1–18, 29–30. See III.6.1278b15–25 for further discussion of the natural "urge" to form cities.

15 *Politics* I.2.1253a18–27.

16 See *Politics* IV.3 and VII.7 for further discussion of the various parts that make up a functioning city and the difficulty of ranking their importance.

17 *Politics* I.2.1252b30–35.

18 *Politics* I.2.1253a27–29.

19 *Politics* I.2.1253a30–31. This statement of the importance of the founder raises questions to be explored further: Who in a political regime needs to know how the city works to perpetuate its goodness? Does the best city for most cities and human beings (a republic) require that all citizens understand its institutions and principles so that they can consciously make decisions that further its success? Or is it possible (even necessary) that the founder, or the founder in conjunction with a small group of well-educated statesmen in each generation, knows the big picture and guides future citizens in a path they do not understand or tend themselves? Can a republic's citizens retain the necessary affection for the regime without a full understanding of its foundations? (See conclusion.)

20 *Politics* I.2.1253a32–39.

21 Leo Strauss, *The City and Man* (Chicago: University of Chicago Press, 1964), 45.

22 *Politics* II.4 contains various reasons that the abolition of family structure and individual households would have bad moral and political consequences.

23 *Politics* I.4.1254a13–17, I.5.1254a21–36, b4–9, 16–23.

24 *Politics* I.6.1255a1–7, 19–28, b4–15.

25 *Politics* I.5.1254a24–26.

26 *Politics* I.7.1255b16–20. In the same context, i.e., the debate over the perpetuation of the injustice of slavery, the American founders experience the problem of politics that Aristotle illustrates here: human beings must engage in the give-and-take of political controversy, but they also know that their arguments and decisions are imperfect. The politically active are constantly reminded of reason's fallibility and every person's self-directed motives. Though it is wise never to forget the politically controversial, it is possible to ascend from the level of political debate, which is always tinged with selfish motives, to the level of thoughtful insight. In a world in which slavery was ubiquitous, Aristotle shows the problem with which the modern world eventually wrestled—the clash of the political principle of liberty for all rational beings against economic interest in a world in which slavery had long been taken for granted.

27 Herodotus, *Histories*, trans. Aubrey de Selincourt (Harmondsworth: Penguin Books, 1971), 2.172.

28 *Politics* I.12–13.1259b1–4, 1260a12–14.

29 *Politics* I.13.1260a25–31.

30 *Politics* I.13.1259b32–1260a4, 14–24.

31 Some examples of this avoidance: making those who are ruled as youth eligible for rule when they are older and preparing them for office by a mixture of ethical and musical education with military training; offering liberation to slaves of a certain character (*Politics* VII.14).

32 *Politics* VII.10.

33 In *The Spirit of Modern Republicanism* (Chicago: University of Chicago Press, 1988), Thomas Pangle does much essential work distinguishing various schools of republican thought, i.e., thought that culminates in partisanship for the republican form of government. Various

twentieth-century interpreters of the founding era seem to be looking for a foundation upon which to build a theoretical vision of what America should be—civic humanism, liberal republicanism, natural rights republicanism. These theorists/historians of the American republic take up what Aristotle calls the third part of political science: "the regime based on a presupposition—for any given regime should be studied [with a view to determining] both how it might arise initially and in what manner it might be preserved for the longest time" (*Politics* 1288b28–30). It is this study of a regime's "presupposition" that Aristotle brings to bear on Sparta, Crete, and Carthage, to show that they failed to fulfill their presupposed goals. The implication of the scholars of the various shades of republicanism is that America needs to return to the right track, if only we can identify it properly, and get on with the task of fulfilling its "presupposition." One lesson Aristotle teaches is that, if the founder sets the bar too high for the city or the citizens, the regime will fail and its lawgivers would be well advised to modify the regime to resemble a republic—a regime that can be mistaken for several types of regime without becoming any one of them. The American republic had to convince both the wealthy and the poor that their interests would be protected and their achievements honored. There is no need to prove that some or any of the American founders learned this truth from Aristotle—it is, for the purposes of this book, necessary only to point out that they discovered from the observation of politics in various regimes called republics the same political truth that Aristotle discovered from observing various regimes. Granted, the framers rejected the political teaching of the Aristotle they would have known, but this was the political teaching derived from reading such excerpts of the *Politics* as John Adams quotes (see chap. 4)—the prayer for the philosophically best regime, analogous to Socrates' depiction of the just city in speech in the *Republic*. The founders weren't political philosophers, or even political philosophy professors, but they were, for the most part, educated men who had given political history considerable thought. They could see that pursuing excellence by taking one political principle to its extreme would result in the opposite of excellence—to aim to be, e.g., purely democratic would deprive members of the minority of the security they need to be able to support the regime.

I believe that I understand the reason that Pangle groups all "classical" republicanism under Socratic philosophy: ultimately most thoughtful defenses in the ancient world of a political life in which a majority of the populace could participate pointed beyond the political order, first toward the perfection of virtues not performed for the sake of the city, but for the sake of the noble and one's own happiness, and ultimately toward the highest activity of the soul, the contemplative life, which eschews politics. Although the American founders used classical Greek and Roman examples, and even to some extent theories, of republics, there is little evidence that even the most thoughtful founders saw the life of pure contemplation or even the magnanimous man's condescending ethical perfection as superior to the effort to contribute to the good of a good political order.

The founders were not Socrateses and their regime is not a Platonic republic, such as can be found outlined in the *Laws*. In a way that distinguishes him from his most famous teacher, however, Aristotle makes a defense of political life on its own grounds and gives an extended account of a type of regime that aims at more widely attainable virtues in the citizens and peace and fairness in the political realm. Unlike the regime of *Politics* VII and VIII, this republic does not point beyond itself, and it also stands in Aristotle's text as an exemplar to other regimes in need of achievable reform.

34 *Politics* III.9.1280a25–35, b5–6.

1: A Practical Republic

1 *Politics* II.1.1260b29–36.

2 For good reason, i.e., to indicate Aristotle's use of the same word for political arrangements in general (regime) and one particular regime ruled by the many for the benefit of all, Carnes Lord and others use "polity" to translate *politeia* in all cases. Since this analysis of the *Politics* takes as a fundamental touchstone that overlap in terms and its indication that this type of regime is most particularly the *political* regime (because a *politeia* must be a political order and this is the most political of the possibilities), the regime called *politeia* will be translated "republic." The term has more resonance with American politics, given John Adams' definition as indicative of its use both generically to mean any non-monarchic regime, and thus, any regime in which there are multiple ruling offices, and the more specific attributions of the term throughout the founding era to denominate the project as a whole. (See discussion of the ambiguities of Aristotle's use of this term in chap. 2, p. 16.)

3 The distinction is Aristotle's between the "political" standard, by which the republic is the superior regime, and the standard of the best simply or of virtue. He gradually introduces the distinction in Book II.6 and 9–11 and refers to it in Book III, but does not fully articulate it until Book IV. This differentiation obviously depends on Aristotle's use of the term "political," which begins in his observations on politics' distinctiveness as a type of human association and activity in Book I. (See introduction.)

4 Consider the challenge for a citizen choosing political rulers when equality is based on a notion of universal human rights consistent with the Declaration of Independence:

> I think the authors of that notable instrument intended to include *all* men, but they did not mean to declare all men equal *in all respects*. They did not mean to say all men were equal in color, size, intellect, moral development, or social capacity. They defined with tolerable distinctness in what they did consider all men created equal,— equal in certain inalienable rights, among which are life, liberty, and the pursuit of happiness. (Abraham Lincoln, speech on the Dred Scott decision [Springfield, Ill., June 26, 1857], Teaching American History, http://teachingamericanhistory.org/ library/document/speech-on-the-dred-scott-decision)

Surely intellect, moral development, and social capacity are criteria relevant to the selection of a good officeholder, but they are qualities that can be very difficult to distinguish and compare, especially while preserving the fundamental equality of all citizens.

5 *Politics* II.2.1261a22–24.

6 *Republic* 463c–e.

7 *Politics* II.2.1261a30–31. As Lord notes, Aristotle refers to his *Ethics*: see V.5.1132b33–1133a2.

8 *Politics* II.2.1261a32–b4.

9 *Politics* II.5.1264b8–15.

10 *Politics* II.2.1261b9.

11 *Politics* I.5.1254b2–9.

12 For a more detailed analysis of Aristotle's criticism of Socrates' regime, see Leslie G. Rubin, "Aristotle's Criticism of Socratic Political Unity in Plato's *Republic*," in *Politikos*, vol. 1, ed. Kent Moors (Pittsburgh: Duquesne University Press, 1989), 100–119.

13 *Politics* II.6.1265a21–28.

14 Cf. *Politics* II.7.1267a18–31 and VII.5–6.

15 *Politics* II.6.1265b27–29.

16 *Politics* II.6.1265a8–18.

17 *Politics* II.6.1265a29–32. See Plato, *The* Laws *of Plato,* trans. Thomas L. Pangle (New York: Basic Books, 1980), 737d. All quotations from the *Laws,* unless otherwise noted, are from this translation.

18 *Politics* II.6.1265a32–38.

19 Or "most generally accessible [*koinotaten*]."

20 *Politics* II.6.1265b29–34. Despite the Athenian Stranger's claims, this republic is not the second-best regime according to the standards appropriate to Socrates' just regime in the *Republic* or Aristotle's simply best regime. The second best according to that ranking would be the timocracy of the *Republic* (544c–547a) or, as Aristotle suggests, the Spartan regime. If the criteria of the simply best regime are employed, Magnesia belongs in no higher than the third rank.

21 *Politics* II.6.1266a1–3. The term used at *Laws* 693d is the more neutral *monarchian*. Plato, *The Laws*, trans. R. G. Bury (Cambridge, Mass.: Harvard University Press, 1967). All quotations from the Greek text are taken from this edition.

22 As Pangle puts it, the critique of the *Laws* provides a "glimpse of the scaffolding for his own practical science and ranking of regimes" (Thomas L. Pangle, *Aristotle's Teaching in the* Politics [Chicago: University of Chicago Press, 2013], 79).

23 *Politics* II.6.1266a1–31.

24 Aristotle's critique of Sparta will observe that, in a regime in which property is distributed to achieve equality but marriages and births are not carefully regulated to maintain that equality, the other three criteria would be impossible: there would be insufficient men prepared to bear heavy arms; there would be insufficient funds in the hands of most and excessive wealth in the hands of a few for a moderate and liberal existence; and the democratic and oligarchic elements of the city would be so radically divided as to rule out political cooperation.

25 *Politics* II.6.1266a23–25. See also Lord's introduction, *Politics*, xxiii, n. 35; cf. Pangle (2013, 80–81).

26 I.e., Plato's Socrates and Athenian Stranger, Hippodamus of Miletus, and Phaleas of Chalcedon.

27 *Politics* II.9.1269a30–34.

28 *Hupothesin*, also "presupposition."

29 *Politics* II.11.1272b26–30.

30 *Politics* II.10.1271b20–24. Aristotle sets himself a preliminary question in examining the *Republic*: "the natural beginning" for an investigation into the best regime is to ask in what things the citizens share, "in everything or in nothing, or in some things but not in others" (II.1.1260b36–39).

31 *Politics* II.11.1273b26–27.

32 Peter Simpson, in *A Philosophical Commentary on the* Politics *of Aristotle* (Chapel Hill: University of North Carolina Press, 1998), 127, suggests Aristotle salvages some of these regimes' institutions for his own "best regime." These political arrangements are not irredeemable, but these cities merely used them poorly, for which Simpson amply chastises their lawgivers. Michael Davis, in *The Politics of Philosophy: A Commentary on Aristotle's* Politics (Lanham, Md.: Rowman & Littlefield, 1996), 44, on the other hand, argues that these regimes' failures in Aristotle's eyes have more to do with the unavoidable paradox of political science when it attempts a rational understanding of the not-completely-rational world of politics.

Books IV through VI show that the irrationality of the rational animal engaging in politics can be redeemed. That very unforeseeable, uncontrollable aspect of human being, however, leads Aristotle to propose several split-the-difference measures to make it more likely that the quintessentially political regime can achieve some stability and some justice. Aristotle the philosopher will always see its weaknesses according to a philosophic standard, but he does not hold the lives of the vast majority of human beings hostage to that standard.

33 Cf. *Politics* IV.9.1294b17–36. Harry Jaffa asserts, misleadingly, that these three real cities are criticized primarily according to the principles of the simply best regime. Jaffa, "Aristotle," in *History of Political Philosophy*, ed. Leo Strauss and Joseph Cropsey (Chicago: Rand McNally, 1963), 127.

34 Indeed, leisure from necessity is related to a "finely governed" city and anticipates Aristotle's best regime (*Politics* VII.15.1334a11–b5).

35 Roger A. de Laix makes the interesting observation that Aristotle calls Lycurgus by name in Book II only when Sparta's institutions are praised, but refers to "the lawgiver" when criticisms are leveled (de Laix, "Aristotle's Conception of the Spartan Constitution," *Journal of the History of Philosophy* 12, no. 1 [1974]: 27–28).

36 Socrates' particular fear was that, if allowed to have private possessions, to call things "mine" in a private way, the guardians would become mean and illiberal, rather than friendly toward their fellows (*Republic* 464c–465c).

37 *Politics* II.5.1263b15–22. Benjamin Jowett's restatement of this principle, "more good will be done by awakening in rich men a sense of the duties of property, than by the violation of their rights," misses the point. See Aristotle, *The Politics of Aristotle*, trans. Jowett (Oxford: Clarendon, 1885), xxviii. Duties and rights are not at issue here. The virtues to which Aristotle refers are habits, somehow based on rationality, but far from the modern conception of duties based in a rational "law of nature" or premised on a Kantian good will. Whereas moderns are enjoined to study duties individually and to practice good actions for personal moral satisfaction, Aristotle is talking about a city in which citizens learn ethics from the laws and customs of the regime and practice it out of habit or are punished.

38 *Politics* II.5.1263b7–8.

39 *Politics* II.5.1263b5–14.

40 More likely, communal property will be detrimental, because of the deprivations of good things it occasions. If no one owns anything, one cannot be liberal; with communal wives, one cannot exercise sexual temperance. *Politics* II.5.1263b7–29. See also I.13.1260b14–20 for the significance of the virtue of women for politics.

41 Simpson (1998, 113).

42 Cf. *Politics* IV.9.1294b34–40; also *Laws* 692a–b and Simpson (1998, 113–15).

43 Cf. Pangle (2013, 88–89).

44 Spartan history provides clear evidence for Aristotle's criticism of Phaleas' communal plan, that he fails to recognize this essential connection (*Politics* II.7.1266b8–14).

45 Jane Jacobs, *Systems of Survival: A Dialogue on the Moral Foundations of Commerce and Politics* (New York: Random House, 1992), chaps. 2 and 5.

46 Plutarch, *Plutarch's Lives*, vol. 1, trans. Bernadotte Perrin (London: W. Heinemann, 1982), I.29.1–6, 31.2.

47 *Politics* II.9.1270b14–17. Simpson (1998, 117) shows nicely how a kingship in which the kings fear the democratic element of the regime is not merely a democracy, but an extreme form of democracy: the ephors in effect force the kings to become demagogues, truckling to the many to keep their power.

48 *Politics* II.9.1270b21–22; see also II.11.1272b43–1273a2.

49 *Politics* II.9.1271a3–9. Compare the praise of Solon's demotic measures at II.12.1274a15–18.

50 *Politics* II.9.1271a10–13.

51 *Politics* II.9.1271a17–18.

52 E.g., *Politics* IV.4.

53 Just as the elder statesmen are encouraged to compete with each other for the honor of becoming a senator, the two kings are not trusted in the Lacedaemonian laws, according

to Aristotle's analysis of the Spartan belief that "factional conflict between the kings means preservation for the city." Neither harmony nor justice but mere preservation is sought in the arrangement of the dual kings drawn from separate hereditary lines who are "repeatedly sent on embassies accompanied by their enemies" (II.9.1271a23–26). A king should be chosen on the basis of his own merits, not his family lines, and one of those merits should presumably be trustworthiness in office. The danger of hereditary kingship of any kind is that, however good and skillful the first of the line, "how should one handle what pertains to the offspring? Must the family rule as kings also? But if those born into it are persons of average quality, it would be harmful" (III.15.1286b23–25). If Sparta cannot make the case that its kingship is like Aristotle's *pambasileia*, the rule of the supremely virtuous over willing and obviously inferior subjects, the next best arrangement is the rule of the few best. The necessary support for a genuine aristocracy—a body of well-educated and virtuous citizens—also does not exist in Sparta. The mixed regime, specifically the mixture of oligarchy and democracy known as polity, is the third choice, as Aristotle argued in his critique of the *Laws*.

54 *Politics* II.9.1271b7–11.

55 *Politics* II.9.1270b30–33.

56 The political virtues discussed in Book IV—reasonableness, moderate ambition to rule without arrogance and willingness to be ruled without slavishness, friendliness to all parts of the regime, self-reliance—are clearly virtues of peacetime.

57 As Pangle notes (2013, 92), Aristotle acknowledges his debt to Plato's *Laws* for the criticism of Sparta's excessive attention to "warlike virtue." This bow to Plato leads Pangle to suggest that Magnesia is "*the* standard" by which Aristotle judges Sparta altogether. It is not so clear that such a connection should lead to seeing Book VIII's regime as an abbreviated version of the *Laws*' regime and not, rather, to see Book IV's polities as more practicable versions of what the Athenian Stranger is attempting to accomplish, which Aristotle labels a polity.

58 *Politics* II.10.1271b20–24. *Hetton glaphuros* or *hetton dierthrotai*.

59 *Pephilosopheken*.

60 *Politics* II.10.1272a16–27.

61 For a related crucial flaw in Phaleas' plan, see *Politics* II.7.1266b8–16, 38–1267a9.

62 *Politics* II.10.1272a8–12.

63 Aristotle later argues that it is only in an absolute kingship of the best man, if even then, that a community can rightly be ruled solely according to the ruler's discretion (*Politics* III.17). Clearly neither Sparta nor Crete has the intention or the wherewithal to aspire to *pambasileia*.

64 *Politics* II.10.1272a39–b1.

65 *Politics* II.9.1269a36–b7.

66 As an island nation, Crete may fail the test of a "political" regime, precisely because it did not feel the need to practice martial virtues or attend to relations with neighboring cities.

67 *Politics* II.10.1272a37, b7, 16.

68 *Politics* II.10.1272b11–14.

69 *He kai delon hos echei ti politeias he taxis, all' ou politeia estin alla dunasteia mallon* (*Politics* II.10.1272b9–11).

70 *Politics* IV.5.1292b5–10.

71 Usually context indicates whether the generic "regime" or the specific "polity" ("republic") is meant, but in certain cases the context fails to resolve the difficulty and may even support the ambiguity. One of the latter cases occurs in the criticism of Crete. There are two possible translations of the sentence quoted above and in n. 69: (1) The Cretan "arrangement has elements of a regime but is not so much a regime as it is rule of the powerful [*dunasteia*]"

(Lord [2013, 55]; cf. *The Politics*, trans. T. A. Sinclair [Baltimore: Penguin Books, 1962], 93; *The* Politics *of Aristotle*, ed. and trans. Ernest Barker [Oxford: Oxford University Press, 1958], 83; and *The* Politics *of Aristotle*, trans. Peter L. P. Simpson [Chapel Hill: University of North Carolina Press, 1997], 67), or (2) the Cretan regime "has a republican element, although it is not actually a republic but rather a dynasty" (*The Politics*, trans. H. Rackham [London: W. Heinemann, 1932], 155, which is similar to Benjamin Jowett's translation in *The Complete Works of Aristotle*, vol. 2, ed. Jonathan Barnes [Princeton: Princeton University Press, 1984], 2019). The first interpretation relates to the Aristotelian position that the extreme form of a regime, particularly a defective regime, is no longer a regime, a settled order of offices and way of life according to law or custom, but individuals ruling for private benefit according to ever-changing whim. The second interpretation suggests that, within the context of their politics, the Cretans' oligarchic party is so strong that the form of government approaches the dynastic or most extreme form of oligarchy rather than the moderate mixture of oligarchy and democracy found in the regime called polity. The point seems to imply that the Cretan regime wanted (or should want) to be a republic, but fails.

72 *Demos.*

73 *Stasis.*

74 *Politics* II.11.1272b30–34.

75 *Hupothesin*, or "presupposition."

76 *Politics* II.11.1273a4–6.

77 *Politics* II.11.1273a13–30.

78 *Politics* II.11.1273a38–39.

79 Pangle (2013, 93).

80 *Politikoteron . . . kai demotikoteron*, meaning "more favorable to the people," the *demos*.

81 *Politics* II.11.1273b8–15.

82 *Politics* II.2.1261a32–37.

83 *Politics* II.11.1273b5.

84 *Politics* II.11.1273b13–17. Cf. Simpson (1998, 127).

85 *Politics* II.11.1273b18–24.

86 Politics IV.1.1288b22–28. Cf. Fred D. Miller's argument in *Nature, Justice and Rights in Aristotle's* Politics (Oxford: Clarendon, 1997), 191, 253.

87 Mary P. Nichols, *Citizens and Statesmen: A Study of Aristotle's* Politics (Lanham, Md.: Rowman & Littlefield, 1992), 46.

88 As one example, Nichols uses Aristotle's criticism of the ephorate. Aristotle acknowledges that it may have saved the Spartan regime by giving the many a share of power, but it shows a flaw in Lycurgus' founding because he failed to anticipate the need for such an institution. Nichols emphasizes Aristotle's remark that the ephorate arose not "through the legislator" but "by chance" (*dia tuchen* [*Politics* II.9.1270b17–20]) so Lycurgus gets no credit for the necessary balance of the many against the few (Nichols [1992, 119]: "Human beings overcome the chaos of chance through the deliberative choices of those options that give permanence to their lives. This is the teaching of Aristotle's *Politics*"). To make sense in the context, "by chance" in this statement must mean the original lawgiver did not think of it when the laws were first devised, but it cannot mean that some irrational, inexplicable event created the institution. Someone *thought* of a board of overseers, probably in response to disaffection among Spartiates who were not accorded much influence over the ruling Senate. It was not that a statesman did not exert reason: a decision was made, led or backed by Theopompus (*Politics* V.11.1313a25–28), in response to the situation on the ground, a decision that moved the original aristocracy/oligarchy toward polity by incorporating a democratic element. Someone deliberated and accomplished just what Aristotle

recommends in Book IV.9. That the ephorate later became "tyrannical" (II.9.1270b14–15) suggests that Theopompus' reasoning was not perfectly prescient and, therefore, a further effort at balancing is required. Aristotle even hints at what could be done: give the ephorate auditing powers over the Senate, but adjust the eligibility requirements for the former and expand the common messes or change the property laws to diminish the temptation for the politically influential to succumb to bribery. In other words, rebalance the oligarchic and democratic elements. He does not recommend changing the education to produce more virtuous citizens (though he does seem to recommend changing the educational system to include the women).

89 Pangle (2013, 86–88).

90 *Politics* II.10.1272b19–22.

91 Specifically, Davis notes Aristotle's mixture of reason and chance to explain Sparta's status in the fourth century: he observes that "one cannot understand Sparta without taking into account how it understands itself, but its self-understanding is a cause of its turning out differently from what it thinks it is" (1996, 41–43). A lawgiver must think about what he wishes to accomplish, but the means he chooses may not look like the end he seeks, or if they do, the means may achieve the opposite result. The more Sparta focused on producing self-restrained he-men, the more time it spent on war, leaving the women, untrained and sick of deprivation, in charge of the city and moving it toward luxury and vice. Davis sees the lesson here as part of his overall argument that philosophical analysis is both necessary (and necessarily entailed) in politics, but that it must be concealed, and its success in improving a political regime is limited by the nature of human beings and the world they inhabit. Aristotle criticizes Sparta's lawgiver for specific failures with regard to the education of women (cf. Robert C. Bartlett, "Aristotle's Science of the Best Regime," *American Political Science Review* 88, no. 1 [1994]: 146). It is interesting that Plutarch's account of Lycurgus' Sparta, one in which Plutarch admits he is cherry-picking the historical record and implies he is idealizing the regime, emphasizes the rigorous training of the women and their roles in supporting the moderation and manliness of the men (Plutarch, *Lives*, "Lycurgus," 14–15), the property transfer laws, and the encouragement of child-bearing, but Plutarch also knows that no statesman can be so careful as to anticipate all consequences (*Politics* III.16.1287a23–28, b18–29).

Moreover, Davis' line of analysis suggests that the implementation of any political goal often needs to be concealed behind what appears to be its opposite: to protect the military virtue of the men, Sparta should have spent more time on the education of its women; the institutional restraints that force citizens to live moderately produced an overwhelming desire for living immoderately. Finally, these suggestions for the lawgiver make a curious mixture: include the women in the educational scheme, tinker with the property laws to keep estates from becoming either too large or too small (which might require a wrenching land redistribution), and rethink the public incentives to produce more children. These questions point to the bigger question of the extent to which *a statesman* can achieve such reforms and the extent to which the citizen body must decide for itself that reform is necessary: whether the citizen body be persuaded by reason alone to act contrary to what it habitually views as its advantage. (See conclusion.)

92 *Politics* II.12.1273b31–37. Lord notes that Aristotle does not say to whom he refers as supposing Solon to be "an excellent legislator" (2013, 59, n. 117). Perhaps it is merely a popular (in both senses of that term) opinion in Athens. Yet, Lord also refers to Aristotle's later praise of Solon and of some of his legislation at 3.11.8–9 and 4.11.15.

93 Pangle (2013, 97–98).

94 *Politics* II.12.1274a3–21. With these warnings in mind, it is interesting that Aristotle makes not only what a modern political scientist might call policy recommendations, but also reform proposals concerning the ruling offices of the Spartan regime: the original aristocratic aspirations are rightly tempered by the ephorate, tempered indeed to such an extent that the regime is no longer an aristocracy. Because the *demos* demands a voice in political decisions, the ephorate "holds the regime together." Because the senate is peopled with senile and corrupt men who have received no successful education in virtue, it requires audit by another body, and Aristotle all but recommends the auditing body be the ephorate. The senate's aristocratic qualities are also corrupted by the process of self-nomination. Sparta illustrates two important pitfalls of a serious attempt to institute an aristocracy: the difficulty of providing over time the requisite complement of virtuous men for rule and the immanent possibility of their corruption if they are not watched by another political authority (*Politics* II.9.1270b14–26, 36–1271a18).

2: CITIZENS, RULERS, AND THE LAW

1 *Politics* III.5.1278a15–34.
2 *Politics* III.7.1279a38–39.
3 Only in a city (*polis*) ordered by a regime (*politeia*) can there be a governing body (*politeuma*) (*Politics* III.6.1278b10–14).
4 *Politics* III.6.1278b15–30. Cf. I.2.1252b27–1253a3, 29–30.
5 Cf. *Politics* III.9.1280b38–40.
6 *Politics* III.6.1278b33–37.
7 *Politics* III.6.1279a18–22.
8 *Politics* III.9.1280a32–34.
9 *Politics* III.6.1279a9–13.
10 Cf. Barker's account of the distinction between "normal" and "perverted" regimes (1958, 113, n. V).
11 *Republic* 346e–347a. All of *Politics* III.6 appears to be a response to Socrates' argument against Thrasymachus at *Republic* 341b–347e. Using the same analogies as Socrates, Aristotle shows that Socrates' comparisons between the political ruler, on one hand, and the gymnastic trainer, doctor, and pilot, on the other, lead him to an erroneous view of the political relationship. Considered strictly, the trainer, the doctor, and the pilot are athlete, patient, and sailor accidentally. Insofar as they are the rulers in the training, medical, or sailing relationships, they are the clear superiors and their orders are as law. They only become engaged in a fully common effort like politics when they take their places among the ruled, exercising, being diagnosed, or worrying about whether the ship will arrive at its destination. None of these well-trained persons would consent to take orders from their inferiors, but they would also not deign to take the difficult job of ruler without some compensation—wages or honors of some sort. There is nothing in the relationship, apart from this compensation, that would cause them to choose the ruler's position. They are not paternal, in the sense that a father does not ask wages for ruling the household well, but they are even farther from a position of equality with the ruled.

Aristotle is aware of the avenues of argument suggested by the analogy between arts and politics. If a ruler is the master of an art, Socrates argues, he derives no benefit from the art itself, but acts only to perfect that of which he is master. Aristotle rejects the analogy, at least insofar as it suggests this conclusion. Thrasymachus chooses to compare rulers and shepherds, showing that the art of sheepherding serves the sheep only in order eventually to serve the shepherd—at his dinner table. Of course Aristotle rejects this argument when he distinguishes politics from slavery, and when he rejects Thrasymachus' much-vaunted tyrant.

12 Cf. the criticism of Carthage, *Politics* II.11.1273a21–b7.

13 This remark parallels the earlier mention of Jason, who "did not know how to be a private individual" and said "he was hungry, except when he was a tyrant" (*Politics* III.4.1277a24–25).

14 *Politics* II.7.1267a14–16.

15 For the restriction of slaves to the satisfaction of material necessities, see *Politics* I.4 and 7, and for the vast desires of a tyrant for pleasures without pain, as opposed to justice or the life of virtue, see II.7.1267a2–9.

16 *Politics* III.8.1279b20–1280a6. Aristotle might not be able to place the United States in his scheme of six regimes because the poor are few and the well-off many. It turns out, however, that in the best republics as well as the best democracies and oligarchies, the extremes of poverty and wealth are minorities and those who are comfortable and self-reliant are the majority.

17 Although later the military does not appear so prominent in a republic, its presence is felt, especially in the emphasis on ruling and being ruled and on the necessity for training in both.

18 Cf. Publius' observation in Federalist 10 (Hamilton et al. [2000, 10.56]).

19 *Politics* III.9.1280a25–35.

20 *Politics* III.9.1280b5–7.

21 *Politics* III.7.1279b3–5.

22 For an extensive development of the relation between military virtue and free societies, see Wendell John Coats, Jr., "Armed Force and Political Liberty," in *The Activity of Politics and Related Essays* (Selinsgrove, Pa.: Susquehanna University Press, 1989), 121–32.

23 *Politics* III.9.1280a35–36.

24 *Politics* III.9.1280b6–8, 31–34. Cf. Jaffa (1963, 104–5), on the necessity, but insufficiency, of economics to the understanding of political life. Also, in *Politics* III.1–4, Aristotle insists that a citizen have a type of virtue in order to be able to serve the regime, yet it need not be understood as virtue entire, required only of the ruler of the best regime. He is careful to attach the qualifier "political" to the term "virtue" in that discussion.

25 *Politics* III.9.1280a31–b7, 38–40. An illuminating essay by Anthony Kronman argues that Aristotle's description of the bond among citizens is akin to that between friends and, further, that between brothers. By overlooking Aristotle's strong arguments against Socrates that a city is quite different from a household or a man, however, Kronman misses a crucial dimension of the argument: the lawmaker cannot expect citizens to be fraternal, to love and trust all other citizens as brothers, nor to feel as warmly toward each other as "true or perfect friends," which entails the intimate, reciprocal love of virtuous, and equally virtuous, human beings (Kronman, "Aristotle's Idea of Political Fraternity," *American Journal of Jurisprudence* 24 [1979]: 131–32, 137–38; cf. *Nicomachean Ethics* VIII.2–3). Although Aristotle surely sees the citizen bond as something like friendship, he is not sanguine that such a wide-ranging friendship bond can be created and sustained, for it does not come to be naturally as among brothers, nor does it enjoy the careful nurturing of intimately acquainted and good people.

Aristotle's arguments in Book II against certain aspects of Plato's *Republic* address the issue of friendship in politics. *Philia*, the love between friends or between family members, does promote a desire to be together and to act for the sake of one another. Some type of this love should obtain among the citizens of a regime, and yet it is threatened with dilution by the communal scheme, the forced family, of the *Republic* (*Politics* II.3.1261b33–1262a6; *Republic* 464d–465c). Genuine affection cannot be purchased wholesale. One must believe that the object of one's love is in truth, not merely by law, "one's own" and "dear" (*Politics* II.4.1262b7–23). Though Aristotle sees the need for citizens to take an interest in the merits of their fellows, at least to be able to decide on their worthiness for office and at best to promote the common effort of living the good life, he does not suggest that they could ever know all the other citizens well enough to be true friends, i.e., to consider them "their own" or to determine that they are lovable. Thus free human beings are liable to resist a law insisting that they consider all citizens brothers. Friendship among citizens cannot be imposed from above, but must grow out of acquaintance and mutual assistance, encouraged by well-enacted laws.

26 Prominent writers at the time of the American founding were aware that the transition from the Articles of Confederation, in essence a treaty of alliance among thirteen sovereign states, to the Constitution, a national government, would require the development of an affection among three million fellow citizens of the Union. Americans' attachment to each other and to the whole may have been forged and sustained temporarily by the war for independence, but surely it was waning in the period of economic hardship that followed. For these political essayists, as for Aristotle, this affection naturally includes a concern with the public virtues of one's fellow citizens.

27 *Politics* II.5.1263a37–b8.

28 *Politics* III.9.1281a1–8.

29 *Politics* III.4.1276b29–33 *et passim.*

30 It is only in the account of the best regime of Book VII that Aristotle advances the claim that no one should be harsh toward strangers, "nor are magnanimous persons savage in their nature, except toward those behaving unjustly." For good political reasons, it seems, a regime could describe its enemies as unjust to its citizenry, in hopes of rousing their ardor to defend themselves, even when the enemy is not, strictly speaking, unjust. (Cf. *Politics* V.8.1308a24–30, where the importance of making far-away dangers seem imminent is argued.) The simply best regime can perhaps afford the luxury of discouraging harshness if it can produce genuinely magnanimous men, an aspiration not attributed to the political regimes.

31 *Politics* III.10.1281a19–22.

32 *Politics* III.10.1281a27–33.

33 *Politics* III.7.1279a26–38. Further, the danger of faction is said to be present in any non-democratic regime, if the many are not given some authority (III.11.1281b25–30). It is not clear in this section, however, whether Aristotle considers this danger greater than that of having the many rule over the few best (III.11.1281b38–1282b14).

34 *Politics* III.11.1281a33–34.

35 *Politics* III.11.1281a40–b2. The defense of the virtues of the middle class as rulers appears only after their characteristics are described in some detail. Jaffa calls these arguments for the claims of the many to rule "in a sense the culminating theoretical analysis of the entire book, and of the entire *Politics*" (1963, 105).

36 *Politics* III.11.1281b1–9. Barker draws an interesting distinction between this argument in behalf of the aesthetic judgment of the many acting together and the argument of the *Laws* to the effect that the many are the worst judges of the theater (1958, 127–28, n. Y; cf. Plato, *Laws* 700e–701a).

37 Aristotle elaborates on an education in the liberal arts in *Politics* VIII, esp. 2–3 and 5–7, which suggests a very high standard of amateur music and art appreciation not attainable by those who must work for a living.

38 *Politics* III.11.1281b2–15. At III.16.1287b25–36, a monarch's "intention" is the coordinating factor for the many eyes, ears, feet, and hands of his advisors. The coordination of many eyes, ears, feet, and hands could also be the definition of an army—the military virtues again enter the picture of a well-ordered multitude.

39 *Politics* III.11.1281b15–21. Cf. Jaffa's interpretation of the two oaths in this section of Book III (1963, 107–8).

40 Cf. *Nicomachean Ethics* II.1 for Aristotle's account of the role of training and habituation in the development of the virtues.

41 Aristotle never describes an educational scheme to train this multitude to be good citizens in the regime they control. Throughout the *Politics*, references to the laws suggest their educative function: both by court proceedings and formal punishments, but rather more by their attention to the citizens who are rewarded with honors and offices, the laws set a standard for citizens to emulate.

42 *Politics* III.11.1281b22–26. What is meant by "the greatest offices" is not explicit, but in the case of Carthage they were generals and kings. The types of offices would surely differ with the regime, but these represent examples. The argument thus far regarding the strictly political regimes indicates that kingship would not be appropriate here, unless it were combined with more widely distributed offices. At III.11.1282a29–32, general and treasurer are said not to be appropriate offices for those from the lowest assessments and of any age, but these are not even "the greatest offices."

43 Cf. the account of Solon's reasons for democratizing the election and audit processes—"If the people did not even have authority over this, they would be enslaved and an enemy to the regime" (*Politics* II.12.1274a15–18).

44 *Politics* III.11.1281b35–39.

45 *Politics* III.11.1282a14–16.

46 The architecture analogy may also suggest that results, and not techniques, are the prime criteria of a good statesman. Citizens judge rulers by the actions they perform in office. The prudence necessary for good rulership cannot be displayed in any other forum.

   Aristotle also likens politics to architecture in the first section of the *Nicomachean Ethics*. Putting the two passages together, it is possible to sketch Aristotle's view of the relationships between these arts. The true architect in politics would be the founder of the regime, the person who first delineates the ruling offices and describes the characteristics of the necessary materials, the citizens. In this analogy, the person who will live in the structure does not choose the architect, but takes up residence in a house of another's design. The carpenters who actually build the house and the household manager who keeps it in good condition under the rubric of the architect's plans are the rulers who take the responsibility of high office and the citizens who act to preserve their regime, attend the assembly, or sit on a jury. If one knows how to behave in a political order, one need not know as much as or be as good as the original founder to live in the regime and preserve it, as long as the foundations are well laid, the materials solid, and the construction sound.

47 *Politics* III.11.1282a25–27.

48 *Politics* III.11.1282a34–37.

49 In an assembly or a council, unlike a jury, a "harmonizing principle" may be required to lead the whole to a sensible judgment about the common good. That Aristotle often points to the tendency of democratic assemblies to be swayed by demagogues suggests that he may be less sanguine in his faith in the many than he appears here. Book IV suggests that it is only under a moderate regime, which instills principles of obedience to law and the just treatment of all free persons, that any multitude may safely be given authority over some great issues.

50 William T. Bluhm emphasizes Aristotle's praise of the many to the exclusion of his reservations, and thus too hastily takes it to an extreme. He argues that Aristotle's simply best regime is some sort of democracy (Bluhm, "The Place of the 'Polity' in Aristotle's Theory of the Ideal State," *Journal of Politics* 24, no. 4 [1962]: 747). James Wilson, among other

American founders, seems to understand Aristotle's task here: speak as generously as possible about the virtues of the ordinary citizen in order to give him or her an appreciation for the contributions he or she has made and/or can make to the community (James Wilson, "Oration on the Fourth of July" [1788], in Sheehan and McDowell [1998, 508]).

51 *Politics* III.11.1282a38–40.

52 Since even good regimes can bring about their own downfall by being too exclusive, "well-enacted laws" also seem to require the popular institutions Aristotle has been discussing: a well-enacted aristocracy, e.g., should have a popular assembly or court system, or should allow the many to elect or at least to audit the few who take higher office.

53 Justice as a particular virtue is that which governs the relations between human beings. In *Nicomachean Ethics* V, it is composed of distributive, corrective, and reciprocal justice.

54 It is likely that Aristotle did not choose his examples of irrelevant criteria at random. Surely height (a "stately" build) and beauty played a large role in some political decisions in his day as they obviously do in ours. Cf. two retired American presidents reflecting on the role of beauty in the creation of an aristocracy: John Adams to Thomas Jefferson, 2 September 1813, National Archives Founders Online (NAFO), http://founders.archives.gov/documents/Jefferson/03-06-02-0374; and Thomas Jefferson to John Adams, 28 October 1813, NAFO, http://founders.archives.gov/documents/Jefferson/03-06-02-0446.

55 *Politics* III.12.1282b30–1283a11.

56 Cf. *Politics* III.4 for the necessity of prudence in a good ruler, and *Nicomachean Ethics* VI.5.8–11 for its rarity and the need of political office for its full exercise.

57 Manuscripts differ as to whether this word is *politike* or *polemike*.

58 See also Bartlett (1994, 147–48).

59 *Politics* III.13.1283a31–38. See Jaffa (1963, 114).

60 *Politics* III.13.1283a38–40. Cf. the discussion of the sense in which perfect justice includes all the other virtues at *Nicomachean Ethics* V.1.1129b25–1230a1, 8–13.

61 *Politics* III.13.1283a23–26.

62 The wealthy's claim to authority grounded on ownership of the land necessary to support the city seems to hold water, but Aristotle punctures this argument with one short phrase: "The wealthy [have a claim] because they have the greater part of the territory, and the territory is something common." In some sense, the land belongs to the whole city, and it is within a regime's purview to decide who holds it and under what circumstances. If a regime were to adopt Aristotle's suggestion in Book II that property be held privately and put to common use, it is possible that individual wealth would have less significance. Neither does Aristotle seem to believe wholeheartedly in the trustworthiness of the wealthy. See *Politics* IV.8.1293b38–39.

63 Aristotle states the claim of the well-born as being "more particularly citizens than the ignoble," though he has just argued that functioning in deliberation and judgment makes one a citizen, and entitlement to do so is distributed differently in the various regimes. His remark that "good birth is honorable at home among everyone" reminds us of his criticism of the defenders of the custom condemning the vanquished to enslavement. Greek noblemen often opined that their nobility should be recognized universally, but that noble foreigners are only noble at home (*Politics* I.6.1255a32–40). Honoring noble families stems from a belief that good qualities are perpetuated through generations, but only a few pages later, Aristotle will argue that an excellent king, whose children could be expected to have all that is necessary for a good upbringing, cannot be sure his sons will be fit to replace him. The claims of noble families are open to serious doubt (III.15.1286b22–27).

64 *Politics* III.13.1283a29–42.

65 *Politics* III.13.1283b13–35, 1284a3–15.

66 *Politics* III.13.1283b1–9.

67 *Politics* III.13.1283b38–42.

68 *Politics* III.13.1284b15–17, 29–32. Note the use of the expression "a certain political justice [*ti dikaion politikon*]" as distinguished from "simple justice [*haplos dikaion*]" at III.13.1284b24–25. To attempt to give the simply best person his or her due, and therefore to relegate all others to the subordinate position that is their due, would be simply just but politically dangerous in all but the simply best regime. That political danger translates into a certain injustice in Aristotle's view: that which destroys the regime cannot be just (III.11.1281a19–22).

69 *Politics* III.17.1288b2–6. Cf. VII.4.1325b34–40.

70 *Politics* III.14.1285b29–33, III.17.1287b37–1288a6.

71 *Politics* III.16.1287a28–41, b8–15.

72 Cf. *Politics* VII.14.1332b16–27.

73 *Politics* III.14.1285b29–33.

74 *Politics* III.16.1287a26–29.

75 *Politics* III.15.1286a21–26.

76 He reiterates this point later (*Politics* III.17.1287b40–1288a5).

77 As Barker suggests (1958, 151, n. GG). See *Politics* IV.13.1297b2–28, near the end of the discussion of the middle-class republic, where a short history of warfare runs parallel to the development first of oligarchies and then of the polity, as the necessary weapons become more widely held and affordable. The key for a republic is to set the property assessment for citizenship where those participating in the regime are more numerous than those who are not. Cavalry service was a shortcut way to determine the pool of rich men to be included in an oligarchy, and hoplite status is an easy way to define the citizens of a republic.

78 When Aristotle refers to those naturally ruled by aristocracy as "ruled in accordance with the rule that belongs to free men," he suggests that they participate in some political office from time to time. They cannot be treated slavishly and they are not the aristocrats, but political freedom seems to require some honor or opportunity to take political office. In a properly ordered aristocracy, such office could not be binding on the best men, for justice requires that they not be ruled by their inferiors, or that the whole not be ruled by a part.

79 In *Politics* V, Aristotle confirms the suggestions made in this section when he takes up the causes of *stasis*, or factional conflict, and the possible modes of its prevention in the various types of regime. Early in Book V, Aristotle claims that factions form because opinions differ, especially opinions about justice. By stating that in imperfect, partially unjust regimes, factions form on the basis of competing imperfect notions of justice (V.1.1301a35–39), Aristotle perhaps implies that in a just regime, no seditious factions would form. At any rate, there is a suggestion in this passage that a vital link exists between stability and the justice of the regime. This suggestion is more fully spelled out in Book IV's account of the most stable polity.

Factious activity may issue in different results. In all cases, however, the changes to which Aristotle refers in describing *stasis* rest on disagreements over arithmetic versus proportional equality and inequality (V.1.1301b26–29, 35–39). The prevalence of oligarchy and democracy is a result, says Aristotle, of their simple principles of justice and equality, and the greater availability of the men to fill their criteria. As Aristotle noted in Book III, democrats assert that equality respecting free birth confers on all free men equality in desert. There are usually many free persons in a city. In the same manner, there are usually more wealthy citizens in a city than virtuous or exceptionally well-born citizens, and they generally espouse the oligarchic principle that the superior in wealth should be treated as superior in all respects. Either principle unmitigated creates an unstable regime (V.1.1302a2–7). Either principle is both unjust simply and provocative to the group it excludes.

Aristotle declares that "the regime [*politeia*] made up of the middling elements . . . is the most stable of regimes of this sort," i.e., oligarchy, democracy, and the middle regime (V.1.1302a14–15). In other words, Aristotle, relying on discussions that appear in Book III, concludes in Book V that no other of the political regimes can achieve both the stability that rests on justice and the justice appropriate to a city of differing sorts of free people as well as the regime of the middling element. It is this middle regime that occupies center stage in Book IV.

3: The Best Regime

1 *Politikos*: also "statesman," "politician," "political ruler."
2 *Politics* IV.1.1288b22, 25–27.
3 For a counterargument, cf. Bluhm (1962).
4 *Kreitton* probably refers to greater numbers (thus, perhaps, greater strength, but not superiority in virtue) in this passage, since in the next passage quoted, IV.9.1294b36–39, Aristotle uses the word *pleious*, clearly denoting greater quantity, in its stead.
5 *Politics* IV.12.1296b15–17, IV.9.1294b37–39, IV.11.1296a7–9.
6 Though it remains questionable whether politics itself is an art like medicine, architecture, or playing music, Aristotle expresses no doubts here about whether political *science* is an art. He likens it not only to gymnastic training, but also to "medicine, shipbuilding, the making of clothing, and every other art" (*Politics* IV.1.1288b19–21).
7 *Politics* IV.1.1288b35–1289a2.
8 *Politics* IV.1.1288b10–12, 21–37.
9 *Politics* IV.1.1289a11–20.
10 *Politics* IV.2.1289b12–27.
11 *Politics* IV.1.1289a15–18.
12 Aristotle does not imply that these lists of genera are exhaustive, unlike the original list of six species. Though he says that it is necessary to know all types and varieties in order to have a comprehensive knowledge of the founding and preservation of regimes, he does not present the varieties according to a simple scheme (one, few, or many rulers with good or bad aims), but rather according to his observations of the needs of political life.
13 This account points back to Book I with its emphasis on households as the primary parts of a political order.
14 *Politics* IV.3.1289b27–1290a7.
15 Ernest Barker, *The Political Thought of Plato and Aristotle* (New York: Russell & Russell, 1959), 476–77.
16 *Politics* IV.11.1296b2–12.
17 *Politics* IV.3.1290a24–26.
18 See Lord's note on the interpretation of this puzzling passage (2013, 101, n. 15).
19 The second list of a city's vital parts bears many resemblances to the list that appears in Book VII in the account of the simply best regime, where Aristotle is quite explicitly developing a hierarchy of types of rule with aristocracy at the top. *Politics* VII.3–4.
20 Criticizing Socrates' first city in the *Republic*, Aristotle does not simply adopt Glaucon's view, that it is a city of sows due to its lack of "relishes," but he takes a similar tack in subordinating the provision of necessities to action for the sake of what is not necessitated, for the sake of the noble (*Republic* 369b–371c). Socrates definitely places great emphasis on need as the basis of his first city in speech—see esp. 369b–d, 370b–c.
21 *Republic* 373b–374d.

22 *Politics* IV.4.1291a22–24.

23 It is a puzzle why Aristotle praises the leisure of the rulers of the best regime of Books VII and VIII, while arguing that the lack of leisure of the middling property holders is their greatest title to rule in a democracy, oligarchy, or republic. If the legislator is aiming for the best regime simply and has reason to believe that that regime is achievable in his city, then he must accord the rulers the leisure sufficient for their oversight of all aspects of the common life in pursuit of excellence for all. If, on the other hand, the legislator cannot hope to institute such a regime, he must go almost to the other extreme and empower those who have only limited leisure time for participation in ruling and being ruled. If those who are not simply virtuous rule, there must be limits on their power; the most effective limit might be their private interest, which would limit the time available for politics. If the ruling element cannot devote all of its time to serving the common good, it is better that it devote as little as possible while performing the essential offices.

As a rule, when discussing both the best regime simply and the more practicable regimes, Aristotle is less concerned with what one does to acquire one's daily bread than with the amount of leisure time the occupation allows him and what activities are pursued while he is at leisure. Cf. *The Politics of Aristotle*, trans. W. L. Newman (Oxford: Clarendon, 1887):

> The main reason why the first kind of democracy (if we group the first two together) is the best is that the ruling class in it is most like that which rules in the polity and least disposed to make itself sole sovereign. It has property enough to distract its attention from politics. It is too busy with its own affairs, and the rural section of it lives too far from the central city, to attend frequent meetings of the assembly, and it cares more for its business pursuits than for a life of politics and office holding; thus it rules in subordination to the law and leaves a share of power to the magistrates, the chief citizens, and the rich, and does not sacrifice them to demagogues. It does so not only because it has not leisure enough to do otherwise, but because it would not wish to do otherwise if it could. (IV.xxxvii–xxxviii)

24 *Politics* IV.4.1291b38–1292a7.

25 Elbridge Gerry warned of the "evils" of an "excess of democracy" in an early speech at the Constitutional Convention, given on May 31, 1787: "The people do not want [lack] virtue, but are the dupes of pretended patriots" (Gerry, *The Debates on the Adoption of the Federal Constitution in the Convention held at Philadelphia in 1787*, ed. Jonathan Elliot, vol. 5 [Philadelphia, 1836], http://oll.libertyfund.org/titles/madison-the-debates-on-the -adoption-of-the-federal-constitution-vol-5). In the same speech, Gerry summarizes his position in a fashion quite consistent with Aristotle's argument, as long as it is remembered that he uses "republican" to label what Aristotle would call "democratic": "He had, he said, been too republican heretofore: he was still, however, republican, but had been taught by experience the danger of the levelling spirit."

26 *Politics* IV.4.1292a4–38.

27 *Politics* IV.6.1292b26–30.

28 *Politics* IV.6.1292b32–34.

29 *Politics* IV.5.1292a39–42.

30 *Politics* IV.6.1293a13–14, 20–21.

31 Newman calls this most moderate oligarchy the rule of a fairly numerous "bourgeoisie" rather than an oligarchy (1887, I.495–96). In volume IV, Newman states quite plainly, "Aristotle has, in fact, in the polity, in which the moderately well-to-do class rules, a standard for estimating the merits of the varieties of oligarchy and democracy (6 [4].11, 1296b4sqq). Those varieties are best which most nearly approach the polity" (IV.xx). He

goes on to characterize Aristotle's general argument for polity as heavily influenced by his confidence in the "moderately well-to-do class" and questions whether the claim for these citizens on the grounds of their level of wealth can have "more than a broad and general truth." As will become clearer, the amount of property is less significant in itself than its capacity to influence the character of its owner. Ultimately Aristotle rests his confidence in the moderately virtuous more than the "moderately well-to-do."

32 *Politics* IV.11.1296a3–5.

33 *Politics* I.7.1255b16–20, III.6.1278b34–1279a10. Cf. Jaffa's explanation of the reason Aristotle calls this regime by the generic name: "It is no accident that the specific and the generic name should coincide in the case of the regime which is a compound of democracy and oligarchy. For it coincides in the case of the one regime which balances the two elements which alone cannot be combined. Polity is a kind of virtuous mean between the two vicious extremes constituted by the claims of wealth and poverty" (1963, 118).

34 *Politics* III.7.1279a37–39, IV.7.1293a38–40.

35 *Politics* IV.7.1293a38–b2.

36 Sparta: *Politics* IV.7.1293b15–20, II.9.1270b20–26; Carthage: II.11.1272b30–33, 1273a4–b23.

37 Cf. *Republic* 450c–d, 499b–c, 540d–e; *Politics* IV.1.1288b21–24, IV.11.1295a29–31, VII.3.1325b33–38 *et passim*.

38 *Politics* IV.8.1293b23–27, 34.

39 If the republic is indeed an uncommon regime, not even listed by many thinkers among the regimes, the source of these "customary" views is obscure. Apparently, whatever usage *politeia* has in referring to a specific regime, it is confused.

40 *Politics* IV.8.1293b35–36.

41 *Politics* IV.8.1293b38–39. As if this were not sufficient condemnation, Aristotle will attack the "overly wealthy" openly in Chapter 11 as tending to arrogance and baseness "on a grand scale," and thus to "acts of injustice" (1295b6–12).

42 The "forms of so-called polity which incline more toward oligarchy" were listed by Aristotle earlier among the merely "so-called aristocracies" (*Politics* IV.7.1293b8–21).

43 *Politics* IV.8.1294a1–9.

44 *Politics* IV.8.1294a25–29. Cf. Barker (1959, 477).

45 According to Newman, "The reason why the mixture of oligarchy and democracy in polity results in a normal form is that it mixes them in a special way. It fuses them in such a manner as to avoid the excesses and the one-sidedness of both, and to hit the mean between them." Yet Newman doubts that polity mixes rich and poor so much as it mixes oligarchy and democracy. There is not much power given to the poor, except in judicial functions. He admits, on the other hand, that the middle class would have to support the poor sometimes to balance out the oligarchs. The influence of the less wealthy will depend completely on the property assessment necessary for citizenship (1887, IV.xv).

46 *Politics* IV.9.1294b15–19. It is here that the republic is first associated with "the mean [*to meson*]" as a principle of political life.

47 *Politics* IV.4.1291b30–38, IV.6.1292b25–33.

48 *Politics* IV.9.1294b35–39.

49 Cf. *Politics* II.5.1264b6–25, III.11.1281b22–34.

50 *Politics* IV.10.1295a1–4. Cf. IV.2.1289b2–3.

51 *Politics* IV.10.1295a15–24.

52 The claim that the middle-class republic is a species of the regime called polity or republic is supported by the following considerations: The polity/republic is first described systematically in III.8 as "when the multitude governs with a view to the common advantage,"

making military virtue preeminent (1279a38–b4). At the beginning of Book IV, mention is made of the need to examine the "best regime that circumstances allow," in addition to the regime "most fitting for all cities," though neither is named (1288b24–27, 34–35). Chapters 7 through 9 are concerned with the regime called polity/republic, defined as a mixture of oligarchy and democracy, admitting both rich and poor to political participation. Since most cities are said to be either oligarchic or democratic (IV.11.1296a23–24), this general outline is likely to be recommending the best regime that the circumstances of most cities allow. If a regime is either an oligarchy or a democracy, it could be most improved and most easily improved by instituting a mixture of the two. This recommendation culminates with the claim that the republic is self-sustaining and not prone to sedition due to its satisfaction of all the parts of the city.

In contrast, Chapters 11 through 13 explicitly depict the best regime and way of life "for most cities and most human beings" (1295a25–26). In this regime, as in the republic, most can participate. Rather than the obvious methods of mixing the wealthy and the needy mentioned in Chapter 9, this regime balances the extremes by giving the greatest influence to a "middling element," the self-supporting citizens of moderate means. Whereas the earlier republic is supposed to resemble both oligarchy and democracy and resembles neither, this "political partnership that depends on the middling sort" avoids the dangers of resembling either, so it more closely approaches a genuinely good regime, one whose stability rests on its own merits and does not derive from threats to the parties out of power: "That the middling sort is best is evident. It alone is without factional conflict, for where the middling element is numerous factional conflict and splits over the regimes occur least of all" (1296a7–9). Thus, this regime *best* satisfies the two primary requirements of a republic, a well-mixed ruling body and political stability. Because, in Aristotle's experience, the middle class is not ordinarily large, the regime through the middle cannot be defended on exactly the same ground as the simple republic—it is not the most readily available, decent arrangement "that circumstances allow." Rather, the regime through the middling elements is the best way of life for the political animal.

Richard Robinson summarizes the arguments for the view that, he says, "interpreters all conclude" regarding the identity of the mixed republic and the regime of the middle class. To summarize his summary: (1) Aristotle would not recommend two different moderate regimes in the same book without saying which is preferable. (2) Both are rare phenomena. (3) The simple polity is a "middle regime" also, since it is midway between oligarchy and democracy. (4) The first two principles of mixture presented in IV.9 were meant to produce a "middle," or a mean between two extremes, so that all republics are regimes of the middle. (5) All regimes must be classed as one of the six fundamental types and the middle regime is clearly closest to the republic (Aristotle, *Aristotle's Politics: Books III and IV*, trans. Richard Robinson [Oxford: Clarendon, 1962], 100–101).

Although these points are sound for the most part, the status of the two regimes may be clarified by working on an assumption that the republic of the middle class is not meant to be identical with all polities, but that it is a type, and the best type, of polity. Five points illustrate this distinction in the status of the two regimes. (1) In a sense, Aristotle does say which regime is preferable by saying which is more accessible to most cities—the mixture of oligarchy and democracy—and yet describing another moderate regime which is not so readily possible for all and calling it "the best" (IV.11.1295b35–40, 1296a7–12, b2–3). Some sort of republic is the best way of life most cities can hope to achieve, but the middle-class republic is the best form of republic. These regimes are different in one important respect, in what modern social science might call the "social character" of the predominant part of the city, but both are respectable moderate regimes and Aristotle recommends both, though to different kinds of city.

(2) Both regimes are indeed called rare, but the rarity of the middle regime, as a species, is emphasized even more than that of a republic in general. Whereas the latter is rare because reformers and founders have not yet discerned the wisdom of modifying the common regimes of democracy and oligarchy into the more stable and more just republic, the former is rarer because it requires the circumstance that the part of the citizen body possessing moderate amounts of property be quite large (IV.7.1293a38–40, IV.11.1296a22–40). (3, 4) In Chapter 9, moreover, Aristotle gives a number of suggestions for methods of mixture to arrive at a regime between oligarchy and democracy. Giving authority to a class neither oligarchic nor democratic, though not mentioned in the list, is indeed another possible method, but one requiring this special circumstance. In this way, the regime of the middle takes on the character of an unusual hybrid.

Finally, (5) if the regime "through the middle citizens" is closest to a republic, it is not identical to the mixture of rich and poor discussed in Chapters 8 and 9, but is a certain special type, just as the most moderate democracy of IV.4 is not at all identical to, but is rather a rare species of, the generic democracy outlined in III.7–9.

53 *Ton meson bion.*

54 *Politics* IV.11.1295a36–b1.

55 *Nicomachean Ethics* II.1.

56 *Nicomachean Ethics* II.6.1107a6–8.

57 *Politics* IV.11.1295b3–5.

58 The longer account of liberality in *Ethics* IV.1 suggests that the liberal quality of an act depends on the materials available to the actor, so that a man of moderate means could be just as generous in proportion to his possessions as a more wealthy man. Indeed, it is difficult for a truly liberal person to remain wealthy, even if he should begin so, or to become wealthy, if he should not (IV.1.1120b7–20, X.8.1178b34–1179a33). For the further development of the meaning of liberality in Greek thought, see Leo Strauss, "The Liberalism of Classical Political Philosophy," in Strauss, *Liberalism Ancient and Modern* (New York: Basic Books, 1968), 28–29.

59 *Nicomachean Ethics* I.8 and 9, IV.2 and 3, and X.8.

60 *Politics* II.7.1266b29–31. Cf. Newman (1887, IV.xvii and 212, n. 5).

61 To confirm the strangeness of Aristotle's statement here, see *Nicomachean Ethics* II.1: In the midst of a discussion of virtue as learned by habit and not acquired either by nature or from teaching, Aristotle says,

> As regards those things we must learn how to do, we learn by doing them . . . by doing just things we become just; moderate things, moderate; and courageous things, courageous. What happens in the cities too bears witness to this, for by habituating citizens, lawgivers make them good, and this is the wish of every lawgiver; all who do not do this well are in error, and it is in this respect that a good regime differs from a base regime. (*Nicomachean Ethics* 1103a32–b6)

62 Cf. Plato, *Laws* 679b–c, where the Athenian Stranger claims that the men after the flood had neither too much nor too little, and thus "neither insolence nor injustice, nor again jealousy and ill will, come into being there."

Though the practice of virtue becomes habitual or second nature to the good man, it is necessary to take a reasonable view of each situation in order to act as reason determines (*horismene logo*; *Nicomachean Ethics* II.6.1106b36–1107a2, VI.2.1139a31–37). Cf. II.9.1109a24–30 and VI.1. Reasonableness, a good trait in itself, is the basis for the practice of the other virtues listed here as well as the ethical virtues discussed in the *Ethics*. For a good summary of Aristotle's middle-class virtues, see Nichols (1992, 97).

63 *Politics* IV.11.1295b15–18.

64 *Politics* IV.11.1295b21–23; see also 1296a1–5.

65 One of the criticisms of Socrates' best regime was that he tries to encourage an empty, formal friendship among the citizens by decreeing that all property be held in common. While making this criticism, Aristotle acknowledges the importance of *philia* for political harmony yet insists that privately owned property, shared freely with friends, is the only sure way to encourage true liberality among free men (Rubin [1989, 110–14]).

66 *Bouletai*: also "means," "professes," "tends."

67 *Politics* IV.11.1295b25–28.

68 *Politics* IV.11.1295b29–33. See also I.8.1256b30–39, II.7.1267b3–9.

69 *Politics* II.7.1267a22–36.

70 See Mary Pollingue Nichols, "The Good Life, Slavery, and Acquisition: Aristotle's Introduction to Politics," *Interpretation* 11, no. 2 (1983): 171–83, esp. 171, 178–82, in which is laid out Aristotle's ambiguous attitude toward the benefits and dangers of commerce for politics and the good life as it appears in the latter half of Book I.

   In his accounts of the republic, Aristotle makes no mention of the need for public or private slaves, and reasonably so, for the citizens are self-supporting and are not meant to have abundant wealth or leisure.

71 *Politics* IV.11.1295b5–11.

72 *Politics* IV.13.1297b1–2, 12–24.

73 *Politics* IV.13.1297b2–28.

74 If courage is implied in this account of middle-class virtues, however, it is not the truest form of the virtue, but rather the best of the false forms, a citizen soldier's courage, which might need the threat of disgrace to spur him to battle. *Nicomachean Ethics* III.6–8.

75 *Nicomachean Ethics* II.7, III.10, IV.1, 4, V.1–3.

76 Jaffa argues that "polity . . . is inherently moderate by the moderation of the interests of the middle class. But this moderation only resembles virtue, it is not virtue itself. It makes men disposed toward virtue, however, and aristocracy can begin to flourish upon the soil of polity" (1963, 119).

77 This political order relies on middling rather than great wealth. The account of the optimum private property holdings for a citizen stands in stark contrast to the *Republic*'s communal property and represents an alternative that will not fall prey to Socrates' errors. In Book II Aristotle criticizes Socrates' Kallipolis in several ways, but the criticisms may be boiled down to two: First, common property, far from curing faction and supporting a complete unity in the city, as Socrates hopes, will likely sow dissension and create a troublesome serf or slave class. Second, rather than enforcing generosity and other virtues, common property deprives the citizens of the opportunity to be free in a quintessential sense, free to practice liberality.

   The formula Aristotle arrives at in *Politics* II—private property put to some common uses—discourages dissension and encourages the political virtues necessary for a workable association among free men, as is also argued in the defense of the republic. In response to the defects of Socrates' property arrangements, Aristotle argues for "the approach that prevails now—if reinforced with good character and an arrangement of correct laws" as "more than a little better. For it would have what is good in both. . . . For it [property] should be common in some sense, yet private generally speaking." Like the property arrangements in the middling republic, this plan is defended by reference to self-reliance and a certain modest virtue: private property reduces contention about who is responsible to work the land—each owner does his own work or has his own servants; owning one's property also encourages one to work harder to prosper the more; most important, if the property owners have good habits and are trained and encouraged by good laws, they will develop liberality with their goods (*Politics* II.5.1263a21–29; Rubin [1989, 111–12]).

In line with Aristotle's criticisms of the Athenian Stranger's regime in Plato's *Laws*, moderate virtues receive stress in *Politics* IV.11, while magnificence does not. Liberality is the virtue that provides the benefits of common use without laws enforcing common ownership. A great fortune is necessary to practice magnificence, e.g., endowing massive public projects. Such a fortune is not necessary to the practice of virtues that sustain the city in essential ways. Reciprocal justice only requires that one return what is done for one; generosity or liberality requires giving to one's friends such things as are appropriate to the friend's needs and to one's ability to provide. The proportionality of the gift or reciprocation is much more significant than the size. In contrast, the competitiveness and excess that can follow from lavish displays of wealth, however publicly useful, are not appropriate to a stable political life.

78 *Politics* IV.11.1295b35–37.

79 *Politics* IV.13.1297a5–6.

80 *Politics* IV.11.1295b40–1296a4.

81 *Politics* IV.11.1295a25–30.

82 Davis (1996, 65–74). Bartlett argues persuasively that Aristotle, while fully conscious of the divine basis of all Greek cities, intends to introduce a political science that rests upon human reason. That Aristotle makes only oblique reference to the revelations these regimes' founders placed at the basis of their laws is an acknowledgment of the tension between political needs: the universally felt necessity of linking the laws to divine will (to encourage obedience and political unity) vs. the observable fact that the gods (or, more likely, the human lawgivers who attributed the laws to the gods) made mistakes. Aristotle's *Politics* is an argument that such mistakes can be repaired by human thought and action. When he advises political regimes to become as much like a middle-class republic as possible, he does not advise them to eschew the former laws altogether—i.e., he does not dispense with any previously claimed, politically salutary connection to the gods of the city (Bartlett [1994, 152–53]).

83 See Pangle's argument, culminating in this suggestion: "The more we ruminate on Aristotle's advocacy of the middle class and its regime(s), the more we may find, in this advocacy, not so much a recurrence to past Greek experience as a proposal for a yet insufficiently realized potential that may profit future eras in which republicanism will be reborn, and to which Aristotle's writing may penetrate" (2013, 191–92).

84 *Politics* IV.11.1296a17–21.

85 *Politics* III.11.1281b22–34. See Aristotle, *Constitution of Athens* 5–12, where Solon is characterized as a "mediator" and it is claimed that "by wealth and education he belonged to the middle class." His moderate measures are also described and then summarized as follows:

> The common people had believed that he would bring about a complete redistribution of property, while the nobles had hoped he would restore the old order or at least make only insignificant changes. Solon, however, set himself against both parties, and while he would have been able to rule as a tyrant if he had been willing to conspire with whichever party he wished, he preferred to antagonize both factions while saving the country and giving it the laws that were best for it, under the circumstances. (*Aristotle's* Constitution of Athens *and Related Texts*, trans. Kurt von Fritz and Ernst Kapp [New York: Hafner, 1950], 11.2)

86 *Politics* IV.13.1297a15–24. Charondas is said at II.12.1274b5–9 to be a better draftsman of laws than Aristotle's contemporaries because of his precision, but in the later passage here discussed, he is accused of using an ill-advised device against the poor. His status as a member of the middling element could not certify that his laws would be excellent, but he had some good qualities as a legislator.

87 In *Nicomachean Ethics* VI, Aristotle calls legislative prudence the highest exercise of prudence. The essence of the quintessentially political rational virtue is to establish the fundamental principles and aims of a political regime. This account would suggest that in Solon, Lycurgus, and Charondas, the middle class has produced the best of political men. Nonetheless, their superiority is measured in political terms, not in terms of the highest virtue of human reason (wisdom) and the highest pursuit of the human mind (philosophy), nor even in terms of the leisure pursuit of the ruling class of the simply best regime (music).

88 Nichols (1992, 98).

89 *Politics* IV.11.1295b35–39, 1296a10–17, 23–31, IV.12.1297a1–6.

90 *Politics* IV.11.1295b40–1296a3, 21–28.

91 *Politics* IV.11.1295a25–26.

92 See esp. *Politics* VII.4–11 for the stringent prerequisites of the city "constituted according to prayer." Pangle reaches the conclusion that Aristotle is promoting "a middle class consciousness—and this is arguably his most emphatic therapeutic intervention in participatory republican politics" (2013, 192 and 305, n. 33).

93 *Politics* IV.11.1296a7–17.

94 *Politics* IV.12.1296b35–1297a10. See also V.9 for further confirmation of this strong endorsement of the middle class to balance the excesses of ordinary oligarchy or democracy:

> Besides all these things, one should not neglect—what is neglected now by the deviant regimes—the middling element; for many of the things that are held to be characteristically popular overturn democracies, and many of those held to be characteristically oligarchic overturn oligarchies. Those who suppose this to be the single virtue pull the regime to an extreme, ignorant that just as a nose that deviates from the straightness that is most beautiful toward being hooked or snub can nevertheless still be beautiful and appealing to look at, yet if someone tightens it further in the direction of an extreme he will in the first place eliminate any moderateness in the part and eventually will go so far as to make it not even appear to be a nose, on account of the preeminence and the deficiency of the opposites (and it is the same with the other parts of the body as well), so this is what results in the case of regimes too. For it is indeed possible for an oligarchy or a democracy to be in an adequate condition in spite of departing from the best arrangement. But if someone tightens either of them further, he will make the regime worse first of all, and eventually not even a regime. (V.9.1309b19–34)

95 *Politics* VII.3.1325b7–10.

96 This is the sense of justice adduced in *Politics* III.6–13. Cf. justice as a particular virtue, described in *Nicomachean Ethics* V.1–5.

97 Newman contrasts Aristotle's mixed constitution with that of Polybius (*The Histories*, trans. W. R. Paton [Cambridge, Mass.: Harvard University Press, 1922–1927], book 6.3.7 and 6.10, http://penelope.uchicago.edu/Thayer/E/Roman/Texts/Polybius/6*.html) and concludes:

> In such a constitution, according to [Polybius], the king is checked by the *demos* and the *demos* by the few, and the whole fabric escapes degeneracy. Aristotle knows nothing of this. He holds that a well-framed mixed constitution is durable not for [this] reason . . . but because its internal equilibrium is perfect; it contents all classes

by giving them a share of power, so that no one of them wishes for another constitution in its place. (Newman [1887, IV.xix] referring to *Histories* 6.4.9.1294b34ff. [cf. 64.13.1297a40ff. and 2.9.1270b21ff.])

John Adams' middling regime has much in common with Polybius' mixed constitution, but he still will derive considerable argumentative force from Aristotle's defense of the middle class and the regime in which it predominates (see chap. 4, p. 94).

98 Cf. *Nicomachean Ethics* V.4.1132a19–24 on the judge as mediator and the mediate as the just. Of the kinds of justice Aristotle lists in *Ethics* V, the middling republic seems characteristically to practice rectificatory, distributive, and reciprocal justice, but not justice entire or the justice that is identical with the whole of virtue.

99 *Politics* IV.13.1297b1–2, 5–7. It is not clear that this insistence on ownership of armaments forces the regime to become an oligarchy or even an oligarchic polity (cf. Pangle [2013, 193]). First, Aristotle immediately reminds that the ruling body must be larger than "those not sharing." Second, the ownership of weaponry is not the only criterion; the citizen of this regime must exhibit sufficient self-control not to act arrogantly toward the poor, but rather to support them. Given his earlier analysis of the differences between the middle class and either the rich or the poor, Aristotle is suggesting that even if they owned weapons, the very wealthy would not make good citizens of this regime because of their tendency to arrogance and complete disdain for the indigent. If the very rich are not included, the city has a ruling body situated in the middle and larger than the rich and the poor added together. And, third, at 1297b21–29, Aristotle observes that early regimes in which the heavily armed warriors held political sway were then called democracies, not oligarchies, and Aristotle calls them polities/republics, stressing the importance of their middling element. I do not see the dark lines in Aristotle's descriptions of the middling regime that Pangle draws, arguing for "deep inner tensions" among the goals of "rule by elected reputable nobles, predominance of a middle class that arbitrates and solidifies a balanced mixture of rich and poor, and citizenship defined by the requirement to keep and bear arms" (194). The discussion of these goals, however, does suggest a "starting point for an authentic Aristotelian analysis of the American founders' regime."

100 In this respect, Aristotle's republic resembles the modern constitutional republics whose principle is to limit the possible injustices the regime could commit. The most famous instance of such an argument is Federalist 51 (Hamilton et al. [2000, 51.330–35]), but the point is made very clearly by several members of the Constitutional Convention who argued for the need for a strong second legislative branch that would uphold the interests of the wealthy (and well born and virtuous) against the "turbulence and follies," indeed "the fury" of the "democratic" lower house: Edmund Randolph on 31 May, John Dickinson on 7 June, Alexander Hamilton on 19 and 26 June, Gouverneur on July 2. *The Records of the Federal Convention of 1787*, ed. Max Farrand (New Haven: Yale University Press, 1911), http://oll.libertyfund.org/titles/1785.

101 *Politics* IV.14.1298a4–6.

102 *Politics* IV.14.1298b5–12.

103 *Politics* IV.14.1298a35–40.

104 *Politics* IV.14.1298b27–41.

105 *Politics* IV.14.1298b14–26.

106 *Politics* IV.15.1299a25–27.

107 *Politics* IV.14.1297b35–40.

108 Cf. Aristotle's criticisms of Hippodamus' very specific suggestions for improving politics in *Politics* II.8.

109 *Politics* IV.12.1296b39–1297a6.

110 *Politics* IV.9.1294b36–39, 11.1296a7–9.

111 In the *Nicomachean Ethics*, though Aristotle lauds those who pursue the wisdom that reflects the divine in humanity and renders a man self-sufficient, he makes clear that few are fit for such a lofty pursuit and fewer still reach the self-sufficiency that makes political life unnecessary. Within the *Ethics*, he actually pays vastly more attention to the ethical virtues practiced in political society. Courage, moderation, practical wisdom, and justice are virtues practiced by an individual who seeks his own happiness, but they are only virtues because they are aimed outside the individual at the "noble." In the process, they foster cooperation within an interdependent whole.

4: "HAPPY MEDIOCRITY"

1 John Adams, "Thoughts on Government" (1776), NAFO, http://founders.archives.gov/ documents/Adams/06-04-02-0026-0004.

2 *Politics* V.8–9.

3 John Adams, *A Defence of the Constitutions of Government of the United States of America Against the Attack of M. Turgot in his Letter to Dr. Price, Dated the Twenty-second Day of March, 1778* (1787; repr., London: John Stockdale, 1794).

4 Adams (1794, III.166).

5 This salutary socioeconomic mobility is taken for granted in the 1780s, but some—James Madison, Nicholas Collin, even Alexander Hamilton—already saw its potential as a double-edged sword.

6 This is effectively the subtitle of Adams' *Defence of the Constitutions*.

7 James M. Barnard, *A Sketch of Anne Robert Jacques Turgot: With a Translation of His Letter to Dr. Price*, trans. Helen Billings Morris (Boston: G. H. Ellis, 1899), 49–59, https://archive .org/details/sketchofannerobe00barn.

8 Adams (1794, I, Letter XXVI *et passim*).

9 Adams (1794, III.158). Compare Adams' discussion of what can be known about constructing a successful republic in his 1776 letter later labeled "Thoughts on Government."

10 *Nicomachean Ethics* I.3, VI.

11 Niccolo Machiavelli, in his dedicatory letter prefacing *The Prince*, provides one very clear example of the charge Adams makes against political philosophers (Machiavelli, *The Prince*, trans. Harvey C. Mansfield, 2nd ed. [Chicago: University of Chicago Press, 1998], 3–4). His treatise rests upon the redefinition of both kingship and republican government to make a case for "new" modes and orders in politics, modes and orders that will benefit a very few of great "*virtù*" at the expense of all the rest. Since these new modes are founded on this significant inequality and are not characterized by ruling and being ruled in turn, Machiavelli's politics does not meet Aristotle's minimum qualifications for politics properly understood.

12 After his initial definition of the city, Aristotle takes up the misuse of the term "king" to mean a political ruler at the beginning of *Politics* I (1252a8–16), while many passages of Books II, III, IV, and V show Aristotle wrestling with his use of *politeia* to denote a specific type of popular regime.

13 Adams (1794, III.159). During the Constitution's ratification process in each of the states, a process that is only beginning as Adams publishes this work, the prominent writers and debaters use the term "republic" in many different ways. (Consider "Cato" II; "A Citizen of America"; "Brutus" I; "Publius" in Federalist 6, 9, 10, 14, 39, 43, and 49; "Americanus" III; "Agrippa" IV; "An Old State Soldier" [cf. Bernard Bailyn, ed. *The Debate on the Constitution: Federalist and Antifederalist Speeches, Articles, and Letters During the Struggle over Ratification*. 2 vols. (New York: Library of America, 1993)]; Charles Pinckney at the South

Carolina Ratifying Convention; James Madison at the Virginia Ratifying Convention; and Melancton Smith at the New York Ratifying Convention.) Almost everyone agreed that a republic is the most just form of government and the form for which the people and the circumstances of America are suited and, thus, that it should be the goal of the new fundamental law for the Union. Few could agree on what the term meant or what a true republic required. Examining these disparate arguments reveals that Adams was right at least in this observation that "prejudice, habit and passions" become attached to definitions of the term on all sides.

Publius' description of the science of politics as "improved" implies that it had risen above past shortcomings (Hamilton et al. [2000, 9.47–49]). It may be that the Federalist science of politics tries to overcome the influence of "prejudice, habit and passions" in every system's foundation by incorporating them in the system's operation, i.e., by giving them a significant role in balancing each other's influence in an admittedly tumultuous political arena. The Anti-Federalists seem to disagree that the new notion of an intentionally conflict-ridden republic is an improvement.

14 Adams (1794, III.171). If we assume that by "only aristocracies and democracies and mixtures of these," Adams is using "aristocracy" to mean rule of the wealthy, or what Aristotle would term "oligarchy," this mixed citizen body would be consistent with Aristotle's simple definition of polity (*Politics* IV.7–9), a regime that could suffer from a lack of decisiveness, a quality Adams associates with "executive power." See chap. 3.

15 Adams (1794, III.159–60). One might harmonize the two aspects of this definition by thinking of *Politics* III.11, the argument concerning the rule of law vs. the rule of men, together with IV.9–11, which associates good governance with a regime in which "law rules."

16 Adams (1794, III.160–61).

17 Adams translates into English extensive passages from Angelo Portenari, *Della Felicità di Padova* (Padua: Pietro Paulo Tozzi, 1623), a work included in the John Adams Library at the Boston Public Library (https://archive.org/details/dellafelicitdi00port).

18 Adams (1794, III.162).

19 John Patrick Diggins cites Adams' rejection of Aristotle's aristocratic regime but does not acknowledge Adams' appreciation of Aristotle's political wisdom in assessing the middling class. Diggins takes Adams' conflation of Aristotle's two discussions of the parts of a city at face value (Diggins, *John Adams*, The American Presidents [New York: Times Books, 2003], 58).

20 Adams (1794, III.168).

21 *Politics* I.2.1253a2–19.

22 Adams (1794, III.163).

23 Aristotle's disparaging remarks about merchants and artisans in other parts of the *Politics* may be explained by his inexperience with artisans who could have occupied a middling economic or social class because of the physical demands of their occupation, and by what he observed as the tendency of merchants, who make money from money, to succumb to the vicious attitude of oligarchs, i.e., to believe that wealth, not the good life it supports, is the goal of economic exchange and of the political order (*Politics* I.8–11). If he thought merchants and artisans could support themselves in the way he sees the middle class, especially farmers, doing, without becoming envious, arrogant, or seditious, he might have reconsidered.

24 Cf. also III.393 for a reiteration of Aristotle's responsibility for excluding farmers, mechanics, and merchants from citizenship, this time in Arragon [*sic*], in the context of a book-length letter on Nedham's "The right Constitution of a Commonwealth, examined."

25 Adams (1794, III.163–65).

26 Adams (1794, III.165). Cf. Jefferson's educational scheme to raise such geniuses from obscurity to political service (chap. 6).

27 Adams (1794, III.167). It seems impossible that Adams, stationed in England, could have read Federalist 10 and 14, published by Hamilton and Madison under the pseudonym Publius on 23 and 30 November 1787, respectively, before writing this part of the *Defence*. Letter III is not dated separately, but the concluding letter of this lengthy volume is dated 26 December 1787. We now know that Madison made the arguments of Federalist 10 and 14 at the Constitutional Convention, but those debates were supposed to be kept secret.

28 Jefferson wrote: "Mankind are more disposed to suffer while evils are sufferable, than to right themselves by abolishing the forms to which they are accustomed. but when a long train of abuses & usurpations, begun at a distinguished period, & pursuing invariably the same object, evinces a design to subject them to arbitrary power, it is their right, it is their duty, to throw off such government" ("Professor Julian Boyd's reconstruction of Thomas Jefferson's 'original Rough draught' of the Declaration of Independence before it was revised by the other members of the Committee of Five [including John Adams] and by Congress," in *The Papers of Thomas Jefferson*, vol. 1: *1760–1776*, ed. Julian P. Boyd [Princeton: Princeton University Press, 1950], 243–47, http://www.loc.gov/exhibits/declara/ruffdrft.html).

29 According to Joyce Appleby:

> Adams was shocked by the Turgotists' shallow grasp of political truths. He could only regard them as closet philosophers, woolly minded idealists, men totally without any conception of man as a political animal. Feisty, combative, dogmatic John Adams saw clearly the threat which such notions of political equality and unchecked legislative power could do to the world. He deplored their hopes of achieving political purity simply by eliminating the special privileges of the nobility, their belief that human nature would respond freshly to a new political environment, their unwarranted assumption that the future could be radically different from the past. (Appleby, "The New Republican Synthesis and the Changing Political Ideas of John Adams," *American Quarterly* 25, no. 5 [1973]: 582).

30 Adams (1794, III.290–95).

31 Adams and Montesquieu both advocate an independent judiciary, though it is not included in this balancing act. It is not that the judicial functions should be subsumed under one of these three divisions of the political order, but that the judiciary should not be used as a political balancing factor at all. It should be independent of the political branches in order to keep judicial decisions free of political influence. Adams and Montesquieu would argue that using judicial power to balance the political ambitions of the executive or legislative branch undermines the integrity of judicial decisions.

32 In a single assembly, "there is, in short, no possible way of defending the minority, in such a government, from the tyranny of the majority" (Adams [1794, III.291]). Therefore,

> the rich ought to have an effectual barrier in the constitution against being robbed, plundered, and murdered, as well as the poor; and this can never be without an independent senate. The poor should have a bulwark against the same dangers and oppressions; and this can never be without a house of representatives of the people. But neither the rich nor the poor can be defended by their respective guardians in the constitution, without any {an?} executive power, vested with a negative, equal to either, to hold the balance even between them, and decide when they cannot agree. (294)

33 A Citizen of New Jersey, *Pennsylvania Evening Post,* 30 July 1776, in *The Founders' Constitution,* vol. 1, ed. Philip B. Kurland and Ralph Lerner (Chicago: University of Chicago

Press, 1987), chap. 15, doc. 19, http://press-pubs.uchicago.edu/founders/documents/
v1ch15s19.html.

34 Jason, the tyrant of Pharae, "said he was hungry except when he was a tyrant" (*Politics* III.4.1277a25–26).

35 The Citizen, apparently a member of the middle class, proffers an assessment of the middle class' general reputation, that "many" of its members are less avaricious than the wealthy. This conclusion might be drawn from the fact of their status—if they were more avaricious, they would be more wealthy. It is more likely another manifestation of the phenomenon Aristotle observes, that the middling element practices more self-restraint and keeps its desires more under rational control than the rich.

36 The Citizen acknowledges the argument for a property requirement to assure independence in the voter—i.e., to assure that he will not be inclined to sell his vote because of a lack of knowledge of the political landscape reinforced by financial need. Compare an argument made quite baldly by John Adams in his letter to James Sullivan, dated 26 May 1776:

> Is it not . . . true, that Men in general in every Society, who are wholly destitute of Property, are also too little acquainted with public Affairs to form a Right Judgment, and too dependent upon other Men to have a Will of their own? If this is a Fact, if you give to every Man, who has no Property, a Vote, will you not make a fine encouraging Provision for Corruption by your fundamental Law? Such is the Frailty of the human Heart, that very few Men, who have no Property, have any Judgment of their own. They talk and vote as they are directed by Some Man of Property, who has attached their Minds to his Interest. (NAFO, http://founders .archives.gov/documents/Adams/06-04-02-0091)

At the other extreme, recall Aristotle's observation of the reasons the wealthy cannot be trusted with rule over free people: the rich, strong, and well-born tend to be arrogant, they do not control their passions with reason, and they strive for mastery, rather than ruling and being ruled in turn (*Politics* IV.11.1295b10–23).

37 Benjamin Franklin, "Information to Those Who Would Remove to America," September 1782, in *The Complete Works, in Philosophy, Politics, and Morals, of the late Dr. Benjamin Franklin* (London: J. Johnson and Longman, Hurst, Rees, & Orme, 1806), III.399, at Project Gutenberg, http://www.gutenberg.org/files/48138/48138-h/48138-h.htm.

38 Franklin (1806, III.400).

39 Franklin (1806, III.401). This section of the letter suggests that American religious toleration may well rest upon judging God by the standard of usefulness, that His superiority is grounded in utility. Such a formulation points toward the arguments of Benjamin Rush and Nicholas Collin for the utility of religious education in the formation of law-abiding citizens. Further, if God is not to be admired for his longevity in ruling office, so to speak, Franklin implies that neither should scions of ancient families be granted political influence without proving their usefulness in the present.

40 E.g., Franklin humorously anticipates the twenty-first-century cry for safe spaces:

> Bad Examples to Youth are more rare in America, which must be a comfortable Consideration to Parents. To this may be truly added, that serious Religion, under its various Denominations, is not only tolerated, but respected and practised. Atheism is unknown there; Infidelity rare and secret; so that persons may live to a great Age in that Country, without having their Piety shocked by meeting with either an Atheist or an Infidel. (1806, III.408–9)

Cf. Jerry Weinberger, *Benjamin Franklin Unmasked: On the Unity of His Moral, Religious, and Political Thought* (Lawrence: University Press of Kansas, 2005), 244–46.

41 Franklin (1806, III.408).

42 Franklin (1806, III.408).

43 Franklin, "Queries and Remarks respecting Alterations in the Constitution of Pennsylvania," 1789, in *The Writings of Benjamin Franklin*, ed. Albert Henry Smyth, 10 vols. (New York: Macmillan, 1905–1907), 10.58–60.

44 Thomas Jefferson to James Madison, 28 October 1785, NAFO, http://founders.archives .gov/documents/Jefferson/01-08-02-0534. Madison's 1792 remarks in the *National Gazette* on the connections between republican arrangements to combat the excessive influence of factions and moderate property holdings reflect the opinions he shares with Jefferson on this point:

> In every political society, parties are unavoidable. . . . The great object should be to combat the evil: 1. By establishing a political equality among all. 2. By withholding *unnecessary* opportunities from a few, to increase the inequality of property, by an immoderate, and especially an unmerited, accumulation of riches. 3. By the silent operation of laws, which, without violating the rights of property, reduce extreme wealth towards a state of mediocrity, and raise extreme indigence towards a state of comfort. 4. By abstaining from measures which operate differently on different interests, and particularly such as favor one interest at the expence of another. 5. By making one party a check on the other, so far as the existence of parties cannot be prevented, nor their views accommodated. If this is not the language of reason, it is that of republicanism. (NAFO, http://founders.archives.gov/documents/Madison/ 01-14-02-0176, emphasis Madison's)

45 Cf. T. R. Malthus, *An Essay on the Principle of Population* (1798), edited with an introduction by Geoffrey Gilbert, Oxford World's Classics (Oxford: Oxford University Press, 1993), II.19.

46 NAFO, http://founders.archives.gov/documents/Madison/01-09-02-0017. See also Madison's remarks in the Constitutional Convention, 26 June 1787, in *Notes of Debates in the Federal Convention of 1787 Reported by James Madison*, ed. Adrienne Koch (Athens: Ohio University Press, 1966), 194.

47 Cf. Thomas Jefferson, *Notes on the State of Virginia*, ed. William Peden (Chapel Hill: University of North Carolina Press, 1954), Query XIV.146–49.

48 Jefferson restates this opinion in one of his 1813 letters to John Adams: A "government adapted to" the "Man of these states" (as opposed to the "old world") takes account of the fact that

> here every one may have land to labor for himself if he chuses; or preferring the exercise of any other industry, may exact for it such compensation as not only to afford a comfortable subsistence, but where-with to provide for a cessation from labor in old age. Every one, by his property or by his satisfactory situation, is interested in the support of law and order. And such men may safely and advantageously reserve to themselves a wholesome controul over their public affairs, and a degree of freedom, which in the hands of the Canaille of the cities of Europe, would be instantly perverted to the demolition and destruction of every thing public and private. (Jefferson to Adams, 28 October 1813, NAFO, http://founders.archives .gov/documents/Jefferson/03-06-02-0446)

49 Elbridge Gerry, 31 May 1787, in Koch (1966, 39). See also Alexander Hamilton's fairly Aristotelian denunciation of "pure democracy" at the New York Ratifying Convention (21 June 1788):

> It has been observed by an honorable gentleman [John Williams], that a pure democracy, if it were practicable, would be the most perfect government. Experience has proved, that no position in politics is more false than this. The ancient democracies, in which the people themselves deliberated, never possessed one feature of good government. Their very character was tyranny; their figure deformity: When they

assembled, the field of debate presented an ungovernable mob, not only incapable of deliberation, but prepared for every enormity. In these assemblies, the enemies of the people brought forward their plans of ambition systematically. They were opposed by their enemies of another party; and it became a matter of contingency, whether the people subjected themselves to be led blindly by one tyrant or by another. (NAFO, http://founders.archives.gov/documents/Hamilton/01-05-02-0012-0011)

50 Brutus 1, 18 October 1787, quoting Montesquieu (*The Spirit of the Laws*, I.xvi), in *The Complete Anti-Federalist*, ed. Herbert J. Storing with the assistance of Murray Day (Chicago: University of Chicago Press, 1981), 2.9.11.

51 Aristotle's account in *Politics* I.8–10 of the use and abuse of business expertise suggests that he does not consider money-making corrupting in itself, but that one must make money for the sake of something higher than the accumulation of wealth. A merchant could avoid the aspects of moneymaking that Aristotle labels "vulgar," "slavish," and "ignoble."

52 When proposing the amendments that would eventually compose the Bill of Rights, Madison follows the protection of "the people" in "applying to the Legislature by petitions, or remonstrances, for redress of their grievances" with the protection of "the right of the people to keep and bear arms," which he links with "a well armed and well regulated militia being the best security of a free country." That he makes a point of allowing for a conscientious objector to be released from "bearing military service in person" suggests that Madison believes both that military virtue is not the only ground for citizen virtue and, in consonance with Aristotle, that citizenship in a republic is ordinarily and properly associated with military service (*Annals of Congress*, First Congress, First Session, 451, http://memory.loc.gov). See also John Adams' insistence upon militia service "with very few exceptions," so that the citizenry may be better trained and armed (1776).

53 In Koch (1966, 183–84).

54 Koch (1966, 184–86).

55 In *The Debates in the Several State Conventions on the Adoption of the Federal Constitution, as Recommended by the General Convention at Philadelphia in 1787*, vol. 4, ed. Jonathan Elliot (Washington, 1836).

56 Michael P. Zuckert and Derek A. Webb note that, though Smith and his Anti-Federalist associates rejected the political recommendations of Adams that sounded too much like "the British model," they "adopted much from his sociology and psychology" (Zuckert and Derek, introduction to *The Anti-Federalist Writings of the Melancton Smith Circle* [Indianapolis: Liberty Fund, 2009], xxx–xxxi).

57 Note that Smith's "natural aristocracy" differs from that of Jefferson, which may account for the difference in their attitudes toward its ascendancy in free society. Jefferson's natural aristocracy, examined in detail in chapter 6, does not include those who rise to prominence solely upon their wealth or prestigious family name.

58 In Storing (1981, 6.12.15–18).

59 Hamilton et al. (2000, 55.356).

60 Smith was, indeed, asked this question two days later. See Livingston's challenge, chap. 6.

61 In Storing (1981, 6.12.18), emphasis added.

62 In Storing (1981, 6.12.15), emphasis added.

63 In Storing (1981, 2.8.95–99). See Zuckert and Webb (2009, introduction) for an incisive analysis of the affinities among Smith, Brutus, and Federal Farmer, who are, they argue, likely only two people.

64 Adams (1794, I.xiv).

65 In Storing (1981, 2.8.97).

66 In Storing (1981, 2.8.62).

67 Adams (1794, III.161–62, 166).

68 Thomas Jefferson leads the founding generation in the use of *aristoi*, the root, meaning "best," of the term aristocracy. As is developed in chapter 6, Jefferson and others wrestled with the problem that the term "aristocracy" had long since been highjacked by the wealthy and "well-born" to mean little more than the rule of the wealthy and the progeny of influential families, which, for Aristotle, is the defective regime "oligarchy." Assuming no one would wish to be ruled by the *worst* people in a community, the founder(s) of a new regime should pay close attention to the meaning of "the best" when applied to republican ruling officials.

5: Citizen Virtue

1 Christopher Duncan raises the issue of distinguishing the liberal from the republican parts/parties in the founding era. He sees the Anti-Federalists as defining "republican" in terms of community governance, let it go where it will, fostering participation for its own sake. The Federalists, on the other hand, being liberals, would sacrifice this notion of republicanism (knowingly) for the sake of stability in the long term. Duncan contends that both parties knew that it was impossible to create a meaningful community of millions of people (Duncan, *The Anti-Federalists and Early American Political Thought* [DeKalb: Northern Illinois University Press, 1995], chaps. 4–5).

2 Centinel I, October 1787, in Storing (1981, 2.7.9). See the 1776 New Hampshire Constitution for an example of the explicit reliance of a state government upon a broad franchise in a populace wise enough to choose representatives with "social virtue and knowledge" in annual elections (Charles S. Hyneman and Donald S. Lutz, *American Political Writing during the Founding Era: 1760–1805* [Indianapolis: Liberty Fund, 1983], I.397–99).

Historical scholarship suggests that the letters of Centinel were written by Samuel Bryan under the strong influence of his father, Judge George Bryan, "the principal leader" of the Pennsylvania Anti-Federalists (Herbert J. Storing, ed., *The Anti-Federalist: Writings by the Opponents of the Constitution*, selected by Murray Dry [Chicago: University of Chicago Press, 1981], 7, 12, nn. 4–5).

3 Hamilton et al. (2000, 39.240).

4 Jeremiah Atwater, "Sermon before the Governor and Legislature of Vermont," 1801, in Hyneman and Lutz (1983, II.1173, 1175–78). See also the 1778 "Election Sermon" of Phillips Payson for another example of a Christian divine linking "exorbitant wealth" with "evils and mischief," because "wealth and riches will have their commanding influence." He recommends a "general diffusion of knowledge" among all the people so as to "beget and increase . . . public virtue" by alerting all to the corruption of self-interest (in Hyneman and Lutz [1983, I.528]).

5 *Politics* III.9.

6 Hamilton et al. (2000, 39.244–45).

7 *Politics* III.9, esp. 1280a31–b12.

8 In 1774, when the Continental Congress composes an appeal to the people of Quebec to join the rebellion against British tyranny, political leaders are assuming a consensus on the need for government to encourage moral qualities and "liberal sentiments" in the citizenry. The letter praises the "grand right" of a free press, the importance of which consists,

besides the advancement of truth, science, morality, and arts in general, in its diffusion of liberal sentiments on the administration of Government, its ready communication of thoughts between subjects, and its consequential promotion of union among them, whereby oppressive officers are shamed or intimidated, into more honourable and just modes of conducting affairs. (*Journals of the Continental Congress, 1774–1789*, ed. Worthington C. Ford et al., 34 [Washington, D.C.: Government Printing Office, 1904–1937]; repr. in Kurland and Lerner [1987, vol. 1, chap. 14, doc. 12], http://press-pubs.uchicago.edu/founders/documents/v1ch14s12 .html)

The letter also boasts that the system the colonies have instituted "defends . . . the industrious from the rapacious, the peaceable from the violent, tenants from lords."

9 Adams (1794, III.168).
10 "A Landholder" [Oliver Ellsworth], Letter VII, Connecticut *Courant*, 17 December 1787, in *Friends of the Constitution: Writings of the "Other" Federalists, 1787–1788*, ed. Colleen A. Sheehan and Gary L. McDowell (Indianapolis: Liberty Fund, 1998), 483.
11 See, e.g., Benjamin Rush's, Noah Webster's, and Nicholas Collin's education proposals, chap. 6.
12 In Sheehan and McDowell (1998, 484).
13 "Fabius" [John Dickinson], Letter VII (1788), in Sheehan and McDowell (1998, 487), emphasis Dickinson's.
14 [Dickinson], Letter VII (1788), in Sheehan and McDowell (1998, 488).
15 In Sheehan and McDowell (1998, 489).
16 [Dickinson], Letter VIII (1788), in Sheehan and McDowell (1998, 495–96).
17 [Dickinson], Letter IX (1788), in Sheehan and McDowell (1998, 500–501).
18 [Dickinson], Letter IX (1788), in Sheehan and McDowell (1998, 501).
19 Cf. Alexis de Tocqueville's concept of "self-interest well understood," another way of combining rhetorically the benefits of prosperous commerce with an appreciation of one's place in a functioning free society (Tocqueville, *Democracy in America*, trans. Harvey Mansfield and Delba Winthrop [Chicago: University of Chicago Press, 2000], II.2.8).
20 "A Citizen of America" [Noah Webster], "An Examination into the Leading Principles of the Federal Constitution," October 17, 1787, in Sheehan and McDowell (1998, 400). Webster here reveals his understanding of leveling the property holdings of the citizens. He does not suggest "land reform," but rather the redistribution that Jefferson also predicted would follow the abolition of the privilege/practice of entail. He sees it achieving what Aristotle deemed the only advantage of equal property—placing most of the citizenry on a moderate level and teaching the moderation of desires that goes with that social position.
21 In Sheehan and McDowell (1998, 392).
22 [Webster] (1787), in Sheehan and McDowell (1998, 401).
23 [Webster] (1787), in Sheehan and McDowell (1998, 401–2). Webster reiterates the importance of such an electorate in his 1802 speech (in Hyneman and Lutz [1983, II.1236]).
24 Hamilton et al. (2000, 10.56).
25 Webster (1802), in Hyneman and Lutz (1983, II.1229–30), emphasis Webster's.
26 Webster (1802), in Hyneman and Lutz (1983, II.1231).
27 Webster (1802), in Hyneman and Lutz (1983, II.1233).
28 Webster (1802), in Hyneman and Lutz (1983, II.1234).
29 In Kurland and Lerner (1987, vol. 1, chap. 13, doc. 36).
30 Madison, 14 June 1788, in Elliot (1836, 3:380–95).
31 James Wilson, "Oration on the Fourth of July" (1788), in Sheehan and McDowell (1998, 506).
32 Wilson (1788), in Sheehan and McDowell (1998, 505).
33 Wilson (1788), in Sheehan and McDowell (1998, 507), emphasis Wilson's.
34 Wilson (1788), in Sheehan and McDowell (1998, 508).
35 Wilson (1788), in Sheehan and McDowell (1998, 508–9), emphasis Wilson's.
36 In Koch (1966, 177–78).

37 Cf. Brutus' assumption that a large republic must recruit rulers using great honor and emolument "to be the proper objects for ambitious and designing men." The problem then becomes that "such men will be ever restless in their pursuit after them. They will use the power, when they have acquired it, to the purposes of gratifying their own interest and ambition." Honor and power are the inducements to service that are most appealing to the best—meaning most aristocratic—citizens, but they will also tempt those citizens to self-aggrandizement (in Storing [1981, 2.9.20]).

38 In Koch (1966, 179).

39 Compare Federalist 55: "As there is a degree of depravity in mankind which requires a certain degree of circumspection and distrust, so there are other qualities in human nature which justify a certain portion of esteem and confidence. Republican government presupposes the existence of these qualities in a higher degree than any other form." Given that Publius anticipates (in Federalist 49) that the usual state of political life will be characterized by "passions most unfriendly to order and concord," "diversity of opinions on great national questions," and a detrimental "spirit of party," these estimable and confidence-inducing qualities will be sorely tested (Hamilton et al. [2000, 55.359, 49.323–24]).

40 Hamilton et al. (2000, 10.58–59). Recall Webster's arguments concerning an official's "integrity," by which he means taking an independent view from his constituents when necessary.

41 Brutus 1, 18 October 1787, in Storing (1981, 2.9.14).

42 Federal Farmer 7, 31 December 1787, in Storing (1981, 2.8.96, 99).

43 Scigliano opines that the author of Federalist 57 might be Hamilton. Note that Publius here equates liberty with the equal application of the laws to the people and to the legislators. If the United States is far too large to put Aristotelian ruling and being ruled in turn into literal effect, the rulers must at minimum be ruled while they are at the same time ruling by being subject to their own enactments.

6: Securing America's Future

1 Adrienne Koch and William Peden, eds., *The Life and Selected Writings of Thomas Jefferson* (New York: Random House, 1944), 32.

2 See the discussion of Jefferson's educational system below, pp. 164–67.

3 Koch and Peden, *Life and Selected Writings of Thomas Jefferso*, 32.

4 Independence Hall Association, Philadelphia, Pennsylvania, http://www.ushistory.org/declaration/related/pendleton.html.

5 Smith (1788), in Storing (1981, 6.12.15–18).

6 Alexander Hamilton, New York Ratifying Convention, 21 June 1788, NAFO, http://founders.archives.gov/documents/Hamilton/01-05-02-0012-0011.

7 *Politics* I.8–11 concerns the accumulation of money and the material support of the household. Aristotle argues that there are natural limits to the amount of wealth one should seek, limits created by the needs of life to which moneymaking is subordinate. A political order, like a household, should not view moneymaking as an end in itself. See Nichols (1983, 171–83), esp. 171, 178–82.

8 Cf. *Politics* VII.15.1334a25–28: "Moderation and justice [are required] at [times of war and peace], and particularly when [the citizens] remain at peace and are at leisure. For war compels them to be just and behave with moderation, while the enjoyment of good fortune and being at leisure in peacetime tend to make them arrogant."

9 Note that those superior rhetorical skills give unscrupulous power-seekers the capacity to "establish such a system of hopes and fears throughout the state, as shall enable them to carry a majority in every fresh election of the house" (John Adams, *A Defence of the Constitutions of Government of the United States of America Against the Attack of M. Turgot in his*

Letter to Dr. Price, Dated the Twenty-second Day of March, 1778. 1787. Reprint [London: John Stockdale, 1794], 3:284). Rhetoric's demagogic dangers include not only swaying a passionate crowd in the moment, but also setting up a "system" of false expectations and unfounded alarms that produces long-standing perverse effects upon the electorate.

10 Jefferson speculates that a scientific breeding program could more reliably produce talented and virtuous offspring, but he shies away from proposing one for an interesting reason:

> Nature . . . seems to have provided more securely for the perpetuation of the species by making it the effect of the *oestrum* implanted in the constitution of both sexes. And not only has the commerce of love been indulged on this unhallowed impulse, but made subservient also to wealth and ambition by marriages without regard to the beauty, the healthiness, the understanding, or virtue of the subject from which we are to breed. The selecting the best male for a Haram of well chosen females also, which Theognis seems to recommend . . . , would doubtless improve the human, as it does the brute animal, and produce a race of veritable ἀριϛτοι. For experience proves that the moral and physical qualities of man, whether good or evil, are transmissible in a certain degree from father to son. But I suspect that the equal rights of men will rise up against this privileged Solomon, and oblige us to continue acquiescence under the 'Ἀμαυρωϛις γενεος ἀϛτων' [*sic*] ["the degeneration of the race of men"] which Theognis complains of, and to content ourselves with the accidental *aristoi* produced by the fortuitous concourse of breeders. (Jefferson to John Adams, 28 October 1813, in *The Adams-Jefferson Letters: The Complete Correspondence between Thomas Jefferson and Abigail and John Adams*, ed. Lester J. Cappon [Chapel Hill: University of North Carolina Press, 1959; paperback ed., 1987], 387–88)

11 Elliot (1836, II.277–78), as cited in Storing (1981, notes to 6.12.21–22).

12 In Elliot (1836, II), http://www.constitution.org/rc/rat_ny.htm.

13 Hamilton et al. (2000, 10.59). It is in Federalist 10 that Publius also suggests that election of representatives from a wide field serves "to refine and enlarge the public views, by passing them through the medium of a chosen body of citizens, whose wisdom may discern the true interest of their country, and whose patriotism and love of justice will be least likely to sacrifice it to temporary or partial considerations."

14 Hyneman and Lutz (1983, II.756).

15 Robert Coram, "Political Inquiries, to which is Added A Plan for the Establishment of Schools Throughout the United States," 1791, in Hyneman and Lutz (1983, II.784). Chief Justice Warren suggests in his *Brown v. Board of Education* opinion that the public duty to provide education for all citizens only became imperative in the twentieth century, in order to explain why the Court must overturn the doctrine of separate but equal as applied to public schools:

> *Today*, education is perhaps the most important function of state and local governments. Compulsory school attendance laws and the great expenditures for education both demonstrate our recognition of the importance of education to our democratic society. It is required in the performance of our most basic public responsibilities, even service in the armed forces. It is the very foundation of good citizenship. *Today* it is a principal instrument in awakening the child to cultural values, in preparing him for later professional training, and in helping him to adjust normally to his environment. *In these days*, it is doubtful that any child may reasonably be expected to succeed in life if he is denied the opportunity of an education. Such an opportunity, where the state has undertaken to provide it, is a right which must be made available to all on equal terms. (*Brown v. Board of Education of Topeka* [No. 1] 347 U.S. 493, https://supreme .justia.com/cases/federal/us/347/483/case.html, emphasis added)

16 Lorraine Smith Pangle and Thomas L. Pangle note the selectively Rousseauian character of Coram's argument and link his egalitarianism with coercive "governmental authority to . . . break up families and assign to individuals their ways of life" (Pangle and Pangle, *The Learning of Liberty: The Educational Ideas of the American Founders* [Lawrence: University Press of Kansas, 1993], 99–100).

17 Coram (1791), in Hyneman and Lutz (1983, II.788, 795, 805–7). Coram assumes that without public schools, only the rich can provide the means for their progeny to support themselves, i.e., education, thus perpetuating an oppressive social stratification. It is, therefore, a moral imperative for a government that protects property to make it possible for all citizens to acquire property—government must provide education for all and that education must include vocational training. Coram assumes that, if available, parents would willingly take advantage of educational opportunities for their children and that no entity can reliably provide those opportunities for all children but the (state) government (803, 805).

18 In Hyneman and Lutz (1983, II.810–11), emphasis Coram's.

19 Benjamin Franklin, "Proposals Relating to the Education of Youth in Pensilvania" (1749), University of Pennsylvania University Archives and Records Center, http://www.archives .upenn.edu/primdocs/1749proposals.html, emphasis Franklin's.

20 Hugo Grotius published *De jure belli ac pacis* [*On the Law of War and Peace*] in 1625; Samuel von Pufendorf published *De jure naturae et gentium* [*On the Law of Nature and Nations*] in 1672. Both are considered foundational works in the application of moral principle to international law through the natural law.

21 Cf. Pangle and Pangle (1993, 85–86) for an argument that Franklin is here engaged in a Baconian project of supplanting political heroes with "captains of commerce and the argonauts of scientific inquiry and technological innovation."

22 Samuel Adams to James Warren, 4 November 1775, in *The Writings of Samuel Adams*, ed. Harry Alonzo Cushing, vol. 3 (New York: G. P. Putnam's Sons, 1908), 235–37, in Kurland and Lerner [1987, vol, 1, chap. 18, doc. 6, http://press-pubs.uchicago.edu/founders/ documents/v1ch18s6.html.

23 In Hyneman and Lutz (1983, I:700–701). Hyneman and Lutz seem not to have been able to identify this writer, but they speculate that he was a Federalist because he emphasizes the learning of literature rather than the Bible. As they well know, however, Benjamin Rush was a staunch Federalist who endorsed the study of the Bible in public schools, as discussed below.

24 Worcester Speculator 6 (October 1787), in Hyneman and Lutz (1983, I.701), emphasis added.

25 Hamilton (21 June 1788).

26 Hamilton (21 June 1788). See also Federalist 35; Scigliano ascribes this number to Hamilton (Hamilton et al. [2000, 209–13, esp. 212]).

27 Cf. James Wilson (Pennsylvania Ratifying Convention, 4 December 1787), to the effect that it is more important for the representative to know "the true interests" than to know "the faces" of the people. Unlike Hamilton, Wilson argues that a representative's virtue is more important than either form of knowledge, for it is virtue that will carry into effect those interests, presumably as the legislator, not his constituents, understands them (in Kurland and Lerner [1987, vol. 2, art. 1, sec. 2, cl. 1, doc. 12]).

28 Cf. Aristotle's assessment of the relative danger of rich men's vs. poor men's vices:

> Many of those who want to set up aristocratic regimes . . . thoroughly err not only by the fact that they distribute more to the well-off, but also by deceiving the people. For in time from things falsely good there must result a true evil, and the

aggrandizements of the wealthy are more ruinous to the polity than those of the people. (*Politics* IV.12.1297a8–12)

29 Admitting exceptions to their general summary, the editors note that some Federalists railed against the practice of slavery on the grounds of America's "sacred principles," and others, such as Oliver Ellsworth, saw a need for law to punish "gross impieties" and to "induce good habits and educate to virtue."

30 See chap. 5.

31 Noah Webster, "Miscellaneous Remarks on Divizions of Property . . . in the United States" (February 1790), in *A Collection of Essays and Fugitiv Writings on Moral, Historical, Political and Literary Subjects* (Boston: I. Thomas and E. T. Andrews, 1790), 326–32, in Kurland and Lerner (1987, vol. 1, chap. 15, doc. 44), http://press-pubs.uchicago.edu/founders/documents/v1ch15s44.html (retaining one of Webster's attempted contributions to American republican education, his improved spelling).

32 Webster makes the same assumption that Chancellor Livingston made in the New York Ratifying Convention regarding the resentment of wealth, but Livingston considers the likely resentment of wealth a plus, because voters will concentrate on fitness for office instead.

33 Adam Smith's exhaustive treatise on the economic benefits of the division of labor and free markets makes a similar argument for the dangers to the physical and moral capacities of workers and the consequent necessity of publicly supported education. Smith, *An Inquiry into the Nature and Causes of the Wealth of Nations*, ed. Edwin Cannan (Chicago: University of Chicago Press, 1976), V.I.III.2.302–5.

34 Compare the proposition offered in "The Address and Reasons of Dissent of the Minority of the Convention of Pennsylvania to Their Constituents": "That the people have a right to bear arms for the defence of themselves and their own state, or the United States, or for the purpose of killing game; and no law shall be passed for disarming the people or any of them" (in Storing [1981, 3.11.13]).

35 Noah Webster, "On the Education of Youth in America" (1790), in *Readings in American Educational Thought*, ed. A. J. Milson, C. H. Bohan, P. L. Glanzer, and J. W. Null (Greenwich: Information Age Publishing, 2004), 93. He reiterates here the dual roots of a successful republic elaborated in his "A Citizen of America" essay (17 October 1787, in Sheehan and McDowell [1998, 400–402]): both property laws that "give every citizen a power of acquiring what his industry merits"—widespread middling property holdings—and an educational system that "gives every citizen an opportunity of acquiring knowledge and fitting himself for places of trust" (106).

36 Webster (1790), in Milson et al. (2004, 96).

37 Webster (1790), in Milson et al. (2004, 100).

38 Webster (1790), in Milson et al. (2004, 107, 101–2), emphasis Webster's.

39 Webster (1790), in Milson et al. (2004, 98–99).

40 In Milson et al. (2004, 99), emphasis Webster's.

41 Webster (1790), in Milson et al. (2004, 102–5).

42 Webster (1790), in Milson et al. (2004, 105–6).

43 Webster (1790), in Milson et al. (2004, 108–9).

44 Webster (1790), in Milson et al. (2004, 113).

45 *Politics* VIII.1.1337a14–21; cf. III.9.1280a25–b12.

46 Pinckney may be attempting to counteract this drawing-apart of the worldviews of farmers and artisans when he observes their interdependence—the makers make the implements upon which the farmers rely, and that reliance supports the development of and trade in manufactured goods. Can an awareness of this interdependence of freely laboring workers reduce the corrupting effect of dependence on customers that Jefferson fears? In a sense,

in an economy that supports agriculture and manufacturing through commerce, everyone ultimately "looks up to heaven," and to their own "industry," if not "to their own soil" (see Pinckney, chap. 4).

47 Jefferson, "A Bill for the More General Diffusion of Knowledge" (18 June 1779), NAFO, http://founders.archives.gov/documents/Jefferson/01-02-02-0132-0004-0079.

48 Pangle and Pangle (1993, 116) point out that Jefferson advocates teaching history from the correct, i.e., republican, point of view—not through John Marshall or David Hume, for instance—to encourage the citizenry to learn the right lessons.

49 Jefferson (18 June 1779).

50 Jefferson (1954, XIV.146–49).

51 Jefferson to Adams, 28 October 1813, NAFO.

52 Jefferson (1954, XIV.146–49).

53 Jefferson (1954, XIV.146–49).

54 For purposes of this study, it is interesting that Jefferson proposes that students be taught Latin and Greek as well as modern languages at the grammar school level. Language study is as much an exercise for the mind as an acquisition of knowledge. It also serves as "an instrument for the attainment of science. But that time is not lost which is employed in providing tools for future operation: more especially as in this case the books put into the hands of the youth for this purpose may be such as will at the same time impress their minds with useful facts and good principles" (148). Texts read in foreign languages should be chosen for edifying content.

55 Neither Madison nor Aristotle either expected or desired every citizen to participate in politics beyond obedience to law and some attention to those chosen to take official office. The Pangles' study of Jefferson's education plan suggests that he was not so concerned with law-abiding citizens as with vigilant citizens, more suspicious than obedient (Pangle and Pangle [1993, 110–11]). Jefferson's ambitious ward scheme, so well elaborated by Michael P. Zuckert, shows both advantages and disadvantages that Aristotle could have foreseen. The education of every citizen to the apex of his or her abilities (natural talents *and* disposition) coupled with the expectation that such citizens, whether highly educated or merely schooled in the rudiments, will recognize and vote for the elevation into the position most suited to his character only the most talented as opposed to the conventionally prestigious or the powerful or the most willing to pander, is both democratically admirable and impossible (Zuckert, *The Natural Rights Republic* [Notre Dame: University of Notre Dame Press, 1996], 224–26, 236–38). At least Jefferson does not expect the citizens to rest upon their initial judgments of those they put in office, but to use their historical insights to detect every tendency toward corruption.

56 Thomas Jefferson, "First Inaugural Address" (4 March 1801), NAFO, http://founders.archives.gov/documents/Jefferson/01-33-02-0116-0004.

57 Jefferson (1954, XIV.148).

58 Writing as "a Citizen of America" in 1787, Noah Webster defines republican virtue as "patriotism, or love of country" but also dismisses it as less significant than property ownership without entail for the perpetuation of a republic (Sheehan and McDowell [1998, 400–401]). The burden of his Fourth of July speech in 1802, however, places the responsibility upon citizens (1) to choose good representatives, (2) to obey the officeholders they choose, even the occasionally "weak or wicked," and (3) to "govern themselves" (Hyneman and Lutz [1983, 1237]). Upon this later generation "has devolved the task of defending and improving the rich inheritance, purchased by their fathers . . . an estate to be preserved only by industry, toil and vigilance" (1239). This task includes "imitat[ing] the virtues" of the revolutionary generation of "citizen soldiers" and learning to merit the esteem of

women of worth. The vigilance seems to consist of caring to learn the "true principles" of free government in order to "guard against the impositions of designing men" (1236).

59 "A Foreign Spectator" [Nicholas Collin], "An Essay on the Means of Promoting Federal Sentiments in the United States" I (6 August 1787), in Sheehan and McDowell (1998, 408).

60 Benjamin Rush, "Address to the People of the United States" (January 1787), in Sheehan and McDowell (1998, 4). It is difficult to avoid thinking of the parallels between this sketch of a national university for collecting all the world's learning for the benefit of America's future governors and Solomon's House in Francis Bacon's *New Atlantis* (Francis Bacon, *The Advancement of Learning* and *New Atlantis*, 1627 [London: Oxford University Press, 1956, 275–78]). Unlike Bacon, however, Rush emphasizes the foundations of the American republics in self-government and the liberty of the citizen.

61 Rush's plan fleshes out in full detail William Penn's thoughts on the importance of education for his vision of Pennsylvania's future: "Article XII. That the Governor and provincial Council, shall erect and order all public schools, and encourage and reward the authors of useful sciences and laudable inventions in the said province" ("The frame of the government of the province of Pensilvania, in America" [1682], Avalon Project, http://avalon.law.yale.edu/17th_century/pa04.asp).

62 Benjamin Rush, "A Plan for the Establishment of Public Schools and the Diffusion of Knowledge in Pennsylvania; to Which Are Added Thoughts upon the Mode of Education Proper in a Republic" (1786), in Hyneman and Lutz (1983, I.675–76).

63 Rush (1786), in Hyneman and Lutz (1983, I.681).

64 Rush (1786), in Hyneman and Lutz (1983, I.681). Note the interesting use of the word "calculated." One might wonder whom Rush sees as having performed this political calculation.

65 Rush (1786), in Hyneman and Lutz (1983, I.678–79).

66 All contribute willingly because all benefit from the "propagation of virtue and knowledge" (Rush [1786], in Hyneman and Lutz [1983, I.678–79]).

67 Rush (1786), in Hyneman and Lutz (1983, I.687). See Sari Altschuler, "From Blood Vessels to Global Networks of Exchange: The Physiology of Benjamin Rush's Early Republic," *Journal of the Early Republic* 32, no. 2 (2012): 207–31, esp. 213, for a correction of a common misreading of Rush's machine metaphor. He is not speaking of men as becoming automatons in service to a mechanistic government, but in contemporary medical terms as self-contained organisms that respond to stimuli and can be trained to salutary sympathies.

68 Rush (1786), in Hyneman and Lutz (1983, I.684).

69 The security of legal oaths is also only one of the reasons George Washington uses in his "Farewell Address" (1796) to encourage the still-new nation to support religion and morality with publicly supported educational institutions. See n. 87.

70 Rush (1786), in Hyneman and Lutz (1983, I.684–85).

71 William Ziobro cites Benjamin Rush's opinion, expressed in a 1789 letter to John Adams, contra Jefferson and Adams, that classical education is a waste of time for the youth of a modern nation (Ziobro, "Classical Education in Colonial America," in *Classical Antiquity and the Politics of America*, ed. Michael Meckler [Waco, Tex.: Baylor University Press, 2006], 15). The disparity between that opinion and the one put forth in the 1786 "Thoughts upon . . . Education . . . in a Republic" is not as wide as it may at first appear. The reason Rush claims classical education is a waste, and possibly a detriment, is its influence on republican manners: "Do not men use Latin and Greek as the scuttlefish emit their ink, on purpose to conceal themselves from an intercourse with the common people?" Ziobro groups Rush with Thomas Paine and Benjamin Franklin as rejecting the study of Greek

and Latin or their mythologies, though we have seen that Franklin did not reject language study for those who would need it professionally. Rush's "Thoughts upon . . . Education . . . in a Republic" does not reject the fables of classical antiquity; it merely argues that they should accompany, not replace, the study of the Bible in publicly supported schools. When Rush refers to the study of the classics as a waste of time in 1789, he lists some modern authors as better models of "style or language," directly contradicting his argument in the "Thoughts," and he asserts that there are more moral lessons to be drawn from the Bible to reduce "infidelity and . . . immorality and bad government" (*Letters of Benjamin Rush*, ed. L. H. Butterfield [Princeton: Princeton University Press, 1951], 524–25). Insofar as these three leaders during the founding era discouraged reading the ancient texts, they did so as much for an ancient as for a modern reason: the education of citizens needs to be concerned with producing a moral understanding compatible with the way of life of the community, in this case with republican freedom. As a classically educated leader of the burgeoning republic himself, Rush had learned that "the progress of morals, knowledge, and religion" would be essential. Citizens could not be expected to govern themselves without a moral framework. Those who continued the tradition of teaching Latin and Greek language taught them through the use of authors and works chosen for their moral edification.

72 In Hyneman and Lutz (1983, I.688–89).

73 Rush (1786), in Hyneman and Lutz (1983, I.686–87).

74 Rush (1786), in Hyneman and Lutz (1983, I.689).

75 Rush (1786), in Hyneman and Lutz (1983, I.690).

76 Rush (1786), in Hyneman and Lutz (1983, I.691). See also Rush's attempt to enlist Abigail Adams and "our American ladies" in his schemes of educational reform: "Their influence will render my opinions sooner or later universal" (Butterfield [1951, 524]).

77 In Hyneman and Lutz (1983, I.691).

78 Rush (1786), in Hyneman and Lutz (1983, 692).

79 Rush (1786), in Hyneman and Lutz (1983, 692).

80 [Collin] (1787), in Sheehan and McDowell (1998, 406). Cf. Gouverneur Morris (Constitutional Convention, 19 July 1787), in Koch (1966, 322–25).

81 The Federalist essay was published in New York, 22 November 1787, and argues that, in an "extended" republican government, a minority faction "may clog the administration, it may convulse the society; but it will be unable to execute and mask its violence under the forms of the Constitution" (Hamilton et al. [2000, 10.57]). Madison makes an argument on June 6 in the closed Constitutional Convention debates that foreshadows Federalist 10 (Koch [1966, 75–77]). Collin appears to be responding to such an argument here, in his first letter, published August 6.

82 [Collin] (1787), in Sheehan and McDowell (1998, 407).

83 [Collin] (1787), in Sheehan and McDowell (1998, 413).

84 [Collin] (1787), in Sheehan and McDowell (1998, 414).

85 A theme running through various Anti-Federalist writings is that the new national government, being so distant from most inhabitants, will never inspire the citizens' trust because the citizens will not know what is going on or whom to blame for errors. If it does not inspire trust, it will not inspire spontaneous obedience to law, hence the need for force and the threat of force—a standing army—to enforce the laws. From this point, the Anti-Federalists argue, it is but a small step to despotism. (See, e.g., Brutus 1, in Storing [1981, 2.9.14, 17–18] and "The Address and Reasons of Dissent of the Minority of the Convention of Pennsylvania," in Storing [1981, 3.11.50–51].)

86 Compare Samuel Adams' assertion above that a lack of private virtue undermines public virtue (chap. 6, pp. 152–53).

87 In Sheehan and McDowell (1998, 415).

88 A literary work, claiming to be the first American novel, both showing the heinous results of an inadequately realistic moral education (esp. for women) and attempting itself to fill the gap, is the epistolary novel *The Power of Sympathy*, being written at just this time in Boston under a pseudonym, but probably by William Hill Brown (*The Power of Sympathy, or, the Triumph of Nature Founded in Truth* [Boston: Isaiah Thomas, 1789]).

89 For arguments parallel to those of the Foreign Spectator, observing the need for "the sense of religious obligation" in courtroom oaths and well beyond, see also George Washington's observations on the American republic after his two terms as its president in the "Farewell Address" of 1796:

> Of all the dispositions and habits which lead to political prosperity, religion and morality are indispensable supports. In vain would that man claim the tribute of patriotism, who should labor to subvert these great pillars of human happiness, these firmest props of the duties of men and citizens. The mere politician, equally with the pious man, ought to respect and to cherish them. A volume could not trace all their connections with private and public felicity. Let it simply be asked: Where is the security for property, for reputation, for life, if the sense of religious obligation desert the oaths which are the instruments of investigation in courts of justice? And let us with caution indulge the supposition that morality can be maintained without religion. Whatever may be conceded to the influence of refined education on minds of peculiar structure, reason and experience both forbid us to expect that national morality can prevail in exclusion of religious principle.
>
> It is substantially true that virtue or morality is a necessary spring of popular government. The rule, indeed, extends with more or less force to every species of free government. Who that is a sincere friend to it can look with indifference upon attempts to shake the foundation of the fabric?
>
> Promote then, as an object of primary importance, institutions for the general diffusion of knowledge. In proportion as the structure of a government gives force to public opinion, it is essential that public opinion should be enlightened. (Avalon Project, http://avalon.law.yale.edu/18th_century/washing.asp)

90 Cf. Aristotle's joke about the "nobility" of the wealthy, *Politics* IV.8.1293b34–40.

91 See esp. Foreign Spectator VII: "Unbelief in a future state is often the offspring of immorality, and never fails to increase national iniquity" (Sheehan and McDowell [1998, 417]).

92 [Collin] (1787), in Sheehan and McDowell (1998, 419).

93 [Collin] (1787), in Sheehan and McDowell (1998, 410).

94 In Sheehan and McDowell (1998, 411).

95 Tocqueville (2000, II.2.8). For Tocqueville's analysis of the reliance of democratic freedom upon religious faith, see also II.1.5. Foreign Spectator's Letter XV expresses the hope that Tocqueville sees in action later:

> If therefore the common object of attachment is interesting, and a sufficient majority has those moral principles, which are the stamina of all rational government; the political union has a natural tendency to grow stronger, because the selfish passions will necessarily be weakened, or take a better direction; and all the sentiments of integrity, honor, private attachment, and public spirit, will encrease; by the exercise of social duties, by civil habits, and the gradual incorporation of the body politic, which will be finally moulded into an excellent form, and animated by the same generous spirit. (Sheehan and McDowell [1998, 427])

96 [Collin] (1787), in Sheehan and McDowell (1998, 414–15).

97 [Collin] (1787), in Sheehan and McDowell (1998, 412–13).

98 [Collin] (1787), in Sheehan and McDowell (1998, 408).

99 Collin associates the Anti-Federalist position with this failure to trust the duly elected government, combined with "an excessive love of liberty" ([Collin] (1787), in Sheehan and McDowell [1998, 408]).

100 In Sheehan and McDowell (1998, 408–9).

101 [Collin] (1787), in Sheehan and McDowell (1998, 415–16). Collin cites (without irony) "truly great minds," Cyrus the Great as well as King Gustavus Adolphus, as appreciating religious belief as "the most valuable security to states" because they saw its value to their armies: it unifies "men of diverse characters and conditions." Compare also the "Proposal for Reviving Christian Conviction," published anonymously 11 October 1787, in Virginia, anticipating the ill effects of factions based upon group identity or interest groups:

> In no form of government whatever has the influence of religious principles been found so requisite as in that of a republic. It requires but a slight degree of observation to be convinced that mankind require the awe of some power to confine them within the line of their duty. . . . What is there to correct the injustice and irregularities of the member of a republic, even where the most salutary laws exist, while he can associate numbers in his interest; or supposing the administration of the laws in the hands of such as have a fellow-feeling, or are unwilling to risk their popularity by punctually enforcing them. . . .
>
> The man who carries his prospects forward to futurity, and considers himself a candidate for the favor of omnipotence, will be actuated, in the general tenor of his life, by motives that elevate him above the little interests and passions which disturb the peace of society, and will discharge the relative duties of his station, unawed by the fear of man, with a consistence and steadiness correspondent to the principle from which he acts. (In Storing [1981, 5.8.1–4])

102 [Collin] (1787), in Sheehan and McDowell (1998, 429).

103 [Collin] (1787), in Sheehan and McDowell (1998, 430). This interrelation of agriculture and manufacturing concurs with Charles Pinckney's observations at the Constitutional Convention (see chap. 4, 156–57).

104 [Collin] (1787), in Sheehan and McDowell (1998, 431).

105 [Collin] (1787), in Sheehan and McDowell (1998, 430–31).

106 In Sheehan and McDowell (1998, 421–22). Sheehan and McDowell supply the biblical citation and quotation: "Give me neither poverty nor riches" (Prov 30:8).

107 Sheehan and McDowell (1998, 422–23).

108 In Sheehan and McDowell (1998, 425).

109 Wilson (1788), in Sheehan and McDowell (1998, 507–9).

110 Hamilton et al. (2000, 10.57).

111 "In such [free] society, virtue loses all her loveliness, because of her selfish aims." George Fitzhugh, *Sociology for the South, or the Failure of Free Society* (Richmond: A. Morris, 1854), 24.

112 Hamilton et al. (2000, 39.246, 240).

Conclusion

1 In Koch (1966, 654).

2 *Politics* IV.14, V.8–9; Publius in Hamilton et al. (2000, X.58–59); Fabius in Sheehan and McDowell (1998, 487). At the Constitutional Convention, Madison shows his awareness

of the same "devices" Aristotle mentions that would pull a polity toward oligarchy (in Koch [1966, 427]).

3 Social dominance would mean that the majority of society admires the middle class' way of life. The poor strive to join it, and the more wealthy do not flaunt the advantages they derive solely from their wealth, appreciating the stability the middle provides.

4 Adams (1794, III.162).

5 *Politics* IV.4.1292a4–34.

6 The debate surrounding the proposal and ratification of the first amendments to the Constitution suggests, first, that many of those who influenced the composition of the Constitution were involved (in Amendments 1 to 12) or were "consulted" via historical research (in Amendments 13 to 15), and, second, that since the 1860s, the understanding of the founders has not been much consulted in the amendment process. Constitutional amendment is no longer understood as bringing the operation of the original principles into line with present political necessities, but rather as fixing the framers' mistakes. The judiciary's modifications under the guise of the "living constitution" openly presume an understanding of equality and liberty superior to that of the founding era.

7 The initial republican lawgiver(s) or subsequent statesmen trying to "keep" the republic must not confuse the task with that of the founder of the best regime of a philosopher's prayers, and the citizens should not be taught that a lofty standard of cultured virtue renders their middle-class republican standard despicable. Aristotle's praise of the attainable virtues of the "regime of the middling sort" gives the leading citizens of a republic a defensible partisanship for their regime by associating it with "the mean" and thus the principle of the virtues analyzed in the *Ethics*, without acknowledging the differences.

8 "Resistance to Civil Government" is the revealing title Thoreau used when he published in 1849 the essay posthumously retitled "Civil Disobedience" (American Transcendentalism, http://transcendentalism-legacy.tamu.edu/authors/thoreau/civil). In contrast to the usage of the latter expression today, which suggests that civil disobedience is a healthy aspect of ordinary citizenship in a democracy, Thoreau saw the defiance of the laws with which one disagrees as a means of jamming the corrupt "machine" of democratic politics to make it grind to a halt.

9 John Stuart Mill, *On Liberty* (1869), ed. Michael B. Mathias (New York: Pearson Longman, 2007), chap. II, esp. 93–108.

10 Karl Marx, "Critique of the Gotha Program" (published by Friedrich Engels in 1891), in *The Marx-Engels Reader*, ed. Robert C. Tucker (New York: W. W. Norton, 1972), 388.

11 Herbert David Croly, *The Promise of American Life* (New York: Macmillan, 1909), 400–403, Project Gutenberg, http://www.gutenberg.org/ebooks/14422.

12 It was a conservative revolution in the sense adduced by Marc Landy and Sidney M. Milkis (*Presidential Greatness* [Lawrence: University Press of Kansas, 2000], 4–6) in that it attempted to conserve progress that had been made toward liberty and equality and to establish institutions that would both maintain the allegiance of those who were satisfied with those gains and workably expand, or at least not threaten, the liberty and equality of future generations consistently with the nation's principles.

13 Adams (1776).

14 Cf. *Daily Advertiser* (New York), 24 September 1787: In a short piece arguing for ratification of the newly published Constitution, produced by "*mutual deference and concession*" in a "*spirit of amity*," the author makes reference to almost all the middling virtues that both Aristotle and the founding writers praise. Before he claims that the only alternatives to a balanced constitution, by which is meant adequate power with checks upon its use, are "Gorgon-headed anarchy, or a miserable aristocratic domination," in other words, "lawless

Democracy, on the one hand, or . . . the Sovereign authority degenerating into Tyranny, on the other," he acclaims the document as "temperate and wise," composed by "genius and patriotism" in an epoch that brought forth "a *revolution*, effected by good sense and deliberation . . . the reign of reason, the triumph of discretion, virtue and public spirit," and encourages "all honest, well-disposed men, friends to peace and good government" to "be wise" and accept the product of the wisdom of the framers with gratitude. This sensible and deliberate revolution should be "recorded as a lesson to future generations in these United States" (*The Debate on the Constitution*, ed. Bernard Bailyn [New York: Library of America, 1993], I.12–14, emphasis in original).

15 When Madison defines and decries faction as the death of a republic, he and Aristotle are looking at the same phenomenon and approaching the solution along similar lines. Federalist 10 makes the apparently paradoxical claim that the way to tame factions is to make more of them—to divide the citizenry among so many parties that no one of them can capture exclusive political power at the national level. Madison cannot advocate eliminating faction (even if he thought it possible) because his foundational principle is the rights of the people to liberty and the pursuit of different modes of making a living.

16 Hamilton et al. (2000, 10).

17 Hamilton et al. (2000, 57.366–68).

18 That Franklin could not help treating "mediocrity" with a mixture of admiration and disdain indicates that his effort to recruit industrious lower- and middle-class immigrants to "remove to America" was a doubtful enterprise even at its start.

19 As Aristotle teaches, admirable ambition is not a blind desire for power, but "longing for honor" neither excessively nor deficiently (*Nicomachean Ethics*, IV.4.1125b5–20; cf. James Madison, Virginia Ratifying Convention, 20 June 1788, in Kurland and Lerner [1987, vol. 1, chap. 13, doc. 36]).

20 Nicholas Collin argued in 1787 that moral behavior in an increasingly commercial society would require a religious moral upbringing to combat selfishness. Alexis de Tocqueville observed in the 1830s while touring the American states before writing *Democracy in America* that American "self-interest well understood" coincided with widespread religiosity in the populace. He argues at length for the necessity of this right understanding for the long-term success of commercial democracy. His sociological analysis of the individualistic tendencies of democracy shows how easily self-interest (*egoisme*) can surrender its political self-government to an increasingly powerful state incompatible with republican principles (Tocqueville [2000, II.4.1–3]).

21 Adams (1776).

22 Thomas Pangle (1988) interrogates John Locke to determine his ultimate position on the highest questions of political philosophy and finds that it is radically different from the philosophical position of Plato. He argues persuasively that, because the American founding rests much on the political teachings of Locke, the founders adopted political principles that culminated in liberty as the highest good without necessarily appreciating the political dangers involved. Liberty for its own sake and not, as in Plato's political thinking, for the sake of wisdom or the highest virtue, or liberty of conscience that rests on independence from divine law, has the potential to lead to a society venerating license.

Without attempting to detract from these considerations distinguishing the Americans from Plato, I would argue that Aristotle, though capable of contemplating the regime in which virtue (virtue compatible with a pious people, in fact) is the goal, does not consider this the best *political* regime. Politics, as a human activity that requires a certain virtue, may point beyond itself because we can imagine virtues that some few human beings can practice and that are higher than politics and potentially undermine a political regime. Aristotle's republic of the middling element is his best political regime because it does not fall prey to the philosophical temptation to point to the most divine potential within human beings. It takes politics on its own terms as a legitimate, even admirable, human pursuit. Aristotle, knowing how the extreme of virtue, just like the extreme of vice, threatens political stability, does not urge on real cities and men the unattainable goals of individual and social perfection. Rather, the best political order is the best place for human beings to live. It does not measure itself against superhuman standards because that would lead to a social order that is not the best place for human beings to live.

Pangle does not attempt to demonstrate that the American founders contemplated either the most profound implications of the classical admiration for Sparta or Rome or the politically dangerous implications of Locke's argument against biblical theology. They probably did not. He attempts, rather, to teach contemporary Americans about the implications and potential risks—e.g., liberty becomes license and toleration becomes intolerant atheism—of their constitutional order through his searching interpretation of its Lockean foundations. I have tried to argue that many in the founding generation foresaw both of these worrying trends and sought, both by the appreciation of the sober life of the middling citizen and by attention to moral education, to fend off the worst of those potentialities.

23 Sheehan and McDowell (1998, esp. 510). See also Franklin's remarks at the end of the Constitutional Convention. Just before he uttered the epigraph to this chapter, he said,

>   I consent, Sir, to this Constitution because I expect no better, and because I am not sure, that it is not the best. The opinions I have had of its errors, I sacrifice to the public good. I have never whispered a syllable of them abroad. If every one of us in returning to our Constituents were to report the objections he has had to it, and endeavor to gain partizans in support of them, we might prevent its being generally received, and thereby lose all the salutary effects & great advantages resulting naturally in our favor among foreign Nations as well as among ourselves, from our real or apparent unanimity. (In Koch [1966, 654])

24 Thomas Jefferson to Henry Lee, 8 May 1825, NAFO, http://founders.archives.gov/documents/Jefferson/98-01-02-5212. It is crucial to an understanding of Jefferson's thought to know that he considered Plato's *Republic* ridiculous (Jefferson to John Adams, 5 July 1814, NAFO, http://founders.archives.gov/documents/Adams/99-02-02-6314) and the Roman republic a crucially flawed model. (See Zuckert [1996, esp. chap. 7], for a deep and thorough analysis of the many strains of Jefferson's thought on republics.) When he drafted the Declaration or proposed legislation in the Virginia legislature, he was not advocating the reproduction of either Plato's Kallipolis or the Roman republic on the soil of North America nor criticizing British rule over the American colonies or British primogeniture according to a single political theory. Since Aristotle was also not adopting Platonic political philosophy wholesale, nor taking Sparta (or any other city) as his model for political reform, but teasing out the implications of constructing a regime that would actually survive given the flaws of real human beings, he was working in the same vineyard as this prominent founder.

25 Perhaps Adams absorbed Aristotle's observation that the political control of wealth in Sparta did not prevent its descent into money loving and all its consequent social ills.

26 James Madison to Thomas Jefferson, 19 June 1786, NAFO, http://founders.archives.gov/documents/Madison/01-09-02-0017.

27 Centinel I in Storing (1981, 2.7.9).

28 Federal Farmer goes so far as to predict that if the middle class loses its majority, its virtue will lose influence in elections and therefore in lawmaking. Citizens will become servile

and the nation "depraved" due to the dominance of either the rich or the poor. (See chap. 4, p. 115.)

Insofar as the Federalist Publius argues in Federalist 45 that the national constitution allows certain federal aspects of American politics to continue, e.g., that the states will retain authority over most citizens' daily lives, he implies that the American union can have the best of both worlds. The Anti-Federalists' predictions of the gradual domination of the national government over the state governments and the uniformity in education without republican moral content seem to have been proven correct.

29 Coram (1791), in Hyneman and Lutz (1983, II.756, 795, 805–7, 811).

30 Hamilton et al. (2000, 39.239–42, 246).

31 James Truslow Adams publishes *The Epic of America* (Boston: Little, Brown, 1932) in order "to trace the beginnings . . . of such American concepts as 'bigger and better,' of our attitude toward business, of many characteristics which are generally considered as being 'typically American,' and, in especial, of that American dream of a better, richer, and happier life for all our citizens of every rank which is the greatest contribution we have as yet made to the thought and welfare of the world" (preface, vii–viii).

I am told this is the first use of the expression the "American dream." I wonder whether this Adams is eliding the connotations of "richer" in this definition. Have Americans always aimed for riches *qua* material wealth alone, or have they aimed for other senses of a rich life as well, such as "high in quality" or "meaningful"? Was the goal of a richer life always open-ended, or did it ever hold within it a limit—"I want to make enough to enable my family to live a good life," rather than "A good life equals ever-increasing riches"? Perhaps his vantage point from the Great Depression (the preface is dated 1 May 1931, from Washington, DC) narrows Adams' field of vision to the economic emergency of bringing a large segment of the populace to a decent standard of living and obscures the founding era's parallel goal of making middling citizens admirable for their qualities of character. It is surely true that the American dream of the rest of the twentieth century focuses ever-more narrowly on economic indicators, income, home ownership, and post-secondary education for the sake of a better income and a better house. The most selfless expression of this upward mobility would be, "I want my kids to have it better than I did." It is hardly selfless, however, if "better" means only "wealthier," and if it implies, "the kids will take care of me in my old age."

32 "The principle of patriotism stands in need of the reinforcement of prejudice, and it is well known that our strongest prejudices in favour of our country are formed in the first one and twenty years of our lives" (Hyneman and Lutz [1983, 680–81]).

33 Aristotle, *Politics* V.9.1310a12–15, 35–36.

34 Webster (1790) quotes "the great Montesquieu" as observing what Aristotle also taught, that "the laws of education ought to be relative to the principles of the government" (in Milson et al. [2004, 106]).

35 It is interesting that in some communities, behaviors that the law-abiding and self-controlled would like to discourage are decried as "ignorant." That holdover from the Enlightenment association of education with "refinement" and (morally) good "life choices" provides some hope that a saving remnant may remain among parents teaching their children, but the most highly rewarded educational leaders seem to move in the opposite direction, asserting that children of ever younger ages must be told the stakes, but then allowed to make consequential moral decisions (e.g., about sexual activity or drug and alcohol use) on their own.

36 A complete Aristotelian political science examines the character of the inhabitants, their way of living, and the virtues they hold in esteem. Given certain unchanging characteristics of

human nature, the American framers consider the ways of life and the education of future generations that would constrain disruptive human tendencies and encourage the beneficial ones in reliable ways. Opinion leaders try to promote an attachment to the Constitution's republican principles; the citizens need to believe that their form of government, albeit new, is not only "their own" but "lovable," i.e., consistent with fixed standards, such as those outlined in the Declaration of Independence (*Politics* II.4.1262b7–23). On the imperative to instill love of the Constitution and the American republic in each generation, in addition to Franklin's epigraph to this chapter and the arguments discussed above from Atwater, Fabius, Wilson, Webster, the Worcester Speculator, a Foreign Spectator, and Rush, see also Webster's 1802 Fourth of July oration excerpted in Hyneman and Lutz (1983, II, esp. 1233–36). Webster uses four quotations from Shakespeare's *Measure for Measure* to support his reservations about the failure to enforce law strictly, implying that the trend stems from increasing reliance on a broad popular franchise that expects to control its representatives and a citizen body that is losing its respect for the Constitution's principles and America's republican way of life.

37 Jefferson to Adams, 28 October 1813, NAFO.
38 To give the middling element a foundation for self-esteem, Aristotle propagandizes that "the best legislators are from the middling citizens," and quotes Phocylides approvingly praying, "'Many things are best for the middling; I would be of the middling sort in the city'" (*Politics* IV.12.1296b35–1297a7).
39 *Politics* IV.6.1292b23–1293a11.
40 *Politics* III.4.1277a23–26.
41 [Webster] (1787), in Sheehan and McDowell (1998, 392).
42 *Politics* I.12.1259a39–b11.
43 Aristotle would reply that his republic should not suffer from the fate of "imagined republics" that Machiavelli criticizes so brazenly:
> And many have imagined republics and principalities that have never been seen or known to exist in truth; for it is so far from how one lives to how one should live that he who lets go of what is done for what should be done learns his ruin rather than his preservation. For a man who wants to make a profession of good in all regards must come to ruin among so many who are not good. (Machiavelli [1998, XV.61])
44 *Politics* I.12.1259a39–b11.

Bibliography

Adams, James Truslow. *The Epic of America*. Boston: Little, Brown, 1932.

Adams, John. *A Defence of the Constitutions of Government of the United States of America Against the Attack of M. Turgot in his Letter to Dr. Price, Dated the Twenty-second Day of March, 1778*. 1787. Reprint, London: John Stockdale, 1794.

Altschuler, Sari. "From Blood Vessels to Global Networks of Exchange: The Physiology of Benjamin Rush's Early Republic." *Journal of the Early Republic* 32, no. 2 (2012): 207–31.

Appleby, Joyce. "The New Republican Synthesis and the Changing Political Ideas of John Adams." *American Quarterly* 25, no. 5 (1973): 578–95.

Aristotle. *Aristotelis Politica*. Edited by W. D. Ross. Oxford: Oxford University Press, 1957.

———. *Aristotle's* Constitution of Athens *and Related Texts*. Translated by Kurt von Fritz and Ernst Kapp. New York: Hafner, 1950.

———. *Aristotle's* Nicomachean Ethics. Translated by Robert C. Bartlett and Susan D. Collins. Chicago: University of Chicago Press, 2011.

———. *Aristotle's* Politics. Translated by Carnes Lord. 2nd ed. Chicago: University of Chicago Press, 2013.

———. *Aristotle's* Politics*: Books III and IV*. Translated by Richard Robinson. Oxford: Clarendon, 1962.

———. *Ethica Nicomachea*. Edited by Ingram Bywater. London: Oxford University Press, 1894.

———. *The Politics*. Translated by H. Rackham. London: W. Heinemann, 1932.

———. *The Politics*. Translated by T. A. Sinclair. Baltimore: Penguin Books, 1962.

————. *The* Politics *of Aristotle.* Edited and translated by Ernest Barker. Oxford: Oxford University Press, 1958.

————. *The* Politics *of Aristotle.* Translated by Benjamin Jowett. Oxford: Clarendon, 1885.

————. *The* Politics *of Aristotle.* Translated by W. L. Newman. Oxford: Clarendon, 1887.

————. *The* Politics *of Aristotle.* Translated by Peter L. P. Simpson. Chapel Hill: University of North Carolina Press, 1997.

Bacon, Francis. *The Advancement of Learning* and *New Atlantis* (1627). London: Oxford University Press, 1956.

Bailyn, Bernard, ed. *The Debate on the Constitution: Federalist and Antifederalist Speeches, Articles, and Letters During the Struggle over Ratification.* 2 vols. New York: Library of America, 1993.

Barker, Ernest. *The Political Thought of Plato and Aristotle.* New York: Russell & Russell, 1959.

Barnard, James M. *A Sketch of Anne Robert Jacques Turgot: With a Translation of His Letter to Dr. Price.* Translated by Helen Billings Morris. Boston: G. H. Ellis, 1899.

Barnes, Jonathan, ed. *The Complete Works of Aristotle.* Vol. 2. Princeton: Princeton University Press, 1984.

Bartlett, Robert C. "Aristotle's Science of the Best Regime." *American Political Science Review* 88, no. 1 (1994): 143–55.

Bluhm, William T. "The Place of the 'Polity' in Aristotle's Theory of the Ideal State." *Journal of Politics* 24, no. 4 (1962): 743–53.

Boyd, Julian P., ed. *The Papers of Thomas Jefferson.* Vol. 1: *1760–1776.* Princeton: Princeton University Press, 1950.

Brown, William Hill. *The Power of Sympathy, or, the Triumph of Nature Founded in Truth.* Boston: Isaiah Thomas, 1789.

Butterfield, L. H., ed. *Letters of Benjamin Rush.* Princeton: Princeton University Press, 1951.

Coats, Wendell John, Jr. *The Activity of Politics and Related Essays.* Selinsgrove, Pa.: Susquehanna University Press, 1989.

Croly, Herbert David. *The Promise of American Life.* New York: Macmillan, 1909.

Cushing, Harry Alonzo, ed. *The Writings of Samuel Adams.* Vol. 3. New York: G. P. Putnam's Sons, 1908.

Davis, Michael. *The Politics of Philosophy: A Commentary on Aristotle's* Politics. Lanham, Md.: Rowman & Littlefield, 1996.

de Laix, Roger A. "Aristotle's Conception of the Spartan Constitution." *Journal of the History of Philosophy* 12, no. 1 (1974): 21–30.

Diggins, John Patrick. *John Adams.* The American Presidents. New York: Times Books, 2003.

Duncan, Christopher. *The Anti-Federalists and Early American Political Thought.* DeKalb: Northern Illinois University Press, 1995.

Elliot, Jonathan, ed. *The Debates in the Several State Conventions on the Adoption of the Federal Constitution as Recommended by the General Convention at Philadelphia in 1787.* Vol. 4. Washington, 1836.

————, ed. *The Debates on the Adoption of the Federal Constitution in the Convention Held at Philadelphia in 1787.* Vol. 5. Philadelphia, 1836.

Farrand, Max. *The Records of the Federal Convention of 1787.* New Haven: Yale University Press, 1911. http://oll.libertyfund.org/titles/1785.

Finley, M. I. *Politics in the Ancient World.* Cambridge: Cambridge University Press, 1983.

Fitzhugh, George. *Sociology for the South, or the Failure of Free Society.* Richmond: A. Morris, 1854.

Franklin, Benjamin. *The Complete Works, in Philosophy, Politics, and Morals, of the late Dr. Benjamin Franklin.* Vol. 3. London: J. Johnson and Longman, Hurst, Reese, and Orme, 1806. Project Gutenberg. http://www.gutenberg.org/files/48138/48138-h/48138-h.htm.

Hamilton, Alexander, John Jay, and James Madison. *The Federalist: A Commentary on the Constitution of the United States.* Edited by Robert Scigliano. New York: Modern Library, 2000.

Herodotus, *Histories.* Translated by Aubrey de Selincourt. Harmondsworth: Penguin Books, 1971.

Hyneman, Charles S., and Donald S. Lutz. *American Political Writing during the Founding Era: 1760–1805.* 2 vols. Indianapolis: Liberty Fund, 1983.

Jacobs, Jane. *Systems of Survival: A Dialogue on the Moral Foundations of Commerce and Politics.* New York: Random House, 1992.

Jaffa, Harry V. "Aristotle." In *History of Political Philosophy,* edited by Leo Strauss and Joseph Cropsey, 64–129. Chicago: Rand McNally, 1963.

Jefferson, Thomas. *Notes on the State of Virginia.* Edited by William Peden. Chapel Hill: University of North Carolina Press, 1954.

Koch, Adrienne, ed. *Notes of Debates in the Federal Convention of 1787 Reported by James Madison.* Athens: Ohio University Press, 1966.

Koch, Adrienne, and William Peden, eds. *The Life and Selected Writings of Thomas Jefferson.* New York: Random House, 1944.

Kronman, Anthony. "Aristotle's Idea of Political Fraternity." *American Journal of Jurisprudence* 24 (1979): 114–38.

Kurland, Philip B., and Ralph Lerner, eds. *The Founders' Constitution.* 5 vols. Chicago: University of Chicago Press, 1987. http://press-pubs.uchicago.edu/founders/documents.

Landy, Marc, and Sidney M. Milkis. *Presidential Greatness.* Lawrence: University Press of Kansas, 2000.

Machiavelli, Niccolo. *The Prince.* Translated by Harvey C. Mansfield. 2nd ed. Chicago: University of Chicago Press, 1998.

Malthus, T. R. *An Essay on the Principle of Population* (1798). Edited with an introduction by Geoffrey Gilbert. Oxford World's Classics. Oxford: Oxford University Press, 1993.

Mill, John Stuart. *On Liberty* (1869). Edited by Michael B. Mathias. New York: Pearson Longman, 2007.

Miller, Fred D. *Nature, Justice and Rights in Aristotle's* Politics. Oxford: Clarendon, 1997.

Milson, A. J., C. H. Bohan, P. L. Glanzer, and J. W. Null, eds. *Readings in American Educational Thought.* Greenwich: Information Age Publishing, 2004.

Nichols, Mary P. *Citizens and Statesmen: A Study of Aristotle's* Politics. Lanham, Md.: Rowman & Littlefield, 1992.

———. "The Good Life, Slavery, and Acquisition: Aristotle's Introduction to Politics." *Interpretation* 11, no. 2 (1983): 171–83.

Pangle, Lorraine Smith, and Thomas L. Pangle. *The Learning of Liberty: The Educational Ideas of the American Founders.* Lawrence: University Press of Kansas, 1993.

Pangle, Thomas L. *Aristotle's Teaching in the* Politics. Chicago: University of Chicago Press, 2013.

———. *The Spirit of Modern Republicanism.* Chicago: University of Chicago Press, 1988.

Plato, *The Laws.* Translated by R. G. Bury. Cambridge, Mass.: Harvard University Press, 1967.

———. *The* Laws *of Plato.* Translated by Thomas L. Pangle. New York: Basic Books, 1980.

———. *The* Republic *of Plato.* Translated by Allan Bloom. New York: Basic Books, 1991.

Plutarch. *Plutarch's Lives.* Vol. 1. Translated by Bernadotte Perrin. London: W. Heinemann, 1982.

Polybius. *The Histories.* Translated by W. R. Paton. Cambridge, Mass.: Harvard University Press, 1922–1927. http://penelope.uchicago.edu/Thayer/E/Roman/Texts/Polybius/home.html.

Rubin, Leslie G. "Aristotle's Critique of Socratic Political Unity in Plato's *Republic.*" In *Politikos,* vol. 1, edited by Kent Moors, 100–119. Pittsburgh: Duquesne University Press, 1989.

Sheehan, Colleen A., and Gary L. McDowell, eds. *Friends of the Constitution: Writings of the "Other" Federalists, 1787–1788.* Indianapolis: Liberty Fund, 1998. http://oll.libertyfund.org/titles/sheehan-friends-of-the-constitution-writings-of-the-other-federalists-1787-1788.

Simpson, Peter L. Phillips. *A Philosophical Commentary on the* Politics *of Aristotle.* Chapel Hill: University of North Carolina Press, 1998.

Smith, Adam. *An Inquiry into the Nature and Causes of the Wealth of Nations.* Edited by Edwin Cannan. Chicago: University of Chicago Press, 1976.

Smyth, Albert Henry, ed. *The Writings of Benjamin Franklin.* Vol. 10. New York: Macmillan, 1907.

Storing, Herbert J., ed. *The Complete Anti-Federalist.* With the assistance of Murray Dry. Chicago: University of Chicago Press, 1981.

Strauss, Leo. *The City and Man.* Chicago: University of Chicago Press, 1964.

———. "The Liberalism of Classical Political Philosophy." In Strauss, *Liberalism Ancient and Modern*, 26–64. New York: Basic Books, 1968.

Tocqueville, Alexis de. *Democracy in America.* Translated by Harvey Mansfield and Delba Winthrop. Chicago: University of Chicago Press, 2000.

Tucker, Robert C., ed. *The Marx-Engels Reader.* New York: W. W. Norton, 1972.

Webster, Noah. *A Collection of Essays and Fugitiv Writings on Moral, Historical, Political and Literary Subjects.* Boston: I. Thomas & E. T. Andrews, 1790.

Weinberger, Jerry. *Benjamin Franklin Unmasked: On the Unity of His Moral, Religious, and Political Thought.* Lawrence: University Press of Kansas, 2005.

Ziobro, William. "Classical Education in Colonial America." In *Classical Antiquity and the Politics of America*, edited by Michael Meckler, 13–28. Waco, Tex.: Baylor University Press, 2006.

Zuckert, Michael P. *The Natural Rights Republic.* Notre Dame: University of Notre Dame Press, 1996.

Zuckert, Michael P., and Derek A. Webb, eds. *The Anti-Federalist Writings of the Melancton Smith Circle.* Indianapolis: Liberty Fund, 2009.

ONLINE ARCHIVES

American Transcendentalism Web. http://transcendentalism-legacy.tamu.edu.

Annals of Congress. http://memory.loc.gov.

Avalon Project. http://avalon.law.yale.edu.

Constitution Society. http://www.constitution.org.

Independence Hall Association, Philadelphia. http://www.ushistory.org/declaration/related/pendleton.htm.

Internet Archive. https://archive.org.

Justia. https://supreme.justia.com/cases/federal/us/347/483/case.html.

Library of Congress. http://www.loc.gov/exhibits.

National Archives Founders Online (NAFO). http://founders.archives.gov/.

Online Library of Liberty (OLL). http://oll.libertyfund.org.

Penelope. http://penelope.uchicago.edu.

Project Gutenberg. http://www.gutenberg.org.

Teaching American History. http://teachingamericanhistory.org.

University of Pennsylvania University Archives and Records Center. http://www.archives.upenn.edu/primdocs.

General Index